# THE IDEA OF COMMERCIAL SOCIETY IN THE SCOTTISH ENLIGHTENMENT

D1615578

# THE IDEA OF COMMERCIAL SOCIETY IN THE SCOTTISH ENLIGHTENMENT

Christopher J. Berry

EDINBURGH
University Press

© Christopher J. Berry, 2013, 2015

Edinburgh University Press Ltd
The Tun – Holyrood Road
12 (2f) Jackson's Entry
Edinburgh EH8 8PJ

www.euppublishing.com

First published in hardback by Edinburgh University Press 2013

This paperback edition 2015

Typeset in Sabon by
Servis Filmsetting Ltd, Stockport, Cheshire,
and printed and bound in Great Britain by
CPI Group (UK) Ltd, Croydon CR0 4YY

A CIP record for this book is available from the British Library

ISBN 978 0 7486 4532 9 (hardback)
ISBN 978 1 4744 0471 6 (paperback)
ISBN 978 0 7486 4533 6 (webready PDF)
ISBN 978 0 7486 8453 3 (epub)

# Contents

# *Preface*

This book is an explication of Adam Smith's remark in the early pages of the *Wealth of Nations* where he writes, 'Every man thus lives by exchanging, or becomes in some measure a merchant, and the society itself grows to be what is properly a commercial society.' I here argue that the judgment that a 'society' can be typified as 'commercial' is significant. It involves a twin conceptualisation. That is to say, it articulates a notion both of 'society' (rather than say regime-type) as an appropriate 'unit' for analysis and of 'commercial' as the encapsulation of a distinctive mode of organisation. To adopt this articulation is to subscribe to the 'idea of commercial society'.

I want to claim that this 'idea' has particular resonance among that group of thinkers standardly grouped as the Scottish Enlightenment. Whether or not W. R. Scott's use of the term 'the Scottish Enlightenment' in his book on Hutcheson, published in 1900, was the first reference the term is now well-established. Even while its content and contours are generally agreed, there remains, of course, a divergence in interpretation and nuance. This book highlights a particular aspect and makes a case for its special significance. It does not pretend to foist on the Scots some homogeneity of perspective – indeed it is one of the striking elements of their writings that they are contesting the meaning and implication of this idea.

In practice, I adopt the following 'rough and ready' parameters. My temporal frame is from the publication of Hume's *Treatise* (1739–40) to the sixth edition of Smith's *Moral Sentiments* (1790). But I feel no qualms about, for example, referring to Hutcheson's work before and Ferguson's after those two dates. Within that half-century my theme requires me to be selective – not everything written is germane. What this means is that Smith followed by Hume, Millar, Ferguson, Kames and Robertson figure prominently and more than occasional reference is also made to Dunbar and Wallace. Where especially apt I discuss Turnbull, Blair and Dalrymple and a few others. There are two others on whose writings I draw. Gilbert Stuart was a Scot but enjoyed no institutional status and lived much of his life in London. He was a fierce, though scholarly, polemicist whose animus is not unconnected to his failure to obtain a university position (Robertson as Principal of Edinburgh being the main villain). However, in virtue of his meticulously documented demurrals, his writings deal with a number of the same issues as his compatriots. It is not controversial to include him within the ambit of the Scottish Enlightenment, as I did in my *Social Theory of the Scottish Enlightenment* (Edinburgh University Press, 1997). James Steuart was also an 'outsider'; a Jacobite sympathiser who spent much of his life on the Continent. Nonetheless because (despite significant differences) his major work, influenced by Hume as he acknowledges, does deal pertinently with some of the common themes that the Scottish-based authors consider I have sparingly availed myself of it.

Over many years and many publications I have pursued the theme of this book. While I reference this earlier work (and occasionally exploit it), I have endeavoured not to repeat myself but to examine afresh the idea of a commercial society; certainly to do so more systematically and thoroughly than in any earlier discussions. I have also incurred many debts. I have enjoyed the friendship and intellect for over forty years of Roger Emerson, Nick Phillipson and the late Andrew Skinner. At Glasgow I also had the benefit of interacting with Alexander Broadie and Colin Kidd, to whom I can add Craig Smith and not only for reading an earlier draft of this book, for which selfless task I am especially grateful. I am also pleased to acknowledge the material support I received from the Carnegie Trust who helped fund a trip to Japan, where I was further assisted by support from the Japan Science Foundation (thanks to Hideo Tanaka). I was enabled, thanks to this support at an important formative stage, to 'try out' some of the ideas in this book at a variety of universities (I am grateful to all who facilitated that).

I have spent all of my academic career in the University of Glasgow and I will always remain grateful to David Raphael for appointing me. Though this book is far more than about Smith it is fitting that I record my conviction that it was his Glasgow years that formed him into the world-historical figure he has become. The sentiments that inspired Smith at his installation as rector of the university to declare that his time there was the 'happiest and most honourable' in his life I wish also to claim for myself. In that spirit I wish to dedicate this book to the University of Glasgow.

Chris Berry

# Abbreviations

For full bibliographical details see References.

DALRYMPLE

FP         *Essay toward a General History of Feudal Property in Great Britain.* Cited by page.

DUNBAR

EHM        *Essays on the History of Mankind in Rude and Cultivated Ages.* Second edition, 1781. Cited by page.

FERGUSON

APMP     *Analysis of Pneumatics and Moral Philosophy.* Cited by page.

CorrF      *Correspondence.* V. Merolle (ed.). 2 vols. Cited by volume, page.

ECS       *An Essay on the History of Civil Society.* D. Forbes (ed.). Cited by page.

IMP       *Institutes of Moral Philosophy.* 3rd edn. Thoemmes reprint. Cited by page.

MSS      *The Manuscripts of Adam Ferguson.* V. Merolle (ed.). Cited by page.

PMPS     *Principles of Moral and Political Science.* 2 vols. Olms reprint. Cited by volume, page.

Reflections  *Reflections Previous to the Establishment of a Militia.* Cited by page.

Remarks   *Remarks on a Pamphlet Lately Published by Dr Price.* Cited by page.

Rom      *The History of the Progress and Termination of the Roman Republic.* 5 vols. New edition, 1813. Cited by volume, page.

HUME

| | |
|---|---|
| *A* | *An Abstract of a Treatise of Human Nature* in *T*. Cited by paragraph. |
| *DP* | *A Dissertation on the Passions.* T. Beauchamp (ed). Cited by paragraph/page. |
| *E* | *Essays: Moral, Political and Literary.* E. Miller (ed.). Essays in this edition are individually identified and cited by page as follows: |
| *E-AS* | *Of the Rise and Progress of the Arts and Sciences* |
| *E-BG* | *Whether the British Government inclines more to Absolute Monarchy or to a Republic* |
| *E-BP* | *On the Balance of Power* |
| *E-BT* | *Of the Balance of Trade* |
| *E-CL* | *Of Civil Liberty* |
| *E-Com* | *Of Commerce* |
| *E-CP* | *Of the Coalition of Parties* |
| *E-FPG* | *Of the First Principles of Government* |
| *E-Int* | *Of Interest* |
| *E-IP* | *Of the Independency of Parliament* |
| *E-IPC* | *Idea of a Perfect Commonwealth* |
| *E-JT* | *Of the Jealousy of Trade* |
| *E-LP* | *Of the Liberty of the Press* |
| *E-Mon* | *Of Money* |
| *E-NC* | *Of National Characters* |
| *E-OC* | *Of the Original Contract* |
| *E-OG* | *Of the Origin of Government* |
| *E-PAN* | *Of the Populousness of Ancient Nations* |
| *E-PC* | *Of Public Credit* |
| *E-PD* | *Of Polygamy and Divorces* |
| *E-PG* | *Of Parties in General* |
| *E-PGB* | *Of the Parties of Great Britain* |
| *E-PSc* | *That Politics may be reduced to a Science* |
| *E-RA* | *Of Refinement of Arts* |
| *E-ST* | *Of the Standard of Taste* |
| *E-Tax* | *Of Taxes* |
| *E-v* | *Variants collected at the end of E* |
| *HE* | *History of England.* 3 vols. Cited by volume, page. |
| *Letters* | *The Letters of David Hume.* 2 vols. J. Greig (ed). Cited by volume, page. |
| *M* | *An Enquiry concerning the Principles of Morals.* T. Beauchamp (ed.). Cited by chapter, paragraph. |

NHR&#x20;&#x20;&#x20;&#x20;&#x20;&#x20;*The Natural History of Religion.* T. Beauchamp (ed.). Cited by chapter, paragraph/page.

SBNA&#x20;&#x20;&#x20;&#x20;&#x20;*An Abstract of a Treatise of Human Nature* appended to SBNT. Cited by page.

SBNM&#x20;&#x20;&#x20;&#x20;&#x20;*Enquiry concerning the Principles of Morals.* L. Selby-Bigge and P. Nidditch (eds). Cited by page.

SBNT&#x20;&#x20;&#x20;&#x20;&#x20;*A Treatise of Human Nature.* Revised edition. L. Selby-Bigge and P. Nidditch (eds). Cited by page.

SBNU&#x20;&#x20;&#x20;&#x20;&#x20;*Enquiry concerning Human Understanding.* L. Selby-Bigge and P. Nidditch (eds). Cited by page.

T&#x20;&#x20;&#x20;&#x20;&#x20;&#x20;&#x20;&#x20;&#x20;*A Treatise of Human Nature.* D. and M. Norton (eds). Cited by book.part.chapter.paragraph.

U&#x20;&#x20;&#x20;&#x20;&#x20;&#x20;&#x20;&#x20;&#x20;*An Enquiry concerning Human Understanding.* T. Beauchamp (ed.). Cited by chapter.paragraph.

## HUTCHESON

PW&#x20;&#x20;&#x20;&#x20;&#x20;&#x20;&#x20;*Philosophical Writings.* R. Downie (ed.). Cited by page.

SIMP&#x20;&#x20;&#x20;&#x20;&#x20;*Short Introduction to Moral Philosophy.* Liberty Press edition. Cited by page.

SMP&#x20;&#x20;&#x20;&#x20;&#x20;&#x20;*A System of Moral Philosophy.* 2 vols. Continuum reprint. Cited by volume, page.

## KAMES

EBA&#x20;&#x20;&#x20;&#x20;&#x20;&#x20;*Essays upon Several Subjects concerning British Antiquities.* Cited by page.

EC&#x20;&#x20;&#x20;&#x20;&#x20;&#x20;&#x20;&#x20;*The Elements of Criticism.* 9th edn. 2 vols. Cited by volume, page.

ELS&#x20;&#x20;&#x20;&#x20;&#x20;&#x20;&#x20;*Elucidations respecting the Common and Statute Law of Scotland.* Cited by page.

HLT&#x20;&#x20;&#x20;&#x20;&#x20;&#x20;*Historical Law Tracts.* 2nd edn. Cited by page.

PE&#x20;&#x20;&#x20;&#x20;&#x20;&#x20;&#x20;&#x20;*Principles of Equity.* 2nd edn. Cited by page.

PMNR&#x20;&#x20;&#x20;&#x20;&#x20;*Essays on the Principles of Morality and Natural Religion.* 3rd edn. Liberty Press edition. Cited by page.

SHM&#x20;&#x20;&#x20;&#x20;&#x20;&#x20;*Sketches on the History of Man.* 3rd edn. 2 vols. Cited by volume, page.

## MILLAR

HV&#x20;&#x20;&#x20;&#x20;&#x20;&#x20;&#x20;&#x20;*An Historical View of the English Government.* 4 vols. Liberty Press edition. Cited by volume, chapter/page reference to one volume.

Obs&#x20;&#x20;&#x20;&#x20;&#x20;&#x20;*Observations concerning the Distinction of Ranks of Society.* Cited by page.

OR          *The Origin of the Distinction of Ranks.* 3rd edn. W. Lehmann (ed.). Cited by page.

## ROBERTSON

*HAm*        *The History of America.* D. Stewart (ed.). Cited by page to *Works* (in one volume).

*HSc*         *The History of Scotland.* D. Stewart (ed.). Cited by page to *Works* (in one volume).

*India*       *An Historical Disquisition concerning Ancient India.* D. Stewart (ed.). Cited by page to *Works* (in one volume).

*VP*          *A View of the Progress of Society in Europe.* D. Stewart (ed.). Cited by page to *Works* (in one volume).

## SMITH

*CL*          *Considerations concerning the First Formation of Languages* in LRBL. Cited by paragraph/page.

*Corr*        *Correspondence of Adam Smith.* E. C. Mossner and I. S. Ross (eds), Liberty Press edition. Cited by letter number/page.

*ED*          *Early Draft of Part of the Wealth of Nations.* In LJA/B. Cited by paragraph/page.

*EPS*        *Essays on Philosophical Subjects.* W. Wightman, J. Bryce, I. Ross (eds), Liberty Press edition.

*FA*          *First Fragment on the Division of Labour.* In LJA/B. Cited by paragraph/page.

*HA*          *The Principles which Lead and Direct Philosophical Enquiries Illustrated by the History of Astronomy.* In *EPS.* Cited by section.paragraph/page.

*Letter*      Letter to the *Edinburgh Review.* In EPS. Cited by paragraph/page.

*Life*        *Account of the Life and Writings of Adam Smith.* Dugald Stewart (ed.). In *EPS.* Cited by section.paragraph/page.

*LJA*       *Lectures on Jurisprudence 1762/3.* R. Meek, D. Raphael and P. Stein       (eds). Liberty Press edition. Cited by section.paragraph/page.

*LJB*       *Lectures on Jurisprudence 1766.* R. Meek, D. Raphael and P. Stein (eds). Liberty Press edition. Cited by paragraph/page.

*LRBL*     *Lectures on Rhetoric and Belles Lettres.* J. Bryce (ed). Liberty Press edition. Cited by section.paragraph/page.

*TMS*       *The Theory of Moral Sentiments.* A. MacFie and

D. Raphael (eds). Liberty Press edition. Cited by book. part.chapter.paragraph/page.

WN          *An Inquiry into the Nature and Causes of the Wealth of Nations*. R. Campbell and A. Skinner (eds). Liberty Press edition. Cited by book.part. chapter.paragraph/page.

## STEUART
PPE         *An Inquiry into the Principles of Political Oeconomy*. 2 vols. A. Skinner (ed). Cited by volume, page.

## STUART
HD          *Historical Dissertation concerning the Antiquity of the English Constitution*. Cited by page.
OPL         *Observations concerning the Public Law and the Constitutional History of Scotland*. Cited by page.
VSE         *A View of Society in Europe in its Progress from Rudeness to Refinement*. 2nd edn. Thoemmes reprint. Cited by page.

## TURNBULL
PMP         *The Principles of Moral Philosophy*. A. Broadie (ed.). Liberty Press edition. Cited by page.
MCL         *Discourse upon Moral and Civil Laws* (appended to his edition of Heineccius' *System of Universal Law*). Cited by page.

## WALLACE
CGB         *Characteristics of the Present Political State of Great Britain*. Kelley reprint. Cited by page.
DNM         *Dissertation on the Numbers of Mankind in Antient and Modern Times*. 2nd enlarged edn. Kelley reprint. Cited by page.
Prospects   *Various Prospects of Mankind*. Cited by page.

# 1. *Scotland, Improvement and Enlightenment*

The Scottish Enlightenment is both a set of institutions and a set of ideas. As such they represent two differing facets of a complex whole. It is bad metaphysics to give one some sort of explanatory priority over the other – the argument that 'luxury' corrupts is just as 'real' as the number of diamond buckles for sale in the market. Given that the title of this book contains the word 'idea' then it is the latter set that will be the main focus. However, in acknowledgment (albeit in practice token) of complexity, this opening chapter provides, in Part I, an outline of the institutional setting. With respect to this setting, it needs always to be borne in mind that there is no necessary correspondence between what the historian can retrospectively identify as the 'objective' facts of the matter and what was subjectively apparent to those living in the time. Discounting as fanciful the possibility of mass self-deception, in this outline, I use 'improvement' as the principle of selection. This is a particular, documentable facet of the Scots' self-consciousness about their own society. Moreover, suitably reflecting the complex totality, 'improvement' exemplifies the linkage between the institutional and ideational dimensions of the Scottish Enlightenment; indeed, if less centrally, of the Enlightenment more generally. This wider picture is sketched in Part II and adumbrates some of the themes to be developed in subsequent chapters.

## I

J. S. Mill, on the opening page of his *Autobiography* (1873), said of his own time that it was an age of transition and that is certainly true of eighteenth-century Scotland, notwithstanding that that descriptor is something of a cliché. The Scottish transition is captured by the deliberate intent to 'improve'. This is not to say this intention is without precedent. To give just one illustration, George Sinclair the first 'professor' of mathematics at Glasgow, upon leaving the university in 1666, among other projects, put his hydrostatic knowledge to the task in 1670 of bringing a water supply into Edinburgh (Wood 2003: 96). In an overtly selective manner I examine how that 'improving intention' can be detected within the formal legal, religious and educational institutions and the more informal network of linkages between them, abetted by a host of clubs, societies and print media. These institutions, of course, exist within a political and economic framework. I start with an indicative survey of this framework.

## THE POLITICAL SETTLEMENT AND STATE OF THE ECONOMY

Without prejudice to the debate about how decisive an event it was, I start this survey with the Union of the English and Scottish Parliaments in 1707.[1] The whys and wherefores of this event were disputed at the time with an extensive pamphlet war and this continues, as a flurry of publications to mark the tercentenary bore witness (Whatley [2006] is the most perspicacious). What is less contentious is that Scotland was relatively poor[2] and that one of the motives behind the Union was the need for Scots to gain unrestricted access to English markets. While trade questions have been deemed to be 'no more than a propaganda duel' to justify a political, or religious, agenda (Riley 1978: 245; cf. Kidd 1993: 50) the bulk of the Treaty's articles in fact refer in some way to economic issues. These included the standardisation of coins and weights and measures (XVI, XVII), the levying of the same excise duties with some allowance for adjustments over time (VI to XV) and, especially important, giving 'all the subjects of the United Kingdom [. . .] full Freedom and Intercourse of Trade and Navigation to and from any Port or Place within the said United Kingdom and the Dominions and Plantations thereunto belonging' (IV). That last clause was to bear dramatic fruit later in the century with the growth of the Glasgow tobacco trade.

While the early years proved difficult (in part helping the cause of the Stuart claimant [the Old Pretender] to the throne following the accession of George of Hanover in 1714), by about mid-century the Union began to have an economic pay-off and rapid change took place (cf. Devine 1985). The growth of Glasgow was the most remarkable, but it was not alone. Edinburgh's population grew from 52,250 to 82,500, while Dundee's doubled and Aberdeen's increased by 80 per cent (Lenman 1981: 3). Glasgow's population grew from (roughly) 12,700 in 1708 to 17,000 when Smith was a student in the 1740s, and then according to Adam Anderson's computation this 'beautiful and increasing City' had reached 27,000 twenty years later (1764: II, 423), growing to over 54,000 at the end of the century according to the *Statistical Account*, and was soon to overtake Edinburgh. The city attracted numbers from the rural Western Highlands as a process of urbanisation began, though even in 1800 the majority of Scots lived in settlements of fewer than 2,500 (Foyster and Whatley 2010: 3). The rapidity of socio-economic changes, accentuating a seeming sharp divide between, what Robertson termed in his *History of America*, different modes of subsistence, has caused some commentators to speculate that the 'four stages theory' (with commerce as the fourth – see Chapter 2) was thus stimulated by these apparently evident changes.

Irrespective of the methodological soundness of that speculation, it is reasonable to remark that the Scottish 'literati', as they were contemporaneously known (Carlyle 1910: 312), and the institutions within which they operated, could scarcely be immune to the 'economy'. Excluding agriculture, the production of textiles, especially linen, was the chief Scottish industry and this expanded dramatically from the early 1730s (Durie 1979). A similar growth took place in the tobacco trade with the Scottish share of the British trade rising from 10 per cent in 1738 to 52 per cent in 1769 (Smout 1969: 244). Glasgow was the focus and the ten-fold growth in its trade between the 1730s and 1770s meant it overtook Bristol to become the major port (Devine 1990: 73). Smith knew a number of the Glasgow 'tobacco lords' and a passage in the *Wealth of Nations* where he remarks on the tendency of merchants to become country gentlemen (*WN* III.iv.3/411) does reflect the activities of a number of these tobacco merchants, such as John Glassford (who like a number of others gave his name to extant Glasgow street names).

The development of 'heavier' industry like mining, chemicals and smelting did not take off until the last quarter of the century and it is frequently noted that Smith's model of 'industry' was small-scale (Kennedy 2005: 132). What urbanisation and textile production did require was the growth of a market, as Smith centrally proposed. Markets need a supportive infrastructure, both physical and financial. Transportation was by boat and cart (Smith rode on horseback to Oxford to take up a Glasgow-awarded scholarship in 1740). While there was a reasonably efficient coach service between Edinburgh and London, as there was between Edinburgh and Glasgow, cross-country travel further afield was arduous and even by 1788 there were only eighteen turnpike trusts and none north of Perth (Durie 2010: 261). The only way to transport in bulk was by boat and, perhaps, the most striking 'improving' project was the construction of a canal linking the estuaries of the rivers Forth in the east and the Clyde in the west, with spurs into Edinburgh and Glasgow. Begun in 1768 and completed in 1790, the canal was a considerable engineering achievement; the author of the entry for the 'parish of barony of Glasgow' for the *Statistical Account* of 1791, declared the (still functional) viaduct over the river Kelvin to be 'one of the most stupendous works of this kind perhaps in the world' (Sinclair 1973: VII, 354).

Like all such large-scale projects the Forth–Clyde Canal was beset by financial problems. The most significant of these was the collapse of the Ayr Bank in 1772. This bank was one of many that were founded in the eighteenth century. The Bank of Scotland predated the Union but the Royal Bank was established in 1727 with the support of Andrew Milton and the Earl of Ilay (later the 3rd Duke of Argyll). The two banks had an uneasy relationship that was not helped by the establishment of the British Linen Company in 1746, in which Milton also had a hand (Durie 1979: 115). This company was set up to encourage the eponymous industry together with a cash economy and its operation as a bank was eventually recognised by the other two. These were all Edinburgh based and the commercial growth of Glasgow stimulated the emergence of banks there and the outbreak of 'bank wars'. It is in the context of this growth of 'private' banks (not possessing the limited liability status of the older establishments) that the Ayr Bank was founded in 1769. Its aggressive expansion, responsible for two-thirds of the notes in circulation in Scotland in 1772 (Cameron 1995: 63), led to an inability to cover its liabilities and its consequent collapse. More generally, this episode is telling because it exemplified the supposedly dangerous instability of commerce and credit over against the supposed stability of landed possessions. This debate will occupy us in Chapter 6.

If we now return to 1707, the Union Treaty's most palpable and dramatic consequence was that the United Kingdom of Great Britain (as it was now titled) was to "be Represented by one and same Parliament" (III). The Treaty (XXII) gave the Scots as Scots little direct political power (only sixteen nobles in the Lords and about 8 per cent of the complement of the Commons). But it did allow them to retain their own legal system. The latter was distinctively different from English Common Law and had always had closer links with European/Roman systems; indeed, until the eighteenth century and until the founding of law chairs in the universities, Scotland's lawyers were educated abroad, especially at the great Dutch universities of Leiden and Utrecht. Concomitant necessarily with the retention of the legal system was the continuation of the two supreme courts, the Court of Session (civil and appeal court) and the Court of Justiciary (criminal court) with, as explicitly specified in the Treaty (XIX), 'the same Authority and Privileges as before the Union'.

This settlement had the effect of enhancing the role and position of lawyers, and senior lawyers became pivotal figures in the administration of Scotland. The reason for this has been attributed to 'the executive vacuum which existed in Scottish government' thus making 'politics and the law almost inseparable' (Murdoch 1980: 55). Although there was a Scottish secretary based in London, there was less formally a Scottish 'minister' who 'managed' the Scottish parliamentary representatives, keeping them supportive of the administration. Ilay was the most conspicuous and influential of these ministers. He was, moreover, as we shall note, a conspicuous advocate (and practitioner) of improvement. The actual governance of Scotland lay in the hands of a sub-minister. This was the role played in the first half of the century by Andrew Milton. He was Lord Justice-Clerk (the senior Lord Justiciary) between 1734 and 1748 and then Keeper of the Signet (a sinecure but effectively in charge of civil administration) until 1766 (Murdoch 1980: 12; see also Shaw 1983: Chap. 7). He and Ilay/Argyll (who died in 1761) were the most powerful figures in Scotland, though that is not to say they were unopposed or always got their own way. In the last quarter of the century Milton's role was performed by Henry Dundas (Lord Advocate and Keeper of the Signet) (cf. Dwyer and Murdoch 1983). This use of local representatives or agents was also adopted by the leading Scottish magnates who upon their decampment to London required individuals, again normally lawyers, to look after their interests.

On a broader front what dominated the political landscape of the first half of the century was the Hanoverian succession to the throne of England and Scotland. The Union Treaty had reaffirmed the 1689 Settlement (on the accession of William and Mary, following the deposition/abdication of the Stuart king, James II/VII) that no Catholic could be monarch. The Treaty, moreover, had anticipated that should Anne (the current monarch) die without issue then the monarchy should pass to Sophia of Hanover and her heirs 'being Protestants' (II). The accession to the throne of George I energised the supporters ('Jacobites') of the Stuart line in support of their claimant Charles. This had particular purchase in Scotland because the Stuarts were a Scottish line from the accession of King James VI to the English throne in 1603.

While there were regular flare-ups and threatened invasions against the new dynasty, there were two significant rebellions: one in 1715, led by the Old Pretender and one in 1745, associated with the Young Pretender or Bonnie Prince Charlie. The former had widespread support and was able to draw upon a general dissatisfaction with the perceived lack of benefits flowing from the Union and the impact of a more efficient excise system. But it would be a mistake to regard opposition to the Union and Jacobitism as conterminous (Whatley 2006: 343). The members of the Scottish Enlightenment were Hanoverians but they predominantly belong to the next generation (for example, Hume was born in 1711, Smith and Ferguson in 1723; only Kames [Henry Home] born in 1696 and Wallace born a year later were of an earlier era). The '15 did garner some academic support especially in the non-Lowland Aberdeen universities (Kings and Marischal Colleges) where there had to be a purge because of significant support for the uprising.

The '45 initially seemed to pose a greater threat to the British state. The Jacobite army with little opposition penetrated into England to within about one hundred miles of London. Smith comments in his lectures à propos the effects of commerce that four or five thousand 'naked unarmed Highlanders' took possession of 'the improved parts' without resistance (*LJB* 331/540). This incursion flattered to deceive. Without any support, both militarily and logistically, the army returned to Scotland but, outside the Highlands, it was, within Scotland, poorly supported. This time the Aberdeen universities were loyal, indeed some members took up arms against the rebels (Emerson 1992: 12). The literati were indeed Hanoverian and, as Colin Kidd (1993: 115) has argued, they used their 'historical sociology' to reject 'a native political culture associated with armed resistance and religious fanaticism'. Robert Wallace, referring to the Union, gave a pithy assessment, 'in truth, the Scots have lost nothing that can be called substantial [. . .] [and] acquired the more solid blessings of security, liberty and riches' (*CGB* 117). After the battle of Culloden (1746), which crushed the rebellion, it was deliberate policy to destroy the political separateness of the Highlands (Youngson 1972: 26); a policy that has been emotively depicted as 'state-sponsored terrorism' (MacInnes 1999: 81) or 'cultural genocide' (Young 1979: 26).

This 'policy' captures in an important way not only the institutional and ideational linkage but also is intimately connected with a debate about the nature, or proper character, of a 'commercial society'. Four Acts were passed in the immediate aftermath of the '45. These included an 'Act for the more effectual disarming the Highlands in that part of Great Britain called Scotland' (19 Geo II c38) and another that abolished 'heritable jurisdictions' for the sake of 'remedying the inconveniences that have arisen' and restored the powers of jurisdiction to the Crown (20 Geo II c43). These 'jurisdictions', which had been explicitly preserved by the Treaty of Union (XX), gave local clan chiefs ('barons') rights to administer justice (including in the case of 'barons of regality' the power to punish by death) and pertinently the power to raise an 'army' from their vassals (Shaw 1983: 169). Smith refers to the exercise of local judicial power by a 'Mr. Cameron of Locheil, a gentleman of Lochabar [sic]' in the *Wealth of Nations* (WN III.iv.8/416) in the context of an explanation of the emergence of a commercial society. It is one of the cardinal features of the idea of a commercial society that the uniformity of a rule of law is effectively in place. Dr Johnson, for all his prejudices, was moved to remark of this measure that the 'crushing of all the local courts' had extended the 'general benefits of equal law to the low and high in the deepest recesses and obscurest corners' (1791: 101). (Gilbert Stuart had expressed this same sentiment some years earlier, along with the judgment that heritable jurisdictions were 'infinitely disgraceful' [*OPL* 39–40, 144].)

A third law (20 Geo II c51) forfeited rebel estates for subsequent resale. Milton was the prime mover in the execution of that task (Murdoch 1980: 38). The Highland Annexation Act of 1752 (25 Geo II c41) led to the establishment of the Annexed Estates Commission of 1755, with lawyers, including Milton, prominent amongst its membership, even if Ilay's sway was lessened (Shaw 1983: 171). What is revealing is that the Act explicitly stated that the income from the estates should be applied to 'the Purpose of civilizing the Inhabitants [. . .] promoting amongst them the Protestant Religion, good Government, Industry and Manufactures'. This language was not exceptional. The Sale to the Crowns Act (20 Geo II c51) was prefaced by the justification that 'whereas it may be necessary for the preservation of the publick peace and the further civilizing of the inhabitants of the highlands of Scotland'; and again the 1753 Act for 'Encouraging and improving the manufactory of Linen in the Highlands' was prefaced with a reference that this will be 'a farther means of improving and civilizing the Highlands'. The Scottish-born Adam Anderson in his monumental 'history of commerce' declared of the former Act that this is 'a very good law' (1764: II, 401). He was not alone. Robert Wallace in 1753 judged that the Highlands 'can only be civilized by being made industrious' (*DNM*: 159).[3] This is not to say there was no debate about both the efficacy and propriety of such a programme. As R. H. Campbell (1982: 19) judiciously observes, this form of intervention seems 'redolent of an earlier mercantilist age' and reflects a major bone of contention in how a 'modern' commercial society should operate, as we will see in Chapter 4.

There was a clear affinity between the literati and this legislation, with its open expression of the value of improvement. Wallace in his

*Characteristics* (1758) commented that 'a taste for improvements in manufactures and agriculture and an inclination to industry is gaining ground every day in Scotland' (*CGB*: 109). The affinity had visible presence in the appointment, as a Commissioner of the Annexed Estates, of Kames who was ennobled as a law-lord with Argyll's backing in 1752. Kames was a focal member of the Scottish Enlightenment. He was also on other boards, such as that for the Encouraging of the Fisheries, Arts and Manufactures (established by Article XV of the Union Treaty), and was an open advocate of the Forth–Clyde Canal and the plans for a New Town in Edinburgh (Ross 1972: 322, 328–9). Moreover, he himself was an 'improver' (on the estate of his wife). He corresponded with Joseph Black, a professor at Glasgow then Edinburgh, over the properties of clay regarding the issue of effective ploughing (see Tytler 1993: II, Appendix 99). As well as writing a lengthy handbook, with the splendidly evocative title *The Gentleman Farmer. Being an attempt to improve Agriculture, by subjecting it to the Test of Rational Principles* (1776), he had previously published a pamphlet on the *Progress of Flax-Husbandry in Scotland* (1766) as well as other similar works proffering policy advice. In line with the temper of the times, the *Gentleman Farmer* advocated the establishment of a 'Board for Improving Agriculture', to consist of nine members 'the most noted for skill in husbandry and for patriotism' though confined to gentlemen who resided in Edinburgh to permit punctual attendance at meetings (1776: 369ff). The *Progress* for its part explicitly evokes that 'spirit for improvement' as a product of the 'blessings of liberty and independence' that followed the Union (1766: 5).[4]

## THE KIRK

Before turning to the role of universities and various formal and semi-formal 'Societies' in promoting 'improvement' I will look briefly at the place of the Church. One still common picture of the Enlightenment paints it as hostile to religion. In Scotland the relation is nuanced. The literati shared an antipathy to superstition but they came to an accommodation with the Established Church. In an important sense this accommodation was itself connected to the drive to improve.

The Union Treaty attached a lengthy declaration that this Act should not alter the 'Worship, Discipline and Government of the Church of this Kingdom as now by Law established'. This was to secure the 'true Protestant Religion' and 'Presbyterian Church Government'. The 1690 Settlement had established Presbyterianism as the officially sanctioned form of Church government in Scotland. This was genuinely a governance. From the national General Assembly down to the kirk sessions in every parish, all aspects of social life were subject to its ordinances. Within what were small communities, those who were suspected of sinful conduct (adultery, drinking, dancing, missing church) were subject to 'discipline', including fines and public humiliations. A telling case in point at the institutional level is that subscription to the tenets of the Calvinist Westminster Confession was made the test of orthodoxy and all university teachers were required to adhere to the Confession of Faith.

The potency of this Calvinism is exemplified by the execution in 1696 of a nineteen-year-old student, Thomas Aikenhead, for blasphemy (even after he had recanted of his alleged view that theology was 'a rapsidie of faigned and ill invented Nonsense' [quoted in Hunter 1992: 224]). Yet the very severity of this response (and this is not an isolated case) could conversely, perhaps, be taken as indicative of a growing awareness that times were changing and sufficiently so to instil some insecurity that orthodoxy was losing its grip and authority.[5] While the rigours of Calvinist theology did indeed soften as the new century advanced, that seeming relaxation did not happen without contestation; there always remained a vociferous faction committed to an orthodox, evangelical approach even to the extent of a Secession in 1733.

The contest was partly doctrinal. Thomas Halyburton (1674–1712), who taught divinity at St Andrews, identified the divisive issue when he is reported in his *Memoirs* (1718: 199) to have lamented at the end of his life, 'that a rational Sort of Religion is coming in among us: I mean by it a Religion that consists in bare Attendance on outward Duties and Ordinances without the power of Godliness; and thence People shall fall unto a Way of serving God, which is meer Deism'.[6] An indicative marker of the change was the charge levied against Francis Hutcheson in 1737 by the Glasgow Presbytery for his contravention of the Westminster Confession by teaching that 'the standards of moral goodness was the promotion of happiness of others' and that humans can have 'a knowledge of good and evil without and prior to knowledge of God'. Not only did Hutcheson successfully defend himself but manoeuvred to get 'his' candidates appointed as the next two Professors of Divinity (the second of these, William Leechman, in a tightly contested affair [Kennedy 1995: 57]). As Hutcheson was well-aware from his own student days at Glasgow this chair had had an eventful recent history in the form of John Simson, who was officially suspended in 1727 and that after a reprimand in 1717. Both cases involved prolonged dispute but the gravamen of the charge was that Simson was undermining the fundamentals of Calvinist theology by adopting a more inclusive

approach, which for someone whose job it was to train Church ministers meant he was a dangerous subversive. Inevitably there was more
to it than 'just' theology, since politics and patronage also had a role
(for an exhaustive study of Simson see Skoczylas 2001). The fact that
this battle was fought out over university positions indicates how the
various institutions interlock but also how the 'case' for 'improvement'
had to be made.[7]

The disputes or contest also concerned Church organisation. What
especially galvanised the orthodox faction was the perceived betrayal of
the very principle of Presbyterianism, namely, that the congregation (the
'elders' – hence the Greek-derived term for this mode of governance)
had crucial oversight of ministers and their appointment. The perceived
root of this betrayal was the Patronage Act of 1712. This reasserted the
right of lay patrons to nominate ministers when a vacancy arose, with
the congregation able to accept or reject. These 'patrons' were effectively the largest landowner but the Crown itself was the responsible
agent in a quarter to a third of the parishes (McIntosh 1998: 12), and in
10 per cent this right of patronage was held by the town council. When
some lairds tried to exercise their right it was resisted by a number of
presbyteries. The fact that the General Assembly, the Church's ruling
body, was less than forthright in supporting the lairds' rights resulted in
the emergence of a group known as the Moderates. It is this group who
were the 'Enlightenment' party.

The key figure is William Robertson, who was not only an
Edinburgh minister but in time Principal of Edinburgh University and
Historiographer-Royal. He along with others, including Hugh Blair the
future Professor of Rhetoric and Belles-Lettres at Edinburgh, sought to
(re)establish the Assembly's authority. In response to the Assembly (or
a Commission in its name) not censuring the presbytery of Dunfermline
for disobedience, Robertson with others wrote a 'Reasons of Dissent'
(1752) (excerpted in Rendall 1978: 213–14). The crux of their case
was that in a 'society' a legitimate regulation has to be respected even
if individuals disapprove of it, since without that principle no society
can cohere. At the risk of some over-statement this is a declaration
of the primacy of the rule of law, without which commercial society
cannot effectively function. Many Moderates were lawyers and they
succeeded in getting one of their sympathisers made Moderator, though
not without generating a counter 'faction' (McIntosh 1998: 104).
Nonetheless the Moderates through astute tactics, rather than weight
of numbers, controlled the Assembly, with Robertson himself becoming
Moderator in 1762.

According to Richard Sher (1985: 213, cf. 211) the Moderates had a 'consistent ideological program'. More moderately they were working to that accommodation referred to above. As Ian Clark (1970: 207) says, acquiescence in patronage was the 'price' which the Church had to pay to continue to occupy a 'central place in the national life'. Again this reflects the characteristic institutional intertwining in as much as keeping the Assembly 'sweet' helped the 'management' of Scotland (Shaw 1983: 100). While the Assembly upheld and enforced the (legal) exercise of the power of patronage it, in return, was left free from direct 'interference'. This freedom facilitated the appointment of candidates sympathetic to improvement and to 'enlightenment' (Brown 1997). This does not mean the Moderates' religious beliefs were insincere; in their own eyes they were completing not overturning the Reformation (Kidd 2004: 514). The difference from their critics was more a matter of mood than doctrine (Voges 1986: 144). Hellfire sermonising may have given way to an emphasis on social duties (Christian neighbourliness) but this is consistent with the Moderates' conviction that duties such as politeness were 'part of God's plan for the Christian enlightenment of humanity' (Suderman 2007: 241) and consonant with the prevalent Enlightenment disposition toward Deism and a Christianised Stoic ethic.

## THE UNIVERSITIES

We have already noted that Robertson and Blair were academics and overwhelmingly the key thinkers of the Scottish Enlightenment had an institutional base in the universities. In this regard, they were not unique, for example, Kant was a professor at Königsberg, Linnaeus at Uppsala and Genovesi at Naples but the Scottish professors, as here being demonstrated, were a key part of the society's institutional nexus. For a country of Scotland's size and population the presence of five universities – St Andrews, Glasgow and Kings College Aberdeen, which predate the Reformation, and Edinburgh and Marischal College Aberdeen, which were Reformation foundations – is striking. The traditional task of these universities was to turn out ministers of religion and this continued throughout the century (Cant 1982: 44). This helps explain why law had to be studied abroad and why the provision of a medical education was moribund. As with law the Dutch universities taught many Scots their medicine (Alexander Monro who in 1722 was the first Professor of Anatomy in Edinburgh had studied at Leiden). The eighteenth century saw a marked change with the establishment of the law chairs and medical schools being officially recognised in Edinburgh (1740) and Glasgow (1760).

There were modernising moves. Lecturing in Latin was gradually abandoned with Francis Hutcheson an important pioneer. The system of teaching was overhauled. The traditional method whereby one teacher (the regent) took the same class for all its subjects throughout its four years of study was replaced by the professorial system of specialist teachers and classes (only Kings College retained it). It is, therefore, no coincidence that Edinburgh which led the way in abolishing regents in 1708 also appointed the first professor of law (1710).

The curriculum too underwent change. Aside from intellectually important developments like the teaching of Newton, there was a marked emphasis on the practical aspect of learning. As Paul Wood (2003: 103) put it, the natural philosophers played the 'the improvement card' to enhance the status of the subject both in the universities and the wider society. Hence, in addition to the development of vocational classes in law and medicine there was expansion in subjects like chemistry and botany which had obvious uses in agricultural improvement and 'industry', and intentionally so as William Cullen, when at Glasgow, acknowledged in a letter to Kames (Thomson 1859: I, 596). Indeed these two corresponded at length on the chemistry of fertilisers. Cullen later bought a property where he put his own principles into practice (Donovan 1982: 100; Thomson 1859: II, 670). Cullen also researched into the application of chemistry to linen-bleaching (Guthrie 1950: 62) and to herring preservation (salt) (Donovan 1982: 101). Similarly Francis Home, a professor of Materia Medica at Edinburgh, wrote *The Principles of Agriculture and Vegetation* (1756) to argue the importance of chemistry to enable the principles of agriculture to be established (1756: 4), and, again also like Cullen, he experimented on linen-bleaching (Cullen presented a paper on the subject in 1755 to the Board of Trustees for Encouraging Improvement [Thomson 1859: I, 76]). James Watt was employed by Glasgow University as (in his own designation) mathematical instrument maker. He had considerable interaction with the professors, especially benefiting from the work of Cullen and Black, the two most eminent chemists in the Scottish Enlightenment, while John Anderson, the Professor of Natural Philosophy, set him to work on the university's Newcomen engine (Law 1969: 13, 17).

The universities were a crucial component of the patronage system, with Ilay in particular seeking to appoint professors who would be committed modernisers. This is not to say mere 'party-men' were appointed. Roger Emerson, the leading scholar of academic patronage, summarises that, 'posts were given to particular people for reasons having to do with utility, politeness or a vision of what the country should become as it changed from a greatly depressed and backward agrarian region in 1690 to one which by 1806 was [...] thriving' (Emerson 2008b: 9). The apparently simple fact that the theorists of the Scottish Enlightenment were overwhelmingly university professors is prima facie evidence that in this system ability counted. It would, of course, be a mistake to deny that nepotism and cronyism was present. At Glasgow, for example, Robert Dick passed on the natural philosophy chair to his son, as did the Professor of Humanity Andrew Ross to his son, and Alexander Wilson's son succeeded him as Professor of Astronomy; and these were not the only cases (Mackie 1954: 186). This pattern was replicated in the other universities. It was not, however, always successful. Cullen's lobbying of Dundas for his son to get the botany chair at Edinburgh was to no avail (Thomson 1859: II, 232). Moreover, little was to be gained by appointing lazy incompetents, if for no other reason than that they would not attract students to pay their fees (a Scottish practice that Smith compared favourably to Oxford, of which he had direct experience as a Snell Exhibitioner upon graduating from Glasgow).

Smith himself got the logic chair at Glasgow in 1751 with the approval of Ilay and with the support of Kames, who had previously enabled Smith to give some public lectures in Edinburgh. Roger Emerson's researches reveal that Ilay either supported or acquiesced in twenty appointments at Glasgow between 1728 and 1761, including in their number Hutcheson, Cullen and Black (1995b: 38). Emerson also estimates that Ilay 'had a hand in at least fifty-five appointments across the Scottish Universities' (1995b: 30). For example, Kames wrote to Ilay as well as Milton and Edinburgh's Provost George Drummond to recommend Cullen for the chemistry chair in Edinburgh (Thomson 1859: I, 87–8). It should not be thought this support meant appointment was an automatic process. Ilay supported the rival to Leechman for the divinity chair at Glasgow, even though Leechman was of the same cast of mind as the modernisers; indeed, as well as Principal of Glasgow, he was also to become Moderator of the General Assembly. Smith's logic position was competitive and Milton was lobbied to support Smith's rival, George Muirhead (who a year later acquired – with Ilay support – the humanity chair). Nor is Glasgow exceptional. This pattern of appointments continued after Ilay. Lord Bute, who was Ilay's nephew and who had inherited the Argyll political machine, was responsible for Robertson's principalship and Blair's professorship at Edinburgh in 1762 and 1760, as well placing John Millar in the chair of civil law at Glasgow in 1761. Indeed in 1764 seven of the nineteen posts at Edinburgh and five of the thirteen at Glasgow had been filled with Bute's support (Emerson 1998: 159–60).

One seeming exception to this deliberate use of the universities to prosecute improvement is David Hume. For all his recognised intellectual abilities his candidacy formally for a chair at Edinburgh and perhaps less formally for Smith's logic chair (which was vacant upon Smith becoming Professor of Moral Philosophy) were unsuccessful. In the former case Hume attributed this to internal politicking on the Town Council (the appointing body) where his reputation for religious heterodoxy was brought up. In the latter case Hume cited, 'the violent and solemn remonstrances of the clergy' and the failure of Ilay to support him as the reason (*Letters* I, 164–5). Even Smith, who was one of Hume's supporters, wrote to William Cullen, a fellow supporter, admitting that he 'would prefer David Hume to any man for a colleague' yet acknowledged that 'the public would not be of my opinion' and that opinion needs to be heeded (*Corr* 10/5). While this illustrates, even if at the extremes, the limits of university 'enlightenment', Hume was no social pariah since he obtained a plum 'establishment' post of Keeper of the Advocates' Library in 1752.

## CLUBS AND SOCIETIES

Even from this sketch the interweaving nature of the Scottish institutions of the law, the church and the academy is apparent. The intellectual elite were woven into this fabric. One overt manifestation of this was the shared membership of clubs and debating societies that proliferated and which formed a point of convergence for the universities, the law, the church and the 'improving' gentry. A society grandly entitled 'The Honourable Society of Improvers in the Knowledge of Agriculture' was founded in 1723. This society was established with (as its title indicated) the practical aim of reforming agricultural practices, but its activities ranged widely. The 'improving' practices included introducing the 'English Method' (Ramsay 1888: II, 227) via new crops like clover, rotation and fertilising, as well as new tools and the reorganisation of tenure. As indicative of a broader understanding, T. C. Smout (1999: 219) judges that the draining of an Edinburgh loch in the 1720s by Hope of Rankeillor 'demonstrated the mind-set of the Enlightenment in respect of the possibility of altering the inherited environment'. Francis Home's *Principles* included chapters on soils, manures and ploughing. Particular landlords, such as David Hume's elder brother and Kames, as we have noted, on taking control of his wife's estate at Blair Drummond, set about these tasks systematically.

Home concluded the *Principles* with a 'plan for the further improvement of agriculture', pivotal to which was the establishment of a committee to act as a clearing-house and disseminator of research, with the power to 'grant honorary and lucrative premiums' to those who have 'delivered the most ingenious and useful experiments' (1756: 177). The 'Society of Improvers' also aided the development of the linen industry in as much as key members were involved in the foundation of the Board of Trustees for Fisheries and Manufactures (1727). This board, and its activities and policies, was the subject of published debate, both 'economic' and patriotic,[8] just as the post-'45 institutions generated discussion as to the appropriate mechanisms to stimulate 'the Scottish Highland economy'.

There were in fact many such societies, of which the most prestigious was the 'Select Society' of Edinburgh, founded in 1754, which generated in 1755 the indicatively named 'the Edinburgh Society for the Encouraging of Arts, Sciences, Manufactures and Agriculture'.[9] This included amongst its number key social theorists like Smith, Hume, Kames, Robertson and Ferguson (cf. Emerson 1973). Home's proposed agriculture committee was to be established by the Select. The Select Society, judged by D. McElroy (1969: 48, 58) as the supreme example of an improving literary society, also spawned, in 1761, the society for 'Promoting the Reading and Speaking of the English Language in Scotland' . The motivation here was partly a self-consciousness about 'Scottishness', in particular concern about the written and the spoken word. Back-handed evidence of this comes from Johnson, who with his characteristic condescension, remarks in 1773, that 'the conversation of the Scots grows every day less displeasing to the English; their peculiarities wear fast away' (1791: 380). Hume and Beattie both published lists of such peculiarities ('Scotticisms') and there were public lectures in Edinburgh attended by, as a contemporary put it, 'ladies and gentlemen of the highest position' because the study of elocution had become a 'rage' (Somerville 1861: 56). This anxiety, heightened by the fear of a glib English assumption that Jacobite equals Scot, produced the appropriation of the label 'North Britain' (see for example the editors' preface to the first edition of the *Edinburgh Review* of 1755 [in Rendall 1978: 223]) and the heavily Hanoverian street names of both the Edinburgh New Town and Glasgow new build.

This preoccupation was not merely an expression of self-consciousness because it was integral to a broader concern with politeness. This was initially spread by English periodicals, like the *Tatler* and the *Spectator*, which were reprinted quickly in Edinburgh and widely circulated (Phillipson 1987, 1981). The Scots emulated these by starting up the

*Scots Magazine* in 1739 (Murdoch and Sher 1988: 133). (This journal published in 1760 Hume's list of Scotticisms which had first appeared in his 1752 *Discourses*.) The attention paid to politeness and 'manners' was the corollary of the burgeoning urban culture so that indeed 'urbanity' (and the related 'civility') became (in practice if not in name) positively valued traits of character and behaviour in a commercial society. As their critics charged this was of a piece with the social preaching of the Moderates. Another contemporary remarked that the purveyors of this polite literature 'descanted in a strain of wit and irony peculiar to themselves on those lesser duties of life which former divines and moralists had left almost untouched' (Ramsay 1888: I, 6).

This attentiveness to social propriety also manifested itself in the proliferation of clubs and debating societies. We can get a flavour of the number and diversity of these from the *Autobiography* of Alexander Carlyle (one of Robertson's co-authors of the 'Reasons of Dissent') about his time as a student in Glasgow in the early 1740s. He refers to a weekly club, convened by Andrew Cochrane, Glasgow's provost, of the city's merchants 'to inquire into the nature of and principles of trade in all its branches and to communicate their knowledge and views to each other'. This club (the 'Political Economy') was later to include Smith among its membership (Ross 2010: 140). Carlyle himself joined a literary club that met in the university, another that combined students and 'some young merchants' and later joined yet another this time comprised largely of Glasgow professors (Carlyle 1910: 81–9). This last one, led by Robert Simson, fed into the Glasgow Literary Society (founded 1752), which combined 'town and gown' and at which Smith, Black and later Reid, for example, all read papers.

While some societies, like the Select, were explicitly concerned with improvement, others were more ostensibly 'philosophical', like the 'Rankenian' early in the century that included George Turnbull and MacLaurin (the leading Newtonian) among its members and later the 'Wise Club' in Aberdeen, the source of work from Reid, Campbell and Dunbar among others (Ulman 1990). The extant and still prestigious Royal Society of Edinburgh was founded in 1783. It was convened by Robertson and among those attending the first session were Cullen, Blair, Ferguson and Smith. In addition, also present were the Lord Provost of Edinburgh, the Lord Justice-Clerk, the Solicitor General and other lawyers, along with Edinburgh's MP (Campbell and Smellie 1983: 5).

What the Royal Society exemplifies par excellence is the wider fact that these various societies were an important part of the institutional fabric and played a leading role within Scotland. The literati as members of these institutions were themselves part of this elite (Spadafora 1990: 11). By forming a point of convergence for the universities, the law, the church and the 'improving' gentry these societies give substance to Anand Chitnis' (1976: 196) claim that they 'institutionalised the informal acquaintance of people of different expertise and, in so doing, furthered the movement of which they were a part'. These 'improving ideas' percolated down so that, for example, on a local scale, a large number of agricultural societies (a Scottish invention) were formed (Smout 2012: 144). This dissemination is a key factor in the development of social capital, an informal system of trust-building vital to economic development (Mokyr 2009: Chap. 16). In this way, it can be ventured, the idea of a commercial society took on institutional form.

This interweaving of the law, the church, the academy and 'clubs' establishes one of the crucial 'sociological' facts about the Scottish Enlightenment. Academies and salons were widespread throughout the Enlightenment as foci of debate and the dissemination of ideas but, as Richard Sher summarises, the Scots inhabited an 'environment of mutual support and common cause on behalf of economic and moral improvement, polite learning [. . .] and enlightened values' (Sher 2006: 147). This almost corporate identity, built on interlocking institutional foundations and personal ties with a pervasive interest in 'improvement', meant, as we have just ventured, that thinking about 'commercial society' was woven into the fabric; it was not some detached academic exercise.

## II

Millions of words (to which I have contributed in earlier work) have been spent on the Enlightenment, including the propriety of the definite article (for the contours of that debate, see more or less representatively, Pocock 1999, Robertson 2005, Sher 2006, Withers 2007). I have no wish here to add copiously to this volume. I do, though, want to use this discussion to signal or foreshadow some of the arguments to follow. In this endeavour I retain once again as a selective leitmotif the notion of 'improvement'.

The most often quoted sentence in John Millar's weighty *Historical View* (1797/1803) is in fact a footnote where he remarks, 'the great Montesquieu pointed out the road. He was the Lord Bacon in this [history of civil society] branch of philosophy. Dr Smith is the Newton' (*HV* II, 10/404n). I will use this quotation to structure this limited discussion. Accordingly I discuss discursively Bacon, Newton and

Montesquieu, though deviate from Millar by interpolating a brief exposition of the role of John Locke.

## BACON (1561–1626): REFORM AND IMPROVEMENT

Bacon had an iconic status. It was what he was perceived to stand for that mattered. The Enlightenment thinkers are not followers in the sense of being committed to the implementation of Bacon's various prescriptions; rather they value him as someone who, in challenging prevailing orthodoxies, prefigured their own attitude and approach. Hence Millar was not alone in this positive evocation. For Voltaire he was 'the father of experimental philosophy' (1956: 337) while d'Alembert, in the second part of his *Preliminary Discourse to the Encyclopedia* (1751), included Bacon as one of four significant predecessors, who 'prepared from afar the light which gradually by imperceptible degrees would illuminate the world' (1963: 74). Hume, in his *History* , follows suit by invoking Bacon's pioneering status in his observation that he 'pointed out at a distance the road to true philosophy' (*HE* II, 112).

Bacon himself was a lawyer not a scientist; indeed he did not accept the Copernican system. However, his cultural importance or honorific status stems from his arguments that the aim of 'philosophy' is the cultivation of knowledge that should contribute to improving the human lot. His own reasons for adopting this practical or utilitarian bent are open to debate – whether he was, for example, driven by his commitment to Puritanism and a providential view of history (Webster 1975: 25) or by his desire to promote an imperial state (Martin 1992: 141). But, in the current retrospective context, the touchstone is his declaration, toward the end of the *Advancement of Learning*,(*AL*) that he was driven by 'a desire of improving' (*AL* Bk IX Conclusion/1853: 375). It was this that resonated with Enlightenment thinkers. For them, as for him, knowledge in order to be worthwhile should be put to use. There were both negative and positive aspects to Bacon's own conception of his task.

He campaigned for old practices to be swept away. The most conspicuous target in this campaign was the 'old' organon of Aristotle, who 'corrupted natural philosophy by logic', and his heirs in medieval scholasticism (*New Organon* [NO] Bk 1, sect. 63/1853: 400). But Bacon also set his critical sights on two other trends in early-modern thought: the alchemical tradition, with its reliance on individual practitioners of natural magic; and scepticism, with its philosophy that all was uncertain or doubtable. In this endeavour to clear the decks Bacon was emulated by Descartes (another of d'Alembert's pioneers). Famously Descartes set his cap against scepticism with his 'thought-experiment' about the limits of doubt; it being indubitable that I am doubting or thinking. He too wished to undermine the reliance on 'authority' such as that of Aristotle (typifying his followers as no more than ivy that is restricted to the tree upon which grows [1912: 55]).

This disparagement of authority was to become central to the self-conceived purpose of the Royal Society as it institutionalised a key element in a 'Baconian ideology' (Webster 1975: 99), namely, that science was a co-operative endeavour and, accordingly, cannot be the prerogative of the solitary magus. The establishment of academies to implement this principle was to become a characteristic of the Enlightenment, of which Edinburgh's own Royal Society (mentioned above) is a prime example. The critique of authority is implicit in the motto '*Nullis in verba*' chosen by the original Royal Society. Thomas Sprat in his propagandist *History* of the Society called Bacon 'a great man who had the true Imagination of the whole extent of this Enterprize' (1702: 35) and this motto itself is an echo of Bacon's own concern to reform language. Words, he declared, 'insinuate themselves into the understanding'; they are one of the four 'idols' that he identifies as the 'deepest fallacies of the human mind'. The remedy, though he admits it is imperfect, is definitions (*AL* Bk V, Chap. 4/1853: 207–10). In related vein he advocated, as Adam Smith, for example, was to do, that the 'plain style' should be cultivated ahead of rhetorical ornament. Smith too, like many other Enlightenment authors, published on the origin and nature of language (see his *Considerations concerning the First Formation of Languages*, 1761 [subsequently appended to the Third edition of the *Moral Sentiments*, 1767]) .

But arguably more important than this negative element were Bacon's positive proposals to advance learning. The basis of this advance was 'genuine induction' (*NO* Bk I, xiv/1853: 386). This method was explicitly opposed to Aristotle's syllogistic method which, Bacon claims, cannot advance knowledge because while it might start with senses, it moves, on the basis of but a 'scanty handful' of experience, with unjustified haste to generalisation. Instead 'we must not [. . .] add wings but rather lead and ballast to the understanding' (*NO* Bk I, civ/1853: 431), that is, prosaically, starting from sense perception, with experience, the true method ascends 'continually and gradually' by a process of 'proper rejections and exclusions' (*NO* Bk I, cv/1853: 432) to produce experimentally generalisations or axioms. These in turn derive new experiments (*NO* Bk II, x/1853: 456) and thus 'define new particulars and impart activity to the sciences' (*NO* Bk I, xxiv/1853: 387). While the senses are obviously fallible Bacon thinks his method can produce certainty (Jardine 1974: 79). While, for Bacon, Aristotle only 'touches cursorily the limits of experiment' (*NO* Bk I, xxiv/1853: 387), his own gradual approach, he avers, treats the senses as the judge of 'experiments' and experiments as the 'judge of things' (*Great Instauration* [*GI*] [1853: 15]). To investigate things, or 'the phenomena of the universe' inductively enables the composition of a foundational natural history (*GI* 1853: 16). The purpose of this 'history' is, via 'every kind of experiment' (*NO* Bk I, lxx/1853: 407), 'to afford light to the discovery of causes' (*GI*: 1853: 17). This stress on 'experimentation' or the testing of experience, to elicit causes is central to the Enlightenment's self-understanding of their endeavours. This is not to say this Baconian approach was adopted without further more proximate refinement (recalling that Bacon is indeed judged to be operating 'at a distance').

Bacon's self-styled new 'natural history' was also a notable legacy. The enterprise itself on Bacon's presentation of it was capacious. It incorporated not only mere data collection and tabulation of nature in 'a free state' (minerals, plants, animals and the like) but also, and this is indeed distinctively Baconian, the study of nature as 'bound and tortured, pressed, formed' (*GI* 1853: 17). Nature 'wrought' (*AL* Bk II, ii/1853: 81) was so in virtue of 'art and human history' since Bacon believed, in language that has made him notorious, that 'the nature of things is better discovered by the torturings of art than when left to themselves' (*GI* 1853: 17).

The most important element in Bacon's legacy is, as mentioned above, his resolute utilitarianism, notwithstanding his acknowledgment that contemplation of truth is more 'exalted' than utility (*NO* Bk I, cxxiv/1853: 442). The legacy is apparent in what has become his best known proposition, 'knowledge and human power are synonymous, since the ignorance of the cause frustrates [*destituit*] the effect ' (*NO* Bk I, iii /1853: 383; 1740: I, 274). The discoveries of philosophy are not for their own sake since the 'real and legitimate goal of the sciences is the endowment of human life with new inventions and riches' (*NO* Bk I, lxxxi/1853: 416). Bacon gives a clue to what he envisages in his deliberate 'take' on More's *Utopia*. In his *New Atlantis*, immediately after repeating once again his key theme that the purpose of Solomon's house is the 'enlarging of the bounds of human empire' by 'the knowledge of causes', he gives examples of this enlargement. He mentions digging caves to produce 'new artificial metals', desalinisation plants and salt fields, orchards which 'by art' produce more fruit more often as well as methods to improve medicines, (1868: 297–9). This 'goal' jelled with the Enlightenment ethos of 'improvement'; the claim or conviction that theoretical knowledge could direct practical activities (Golinski 1988: 12). As we saw, the Scottish 'improvers' were centrally concerned to apply 'science' in order to make land increase its yield or chemistry improve linen. John Gregory (himself a doctor) captured this when he observed, 'the civil and natural history of Mankind becomes a study not merely fitted to amuse and gratify curiosity, but a study subservient to the noblest views, to the cultivation and improvement of the Human Species' (1788: 19).

Gregory's language here is a clear echo of Bacon, who divided history into natural and civil but since prosecuting the former meant human intervention then it was a mistake to separate nature from artifice; the history of arts (or 'mechanical history' (*AL* Bk II, ii/1853: 82) is the history of nature 'in constraint' (*AL Bk* II, 2/1853: 79). Thomas Reid judged that Bacon had 'delineated the only solid foundation on which natural philosophy can be built'. Reid then immediately went on to claim that Newton had reduced these principles to a few axioms (*Intellectual Powers* Bk VI, 41/1846: 436). This linkage between Bacon and Newton was widely accepted (Gaukroger 2001: 2). While Newton never mentioned Bacon neither did he disavow the association (Perez-Ramos 1996: 319); an association that, as Millar's footnote demonstrates, was so much part of received Enlightenment wisdom that it could be put to rhetorical use.

## NEWTON (1642–1727): NATURAL AND MORAL SCIENCE

The Scots were self-conscious members of Peter Gay's Enlightenment family (1967: 4). These kindred spirits thought of themselves as shedding improving 'light', so as to lift the darkness of ignorance and superstition. Science was the key source of illumination and its brightest source was Isaac Newton. His achievement was to encompass celestial as well as terrestrial phenomena within one comprehensive explanatory schema, derived from a few simple principles (laws of motion plus gravity). It was because Smith, in Millar's estimation, had reduced the seeming haphazard commercial interactions to a few key principles that he warranted the appellation the 'Newton of political economy'.[10]

Bacon, as we have noted, sought to narrow the distance between natural and civil history and this had an echo in Newton. In the Preface to his *Optics* (1704 Qn.31 [1953: 179]), Newton declared that the method of natural philosophy or science would when perfected enlarge the bounds of moral philosophy (that is, of social science as now understood). It would be a mistake to read this in too positivistic a manner.

Newton himself had the consolidation of true religion over paganism in mind and many of his followers did indeed see Newton's system as, in the words of his major early Scottish successor, 'leading us in a satisfactory manner to the knowledge of the Author and governor of the universe' (MacLaurin 1750: 3). Nevertheless, some of Newton's readers did draw a more directly programmatic message from this declaration. They were inspired to achieve for the moral or social sciences what he had done for natural science. Millar clearly thought Smith had succeeded (just as Kant thought Rousseau had succeeded with respect to the pivotal role of human will). And even when Newton was not mentioned by name his 'influence' was discernible as when Fernando Galiani, for example, in his *Della Moneta* (1751) compared *le leggi del commercio* to the laws of gravity and fluids (1915: 45) or as when Hutcheson compared 'universal benevolence' to the 'principles of gravitation' (1728: 222).

While Hume also gives no names, Newton is, even if not uniquely, a key inspiration behind his *Treatise of Human Nature* (1739–40), with its subtitle that the book is 'an attempt to introduce the experimental method of reasoning into moral subjects'. This method, he believes, has borne striking and decisive fruit in 'natural philosophy' and to pursue it 'morally' meant developing a 'science of man'. This, in turn, meant adopting the three approaches as indicated in the *Treatise*'s Introduction.

Firstly, in the study of moral subjects (humans and their institutions) the scientist must carefully and exactly attend to experience. The human or moral sciences are empirical. Secondly, like Bacon, this should not be a mere cataloguing but should attempt to trace these observational 'experiments' to universal principles, that is, by 'explaining all effects from the simplest and fewest causes'. This second approach comes to attain almost definitional status. Smith, for example, judges the 'Newtonian method' the 'most philosophical' because it deduces phenomena from a principle and 'all united in one chain' (*LRBL* ii.133/146). While for Adam Ferguson the 'object of science' is 'to collect a multiplicity of particulars under general heads and to refer a variety of operations to their common principle' (*ECS* 27). Thirdly, although Hume recognises that moral subjects are at a 'peculiar disadvantage' by being less amenable to experiment than natural ones, he nonetheless declares 'experiments' are still possible. These are derived from 'cautious observation of human life', as it appears 'in the common course of the world', which when 'judiciously collected and compar'd' can achieve certitude. Moreover, because of the solidity of its experimental conclusions, the science of man can be the most useful of all the sciences (*T* Introd.10.*SBNT*.xix). Here again we can see broad subscription to the utilitarian Baconian commitment to improve the human lot (Ferguson even cites the Baconian dictum 'knowledge is power' [*PMPS* I, 3, 280; II, 40]). This commitment is one of the central ingredients in the vindication of the idea of commercial society (see Chapter 3 especially).

The Enlightenment moral scientists did not approach their subject quantitatively; their social science was not 'statistical' (Sinclair's use of the term in the 1797 *Statistical Account* was a self-conscious English neologism). It has been frequently observed that the *Wealth of Nations* indulges in no econometrics, indeed Smith disparaged 'political arithmetic', and while there are plenty of tables and 'calculations' in the Physiocratic works of Quesnay and Mirabeau the latter is explicit that the work is deliberately not algebraic (1760: 20). It is not that there were no competent mathematicians among the Enlightenment scholars. D'Alembert and Maupertuis, for example, were accomplished practitioners. However, this did not intrude (so to speak) into their social thinking. The one outstanding exception is Condorcet. He is a historically significant figure because of his work on probability and his presentation of the paradox of circulating majorities, still cited in electoral studies.

It would also be misleading, and contrary to the Enlightenment's broad Baconian outlook, if it was thought there was a clear-cut division of labour between natural and moral science. 'Science' expressed an *esprit systématique* that encompassed all intellectual inquiry. The social scientists were conscious of operating on the same plane as those working in medicine, chemistry, mathematics and so on. As we have stressed, this conjunction was implicit in an equally shared concern with 'improvement'. Quesnay was a doctor (and published a number of medical works) as well as the founder of the Physiocratic 'school' of economics. Hume wrote a now lost early manuscript on mathematics and Smith exhibited some interest and perhaps some proficiency in the same subject and later studied botany (he had met the 'biologist' Charles Bonnet in Geneva) (Phillipson 2010: 189, 201). Cullen, who we have already mentioned for his improving applied science, also lectured on 'philosophical chemistry' and gave an account of its history akin to that written of religion or property by his compatriots (for an outline see Kent 1950: Chap. 2 and for a general discussion see essays in Withers and Wood 2002). A final illustrative Scottish example is James Hutton (the co-executor with Joseph Black of Smith's estate). In addition to his epoch-making *Theory of the Earth* (1795), Hutton wrote a massive treatise, *An Investigation of the Principles of*

*Knowledge and of the Progress of Reason* (1794) in which the 'science of morals' was a component. But what best perhaps captures this sense of a shared enterprise is revealed in the full title of another his works, *Considerations on the Nature, Quality and Distinctions of Coal and Culm, with enquiries philosophical and political into the present state of laws and the questions now in agitation relative to the taxes upon these commodities* (1777).[11]

## LOCKE (1632–1703): EDUCATION AND PROGRESS

The Scots, as advocates of improvement, are believers in progress. They share the commitment to knowledge and science over against ignorance, prejudice and superstition. They excoriate practices such as slavery, torture, witchcraft or religious persecution and they regard poverty, disease and crime as remediable dark spots. Indeed a key aspect of the Scots' idea of a commercial society is that it is better than (is an improvement upon and a progress from) earlier forms of social organisation. One of the ingredients of the received wisdom about the Enlightenment is that it was the 'age of progress'. It is not as if every thinker subscribed to every dimension (Henry Vyverberg [1958] wrote a book on *Historical Pessimism in the French Enlightenment* while Rousseau made his name by arguing there had been decline rather than progress), but as a generalisation it is true enough.

This belief in, and possibility of, progress required a theory of history. This frequently took a stadial form and we shall have much to say about this in Chapter 2. To link progress and history in the form of growth of knowledge required a principle of transmission. This principle was found in 'education' understood, as it was by William Godwin (1976: 111), to be 'every incident that produces an idea in the mind'. Although the Scots do not share Godwin's consequential confidence in the 'omnipotence of truth', they do interpret education capaciously to incorporate the processes of socialisation. These processes play a significant role in giving the Scots' historical works a gradualist cast. What enabled education to act as progressive conduit was the widespread Enlightenment acceptance of a modified Lockean epistemology.

In his 'Epistle to the Reader' prefaced to his *Essay concerning Human Understanding* (1689), Locke called himself an 'underlabourer' (*Epistle*/1854: I, 121). While there was an element of disingenuousness in this self-description it does reflect a genuine appreciation that the 'cutting-edge' of intellectual progress lay now with the 'master-builders', with 'scientists', like the 'incomparable' Newton or Boyle. The task of the underlabourer was to clear away 'some of the rubbish that lies in the way of knowledge' (*Epistle*/1854: I, 121). As a major component of this 'rubbish', Locke identified the doctrine of innate ideas or the argument that the mind contained within it certain universal truths or primary ideas. This doctrine was an obstruction to the construction of knowledge. For Locke we are only able to build once it is accepted that the infant's mind does not come ready-equipped with 'ideas' but is, rather, a 'white paper' (*Essay* II.2.2/1854: II, 205) or 'empty cabinet' (*Essay* II.1.15/1854: II, 142). Once that is acknowledged then we are able to recognise that our ideas come from 'experience'; it is in experience that 'all knowledge is founded, from that it ultimately derives itself' (*Essay* II.2.2/1854: II, 205).

This was a more sophisticated and consequential notion of experience than the one Bacon had put forward. It was in virtue of this assertion of empiricism that d'Alembert (1963: 83–4) included Locke along with Bacon, Descartes and Newton as a key precursor. Locke was compared to Newton as an innovator, having done for 'metaphysics' ('the experimental physics of the soul') what Newton had done for physics. This is not to say that Locke was adopted tout court. His own account, which had distinguished sensation from reflection, was simplified to subsume the latter in the former. The Abbè Condillac's *Essay on the Origin of Human Knowledge* (1746) was an important French source for adapting and improving Locke (and it too acknowledged in its Introduction Bacon's early role in recognising that knowledge comes from the senses [2001: 6]). Before Condillac, Hume's *Treatise* had proceeded on the basis that 'ideas' were but faint images of 'impressions' or sensations. Although a Lockean-derived empiricism provided the parameters for the bulk of Enlightenment thinking, it was a reaction to Hume that prompted the two notable exceptions to this consensus, since both Kant, toward the end of the century, and Reid, in the mid-century, were driven to attack Hume's supposed premise in the Lockean 'way of ideas'.

What the Lockean image of the mind as 'white paper' enabled was an explanation of unreason and the potential for the principles of reason to accumulate. This permitted superstitions, for example, to be identified as the product of credulous ignorance. For the French *philosophes* this was attributable to the social power of priests who had an 'interest' in keeping the bulk of the population in the dark, whereas if the mental blank page was inscribed by agents of reason, not unreason, then enlightenment was possible. For the Scots the argument was more subtle; for them the explanation lay rather in a complex of social conditions and circumstances that it was the task of Newtonian social scientists to discern (the same task that would enable them to articulate an idea of commercial society). Similarly for them it followed that the causal forces to effect enlightenment/improvement were more complicated. Nonetheless there was a shared ground for optimism. The Baconian dictum that knowledge of causes is power underpinned this for it meant, given that sound ideas can be produced by sound experience, then the more 'educated' society becomes then the more educated, less ignorant, will be the experience that it transmits to the next generation. Hence Helvétius' declaration that '*l'education nous faisant ce que nous somme*' (1843: 310]) or Smith's more specific observation that the difference between the porter and professor 'seems to arise not so much from nature, as from habit, custom and education' (*WN* I.ii.4/28). This observation exemplifies the principle of moral causation, an important dimension in the Scots' analyses and an examination of which will recur in the subsequent chapters.

While there was a shared general assumption that the 'malleability of man' (Passmore 1971) underlay this belief in the power of education and thence of progress (cf. Vereker 1967, Frankel 1948, Spadafora 1990), this was consistent with considerable variation between thinkers. What differed was the estimate of the degree of recalcitrance or 'stickiness' (Berry 2003a). This ranged from Kames' depiction of custom as 'riveting men to their local situation' (*SHM* II, 87) and Smith's location of social change in the 'silent and insensible' shift in property of manners (*WN* III.iv.9–10/417–18) to Godwin's view that through the power of education on the infant mind human weakness is not invincible (1976: 112, 140) and Condorcet's conviction that '*l'empire du hasard*' is surmountable through the reciprocal progress of science and education enabling a continual reduction in inequalities and development toward perfection (1933: 238, 231, 211). The Scottish pairing reflects Duncan Forbes' (1954) argument that the Scots' version of progress had a number of distinctive characteristics derived from their attaching less weight to deliberative reason and more to the recalcitrance of habit, together with an acute awareness of what Forbes (after Wundt) called 'the heterogeneity of ends' or unintended consequences.

## MONTESQUIEU (1689–1755): LAW AND REPUBLICANISM

If 'improvement' is a leitmotif of the Enlightenment then it obviously has political resonance if only in the sense that the status quo is not the best of all possible worlds and there are reasonable grounds to wish for or to advocate or to take action to bring about change. As this range of options indicates there is no one principled course of action. Accordingly we find among the array of Enlightenment thinkers support for benevolent despotism (Voltaire), austere republicanism (Rousseau), constitutionalism (Kant), anarchy or at least minimal government (Godwin). Similarly there are degrees of support for and differing interpretations of equality and liberty. The Scottish Enlightenment is, though, remarkably uniform in its outlook. As is apparent from Part I, their commitment to the House of Hanover meant they were fundamentally committed to the British constitution (indeed are frequently fulsome in praise of it) and, as we will see in later chapters, they held similar views on the relation between equality and hierarchy, and while their disagreements over liberty were more extensive these overlaid shared parameters.

This is not intended to downplay their differences; indeed what was entailed by a society being 'commercial' was a prime site of debate. This will be a running theme in subsequent chapters and the focus of Chapter 6. Here it will be useful to limn out some general contextual features. One of the key ideas that this book is exploring is that to think in terms of 'society' rather than regime type was departure. Ever since Plato and Aristotle complex typologies of constitutions had been drawn up and versions of these persisted into the eighteenth century. The classical twin focus on the quantity of rulers (one, few, many) and the quality of the rule (for the good of all or for the good of the rulers) over time produced respectively an emphasis on the instrument of rule (in the guise of law) or an emphasis on the appropriate character or virtues of ruling and being ruled. These were never stark opposites but they did come to generate two sets of discourse, one talking principally of law and rights, the other centrally of virtues and corruption.

Because these reflect emphases not contraries, most thinkers exhibit strains of both. In work on the Scottish Enlightenment much interpretative labour has been expended on assessing which vocabulary best captures the thought of Hume or Smith or Ferguson, to name only the three most prominent. Montesquieu is another obvious case. The immense impact of his thought is exemplified by Millar attributing to him the Baconian role of pioneer to Smith as Newton.[12] The title of Montesquieu's best known, and deeply influential (with the Scots to the fore), book *De l'Esprit des Lois* (1748) betrays a jurisprudentialist frame. Speaking with inevitable generality, the roots of this legal focus lie in the systems of Roman imperial jurisprudence as it sought to systematise and codify the various local laws of lands now under its sway. This legalism penetrated the Church and then entered either directly or indirectly into the newly established university curricula. Without denying a variety of endogenous processes (see Thornhill

2011), the decisive developments in jurisprudential thinking came in early modern Europe as it adapted to both the post-Reformation collapse of Christendom and the discovery and colonisation of the 'New World'. It is in context of this adaptation that the major texts of Suarez (*Of Laws* [1611]), Grotius (*Of the Rights of War and Peace* [1625]) and later Pufendorf (*Of the Laws of Nature and Nations* [1672]) were produced. The last was especially influential. Gershom Carmichael, Glasgow's first Professor of Moral Philosophy, wrote a commentary on Pufendorf's *Duties of Man and Citizen* (1673), that his successor Francis Hutcheson declared to be 'by far the best' (*SIMP* 3) and who in his own lectures closely followed Pufendorf's discussion. Smith, who after a brief hiatus succeeded Hutcheson, cites Grotius and Pufendorf, alongside Hobbes and Cocceii's commentary on Grotius, in his opening lecture on jurisprudence (*LJB* 1, 3/397–8). Elsewhere in these lectures Smith scatters references to Montesquieu drawing from the treasure trove of examples contained in *De l'Esprit*.

Montesquieu himself opens his book with a discussion of laws in general and announces the cardinal principle that a principle of equity is prior to any human laws. This itself goes back to the roots of Natural Law, arguably to Aristotle or Cicero and certainly to Aquinas, and retained its force in the Enlightenment. Quesnay, for example, in the midst of *Philosophie Rurale*, declares '*le droit naturel*' to be absolute and the foundation of all positive laws (1764: III, 8). Even a thinker like Beccaria, who emphasised the criterion of utility, nonetheless declared the law against suicide '*ingiusta*' (1965: 82). There was, though, more to justice than its role as a benchmark. It was also a decisive principle in a conception of a commercial society; its 'strict' application as we will examine in Chapter 4, was judged necessary to sustain confidence.

Part of what made Montesquieu have such an impact on the Scots was that he distanced himself from some of the basic assumptions of the Natural Lawyers. Unlike Grotius (whom he never cites) and others, Montesquieu did not talk of a 'state of nature' or social contract as the basis of legitimate rule; like his Scottish followers the individualistic premises of the Lawyers were not judged a sound basis for articulating what he called '*un esprit général*' (Bk 19, Chap. 4/1961: I, 319). And yet Montesquieu still produced a typology of governments, albeit an idiosyncratic one with a tripartite classification of monarchies, republics and despotism. This, characteristic of his novelty as a thinker, deliberately melded the quantitative and qualitative dimensions. Number differentiated the first and third from the second (which he subdivided, again numerically into aristocracies and democracies) but the third was distinct because its '*principe*' (or animating force or passion) 'fear' was sufficiently distinct from the 'virtue' of republics and the 'honour' of monarchies to warrant it being a distinct type (Bk III, Chap. 9/1961: I, 31). This association of virtue with republics reveals the presence in *De l'Esprit* of that other equally venerable, and still in the eighteenth century widely-followed, vocabulary. As we proceed, it will be notable that there is also an association between these republics and commerce or trade. However, we will seek to indicate that this association is not identical to the idea of commercial society as put forward by the Scots.

The roots of this 'other' vocabulary lie in Aristotle's argument that the political or civic life was the authentic expression of human nature. Human fulfilment was thus integrally linked with political participation. Those who participated ideally possessed an educated ethical disposition to maintain the public good or act virtuously. These active citizens constituted a republic. Those who failed in that task lacked virtue and the republic was corrupted. What was especially significant and will loom large in Chapter 6 is that this corrupt favouring of self over public interest was associated with commercial or 'economic' pursuits. It is this association upon which Montesquieu is drawing when he identifies virtue as the *principe* of the republics. However, later in the book he devotes many pages to commerce where, while it might corrupt '*les moeurs pures*', it nonetheless polishes and softens '*les moeurs barbares*' (Bk XX, Chap. 1/1961: II, 8). As we will see Montesquieu's use of '*polit*' and '*doucit*' here is significant (recall from Part I the notion of polished manners) as is his clear statement that '*L'effet naturel du commerce est de porter à la paix*' (Bk XX, Chap. 2/1961: II, 8). What these isolated snippets indicate is not merely the internal intricacies of *De l'Esprit* but also, on the broader Enlightenment stage, the complexity, if not confusion, of thinking about economics and politics, about virtue and commerce, and about law and history. The Scots' idea of a commercial society was articulated in the context of this complexity. It will be too much to say that they eliminate it but – or so it will be argued in what follows – they do plot a course that helped establish the parameters of future thinking.

## NOTES

1. Among those who judge the Scottish Enlightenment to 'start' in the late seventeenth century are Allan (1993), Emerson (1986, 1995a), Chitnis (1976).
2. Incidental evidence of that comes from the comment made by James Wodrow (Professor of Divinity at Glasgow in the crucial period, 1692–1707) to his son (Robert) that printing in Scotland was hindered by 'want

of money' both to incur the costs of publication and for people to buy what was produced (Wodrow 1828: 171).

3. Robertson reports an earlier attempt by James VI in 1602 to 'civilize the Highlands and Isles' by introducing towns and even planting a colony of fishermen from Fife in Lewis. Though this failed, James, being distracted and not able to persevere in this policy when such perseverance is necessary to 'change the manners of a whole people', Robertson does commend James' policy as 'salutary' and that he had 'pointed out the proper method of introducing the civil arts of life' (*HSc* 210). Dalrymple similarly remarked on James' lack of perseverance in the related task of removing even then heritable jurisdictions (*FP* 292).

4. The pamphlet is a typical Kames performance. He commends his plan for inter alia rescuing the 'poor weavers from the oppression of the wholesale-dealer by affording them a choice of markets', while concluding with the warning that the opulence created should not be so extensive as 'to sap the foundations of virtue, to erect a throne for luxury and for depraved selfishness which reduce a nation to an abject state of degeneracy and terminate in a total corruption of manners' (1766: 28, 31). See Chapter 6 for the intellectual context of that 'warning'.

5. This defensiveness can be detected in Principal (of Edinburgh) Gilbert Rule's remark in 1693 that ''tis true we preach not morality alone, as some do; but instruct people in the mystery of Christ [. . .] But we preach the necessity of good works and that moral virtues are not only the greatest ornament of practical religion but a necessary part of it' (*A Just and Modest Reproof*, quoted in Kidd 1993: 62).

6. In the *Memoirs* themselves Halyburton discusses the 'profane and vain Babblings' of Deism (1718: 52). (In his account of his own youthful sinfulness he refers in passing to the 'invisible hand' [1718: 12].) He wrote a book, *Natural Religion Insufficient* (1714), which was expressly directed against the Deist doctrine of Herbert of Cherbury. In the course of his argument he refers to Aikenhead as an 'inconsiderable trifler whose undigested notions scarce deserve the consideration we have given them' (1798: 103–6).

7. George Turnbull (1722) in a letter declaimed against 'domineering pedantic priests' who wanted universities to instil in their students 'a profound veneration to their Senseless metaphysical Creeds & Catechisms' (quoted in Skoczylas 2001: 224).

8. See for example Patrick Lindsay's (Lord Provost of Edinburgh) lengthy *Interest of Scotland Considered* (1733) which praises the board and aims to exhort through his publication 'a spirit of Industry in the People' (1733: xx), observing that industry is stimulated by (in a Barbon-esque manner [see below p. 159]) the invention of 'new wants' (1733: 60). His defence of linen as Scotland's staple product generated a critical reply, in defence, and advocacy of the 'publick Encouragement' of wool (Thomas Melvill's *The True Caledonian* [1734: 16]). Melville deemed that Lindsay seemed

to have a 'deep concern' for the 'Interest of the English' (whose staple was wool) (1734: 35). He laments that 'it is a Pity' that Scotland cannot excel in trade, as it has in 'martial Affairs', especially since 'Trade is the only Thing that can make a Nation truly Great in itself' (1734: 39). See the discussion of this period in Seki (2003).

9. In line with his general interpretation that there was an 'identity crisis' in post-Union Scotland, Nicolas Phillipson claims the Select became a 'para-parliament' (1976: 111; cf. 1973).

10. Millar was not alone. Governor Pownall opened his assessment of the *Wealth of Nations* by noting that Smith's treatise had fixed 'some first principles', becoming a *'principia* to the knowledge of politick operations (see Smith *Corr* App. A, 337).

11. This pamphlet argues that to describe accurately a particular species of coal is 'the province of the naturalist' on which basis there is no distinction between coal and culm. There is, though, an 'eminent difference in this commodity as fewel', that is, commercially or in the domestic economy. That difference can form the basis of differential taxation (he cites 'Dr Smith') (Hutton 1777: 6, 8, 37).

12. Millar reported to Dugald Stewart for his *Life* of Smith that, regarding justice, Smith 'followed the plan that seems to be suggested by Montesquieu; endeavouring to trace the gradual progress of jurisprudence both public and private from the rudest to the most refined ages' (*Life* I.19/274). As we shall see, the Scots criticise Montesquieu for being insufficiently historical and this indeed might be one reason Smith is the 'Newton' to Montesquieu's 'Bacon', that is, by incorporating a diachronic dimension he has advanced beyond the 'suggestions' in Montesquieu to develop the 'science' of political economy and civil society.

# 2. Commerce, Stages and the Natural History of Society

One of the ideas for which the Scots are best known is their notion of the four stages (hunting, herding, farming, commerce). However, 'best known' is not the same as 'best understood'. The argument here is that the 'four stages' is best interpreted as an instance of 'natural history', as presented in Dugald Stewart's summary characterisation of that enterprise. The third section of this chapter will discuss in some detail the Scots' explanation of the break-up of feudalism (third stage) and the establishment of commerce as a way of life. This establishes the 'distinctiveness' of commerce and situates it within a temporal narrative. But before that I outline, in Part I, the meaning of conjectural or natural history before, in Part II, analysing the place and role of the four stages.

## I

In his *Account of the Life of Smith*, Dugald Stewart, in the context of a discussion of Smith's essay on language (*'Considerations'*) makes some generalising comments. These have become the locus classicus for what he terms '*Theoretical* or *Conjectural History*'. He explains that this is an enterprise that 'coincides pretty nearly in its meaning with that of *Natural History*, as employed by Mr Hume, and with what some French writers have called *Histoire Raisonnée*' (*Life* II.48/293; Stewart's emphases) and a little later he gives as further examples of this approach Kames' *Historical Law Tracts* and 'the works of Mr [John] Millar' (*Life* II.51/295). Stewart had previously set the scene for this characterisation. He opens by declaring it an 'interesting question' to discern by what 'gradual steps' the transition from the 'simple efforts of uncultivated nature' to a 'complicated' state has been made (*Life* II.45/292). He also remarks that little information can be gleaned, especially in the earliest ages, from 'the casual observations of travellers'.

Stewart is here faithfully representing recurrent aspects of the Scots' writings and we will consider, in particular, the initial declaration as we proceed.

For Stewart the consequence of the 'interest' in development from simple to complex, in conjunction with a paucity of evidence, is that

> we are under a necessity of supplying the place of fact by conjecture; and when we are unable to ascertain how men have actually conducted themselves upon particular occasions, of considering in what manner they are likely to have proceeded, from the principles of their nature, and the circumstances of their external situation. (*Life* II.46/293)

This sentence deserves scrutiny, if only because it has led to some misreadings of the argument. The 'necessity' in question derives from the imperative that an 'explanation' should be 'complete'; if 'gaps' are left in the narrative of development then this leaves 'space' for fanciful interpolations. Smith, in his *Rhetoric* lectures, acknowledges that imperative when he mandates that a narrative should not leave 'any chasm or gap' (*LRBL* ii.37/100). This aversion to episodic representation and commitment to a narrative continuum was typical (Manuel 1959: 112). In his *History of Astronomy* Smith provides an extended discussion according to which 'gaps' or breaks disturb the expected run of things. This disturbance causes initially 'surprise' and then 'wonder' at how the disruption has occurred (*HA* II.6–7/40–1). He then characterises philosophy or science (using the terms interchangeably) as the attempt to discover a 'connecting chain of intermediate events' such that the previously disturbed imagination can reassume its habits of association and in this way remove the wonder (*HA* II.9/42). The connecting 'chains' are those of cause and effect. This now provides a further dimension to the force of Stewart's use of 'necessity'.

The development from simple to complex is not to be understood as haphazard, but as 'orderly' or structured. This is an instance of the aspiration to emulate Newton in the social world on which we remarked in Chapter 1. If the social world was to be subject to scientific investigation then it had to be susceptible to causal analysis. Recourse to causes in explanations was hardly exceptional. Aristotle had systematically identified four causes (formal, material, efficient and final) and this established the analytical framework until the Renaissance. But in the Enlightenment this analysis had to be 'experimental' that is, as Bacon and Locke had outlined, rooted in experience, with Hume's account famously (or infamously) the most rigorous.[1] The import of these observations is neatly encapsulated by Kames. In his *Historical Law Tracts* he asserts that for law to be 'a rational science' (cf. *ELS* xiii) events must be 'connected in a regular chain of causes and effects' and 'we must endeavour to supply the broken links [in a 'historical chain']' by 'cautious conjectures' drawn from the 'collateral facts' supplied by 'poets and historians' (*HLT* v, 22). Again note here the concern not to leave 'gaps'. This passage is also a likely contender for the source of Stewart's decision quoted above to label this whole enterprise 'conjectural history'.

We have not yet completed the examination of that quotation. We can also see that therein Stewart spells out some cautionary principles when conjecturing. Conjecture is not here to be confused with idle speculation. This was the meaning Ferguson adopted when at the start of the *Essay on the History of Civil Society* he criticised the accounts of the State of Nature put forward by Hobbes and Rousseau (implicitly) as 'conjectures' distinct from the 'facts' (or as 'hypotheses' not 'reality') (*ECS* 2).[2] Stewart's usage rather pretends to respect the facts. This respect stems from recognising the need to anchor conjectures, thus stopping them from floating free like Hobbes' view that humans are naturally solitary and brutish. The principal anchor is constituted by 'the principles of human nature'. These are fixed and constant and thus a proper subject for a 'science of man' (Hume *T* Introd.4/*SBNT* xv). This anchor is complemented by a second – 'external circumstances'. These are uncovered by empirical investigation. In practice this investigation was a combination of history and contemporary ethnography (in essence what Kames above called 'collateral facts'). If, in the cases in point, this circumstantial information is unavailable it remains possible to make inferences (conjectures) derived from these fixed principles of human nature and knowledge of other 'circumstances' that may be 'cautiously' and 'judiciously' judged similar (*T* Introd.10/*SBNT* xix). The Amerindians were especially important in this respect. Robertson, again testifying to the need to fill gaps, states explicitly that they 'fill up a considerable chasm in the history of the progress of the human species' (*HAm* 812). The universalism here is an important element in the Scots' analyses and is signalled by Stewart in his declaration that the subject matter of natural history is 'the history of mankind'. This same phrase is used in the title of Kames' *Sketches* and Dunbar's *Essays* and recurs across the Scots' writings (e.g. Millar *OR* 180; Ferguson *ECS* 3; Smith *WN* IV.vii.c.80/626).

In the examination of this 'history', Stewart remarks that when 'we cannot trace the process by which an event *has been* produced, it is often of importance to be able to show how it *may have been* produced by natural causes' (*Life* II.47/293; Stewart's emphases). This remark is important. To appreciate what is at stake, we can turn again to Kames' *Tracts*. He there remarks that it is through collecting and collating facts from different countries that we can 'make a regular chain of causes and effects' so that we may then 'rationally conclude that the progress has been the same among all nations in the capital circumstances at least; for accidents or the singular nature of a people or of a government will always produce some peculiarities' (*HLT* 23). This dictum is typical of the Scots. The remark also throws light on perhaps the most contentious passage in Stewart's discussion of natural/theoretical/conjectural history. He declares that in most cases, it is of more importance to ascertain the progress

> that is most simple, than the progress that is most agreeable to fact; for paradoxical as the proposition may appear, it is certainly true, that the real progress is not always the most natural. It may have been determined by particular accidents, which are not likely again to occur, and which cannot be considered as forming any part of that general provision which nature has made for the improvement of the race. (*Life* II.56/296)

This declaration has been a butt of much criticism. While chiefly reflecting the impact of post-Rankean or post-Collingwoodian[3] historicist sensibilities there were contemporary doubts.[4] But these critics miss their mark. Natural history, as here summarised by Stewart, is best understood as an expression of the Scottish aspiration to scientific social theory, as Frederick Teggart (1941: 92) initially argued and who was followed in 1945 by Gladys Bryson (1968) in her pioneering study.

Kames again provides a useful clue as to what is at stake. He distinguishes 'rational' history, which traces causal chains, from 'geography' or the antiquarian 'collection of facts merely'. The latter cannot explain why a particular event happened when it did or, what is the same thing, simply puts it down to chance (*HLT* vi–vii). Hume is instructive on this contrast. He opens his early [1742] essay 'Of the Rise and Progress of the Arts and Sciences' with some methodological considerations. He says there is a need to distinguish 'exactly' between what 'is owing to chance and what proceeds from causes' (*E-AS* 111). He does not deny there is a distinction here but the decisive defect of the recourse to chance is that, contrary to the scientific imperative to seek explanation, it precludes all further enquiry. He illustrates it with the performance of a biased die. In a few throws the bias will not reveal itself but it 'will certainly prevail in a great number' (*E-AS* 112). Millar uses a very similar example.[5] He supposes that in one or two throws of a die very different numbers will be produced but 'in a multitude of dice thrown together at random the result will be nearly equal' (*OR* 177). Millar uses this example in his critique of 'Great Man' explanations, as especially manifest in the recourse to legislators, like Lycurgus for Sparta, to account for political constitutions. The die analogy serves to underline the difference between 'the character and genius of a nation', where 'fixed causes' can be identified, and that of an individual, where such fixity is absent. Hence Stewart's contrast between 'real progress' (the 'most agreeable to fact') and 'natural progress' (the 'most simple') is that between one roll and many rolls of biased die.

The example of a die indicates that the 'necessity' in natural history is probabilistic.[6] Again using this example, Hume made this explicit in the *First Enquiry* where he states,

> There is certainly a probability which arises from a superiority of chances on any side; and accordingly as this superiority encreases, and surpasses the opposite chances, the probability receives a proportionable encrease and begets still a higher degree of belief or assent to that side in which we discover the superiority. (*U* 6.1/*SBNU* 56)

In the early essay Hume called it a 'general rule' that 'what depends upon a few persons is in a great measure to be ascribed to chance, or secret and unknown causes: what arises from a great number may often be accounted for by determinate and known causes' (*E-AS* 112). This 'rule' provides the social scientist with a 'working tool'. For example, Hume's essay on population is phrased as an enquiry as to 'whether it be probable from what we know of the situation of society in both periods [ancient and modern] that antiquity must have been more populous' (*E-PAN* 381). As this example demonstrates social science deals properly with probabilities. While Hume's is typically the most rigorous application he is not alone. Indeed Wallace in his own population essay also explicitly set out to enquire whether 'it is not probable' that the ancient world was more populous (*DNM* 33) and Turnbull, too, links probability with the use of 'general observations and rules' (*PMP* 81).

Having to deal with probabilities does not mean social science is not a search for causes. The evidential fact, to give Hume's own example, that rhubarb is not invariably a purgative (unlike fire which always burns) prompts 'philosophers' to seek the 'secret cause' in the exceptional case. In the case of both rhubarb and fire 'our reasonings [. . .] are the same' (*U* 6.4/*SBNU* 58). For Hume, there is 'no such thing as chance in the world' (*U* 6.1/*SBNU* 56). Hence the reference here to 'secret' causes', echoed earlier, as we have seen, in *Arts and Sciences* and originally in the *Treatise* (*T* 1.3.12.1/*SBNT* 130; cf. Kames *PMNR* 195). Hume's wording makes it clear that this difference between chance and cause is one of degree of knowledge (probability). Causal explanations are in principle always available. Of course, care must be taken neither to 'assign causes which never existed' nor to 'reduce what is merely contingent to stable and universal principles' (*E-AS* 113).

The probabilism that the die example throws up, and the polemical naturalism that animates it, reveals a weakness in Mary Poovey's generally insightful account of conjectural history (as she unfailingly terms it). Her analysis is vitiated by her preoccupation with identifying an essentialist reliance on 'human nature' that, she holds, privileged uniformity over difference (1998: 224). Despite her own explicit divergence from the 'unmasking' pretensions of contemporary critics (1998: 226), she seems to regard this putative privileging as suspect. In part this stems from over-interpreting references to 'human nature' or 'human mind'. These terms are contextually best understood as a manifestation of the Scots' 'universalism' which, as will become clear as we proceed, does not entail that they are insensitive to the particularities of different historical contexts. They counsel against importing current values and behaviours into earlier eras (see, for example, Robertson *VP* 381, 417; Stuart *VSE* 50; Dalrymple *FP* 8; and further examples in Chapter 7).

The Scots' universalism is a key presupposition of a crucial component of their social science. To dwell solely in Kames' 'geographic' realm of particulars, or catalogues of facts, is to leave human experience and, especially, the changes in it bereft of explanation. Central to this explanation is the use of comparison to discern effective causation. This is succinctly captured in their critique of Montesquieu's recourse to 'climate' as a 'physical cause' to explain societal differences (see Hume *E-NC* followed by Millar, Dunbar and Kames among others [Berry 1997: Chap. 4]).[7] Importantly, as we shall see, this critique highlighted the greater explanatory power of moral causes, especially to account for social change over time (see Robertson *HAm* 850f, Dunbar *EHM* 296). Poovey underplays this. There are, of course, extant issues with the status of universalist propositions and the intelligibility of cross-cultural comparisons, as can be gauged by the gulf today between (say) John Tooby and Leda Cosmides (1992) and Clifford Geertz (1975). It is, as Poovey is sensitively aware, a mistake to import these debates into the Enlightenment (see Berry 2007).

From this discussion we can reasonably conclude that the 'determinate and known causes' invoked by Hume in his 'rule' correspond to Stewart's natural causes.[8] To seek them is to undertake a scientific enquiry; to refrain from such a search is to remain with the vulgar in a state of ignorance (Kames *SHM* II, 336). This contrast is evoked by Stewart when he says that the quest for natural causes gives a 'check [. . .] to that indolent philosophy which refers to a miracle whatever appearances, both in the natural and moral worlds, it is unable to explain' (*Life* II.47/293). Accordingly when Millar, for example, refers to the 'natural progress' from 'ignorance to knowledge and from rude to civilized manners' (*OR* 176) he is abstractly outlining the scope of a 'natural history'. This natural progress is that which is produced by natural causes, rather than that which is in any particular instance most agreeable to fact. All institutions are susceptible to a natural history. Stewart himself says as much explicitly in his *Dissertation*. He writes that, 'it is the peculiar glory of the latter half of the eighteenth century, and forms a characteristical feature of its philosophy, which even the imagination of Bacon was unable to foresee' that 'natural or *theoretical history*' dealt with 'society in all its various aspects [. . .] the history of languages, of the arts, of the sciences, of laws, of government, of manners, and of religion' (1854: I, 70; Stewart's emphasis). This breadth to the scope of natural history is important because it puts the Scots' accounts of the emergence of commercial society into their proper context.

To understand their own commercial era meant for the Scots placing it in a narrative that began with the destruction of the Roman Empire, but in which the pivotal 'event' is the collapse of feudalism. There are two dimensions to the explanation of that collapse. First, there is a wider generalised analysis of the role, and significance of, social institutions, especially property. Second, there is specific analysis of the operative forces in play in the fifteenth and sixteenth centuries. The former analysis (Part II) requires, as intimated in the opening paragraph, that the role of the four stages be examined, the latter (Part III) requires an account of the processes of social causation in operation.

## II

It is fair to say that in the history of commentary on the Scottish Enlightenment the notion of the four stages has been given an undue prominence, which not coincidentally has also produced a history of dubious interpretation. The initial point to make is that articulations of *four* stages are relatively infrequent, as indeed Peter Stein pointed out (1988: 400). The identification of the three stages of hunters, herders and farmers is common both in the Scots and in many other thinkers in the Enlightenment and earlier. It is the addition of commerce as a distinct fourth stage that is uncommon. Indeed a number of claims for the presence of four stages turn out on inspection not to be case.

Ronald Meek, who I single out not because he was alone but because he did much to highlight stadial theory and wrote a book with four stages as its focus, is, in practice, prone to announce its presence when it is absent. For example, though he claims 'there is succinct and relatively unambiguous statement of the four stages theory' in Helvetius' *De l'Esprit* (1758) the passage quoted does not move beyond three stages or, charitably, remains ambiguous (Meek 1976: 93).[9] The source of the ambiguity is the reference to an agreement 'on a general means of exchange to represent all commodities'. But this is not plausibly read as another 'stage'. Moreover, this reference indicates the presence of a different schema. This is evident when elsewhere in that work, not noted by Meek, Helvetius refers to *les républiques commerçantes* (Carthage for example) (Helvetius 1845: 272). But, as in Montesquieu (see Chapter 1), the emphasis is on the political or constitutional form and these formations do not fit easily into the 'four stages'.[10] I return to this point later.

Excluding Smith and Millar, in Scotland Meek attributes the four stages theory to Robertson, Dalrymple, Ferguson and Kames. But the first two do not adopt that account (as Meek in fact concedes [1976: 101, 143]) and nor does Ferguson, whose supposed version Meek calls 'idiosyncratic' (1976: 154).[11] Although Kames does identify four stages, this identification is not to be found explicitly in the work to which Meek principally refers, and from which he extensively quotes, namely, the *Historical Law Tracts* of 1758 (Meek 1976: 102–7).[12] Meek is seemingly followed by Lieberman, who affirms that in the *Tracts* 'Kames presented one of the first published versions of the "four stages" theory of societal development', when the passage cited clearly outlines three stages (Lieberman 1989: 149).[13] Peter Stein, despite an implicit critique of Meek, himself 'suggests' that it was in the *Tracts* that Kames made the 'first unequivocal declaration' of the four stages (1988: 405). I will consider his argument later.

The prevalence of a three-stage model is attributable to the fact that commerce is less obviously a primary mode since one can only exchange what has been previously caught, reared or grown (cf. Hont 2005: 161). Despite this difference the fact that in a genuine or explicit four-stages account commerce is lined up on the same basis as the other three, that is as a distinct social state rather than a mode of political life, is significant because it provides the diachronic dimension to the idea of a commercial society. However, that provision is not the prerogative of a four-stages account. As we will see, the decisive shift is from a feudal agricultural society to a society based on commerce.

We find unequivocal expressions of four stages in Smith, Millar, Kames and Blair (not mentioned by Meek). This apparently limited list does not mean the 'idea of a commercial society' is confined to these expressions (one of the reasons to deny prerogative status to the 'four-stages theory'). Hume, for example, does not employ a 'stadial theory' while acutely aware of the step-change from feudal to commercial. Similarly Ferguson, who either adopts the traditional three-stage model in the *Institutes* or identifies savage, barbarian and polished/commercial societies (in *ECS* 121 and *APMP* 11) is aware that 'our manners are so different' from 'ancient nations' (*ECS* 194) and pervasively so to the extent of recognising (not always to its advantage) the distinctiveness of contemporary society.

Before considering the two most significant unequivocal expressions of the four stages in Smith and Millar, I want to say something about Kames and Blair, the two other accounts. Kames' actual four-stage enumeration occurs in the context of his discussion of the American Nations in Chapter 12 of Book 2 of his *Sketches* (1774). He points out how America differs from the 'temperate climates of the old world' where there is 'great uniformity' in the 'gradual progress of men' from a 'savage state' to 'the highest civilization'. This progress begins with 'hunting and fishing, advancing to flocks and herds and then to agriculture and commerce' (*SHM*: II, 92). However, this, in situ, is a throw-away remark and is not put to argumentative use.[14]

Hugh Blair does put the theory to use in his defence of the authenticity of Ossian's poems (1763). He simply states that 'there are four great stages through which men successively pass in the progress of society. The first and earliest is the life of hunters; pasturage succeeds to this, as the idea of property begins to take root; next agriculture; and lastly commerce' (1996: 353). Ossian's verses reveal, Blair argues, that they derive from the first, hunter, period.

Blair gives no indication as to his source for this four-stage sequence but its early appearance is striking. It is possible that he had picked it up from Smith in the lectures on rhetoric and jurisprudence he gave in Edinburgh, between 1748 and 1750, prior to his appointment at Glasgow in 1751. There is no record of Smith's course but two, albeit very thin, circumstantial observations can be made. Smith was apparently (that is the information is indirect [see Ross 2010: 108–4; Scott 1965: 55–6; *Corr* 153/192n]) annoyed that Robertson's *View of Progress* (1769) had plagiarised from his lectures (Ross 2010: 103–4). It is not known whether Robertson attended the lectures (he is not mentioned in a short list provided by Tytler in his *Life of Kames* (1807) [1993: I, 190n]) but it is possible there was a manuscript version in circulation (Phillipson 2010: 119). In fact the *View* does not employ a stadial theory[15] and so if indeed Smith did object, it was not on that score. *If* Smith's Glasgow law lectures were an adaptation of his Edinburgh course, as Phillipson thinks is 'reasonable' (2010: 92), then *perhaps* the four stages 'theory' was indeed outlined (and circulated) in Edinburgh.

According to Tytler's list, Blair did attend Smith's Edinburgh lectures. We know, again indirectly, that Smith had reportedly said Blair was welcome to use his jurisprudence material (Rae 1965: 33). At first hand we do know that Blair, upon his appointment as Professor of Rhetoric and Belles-Lettres at Edinburgh in 1762, acknowledged that Smith had lent him his rhetoric manuscript (Blair 1838: 238n). The second observation is that Smith himself refers to Ossian in the 1762–3 version of his Glasgow lectures (*LJA* iv.101/239).[16] Again on the assumption that Blair was privy to Smith's manuscript then this could have been a source for Blair's clear four-stages passage. None of this, even collectively, adds up to much. We will probably never know how Blair came to give such a clear expression so early. It would be counter to what we do know of Blair that he was the source. The danger here is to be too parochial.

In principle, of course, to look for who 'influenced' who overlooks the possibility that there is another common source so that each thinker could have independently arrived at the same conclusion. In practice, there is a contender for this role. The importance of Montesquieu to the Scots was covered in Chapter 1 and the *De l'Esprit* was eagerly read upon its appearance in 1748.[17] In one typically short chapter (Bk 8, Chap. 8), he remarks (I quote from the accurate translation in full),

> The laws are very closely related to the way that various peoples procure their subsistence. There must be a more extensive code of laws for a people attached to commerce and the sea than for a people satisfied to cultivate their lands. There must be a greater one for the latter than for a people who live by their herds. There must a greater one for these last than for a people who live by hunting. (1989: 289)

Meek had quoted this passage though without giving it any particular salience (1976: 33; Teichgraeber [1986: 201n] – citing Meek – gives it a more emphatic role). With its implicit reference to the extensiveness of legislation as the criterion to differentiate modes of subsistence it appears to capture, though with a significant difference, the Scots' position. It is the lack of any dynamic element in Montesquieu that is the seat of that difference[18] (though note also the reference to the 'sea' suggesting Montesquieu is here thinking of maritime trading states [republics] – see Chapter 3). When Smith referred to Ossian in his *Lectures* he did so by remarking that the Scots and Picts described in the poems were 'in the same state as the Americans' (*LJA* iv.101/239). Given that the latter are contemporary and the former are not then this comparison, like that made systematically by Robertson between the Germans and the Amerinds (see below), necessarily imparts a dynamic or historical element to the four stages that Montesquieu's account seemed to lack. Hume's advocacy of the superiority of variable moral causes over static physical causes also appeared in 1748 and, whether or not a direct rebuttal of Montesquieu (see n.5), it would have been fresh material for Smith's Edinburgh jurisprudence lectures that he probably gave in 1749 (Scott 1965: 51).

If we, therefore, stay with what we can know then it is Smith's employment of four stages in his Glasgow jurisprudence lectures that deserves scrutiny since this is the first exposition (of which we have a record). In his Glasgow lectures of 1762–3, he unequivocally refers to 'four distinct states which mankind pass thro' – hunter, shepherd, agriculture and commerce (*LJA* i.27/14–16). In the 1766 version they are called hunting, pasturage, farming and commerce (*LJB* 149/459). In both versions the context is the same, namely, the property rights of occupation.[19] Similarly Millar's most unequivocal expression is in his lectures on government, where they are explicitly said to be 'stages in the acquisition of property'. Millar's list is 'Hunters and Fishers or mere Savages; Shepherds; Husbandmen; Commercial People'. This is from the 1787 version but it is repeated identically in the two other surviving versions (1789, 1790).[20] In Smith's versions the four stages are employed to exemplify the general principle that the 'regulations' concerning the acquisition of property 'must vary considerably according to the state or age of society is in that time' (*LJA* i.27/14).

Smith's actual treatment is terse, taking up a little over two pages of exposition (the 1766 version is even more compressed). Millar is more systematic and this suggests the pedagogic utility of 'the stages', a function that can also be reasonably ascribed to Smith's account. Support for this comes from the fact that when Smith refers to 'periods of society' in the discussion of subordination in the *Wealth of Nations* (see below) he no longer directly uses or needs this short-hand jurisprudential framework (much as might be said of Millar's *Ranks* – hence there the absence of an *explicit* four-stage) (also see below).

I do not want here to enter in any detail into the various interpretative debates about the four stages (I have summarised these previously [Berry 2000]). I have also argued elsewhere (Berry 1997: Chap. 5) that the history of property and other social institutions, as portrayed in the four stages, rests on a particular model of 'natural' development, derived from Lockean philosophy, and again I do not rehearse the argument in detail, but I will, though briefly, invoke an aspect of this shortly. This account of social development follows a natural history track from concrete to abstract,[21] from simple to complex, from rude to cultivated or civilised. This historical pattern is 'plotted' against a Lockean-inspired development of human cognitive and emotional capacities.[22]

The Blair quotation gives a clue to this in its reference to 'the *idea* of property' taking root. This structure enables us to characterise a commercial society as abstract, complex and civilised; it is not, we can also claim in passing, a reiteration of a commercial or mercantile republic in the manner of Helvetius and many others. These synchronic aspects will occupy us in later chapters; the current task is exploring a commercial society diachronically as a historical formation. Part III below will examine the detail of commerce's emergence. In the remainder of this Part, I pursue the place of commerce within a stadial natural history account in which the institution of property plays a key role.

Istvan Hont (2005) recognises the jurisprudential framework of the four stages and argues that it was Pufendorf who laid the theoretical foundations for the decisive move to the incorporation of a fourth, commercial stage. The very complexity of his argument, however, militates against it as a historical account. That is to say while textually and contextually scrupulous, and in that sense historically sensitive, it is a reconstruction, as it puts bits of Pufendorf together without producing a decisive citation. Moreover, the foundations are theoretical because there is no evidence that Scottish or French successors built upon them. Accepting that Smith is the key figure Hont confines himself to him. None of the passages from Pufendorf's *Law of Nature and Nations*, collected by Hont, is cited by, or alluded to, by Smith in his Glasgow Lectures, though even in that pedagogic context that is not of itself decisive. But, aside from occasions where Smith is recording views, his comments on Pufendorf are critical. For example, he disparages as 'whimsical' Pufendorf's recourse to theology to explain testamentary succession (*LJB* 164/466; cf. *LJA* i.150/63). In addition, following Hutcheson among many others, he aligns Pufendorf with Hobbes and Mandeville as an adherent of the untenable 'systems which deduce the principle of approbation from self-love' (*TMS* VII.iii.1/315n). Even so Smith correctly interprets the first part of Pufendorf's 'large treatise' as a confutation of Hobbes, but he judges 'in reality' no purpose is served by discussing laws and property which 'would take place in a state of nature' as 'there is no such state existing' (*LJB* 3/398). Moreover, given Smith's published account is a version of natural social history then the 'radically individualistic' (as Hont himself terms it [2005: 173]) character of Pufendorfian jurisprudence, regardless of any imputed theoretical innovation, is not going to inform Smith's own formulation of four stages even in the *Lectures* which have already rejected the notion of a social or original contract (*LJA* v.115–18/316–17; *LJB* 15–18/402–03).

Peter Stein (1988: 400) judges Hont's recourse to Pufendorf an 'exaggeration' and he himself, as we noted above, sees as decisive the move from a focus on property to that on contract and judges it was here in the *Tracts* that Kames broke 'new ground' to produce 'the first unequivocal declaration of the four stages theory'. This is an exaggeration on Stein's part. As noted above, where Kames is unequivocal is in the later *Sketches* and in a different context from that educed by Stein. The pivot of Stein's argument for Kames' novelty is his recognition that the 'arrival of merchants, as middle men between producer and consumer, demanded a whole new set of contractual arrangements' and 'this created a 'new type of society' (1988: 405). What was 'new' here was not the trafficking of surplus goods but the growth of credit, bills of exchange and the like. In this last move Stein goes beyond Kames, who when he discusses debt and creditors refers to Roman and feudal practice in England and Scotland. But Stein does importantly pick up on the role of promises and contracts. This role is best considered, once again, in the light of natural history and its basic trajectory from concrete/simple/rude to abstract/complex/civilised.

I wish here briefly to associate the notion of promises, contracts and the like to the underlying Lockean schema. Just as a 'conception' of 'property without possession' is 'too abstract for a savage' (Kames *HLT* 82) so too are 'ideas' of contract – 'a naked promise which is but a transitory act makes but a slender impression upon the mind of a rude people' (*HLT* 61n). Contracts and promises imply a commitment to the future but it is the postulated 'savage' condition that they live in the 'here and now'; they 'even seem incapable of attending to any distant consequences' (Ferguson *ECS* 89). The preoccupation with what is immediately wanted means, as Robertson puts it, they exhibit 'an inconsiderate thoughtlessness about futurity' (*HAm* 821; see also Dunbar derivatively *EHM* 15, 68). A particular instantiation of this is testamentary succession. Smith remarks that in 'the savage nations of Asia and America' such succession is unknown and the explanation for this is that 'piety to the dead' is 'too refined a doctrine for a barbarous people' (*LJA* i.153/65; cf. *LJB* 166/467) (hence the whimsicality of the evocation of theology in Pufendorf). The requisite 'refinement' comes from the recognition of a right of disposal on the part of one who being dead cannot properly be said to have a right (*LJB* 164/ 466). As John Dalrymple put it, such recognition was 'no very natural conception' to a rude people (*FP* 143), where by 'natural' he means in line with Lockean developmental assumptions.

Elsewhere in his *Lectures* Smith had given a variety of reasons why the validity of contracts is 'retarded'. He claims that, although all languages are ambiguous, this was more apparent in 'early periods of society' (*CL* 30/217–18; also Kames *HLT* 61, 99)[23] and because at that time there was little of great value then when 'contracts' were made keeping them was not obligatory (*LJA* ii.47/88). Smith proceeds to outline the various 'causes' that led to contracts becoming valid and binding. I will not follow the details of his discussion but do want to note two aspects.

First, it is 'the extension of commerce' (he cites trade between Rome and Alexandria) that increased the volume of binding contracts, because they were no longer made when both parties were present (*LJA* ii.53, 54/91). Yet contracts remain 'imperfect' and it was not until the English Court of Chancery was established that, for example, an action for damages was allowed for a breach of contract (*LJA* ii.75/98–9).[24] Robertson's gloss is that 'some progress towards refinement' needs to have been made before creditors had the right to seize the goods of their debtors (*VP* 385). It is the development of civil government (of which this illustrates but the 'first stage') that permits the pervasiveness of contracts that is a distinctive feature of a commercial society. In a crucial remark, which will be developed in Chapter 4, Smith maintains that the obligatoriness of contract arises 'entirely from the expectation and dependence which was excited in him to whom the contract was made' (*LJA* ii.56/92). However, both the ubiquity and bindingness of contracts and the establishment of regular civil government are effects of more underlying causes. An explication of these causes will be undertaken in Part III below but here the second aspect of Smith's discussion of contracts has to be addressed.

This aspect is the extension of contracts to landed property. In line with stadial theory this has to await the third or agricultural age. But even here the scope for contracts is limited because there is little intercourse even between neighbouring areas let alone further afield. Land, as such, was not an article of commerce; indeed it became hedged about with restrictions such as entails – an institution frequently attacked.[25] What is distinctive about the fourth stage is that land itself becomes alienable. Kames declares that the power of alienation is 'now universally held to be inherent in the property of land as well as movables' (*HLT* 104; cf 191 'the free commerce of land [is] repugnant to the genius of feudal law') and Dalrymple makes clear that the source of this universality is the transactions between merchants and that a 'commercial disposition' had made it necessary to allow 'unbounded commerce in land' (*FP* 94, 114, 159). Similarly for Millar it was 'the general advancement of arts' that rendered land an 'object of commerce' (*HV* I, 12/160).

Millar, in passing, enunciates the underlying point: it is 'the improvements of society' that enlarge 'the ideas of mankind with regard to property' (*HV* II, 6/292). He is not alone; indeed, with its reference to 'ideas' this reflects the natural history that charts the movement from concrete possession (immediate occupation) to abstract property (mediated relations). Kames would appear to be the key thinker. From his early (1747) *Essays on Antiquities* (*EBA* 127n), where he points out that in the 'infancy of society' property was not distinguished from use, to his much later *Elucidations* (1777) (*ELS* 228), where he remarks 'independent of possession they [savages and barbarians] have no conception of property' Kames had pursued this line of argument. It is because, he argues, savages ('first stage' hunter-gatherers) are 'involved in objects of sense and strangers to abstract speculation' (*HLT* 82) that they have no 'conception' of 'property without possession'. We can signal here the significance of this natural history for the idea of commercial society. As the most developed social formation, the idea of property is there the most abstract, as manifest, for example, in form of credit notes and bills of exchange, which rely on a series of beliefs.

This is not some autopoietic process but is, as Millar enunciated above, implicated in social development. As societies 'improve' they have more 'objects' to engage their inhabitants' attention (Millar *OR* 176; *HV* III, Intr/438). This is not merely a quantitative extension because the objects become qualitatively variable as they move away from what is 'sensible' (Robertson *HAm* 819; Millar *HV* IV, 6/760). The 'natural history of mankind' reveals a development from the almost total preoccupation with subsistence that is definitive of the first stage to, for example, the enjoyment of 'science and literature, the natural offspring of ease and affluence' present in the fourth commercial era (Millar *OR* 180, 176). In a favoured organic imagery, society matures from its infant state so that when the 'seeds of improvement' are 'brought to maturity' then 'those wonderful powers and faculties' will 'have led to the noblest discoveries in art or science and to the most exalted refinement of taste and manners' (Millar *OR* 198). A commercial society it follows is a 'refined society' (I will illustrate this in Chapter 7) and one wherein 'ideas and feeling' and 'appetites and desires' have been 'awakened' and 'desires and wants are multiplied' (Millar *OR* 198; Stuart *HD* 84; Robertson *HAm* 728). (That this may be viewed not entirely positively will be picked up in Chapter 6.)

To disaggregate this (natural historical) process into stages that coalesce around what Robertson calls 'mode of subsistence' (*HAm* 823) is a heuristic tool (Haakonssen [1981: 155] and others). Its utility is to identify certain coherences in social institutions. Property was given a central role because how ownership is identified and maintained is inseparable from how law and power both formally (government) and informally (ranks and manners) function. For example, when referring to the relative power possessed by the king or nobles, the subject of Part III below, Robertson declares that 'upon discovering in what state property was at any particular period we may determine with precision [...] the degree of power possessed' (*VP* 375).[26] Hence the central-ised provision of security of life and property is crucial for commerce to flourish as it is also for science and refinement in taste to blossom (*VP* 314).

We can illustrate these connections between the stages, property and natural history by a brief analysis of the account of social hierarchy or ranks. In perhaps the most sustained analysis of social stratification in the Enlightenment, Millar in his *Ranks* argues, 'In that rude period, when men live by hunting and fishing, they have no opportunity of acquiring any considerable property; and there are no distinctions in the rank of individuals but those which arise from their personal quali-ties, either of mind or body' (*OR* 246–7). This argument has a number of corollaries. Property does not create hierarchy (see Stuart *HD* 130) but in its absence there is fluidity of rank order because these 'qualities' (prominently strength, courage and age) are, of themselves, transient. However, with the 'invention of taming and pasturing cattle' comes the 'opportunity' for property and differential ownership and with that comes 'a permanent distinction of ranks' (*OR* 203–4).

Millar's argument is commonly shared by the Scots. The prevalence in rude ages of similar 'personal qualities' are identified by Robertson (*HAm* 827/8), by Kames (*SHM* I, 414; *EBA* 133), by Hume (*E-OG* 39), by Ferguson (*ECS* 84) and by Stuart (*VSE* 37). Smith's version is partic-ularly instructive because it exhibits how he employed 'stadial theory' outside the classroom. What is worth noting about this employment is that he does not explicitly evoke the 'four stages'. He does talk openly of the 'first' (that of hunters) and 'second' (that of shepherds) period of society (*WN* V.i.b.7/712–13) but refers, only in passing, to 'nations of husbandmen who are but just come out of the shepherd state' (*WN* V.i.b.16/717) and also in passing, contrastively, to 'an opulent and civilised society' (*WN* V.i.b.7/712). In these passages he examines what factors 'naturally introduce subordination' (*WN* V.i.b.4/710; cf. *LJA* v.129/321) and identifies four 'causes', or 'circumstances' of which the first two are types of personal quality or attribute – superiority of either body or mind and superiority of age. Millar's reference to (the absence of) property is again helpfully developed by Smith since his two remain-ing 'causes' hinge on a link between property and subordination. The third is 'superiority of fortune' which is especially marked in the age of shepherds although it is 'great in every age' (*WN* V.i.b.7/711). His main example is the Tartar chief under whose rule occurs the greatest degree of subordination, replacing the 'feeble' foundation provided by the first two causes. The differential acquisition of herds creates a 'train of dependence' (Millar *OR* 204) such that, in Smith's version, 'chieftainship' is a 'necessary effect' of superiority of fortune. On this basis he bluntly declares that 'civil government so far as it is instituted for the security of property is in reality instituted for the defence of the rich against the poor, or of those who have some property against those who have none at all' (*WN* V.i.b.12/715). This same argument had been made in the *Lectures* where property in the age of shepherds is said to make government 'absolutely necessary' and to be so because otherwise the poor would attack the rich (*LJA* i.21/ 208).

Smith's fourth cause – superiority of birth – consolidates the third because it only has any social significance once inequality of fortune has been established. To regard the mere fact of birth as a cause of social superiority can only mean being born into wealthy family who from force of habit come to enjoy deference (*WN* V.i.b.8/713; cf. Hume *E-OG* 39). Given this it follows that this fourth cause is necessarily absent from the first age where there is equality of fortune and that, once again, it is pastoral societies which embody this inequality to the greatest extent (*WN* V.i.b.7/713). The conjunction of these third and fourth causes is the prime source of pre-commercial social power, as Ferguson recognised when he commented that a chief enjoys a pre-eminence beyond that of the battlefield when 'the distinctions of fortune and those of birth are conjoined' (*ECS* 100). In the *Moral Sentiments*, Smith remarks that the 'distinction of ranks' rests more securely on 'the plain and palpable difference of birth and fortune' than upon invisible factors like wisdom and virtue (*TMS* VI.ii.i.20/226) (palpability was also invoked in the *Wealth of Nations* [*WN* V.i.b.6/711] but there it is associated with his second cause [age], whereas Stuart follows the *Moral Sentiments* by associating it with 'riches and property' rather than merit [*VSE* 33]). While commercial society also exhibits hierarchy this, as we will see, is in an important sense depersonalised. Politically, in line with the earlier analysis, we can say that 'rule' moves from being concrete and particular to being abstract and general. This provides a subtly historicised account of the move from rule by men to rule by law.

To conclude this part: the Scots' employment of stadial theory in its four-stages guise is best viewed as a 'theoretical' natural history conforming to Dugald Stewart's characterisation of it as an enquiry into how institutions may have developed by 'natural causes' (an enquiry that need not stand four-square with any particular 'real' progress).

Property plays a prominent part, owing to its contextual origins in law lectures, in this enquiry but, following Stewart himself (see above), it is mistake to think it is the exclusive subject matter of natural history (Emerson 1984; Berry 2000). What stadial theory, as a species of natural history, enables the moral or social scientist to do is draw reasonable inferences, both positive and corrective.

We can detect both at play if we return to the discussion of Ossian. In his *Critical Dissertation* (1763), which defends the authenticity of Ossian's poems, Blair locates, as we noted earlier, the poems in the first, hunter, period (1996: 353). Drawing implicitly on the Aberdeen professor Thomas Blackwell's *Life of Homer* (1735), he affirms that the language and style of the poetry conform to the manners of that stage. Echoing the Lockean framework, he also declares that the 'ideas of men at first were all particular. They had not the words to express general conceptions'. This he takes as proof of Ossian's authenticity since the poet 'never expresses himself in the abstract' (1996: 354). But, echoing the above caution about not over-weighing this particular stadial version of natural history, applied to this same case, Hume's inferences were employed correctively rather than positively. He treated as evidence against Ossian's authenticity the fact that in his poems women are depicted with 'extreme delicacy' when (here echoing Millar) such treatment is 'contrary to the manners of the barbarians'.[27]

More generally, we can say this natural historical approach enabled the Scots to evaluate evidence probabilistically. Hence, to give a different example, the weight of evidence makes it a reasonable inference that polytheism predates monotheism (Hume *NHR* I.1/34; Smith *HA* III.2/49; Kames *SHM* II, 390; Ferguson *PMPS* I, 168). Moreover, where evidence of religious beliefs in a particular case is absent then that 'gap', or contingent absence, can be filled in by sound inductive generalisation – if it is known that members of a particular society have few possessions, treat their women abjectly and are illiterate then it is a reasonable inference they are polytheistic. I will pick up this synchronic coherence of social institutions in Chapter 7. Pace Mary Poovey, there is nothing inherently cavalier about this; it manifests the basic assumptions of the 'comparative method' in being necessarily reliant on some underlying principles of uniformity. Implicit in all this is how this natural history gives the Scots a powerful tool to understand societies synchronically (holistically) and place these in a diachronic pattern.

The 'stadial theory' in this way serves as an ordering-device for the history of institutions. It functions, in a manner akin to what is later called an 'ideal-typical' way, on two levels. On one level, societies develop from a world of concrete simplicity to one of abstract complexity. This 'simplicity' gives a basic similarity to societies in the early stages of development. Millar makes the point explicitly,

> rude and barbarous nations [. . .] [having] the same pursuits and occupations and consequently the same objections of attention they undergo a similar education and discipline and acquire similar habits and way of thinking . . .] [and] however such people may happen to be distinguished by singular institutions and whimsical customs, they discover a wonderful uniformity in the general outline of their character and manners; an uniformity no less remarkable in different nations the most remote from each other. (*HV* IV, 8/832)

The second level cashes out the first as the Scots trace societal development as representing an increasing mastery of necessity (Medick 1973: 253) and attendant diversification. A commercial society, accordingly, as we shall explore in detail later, in various ways is healthier, wealthier and more liberal, in both its sentiments and institutions, than earlier stages of society.

The execution of a natural history of society hinges on there being general causes or principles responsible for uniformity both synchronically and diachronically. The latter dimension outlines the progress of society from rude to cultivated (to cite Dunbar's sub-title). This means that the development of commerce into a distinctive form of society is incorporated into such a schema. A discussion of how commerce emerged was in this way theoretically underwritten but it was also, and in a complementary fashion, in its own right a subject of intense interest for the Scots.

### III

How a commercial society emerged, both as a historical narrative and as an investigation of social causation, was one of the great themes in the writings of the Scots. It featured in Hume's *History*, was a famous set-piece in the *Wealth of Nations*, was key factor in Millar's *Historical View* and Robertson's *View of Progress* as well as a recurrent feature of Gilbert Stuart's work (if only as he disputed their arguments) and that of others. I do not intend here to provide a detailed exegesis of the various discussions. In part this abstention is motivated by the basic similarities they exhibit and in part because I want to adopt a more focused view. This focus is the interplay between liberty and commerce. To anticipate: I aim to show how liberty and commerce are both causes and effects but without the vicious circularity that such a characterisation might suggest.

Hume refers to a 'secret revolution [of government] (*HE* II, 603) and Smith to a 'revolution' occasioned by the 'silent and insensible opera-tion [of foreign commerce]' (*WN* III.iv.17.10/420, 418). By their use of the terms 'secret' and 'insensible' Hume and Smith are intimating how the process of social change operates. The 'change' in question is the same – the erosion of the power base of feudal lords and emer-gence of commercial society. The 'process' is the same – the causally explanatory role played by property and manners. This context and this agency are replicated in the writings of Millar, Robertson and others.

'Secret' and 'insensible' indicate that 'events' unfold gradually and imperceptibly, beneath the radar (so to speak) of individuals with their intentions and deliberative purposes. This indication is one of the grand themes of the Scottish Enlightenment theorists – their alertness to the presence and role of unintended consequences – but here I want to highlight how this links up with the biased die, discussed in Part I of this chapter. Hume's general rule (we recall) was that 'what depends upon a few persons is in a great measure to be ascribed to chance' but 'what arises from a great number may often be accounted for by deter-minate and known causes' (*E-AS* 112). Those secret and silent events are the work of the latter but the process itself is kick-started by the former, which means inter alia that there was nothing inevitable about the emergence of commercial society. History for the Scots, we can say, was at once ineliminably open to contingency while also being properly susceptible to causal explanation.

Recalling that 'chance' is just a word to depict ignorance of the causal agent, then, this contrast between 'chance' (one-off contingency) and 'determinate' (probabilistically recurrent) 'causes', can also be depicted as that between 'peculiar' and 'general' causes. Hume uses this terminology. In the context of the reign of Henry VII, he refers to many 'peculiar causes' which enhanced the authority of the crown, but pro-claims that the 'manners of the age were a general cause' by 'subverting the power of the barons' (*HE* II, 602, 603). It is this subversion that is the 'secret revolution'; a change that announces the emergence of a commercial way of life, a change that in Carl Wennerlind's (2002: 267 n.18) terms 'initiated the modernization process'. Pivotal in this process was the feudal barons' acquisition of 'habits of luxury'. Hume's discus-sion evokes that given in 1752 in his 'Refinement of Arts' essay but the role played here by luxury was reiterated by Smith (*LJA* iv.73/227; cf. *LJB* 51/416, 59/420, Millar (*HV* III, 2/489), Kames (*HLT* 191), Dalrymple (*FP* 207) and others. This role is captured in a celebrated passage in the *Wealth of Nations*:

for a pair of diamond buckles perhaps, or for something as frivolous and useless, they [the great proprietors] exchanged the maintenance, or what is the same thing, the price of the maintenance of a thousand men for a year, and with it the whole weight and authority which it could give them. The buckles, however, were to be all their own and no other human creature was to have any share of them [. . .] and thus for the gratification of the most childish, the meanest and the most sordid of all vanities, they gradually bartered their whole power and authority. (*WN* III.iv.10/418–19)

This sequence of events was outlined not only by Smith but also his fellow Scots, with a succinct early (1747) formulation by Kames (*EBA* 155). There is an agreed 'initial condition'. The medieval barons expended their surplus on the maintenance of retainers or dependants, who in return for their keep could only offer obedience. The consequence of which was that these proprietors, in addition to being leaders in war, also 'necessarily became the judges in peace' as the only people who 'could maintain order and execute law within their respective desmesnes, because each of them could there turn the whole force of all the inhabitants against the injustice of any one' (Smith *WN* III.iv.7/415; similarly Hume (*HE* II, 602), Robertson (*VP* 323), Millar (*HV* III, 1/447) and Dalrymple (*FP* 266). With the advent of luxury goods the nobles retrenched on their hospitality and reduced the number of their retainers. These former retainers either stayed on the land because the nobles, to raise funds for their luxuries, had granted them long leases (or even permanent rights to their holdings) (Millar *HV* III, 2/489; Smith *WN* III.iv.13/421) or left for the towns and became manufacturers and mechanics who lived off their own industry supplying the goods to meet the 'new methods of expense' (Hume *HE* II, 602). In both cases the unintended consequence (effect) is the same. Smith contrasts the sway of the feudal lord with the situation in the present state of Europe, where 'a man of ten thousand a year' can spend

his whole revenue, and he generally does so, without directly maintaining twenty people, or being able to command more than ten footmen not worth the commanding. Indirectly, perhaps, he maintains as great or even a greater number of people than he could have done by the antient method of expence [. . .] He generally contributes, however, but a very small proportion to that of each, to very few perhaps a tenth, to many not a thousandth part of their whole annual maintenance. Though he contributes therefore to the maintenance of them all, they are all more or less independent of him, because generally they can all be maintained without him. (*WN* III.iv.11/419–20)

The securing of 'independence' is the key and is picked up by others. For Millar, the 'released' artificers and farmers were independent, able to live without 'the necessity of courting the favour of their superiors' so that they did not feel themselves 'greatly dependent upon them' (*HV*

III, 3/487–9). A particularly crisp statement of this key point was made by James Steuart, who sharply contrasted the 'necessary dependence of the lower classes' under feudal government with the 'modern liberty' of the same classes that derives from their 'independence' consequent upon the 'introduction of industry' (*PPE* I, 208–9). I will return to this notion of 'modern liberty' in Chapter 5.

The Scots explicitly present this as a causal story. Hume's *History* narrates the tale of a change in a set of manners, through the causal mechanism of gradual changes in the socialised pattern of customs and habits (see Berry 2006b for detailed account of the causal mechanisms at work). For Millar 'the same causes that exalted the common people, diminished the influence of the nobility' (*HV* III, 2/489). In Smith the relation can be rightly deemed causal (rather than 'chance') since it is duplicated in the histories of the French and English monarchies and is exemplified by the case 'not thirty years ago' of Cameron of Lochiel (who we mentioned in Chapter 1) (*WN* III.iv.8/415–16). It is therefore a regularity amenable to scientific explanation; as Smith says explicitly here 'such effects must always flow from such causes'.[28] Hence he can explain in a seemingly different context the power of the Tartar chief. Since 'the rude state of his society' (in the second of the four stages) offers no 'manufactured produce, any trinkets and baubles of any kind for which he can exchange that part of his rude produce which is over and above his own consumption' then the surplus is used to maintain a thousand men (that he can command in war to enhance his power and thence his status) (*WN* V.i.b.7/ 712).

As Smith's account makes evident, the gradual decline of feudal power and the emergence of commerce is explicable in terms of 'general causes'. This can be seen in his criticism of the view that would explain this change by recourse to feudal law. The source of this mistake is a misunderstanding of social causation. The cause of feudal power lies not in the deliberative and purposive decrees of law but in 'the state of property and manners'. The former (the particularity of decrees) are subordinate to the latter (the generality of manners). Hume gives a revealing case in point. He remarks on the ineffectiveness of Elizabeth's attempts to restrain luxury by proclamation (*HE* II, 602), just as earlier attempts (including three by Henry VIII) at sumptuary legislation had been to no avail (*HE* II, 231; cf. I, 533 on Edward III's attempt). These 'failed' because they were out of step with what Hume himself calls 'the spirit of the age' (*E-RA* 271; *HE* II, 595) or what Dalrymple, in the similar context of law's inaptness, calls 'the genius and circumstances of the people' (*FP* 128). While particular pieces of legislation are by definition 'individual' or 'peculiar', law/government is a social institution and that means appropriate and commensurate social causes are needed to account for changes (revolution) in it. Stuart neatly summarises this point when he remarks that the disorders between the king and the nobles which affected the whole of Europe in the high Middle Ages are 'not to be referred entirely to the rapacity and the administration of princes. There *must be a cause more comprehensive and general* to which they [the disorders] are chiefly to be ascribed' (*VSE* 71 – my emphasis). In Stuart this role is played by the unfolding of property 'in all its relations and uses'.

This idea of 'general causes' is an important element in the Scots' social science. We find it invoked in Millar where 'the general cause' of the Reformation is 'the improvement of arts and consequent diffusion of knowledge' (*HV* II, 10/407). Hume refers to 'general causes' to account for the activities of the Catholic Church in the reign of Henry III (*HE* I, 338) and Robertson, for his part, attributes the power of the clergy in pre-Reformation Scotland to a range of 'general causes', including the wealth of the Church and the superstitions of the times (*HSc* 41). In the same vein Robertson explains his intent in his preliminary essay to his history of Charles V as an attempt to 'explain the great causes' of 'improvements in the political state of Europe' (*VP* 307). These 'historical' cases exemplify or specify more generic references to general causes as 'situation and genius' (Ferguson *ECS* 124) or prevalent 'manners and customs' (Millar *OR* 177) or the 'slow result of situations' (Dunbar *EHM* 62) or 'slow operation of events' (Stuart *OPL* 108). In line with this Millar is able to argue the institution of juries rose from the '*general situation* of the Gothic nations' rather than from the particular actions of Alfred (*HV* I, 9/141– my emphasis). Similarly the mode of military organisation cannot be properly attributed to Alfred's 'singular policy', since it was not 'peculiar' to England and is rather to be interpreted, in terms akin to Hume's use of 'secret' and Smith's 'insensible', as arising 'almost imperceptibly from the rude state of the country' (*HV* I, 6/97–98). Hume makes the same point about the similarity of customs across Europe counting against 'regarding Alfred as sole author [of a legal system]' (*HE* I, 53).[29] Alfred's 'justice', he judges, was suitable for a 'fierce and licentious people', but which by confining individuals to their locale would be 'destructive of liberty and commerce in a polished state', when 'men are more inured to obedience and justice' (*HE* I, 51). As promised, I will return to how liberty fits into the causal story, but first there is a need to backtrack and examine the 'peculiar cause' or 'trigger', as it were, for this general process.

Smith, we earlier noted, referred to 'foreign commerce and manufactures' as the 'silent' source of the erosion of the power of the 'great proprietors'. We can infer that those frivolous 'diamond buckles' are an example of these foreign goods. Hume in 'Of Commerce' refers to foreign trade giving birth to domestic luxury (*E-Com* 263; cf. *E-JT* 328) and in the *History* gives an example: the importation from Germany of pocket watches in Elizabeth's reign (*HE* II, 599). From these two accounts the trigger appears to be exogenous. External commerce was required to begin the endogenous process whereby England (especially) developed to become a commercial nation.

While Hume and Smith are not very forthcoming, Robertson provides a relatively detailed account of the source of this commerce and its importation.[30] The proximate source was the Italian cities (Smith too made this observation, *WN* III.iii.14/406). Venice, especially, had acted as conduit between the 'West' and the East, centred on Constantinople. A decisive boost to this was given by the Crusades, which led to 'beneficial consequences' that had 'neither been foreseen nor expected' (*VP* 316). From Robertson's discussion (and Smith's briefer treatment [*WN* III.iii.14/406]) we can infer that this took two forms. The crusading nobles when they returned home brought with them a taste for the magnificence they had encountered, which for Robertson explains why soon after their return 'greater splendour in the courts of princes' was seen (*VP* 317). The second form is that these 'courts' were supplied by goods provided by Venice, Genoa and other cities, whence they gradually spread through the activities of Lombard merchants. The resultant trade routes, especially to the Hansa towns of the Baltic, also made Bruges and Antwerp, as entrepot centres, wealthy cities (*VP* 410). Through the activities of the merchants these goods spread through the wider echelons of society. The arrival of those diamond buckles is thus an unintended consequence of the Crusades, just as the desire for them results in the unintended consequence of the loss of baronial power.[31]

There was a further diffusion. In Robertson's estimation, these merchants 'attentive only to commercial objects' could not 'fail of diffusing new and more liberal ideas concerning justice and order in every country of Europe where they settled' (*VP* 411). The cities flourished because they enjoyed a degree of self-governance and acquired liberty to become, as Robertson put it, 'so many little republics'. With this acquisition a set of general causes are set in motion: 'the spirit of industry revived: commerce became an object of attention and began to flourish'. The wealth that thus accrued was accompanied (as usual) by 'ostentation and luxury'. This, in turn, led to 'refinement in manners', the consequence of which was the introduction of 'a regular species of government and police'. The laws and 'polished manners' then 'diffused themselves insensibly through the rest of society' (*VP* 319). (Again note the Smithian use of 'insensibly' here.)

For Millar this pattern whereby the 'progressive advancement of the freedom and independence of the manufacturing and mercantile people' was followed by that of the peasantry or farmers was 'the natural course of things' (*HV* III, 2/488). Notoriously Smith called this same sequence, which, though it was what occurred, to be 'contrary to the natural course of things' (*WN* III.iv.19/422), which he had earlier outlined to be agriculture, manufactures then foreign commerce (*WN* III.i.8/380). However, Smith does say that this sequence is followed 'to some degree [. . .] in every society'. Yet this divergence fits Dugald Stewart's distinction between the 'natural' and the 'real' progress. Smith himself says the sequence that prioritises the country over the town is 'promoted by the natural inclinations of man' (*WN* III.i.3/377). This natural order applies in North America (*WN* III.i.5/378) but its reversal in Europe is initiated by the peculiar cause of the external introduction of foreign commerce. Once that has kick-started the process then as a commercial society naturally develops then, too, foreign commerce comes to reflect an international division of labour based on the most locally productive branches of manufacture.

What this identification of a trigger as an external peculiar cause means is that commerce begat commerce. By the same token, liberty begat liberty. As we have charted above, the industry and wealth initiated by 'free towns' bred a spirit of independence to form, in time, Steuart's 'modern liberty' or Robertson's 'regular government'. This recognition that there was a qualitative shift was made by Hume who, himself, refers to a 'new plan of liberty' (*HE* II, 602; III, 99). As with Robertson, for Hume this was (explicitly) caused by the growth of cities and development of 'a middle rank of men' (*HE* II, 602), who, he affirms elsewhere, are the 'best and firmest basis of public liberty' (*E-RA* 277). Smith, though his immediate context is different, openly declares that it is, for example, the presence of a choice of occupation, that makes individuals 'free in our present sense of the word Freedom' (*WN* I.vii.6/73; III.iii.5/400). As a final illustration, we can cite Millar, who referring to the start of the seventeenth century, links the emergence of 'a new order of things' to 'different arrangements of property' (*HV* III, Introd/437). I will revisit these comments and this chain of argument in Chapter 5.

Before picking up on that reference to 'property', we can interpolate here that the (general) causal explanation of the decline of feudalism/ rise of commerce is consistent with the two anchors (as they were termed above) of natural history, as delineated by Stewart. We have an account of 'circumstances' – feudal tenure and the availability of luxuries – and also of the operation of the principles of human nature. The former circumstance is accepted by all, the content of the latter is more implicit. Smith's explanation for why the proprietors sold their birthright for 'trinkets and baubles' (*WN* III.iv.15/421) is that they consume these themselves, with no need to share, because 'all for ourselves, and nothing for other people, seems in every age of the world to have been the vile maxim of the masters of mankind' (*WN* III.iv.10/418). In the *Lectures,* in the same broad context, he makes the claim less equivocally universal by observing that 'men are so selfish' that they give 'nothing away gratuitously' (*LJA* i.117/50). Hume does not specify which, among the 'constant and universal springs of human nature' (*U* 8.7/ *SBNU* 83), were the barons' motivating passions but, consistent with Smith, 'avarice' is a strong contender given his affirmation that it is 'an universal passion which operates at all times, in all places and upon all persons' (*E-AS* 113). But both Hume and Smith are elsewhere aware that this is too simple. They point out that the desirability of the diamond buckles (say) was as much a matter of maintaining peer-group status as it was of the private enjoyment of personally owned goods (Hume *E-RA* 276, *T* 2.2.5.21/*SBNT* 365; Smith *TMS* I.iii.2.1/50). And both note the effect of imitation or emulation. Hume remarks that the lesser gentry followed the nobility in wanting these items of luxury (*HE* III, 99), while Smith more generally observes the 'disposition of mankind to go along with the passions of the rich and powerful' (*TMS*: I.iii.2.3/51) (an argument that Millar explicitly follows [*OR* 250n]). The part played here by avarice and selfishness, and their place within a commercial society, will be examined in detail in Chapters 4 and 6.

This linkage between 'new' liberty and property indicates a clear legal and political dimension to the argument, as these later chapters will explain. Here its historical aspect will be considered. This consideration for fairly evident reasons is to the fore in Hume and Millar's Histories. They do disagree[32] but they concur on 'the big picture'. For Hume the key to his 'secret revolution' is the emergence of 'general and regular execution of laws' (*HE* II, 603). This arose causally from a two-stage process. First, the barons by letting go their retainers and dependants lost their localised power bases, which thus removed the key obstacle to central authority (*HE* II, 603). The second stage has itself two phases. Initially, in the wake of the decline of the barons, the sovereign took advantage to assume an 'authority almost absolute' (cf. Millar *HV* II, 9/402 re Henry VII) but, then, in England this discretionary power too began to be curtailed by 'regular execution of laws'. The cause of this subsequent curtailment was the rise of the Commons, composed of the middle rank whose wealth increased pari passu with the growth of commerce, as they domestically produced and distributed these consumer goods. These tradesmen and merchants 'covet equal laws', since without the security that comes from the consistent and predictable (regular) operation of law, 'markets' will not function (*E-RA* 277–8). This is a major theme of Chapter 4.

In Millar, 'the advancement of society in civilization' was marked by 'the greater accumulation of property in the hands of individuals' (*HV* III, 2/490). This refers not to aggrandisement by few but the diffusion of property to many. The consequence of this diffusion meant the monarch, faced with increasing costs, had to seek financing from the Commons, which comprised, as Hume had noted, the newly wealthy. The advance in commerce and manufactures that this wealth represented, marked a 'state of property' that was 'highly favourable to liberty' (*HV* IV, 3/726; III, 4/552; IV, 2/712). These property-holders – merchants and the like – 'imbibed a higher spirit of liberty' (*HV* III, 2/497; IV, 5/743) (a 'spirit' that in itself is 'congenial to the minds of men' [*HV* III, 2/487]). Hence as arts, manufacture and commerce continue to advance so is liberty in the shape of the 'rules of law' and virtue of justice gradually extended (*HV* IV, 6/773; IV, 7/787; III, 4/555). In this regard, with implicit reference to stadial theory, Millar explicitly contrasts the manners of a 'commercial people' with those of 'rude nations' (*HV* IV, 6/774). Indeed in 'opulent and polished nations', where 'equal and regular government' is well-established then the 'impartial distribution of justice is looked upon as almost a matter of course' (*HV* I, 8/131). The linkages here will be examined in Chapter 5.


IV


The Scots thought of themselves as living in an 'age of commerce'. This jelled with their commitment to 'improvement' that we covered in Chapter 1. On both scores there is an appreciation of change. It followed that to understand their own society, to evaluate the course and direction of any future ameliorative direction, meant understanding that change. The requisite understanding was to be gleaned by explaining the dynamics of that change by identifying causes. This gave to the Scottish theorists a strong motive to undertake historical research, as Kames remarked rhetorically, 'how imperfect must the knowledge be of that man who confines his reading to the present times?' (*HLT* vi). The focus of this research was, as Steuart put it 'the late revolutions in the politics of Europe' which he believed – in language with which we now familiar – exhibited the 'regular progress of mankind from great simplicity to complicated refinement' (*PPE* I, 28). The focus identified the key point of concern: how the commercial age had emerged from the distinctly different social formation that had preceded it. Perhaps, above all else, it is this interest in the process of social change that gave to the Scots their conception of a commercial society as some-thing distinctive, as an integrated, inclusive form of life that was not prefigured by mercantile city-states. The distinctiveness of the Scots' idea is a theme in Chapter 7. Relatedly, that the Scottish theorists were preoccupied with Britain in particular was not only because it was 'their' society but also because, as Smith's nation of shopkeepers (*WN* IV.vii.c.63/613), it embodied the modern world of commerce.

But they realised that even if the history had a national focus, to give a satisfactory account was a comparative task. Robertson made this explicit. He justified the *View* as a preliminary essay to his *History of Charles V* by observing that, 'the state of government in all the nations of Europe having been nearly the same during several ages, nothing can tend more to illustrate the progress of the English constitution than a careful inquiry into the laws and customs of the kingdoms on the continent'. This 'comparison', he goes on, would be of 'great utility' (*VP* 429) (see also Hume's three methodological prescriptions in the Introduction to the *Treatise*, above p. 22). Robertson also provides a clear expression of another Scottish trait. In their search for Kames' 'collateral facts' Scots viewed contemporary ethnography as a comple-mentary source (recall from above Smith's reference to Americans and Picts in the context of Ossian). Given the absence of direct information about the 'ancient state of the barbarous nations', Robertson hypoth-esises that should there be similarity between the barbarous Europeans and the 'various tribes and nations of savages in North America' (*VP* 371), then 'it is stronger proof' that a 'just account' of the former has been given than 'the testimony even of Caesar or Tacitus'. He then, after itemising five points of similarity, judges that 'a philosopher', will, in line with the evidence, conclude that although not perfectly similar, the 'resemblance is greater perhaps than any that history affords an opportunity of observing' (*VP* 372).

This general analysis comports straightforwardly enough with the idea of natural history. Recalling Stewart's account, these 'collateral facts' are the 'circumstances' and what makes (any) comparison pos-sible is a common principle, which for the Scots lay in the 'principal anchor' of natural history, namely, the uniform principles of human nature. Millar is clear: 'Man is everywhere the same; and we must nec-essarily conclude that the untutored Indian and the civilised European have acted upon the same principles' (*Obs* iii).[33] Natural history was the history of Mankind as social beings. Their behaviour, values and institutions have developed, have 'improved'. The course of this development is plotted as a change from the simplicity of Mankind's early social formations to one of increasing complexity. The 'four stages' was but one particular expression of that plotting. When it was (infrequently) employed, it was done for the particular purpose of highlighting the importance of changes in the regulations of property. While property does play a key role, it is not the only significant factor. A commercial society does indeed have a distinctive property regime but that is only one aspect of the complex inter-related whole which defines that type of society. The following chapters examine that totality.

## NOTES

1. Hume took the notion of the 'association of ideas', which had been used negatively by Locke and others, and treated it descriptively. In experience we associate A as the cause with B as its effect. He then analysed this: A is prior to B and contiguous with it but what vitally makes the relation causal is that experience reveals over time that A and B are constantly conjoined (*T* 2.3.1.16/*SBNT* 403). This associationist reading of causation clearly influenced Smith's analysis in *Astronomy* but Hume's particular analysis of 'causal necessity' as a 'habit in the mind' was not generally accepted.

2. The latter has echoes with Newton's dictum (1953: 43) '*hypothesis non fingo*' and Ferguson does in his later *Principles* precede a contrast between Newton and Descartes by remarking that 'it is safer' to acknowledge ignorance than hypothesise (*PMPS* I, 117). Reid used the Newtonian phrase throughout his work to declare that 'philosophy has been in all ages adulterated by Hypotheses; that is by systems built partly on facts and much upon conjecture' (*Intellectual Powers* II, 3/1846: 224). See Laudan (1970). Ferguson's opening contrast between conjectures and facts bears a striking resemblance to the opening of Goguet's *De l'Origine des Lois* (1758) which was published in Edinburgh in an English translation in 1761.

3. Ranke's (1824: vi) remark in the Preface to his *Geschichte der Romanischen und Germanischen Völker* that he was merely aspiring to depict '*wie es eigentlich gewesen*' has taken on an emblematic status, while Collingwood (1946: 77) judged that 'the historical outlook of the Enlightenment was not genuinely historical'. Cf. Höpfl (1978) and Sampson (1956: 72, 74) who quotes that last extract from Stewart and calls it a 'damaging admission' and says that there is some justification for regarding the eighteenth century as 'fundamentally anti-historical'.

4. In 1807 Kames' first biographer remarked, 'the recording of authentic facts, the display of historical truth is much less an object with such writers than ingenious argument and plausible theory [. . .] such philosophers are

bold enough to determine not only what men ought to be but to prove by a priori reasoning what in certain situations has been and in similar situations ever must be' (Tytler 1993: I, 200n).

5. Mandeville (one of Hume's designated pioneers in the science of man) had argued that because there can be no effect without a cause then 'nothing can be said to happen by chance' and illustrates with the example of casting dice (1988: I, 262).

6. For a discussion of Hume and 'probability' (and the Enlightenment context more generally) see Daston (1988: Chap. 4) and Baker (1975: esp. p. 160ff).

7. In *De l'Esprit des Lois* Montesquieu argued that was a direct physiological relationship between climate or air, as causes, and social institutions or national character and human behaviour, as effects. Hence the different effects of the same opera in England (*si calme*) and Italy (*si transportée*) or the fact that punishment has to be severe in the cold climate of Muscovy (Bk 14, Chap. 2). The *De l'Esprit* was published in 1748 and only a little before Hume's *National Characters* in that same year. There is at best only circumstantial evidence that Hume had previously read Montesquieu (see Chamley 1975) but aside from historiographical reasons the point is not here vital, since in principle the argument is not ad hominem (even if in practice it often took that form), plus Hume had prefigured his argument against 'soil or climate' in the *Treatise* (T 2.1.11.2/SBNT 317).

8. I should clarify that these 'natural causes' are not to be equated with 'physical' as opposed to 'moral' causes. The latter are just as 'natural' as the former. Humans are social beings and as such are subject to the (natural) processes of socialisation or moral causation. See further Chapter 4. This is 'natural' in Hume's sense of 'inseparable from the species' (T 3.2.1.19/ SBNT 484) and here he does not differ from his compatriots.

9. The same caveat of over-interpretation applies to Meek's discussion of Goguet's *De l'Origine des Lois* (1758) despite supplying some lengthy quotations (1976: 94–5) or Turgot, whose discussion in his *Universal History* (1751) is declared to formulate a 'four-stages theory' (1976: 75). In his earlier Introduction to his edition of Turgot's *Essays* Meek is slightly more circumspect – Turgot has a 'three stages theory' and 'in effect' followed Quesnay and Mirabeau so that a fourth stage followed (Meek 1973: 12, 20). Enzo Pesciarelli (1978: 511), who openly acknowledges he is following Meek, seeks to find a four-stage theory in Antonio Genovesi. Genovesi in his *Delle Lezioni di Commercio* does distinguish '*selvagge*' who subsist on hunting; '*barbare*' who have herds and a little agriculture; '*le Nazioni*' who are 'cultivated' ('*culte*') but have no commerce or arts of luxury (he cites the tribes of Germany); and '*le Nazioni perfettamenta culte*' who experience splendid luxury, literature, science and refinement (1765: 51–2). The link with 'refinement' is suggestive of Hume, with whose work Genovesi was familiar. Another little noted explicit exponent is Danvila

in his *Lecciones de Economia Civil o del Comercio* (1779). In his opening *Leccion* he enumerates '*quatro estados*' through which humans have successively passed – *Cazadores, Pastores, Labradores, Comerciantes* (2008: 86). It is possible he took this from Genovesi, who is a significant influence. However, these stages do not reappear in the remainder of his book. Like the Physiocrats he divides '*las artes*' into primary and secondary, with the former comprising '*la caza, la pesca, la arte pastoricia, la de fundir los metals y la agricultura*' (2008: 151) – no reference to commerce – and here he follows Genovesi almost verbatim (1765: 104).

10. See also Goguet (1758: I, 570), who views (again not noted by Meek) commerce as an activity that is almost as old as society and develops insensibly until it seems to unite the world. This is not the stadial model that Meek is seeking to trace.

11. Ferguson has the standard three-fold model and although a little later he says 'progress of arts [. . .] render commerce expedient or even necessary' (*IMP* 28, 32) it is clear this is not sequential – indeed Ferguson argues *against* that (Berry 2009a). Ferguson's stadialism is discussed in Hill 2006 and Wences Simon 2006.

12. Meek also refers to Kames' *Essays on the Principles of Morality*. In the second edition (1758 also the year of *HLT*'s first edition) but not in the first (1751) he succinctly identifies the standard three stages (1758: 77–8/ *PMNR* 47) though Spadafora (1990: 271) citing this passage says it was 'identical' to the four stages of Smith's *Lectures*.

13. See also Rahmatian (2006: 193) who, again citing Meek attributes 'four-stages' to Kames in the *Tracts* but qualifies it a little later stating Kames' reference to a fourth commercial stage is implicit (2006: 194n131).

14. The fact that the enumeration is not exploited is reflected in the only other scholar (Sebastiani 1998) who seems to have picked up on this passage in Kames, since she devotes her analysis to Kames' polygenetic theory and account of race.

15. Pace Neil Hargraves (2002: 267) who states 'Robertson was an acknowledged master [of the four stage theory]' though his reference is wider than the *View*. In *America* he refers unspecifically to 'stages of society' (*HAm* 812) but Robertson's salience in this literature stems from his declaration in that same work that, 'In every inquiry concerning the operations of men when united together in society, the first object of attention should be their mode of subsistence. Accordingly as that varies, their laws and policy must be different' (*HAm* 823). For a gloss and contextualisation of this passage see Berry (1997: 93–4).

16. Still in the same realm of circumstantial evidence, Smith went to Inverary in 1759 and the editors of his *Correspondence* speculate that was 'perhaps' when he heard a piper recite the poems that Macpherson collected (*Corr* 42/59). They cross-reference to Hume's *Letters* (I, 329). In the so-called *Early Draft* of WN from about the same period Smith also refers to Ossian and a comparison with Homer (*ED* 27/573).

17. The appearance of *De l'Esprit des Lois* had been anticipated and plans were made to send 200 or 300 copies to Britain in the expectation of good sales (Shackleton 1961: 243).

18. I am grateful to Naohito Mori for urging that point upon me.

19. The fuller context is Smith's argument that of the three types of rights (called by the civil lawyers 'natural' [*LJB* 8/399]) the first two (of person and of reputation) are unproblematic, it is only the third, property as an 'acquired right' that requires explanation (*LJB* 11/401; *LJA* i.25/13). Regarding property, he enumerates the conventional (Roman) causes of property – occupation, tradition, accession, prescription and succession (*LJA* i.25/13; *LJB* 149/459; see also Hume *T* 3.2.5.5/*SBNT* 505, though he omits 'tradition'). In both versions of the *Lectures* this then leads into the succinct statement of 'four stages' and the variations in the regulations of property they embody. That is they provide a framework for the explanation that is needed for this third branch of 'natural rights'.

20. All three are in Glasgow University Library (GUL MS Gen 289–91). They are quoted in Meek (1976: 166). But this is not isolated and Millar repeats the classification in his lectures on the Institutes of Justinian. While throughout he talks of rude and polished peoples it is only when his topic is 'property' does he explicitly refer to four stages which in the 1789 version (GUL MS Gen 812) are identified as 'state of property among hunters and fishers', then in the next lecture 'state of property among shepherds' then next 'among husbandmen' then 'in a commercial nation'. The four-fold classification is, if anything, clearer in the 1793 version (GUL Hamilton MS 117), where the discussion is prefaced with the heading 'of the nature of property and the different ideas which men entertain concerning that right in different ages'. (Note the reference to 'ideas' here.) In both versions it is said of the commercial age that a 'new species of property' was introduced as a consequence of the development of the arts that promote the 'conveniences and elegancies' regarding 'food, raiment, lodging and entertainment'. Paul Bowles (1985: 197, 208; cf. Bowles 1986) claims that Millar's account of property rests 'exclusively on the four-stages theory' but his discussion assumes the 'four-stages' was the standard expression wherein he follows Meek.

21. While the Scots do consistently use the term 'abstract', they do not employ the term 'concrete' (Dunbar is an exception [*EHM* 89]). I employ it as a convenient imputed antonym. Locke, who is the chief source of this pattern of development, does explicitly refer, in a chapter heading, to 'abstract and concrete terms' (*Essay* III, 8 [1854: II, 77]). I am grateful to Seiichiro Ito for his query on this point.

22. To clarify this is not an autonomic process. These capacities develop as a response to the environment (as we would expect from its Lockean empiricist origins). Hence Robertson, who gives one of the fullest accounts of the Amerindians, remarks that many tribes, who have 'no property to estimate, hoarded treasures to count [...] cannot reckon further than

three', and he takes this as testament to their lack of universal or abstract ideas (*HAm* 819–20). The same example can be found in Condillac's resolutely Lockean *Essai* (2001: 79). The common source is probably de la Condamine (1745: 66), who, as well as taking measurements to test Newton's anti-Cartesian theory that the earth was elongated at the poles and flat at the equator, also wrote a description of the flora, fauna and tribes of the Amazonian basin and cites the Yameos on this point, saying they do not need any more numbers.

23. As I have pointed out elsewhere (Berry 2006a, 2012), the *Considerations* (like other Enlightenment works on language such as those by Condillac and Dunbar) reveals the Lockean progress toward abstraction (see *CL* 19, 20/212–13 for example).

24. Millar in his 'Jurisprudence' lectures also refers to the 'imperfect notions of obligation to fulfil a contract' among rude people.

25. See for example Smith (*LJB* 166/467), Kames (*HLT* 135ff, *ELS* 334, *SHM* II, 523–33), Steuart *PPE* I, 3276). As befits a practising judge Kames took more overtly practical steps on this issue – in addition to an appendix in *SHM* (II, 523ff) see, for example, his letter and submission to the Lord Chancellor reprinted in Lehmann (1971: 327–32). (See further Lieberman [1989: 156–8] and Horne [1990: 106–8].) Though Dalrymple saw entails as out of kilter with 'commerce' he warned against over-hasty abolition (*FP* 185f), a position he later elaborated in *Considerations upon the Policy of Entails in Great Britain*, which was a response to a proposal to amend the law on entails; a proposal he judges 'not expedient at this time' (1764: 10).

26. This may appear distinctively Harringtonian (see his concept of 'balance' as outlined in his *Oceana* [1656]) though Robertson himself in the next paragraph refers to Montesquieu. Dalrymple also expresses the Harringtonian maxim that 'power follows property' (*FP* 156, 326). Harrington's work was known to the Scots. Hutcheson refers to him in his discussion of constitutions (*SMP* I, 264), Millar gives a complimentary assessment in *HV* (II, iv/569) and Hume uses *Oceana* as point of departure in his Essay on Perfect Commonwealth (see Chapter 6).

27. Perhaps with deference to his friendship with Blair this verdict was not published in Hume's lifetime. 'Of the Authenticity of Ossian's Poems' (1875: IV, 417).

28. Dalrymple on several occasions makes a point of saying 'the same causes must have the same effects' (*FP* 167, 255, 303). Compare also Stuart referring to division of property 'the same causes will still be attended with the same consequences' so that although there is no record of this in Scotland it 'must have exhibited a resemblance to those which took effect among the other adventurers of Celtic and Gothic origin, who fixed themselves in their conquest' (*OPL* 6). Note in the manner of Stewart the use of 'must' in this last example.

29. Hume summarises the 'manners of the Anglo-Saxons' as those of a 'rude, uncultivated people, ignorant of letters, unskilled in mechanical arts,

untamed to submission under law and government, addicted to intemperance, riot and disorder' who exhibited a 'want of humanity' throughout their whole history (*HE* I, 127).

30. Robertson repeats this story in nuce in his *America*, which opens with a brief history of commerce (he acknowledges an indebtedness for detail to Anderson's [1764] account). This helps qualify Womersley's argument that Robertson's historiography shifted from one concerned with causality in *Scotland* and the *View* to one in *America* that is sensitive to 'often wonderful facts' (Womersley 1986: 500). Yet in both *Scotland* and *America* Robertson says almost verbatim that the historian should not deal in 'fancy and conjecture' but in 'facts' (*HSc* 53, *HAm* 733, 933).

31. Robertson (1840: li), admittedly in the context of sermon ('The Situation of the World at the Time of Christ's Appearance', 1775), preached that 'Careful observers may often, by the light of reason, form probable conjectures with regard to the plan of God's providence and can discover a skilful hand directing the revolutions of human affairs.' For a discussion of 'unintended consequences' in Robertson's writings see Francesconi (1999).

32. They differ most evidently over the assessment of Charles I of whom Hume, in Millar's estimation, presents a 'very artful picture calculated to mislead an incautious and superficial observer' (*HV* III, iv/582). Salber Phillips (2006: xvi) in his Introduction to *HV* perhaps overplays their disagreement when compared to other contemporary responses (see Chapter 5).

33. The locus classicus of this view is Hume in the *First Enquiry*: 'it is universally acknowledged that there is a great uniformity among the actions of men, in all nations and ages, and that human nature remains still the same in its principles and operations' (*U* 8.7/*SBNU* 83).

# 3. Prosperity and Poverty

A key distinguishing feature of a commercial society is that, compared to earlier 'stages', it is richer in the crucial sense that its inhabitants are better fed, clothed and housed. The institution at the heart of this amelioration is the division of labour. It is not just that the division of labour produces 'opulence' but that this is a 'good thing'. This judgment reveals what Ryan Hanley (2009a: 6, 93) in his discussion of Smith terms a 'commitment to normativity'. Albeit Smith is very much the focus of attention in this chapter, this commitment is not his alone; there is a moral and normative core to the Scots' account of commerce and that will be explored in the following chapters. This chapter will, nonetheless, explore the obverse of the positive assessment of opulence or prosperity, namely, a negative view of poverty. For the Scots there is nothing redemptive about 'poverty' and any social ethic which endorses that view is deficient.

The records of Smith's Glasgow lectures that have survived report him professing that 'opulence and freedom' were the 'two greatest blessings men can possess' (*LJA* iii.112/185). Crucially these blessings are linked and it is this linkage that is central to Smith's vindication of commercial society. This chapter concentrates on 'opulence', the first blessing. I will discuss the second blessing in Chapters 4 and 5. In both discussions, however, the significance of their being linked is addressed.

## THE DIVISION OF LABOUR

What is distinctive about a commercial society, as Smith characterises it, is not that it exhibits opulence, for that is true of some earlier states of society. Rather what distinguishes a commercial society is that it witnesses a 'universal opulence which extends itself to the lowest ranks of the people' (*WN* I.i.10/22; *ED* 10/566). The fact that it is opulence which is diffused also distinguishes a commercial society from the equality of the poverty of the hunter-gatherers of the first state (*WN* V.i.b.7/712; cf. Ferguson *PMPS* II, 422). It is a mark of an 'opulent and commercial society' (*ED* 11/567) that the lowest ranks are supplied 'abundantly' with what they have 'occasion for' (*WN* I.i.10/22), with 'all the necessaries and conveniencies of life' (*ED* 12/567). A crucial precondition of this is that this occurs in a 'well-governed society' (*WN* I.i.10/22), that is, where the linked blessing of liberty is also present.

Smith identifies the division of labour as the source of this abundance. It is the crucial factor in economic growth (Hollander 1973: 209; Brown 1988: 74; Schumpeter 1986: 187). As the editors of the *Wealth of Nations* note (see also Rashid 1986), this practice had been attended to by a number of Smith's predecessors. They mention Petty (as the first modern expositor), Mandeville and note Harris and Turgot among Smith's contemporaries (*WN* I.i.1n). This is not to assume there are no others. W. R. Scott claims Hutcheson's articulation was a key influence on Smith,[1] while notable among the Scots who published before the *Wealth of Nations* is Ferguson who observes in his *Essay* (*ECS* 181) that it is 'by the separation of arts and professions [. . .] [that] every commodity is produced in the greatest abundance'. I will return to Ferguson in Chapter 6. We know, though, that Smith had worked on the role of the division of labour long before the *Wealth of Nations* saw the light of day (see the so-called 'Early Draft' and 'Fragments').

Before proceeding there is an ambiguity to address. There is a distinction between what I shall label the 'sociological' and the 'technological' division of labour.[2] The former refers to sectorial specialisation and since Plato this has been seen as the corollary of the fact that humans are not self-sufficient (Plato identifies, in a deliberately simplified 'model', farming, building and weaving as tasks undertaken by different people [1902: 369d]). The latter refers to the divisions in the process of production – the eighteen stages in pin manufacture, to give Smith's own example. This distinction is one of focus and not of principled difference since both are expressions of inter-dependency. Indeed it is their conjunction that conveys the character of a commercial society. The technological sense is crucial in the explanation of 'the productive powers of labour', and thence of commercial opulence, while the sociological sense, aptly enough, pertains to its 'effects [. . .] in the general business of society' (*WN* I.i.1–2/13–14).

The second chapter of the opening book of the *Wealth of Nations* is titled 'Of the Principle which Gives Occasion to the Division of Labour'. Smith begins with a definite identification of the operant principle but then almost immediately qualifies it. He initially declares the division of labour is a consequence of a 'propensity in human nature' to 'truck, barter and exchange' (*WN* I.ii.i/25). Though this is the only context in which Smith uses the term 'propensity' in the *Wealth of Nations* (it is also in the *Early Draft*), it is employed on a number of occasions in the *Moral Sentiments*, as when humans are said to have the 'greatest propensity to sympathize' (*TMS* I.ii.2.5/33). Its meaning is the standard one of an 'inclination' or 'disposition', which are the terms Smith used, still discussing the division of labour, in his *Lectures* (*LJA* v.56/352) as well as the *Wealth of Nations* itself (*WN* I.ii.3/27). In context the reference to 'propensity' signals that the division of labour with its 'many advantages' is not the fruit of deliberation ('human wisdom'); nor is it an intended outcome but is, rather, a 'very slow and gradual consequence' (*WN* I.ii.1/25). Furthermore as a propensity of human nature it is ex hypothesi universal ('common to all men' *ED* 21/571) and thus cannot be the prerogative of the fourth stage alone. The division of labour in a rudimentary form exists in the first stage. Smith cites the case of an individual skilled in bow-making who discovers that by exchanging his bows for the meat from deer slain by more adept hunters he can obtain more venison than from trying to kill his own beast (*WN* I.ii.3/27; *LJA* vi.55/351). The reason why this is rudimentary is that the 'market' is limited. Why that in turn should be true of the earliest stages and untrue of the fourth stage hinges on the state of 'property and manners' and security generated by the rule of law (see Chapter 2 above and below in Chapter 4). We will return to the role of market extent shortly.

This initial definite statement of the operant principle Smith immediately makes more equivocal. He speculates that this propensity may not be one of those 'original principles of which no further account can be given'. Smith is here alluding to the message from Newton that Hume had made pivotal in his own thought – it is pointless metaphysics to seek 'ultimate answers'. Newton did not know what gravity was, it was enough to calculate its effects; Hume did not pretend to know why pleasure pleases but that it does is sufficient for the science of man. The Smithian science of political economy can be equally unconcerned about 'why' humans possess this propensity – indeed he explicitly declares that this question 'belongs not to our present subject' (cf. Evensky [2005: 113]). Unlike Joseph Harris, for example, Smith does not refer to the 'wise appointment of divine Providence' to underwrite the fact that 'every man stands in need of the aid of others' (Harris 1757: 14). Smith's declared abjuration, in fact, follows his speculation that it 'seems more probable' that the generic trucking propensity is the 'necessary consequence of the faculties of reason and speech' (*WN*

I.ii.2/25). The version in a *Lecture* in 1763 is less circumspect because there the foundation of the trucking disposition is said to be 'clearly the naturall inclination every one has to persuade' (*LJA* vi.56/352). This echoes an observation already made in the *Moral Sentiments* (1759), where the 'desire of persuading [. . .] seems to be one of the strongest of all our natural desires' (*TMS* VII.iv.25/336).

'Persuasion' itself clearly presupposes linguistic competence.[3] At the same time that Smith was lecturing on jurisprudence he was also giving classes in rhetoric. He opens his published essay on language, which grew out of his lectures (see *LRBL* i.17f/9f [lecture 3]), with a reference to the source of language. This he locates in the utterances whereby savages would 'endeavour to make their mutual wants intelligible to each other' (*CL* 1/203). When Smith does refer to 'persuasion' in the *Wealth of Nations* it is to make the traditional point that animals are brutes – they do not possess language (*WN* I.ii.2/26) (speech is the 'characteristical faculty of human nature' [*TMS* VII.iv.25/336]). This then reinforces Smith's point that exchange is a distinctively human phenomenon. Even the savage's utterances are distinct from the 'natural cries' of one animal to another which are unable to signify thereby mutual wants; a dog does not engage in a 'fair and deliberate exchange of one bone for another with another dog' (*WN* I.ii.2/26; see also *LJA* vi.57/352 where monkeys have no contract to divide apples they have taken). Even apparently concerted action, as by the monkeys or greyhounds running down a hare (*WN* I.ii.2/25; *ED* 23/571) is 'mere accidental concurrence of passions' (*WN* I.ii.2/26; *LJB* 219/493) (for the importance of a cognitive element in human exchange see Fleischacker 2004: 91).

Smith's argument is underdeveloped and has produced a variety of interpretations (see Henderson and Samuels 2004). He argues that the division of labour is a consequence of the trucking propensity. Strictly, however, it is a consequence of three other propositions. The first two are closely connected. Humans are social creatures (the key assumption of his moral philosophy) and they lack self-sufficiency, 'man has almost constant occasion for the help of his brethren' (*WN* I.ii.2/26). We are not to read that last term narrowly; for Smith humans live in tribes or groups and not just in families. These two granted, the third proposition comes into play. The way individual shortages ('wants' in the sense of 'absences') can be most reliably met across a range of circumstances is by appeal to the 'self-love' of another – 'give me that which I want and you shall have this which you want' (*WN* I.ii.2/26). This is indeed an exchange. But it is not obvious that a propensity to that end is doing any work.[4] Of works with which Smith was acquainted the nearest expression to his own is made by Josiah Tucker, who refers to 'the natural Disposition, or instinctive Inclination, of Mankind towards Commerce' (1755: 3, 9).

This underdeveloped character of Smith's argument perhaps explains why he speculates that 'persuasion' or use of language may be more 'basic'. But even so persuasion still effectively presumes some level of mutual complementarity (it is unlikely Glaswegians will be persuaded to buy domestic air-conditioning). It is true that Smith here is most obviously discussing the situation in a 'civilised society'. This is borne out by this discussion culminating in one of his most famous utterances, 'it is not from the benevolence of the butcher, the brewer or the baker, that we expect our dinner but from their regard to their own interest' (*WN* I.ii.2/27; *LJB* 220/493).[5] (I will return to the full version of this passage in Chapter 5.) But this 'regard' is clearly not the prerogative of a commercial society (witness the bow-maker mentioned above and his comments on the faint beginning of the division of labour in the Hottentots and Tartars of the shepherd stage [*FA* 4/583]).

We can identify two implications of Smith's recourse to the propensity/ disposition to truck. Firstly, it gives a naturalistic foundation to exchange. The formal 'logic' of exchange had been clearly spelt out by earlier theorists of trade like Dudley North.[6] In the eighteenth century, Condillac is typical while more analytical than many: commerce presumes surplus on the one hand and consumption on the other because exchange of surplus is only possible with someone who needs to consume it and it is '*le besoin nous fera une nécessité de conclure*' (1847: 262, 256).[7] These formal requirements are not of themselves motives. Smith, as we have seen, invokes self-love, so each party is moved to act, but since exchange itself goes with the grain of human nature then this interaction can reliably enough ensue. The root of this reliability is the constancy of human nature. Hence uncovering this trucking disposition is part of the science of human nature (as Smith himself called it [*TMS* VII.iii.2.3/319]) and can license the conclusion that market transactions are not a series of ad hoc chance contingencies but are open, in principle, to generalisable causal analysis; they conform that is to Hume's 'general rule' (see p. 36 above). Hence a science of political economy can proceed.

The second implication is a corollary of the first. Abstractly, if I have X and you want/need it then it can be obtained by force (you can just take it), by gift (a benevolent act from me to you) or by exchange. By regarding exchange as a disposition Smith is undermining the argument that the first stratagem is the default. Of course, Smith's entire moral philosophy, in common with that of all his fellow Scots, is posited on denying that position (see Chapter 5). Contrary to the 'selfish philosophy' and, in particular, Hobbes (1991: Chap. 13) with his postulate that the 'natural condition of mankind' is the war of all against all, humans do, as the opening sentence of the *Moral Sentiments* bears eloquent witness,[8] possess a disinterested concern for the well-being of others. Smithian self-love – the motivation for exchange – is perfectly compatible with that, as it is with the concurrent presence of benevolent gift-giving. Indeed Smith allows that in comparison to the nobility and generosity of giving gifts, barter is 'mean' but that is because, like hunger, thirst and sex, it is 'so strongly implanted' that it requires no supplementary endorsement, no evocation of 'honour' and similar socio-cultural epithets to act as an additional incentive (*LJB* 301/527).[9]

We can identify another more telling difference. Acts of generosity are most likely between individuals who already know each other (Young 1997: 61). What, as we will see, is crucial about a commercial society is that many of the transactions are between those not known (strangers) and in that situation the exchange will be most reliably effected by mutual appeal to our interests – I give the butcher money, he gives me meat. The source of this reliability lies in human nature and once again this underwrites how commercial behaviour is subject to regularity and thus scientific exploration. That this mode of mutuality was, according to Rousseau, a debasing interaction of dependency was for Smith, and the other Scots, a misreading of a relation that is more properly regarded as an inter-dependency. I touch on this Rousseauan objection in later chapters.

Before examining Smith's 'technological' account, a dimension of his 'sociological' account – of the propensity's societal consequences – bears scrutiny. Plato had linked his account of specific trades with natural aptitude (*diatheron phusin*), which is understood in a strong sense. That is, individuals are naturally diverse and, in consequence, adapted to different tasks which are best executed by those with the appropriate *psuche*; so there are those who are weavers by nature (*kata phusin*) (Plato 1902: 370a, b).[10] Plato was admittedly exceptional even in his own times. Aristotle (1944: 1260b), for example, while allowing that there were natural slaves, made the point of denying that shoemakers, for example, were such 'by nature'. Smith belongs in the mainstream but his expression of the point is especially forceful.

In an example he employed in all the iterations of his argument he compares the 'most dissimilar characters' of a philosopher and a 'common street porter' (*WN* I.ii.4/28–9; *LJA* vi.47/348; *ED* 26/572). While in the 1762–3 *Lectures* this dissimilarity is simply said not to be an 'original difference', in the 1766 version (*LJB* 219/492), as well as in the other two citations, he is more specific, stating it derives 'not so much from nature as from habit, custom and education'. Indeed his argument is more emphatic; the 'genius' that, in their maturity, 'appears to distinguish men of different professions' is upon many occasions 'not so much the cause as the effect of the division of labour'.

The reference here to causation evokes an important aspect not only of Smith's social theory but one shared by all his compatriots. I have called this aspect 'soft determinism' (Berry 1997). Its basis is the distinction between physical and moral causes (referred to on p. 37 above). Though by no means original, the classic exposition of this difference among the Scots is by Hume in his essay 'Of National Characters' (1748). As spelt out by Hume, 'physical causes' 'work insensibly on the temper', whereas moral causes are 'all circumstances which are fitted to work on the mind as motives or reasons and which render a peculiar set of manners habitual to us' (*E-NC* 198). The context here was a critique of a climatic theory of character formation that the Scots associated pre-eminently with Montesquieu, though there was a significant earlier formulation by the Abbé Dubos.[11] This theory can be labelled 'hard determinism' because it operates with direct physiological effect ('insensibly'), whereas moral causes are a species of soft determinism because they operate through habituation or socialisation. These are nonetheless still *causes*. In Smith's example it is as soon as infants come to 'be employed in very different occupations' (*WN* I.ii.4/29) that they begin to differ as their 'manner of life began to affect them' (*LJA* vi.48/348). One is not 'born' but 'made' a philosopher (or porter). In Hume the 'principle of moral causes fixes the character of different professions' and he gives as an example the difference between priests and soldiers (*E-NC* 198). As we will see in Chapter 6 this acceptance of moral causation underlies the criticisms made not only by Smith but by many others of the deleterious 'effects' of the technological division of labour on the labourers (the 'simple operatives').

Samuel Fleischacker (2004: 74, 76; 2013) (see also to similar effect Danford 1980), citing the philosopher/porter passage as an illustration, discerns in Smith a 'very strong endorsement' of equality as a normative principle, which goes alongside a 'remarkably strong version' of the claim that humans are 'essentially equal in abilities'. While it is clear there is a rejection of the Platonic argument when it comes to specific occupations there remains some room for some nativism. Smith is typically qualified. He does not deny there are 'natural talents' just that they are less differentiating and more shallowly rooted than is commonly supposed. Indeed we might say that it is the work of the science of man to be alert to the prejudices that underlie that common supposition.

But it is equally 'scientific' not to attribute complete efficacy to moral causes, as, for example, William Godwin might be thought to do (1976: 106ff) (see also Helvetius on education [p. 26 above]).[12]

We can now turn to the technological division of labour and here, too, Smith's exposition is key and will be the focus of attention. He illustrates how an extensive division of labour produces opulence with the example of a 'very trifling manufacture' – pin-making (*WN* I.i.3/14). This example is chosen because of its supposed transparency; it is not that it exhibits the division of labour at its most extensive but, rather, because, as essentially a workshop enterprise, all the component stages of production are evident. This has resulted, as Smith openly admits, in pin-making being a well-established example[13] and that very fact suits his expository purpose. Notwithstanding this pragmatism on his part, it is undeniable that Smith was the source of the recurrent citation of this example by his compatriots.[14]

Smith calculates that through the division of labour ten individuals could make 48,000 pins a day – equivalent to 4,800 each – whereas if each performed all the tasks required 'not twenty each, perhaps not one pin in day' would have been manufactured (*WN* I.i.3/15). He gives three reasons for this, which are paraphrased by Ferguson (*PMPS* II, 423): increased dexterity that comes from reducing each individual's task to 'one simple operation'; time-saving that stems 'from not having to transfer from one task to the next (with a tendency to 'saunter' between them); and inventing better ways of executing the task prompted by the concentration on one task (*WN* I.i.5–8/17–20). We will return to these features – just as Smith does – when we consider in Chapter 6 other less advantageous consequences of this specialisation.

The division of labour in this illustrative way increases the 'productive powers of labour' (*WN* I.i.4/15). But this is not an independent process. Its extensiveness, the key to its provision of opulence (a multitude of pins), is dependent on the range of exchange or a market. When the market is small there is no incentive to specialise so as to produce a surplus to exchange for the surplus of another specialist (*WN* I.iii.1/31). Moreover that production itself requires a prior accumulation of stock (*WN* II.Intro.2/277). In these circumstances the trucking propensity will have little occasion to manifest itself. In Chapter 4 we will discuss the role of law-induced stability to facilitate that propensity but here a key social condition that makes it sensible to specialise needs to be noted.

For Smith market-extent, and thus intensity of specialisation, is a function of population density – a point also made by Kames (*SHM* I,

110).[15] In part this doubtless reflects the urbanisation within Scotland in his lifetime (see Chapter 1) – Smith uses the Highlands of Scotland to illustrate how individuals are forced to perform for themselves many tasks, 'every farmer' must be his own 'butcher, baker and brewer' (*WN* I.iii.2/31). (That Scotland is less developed than England, and the northern part of the former less than the southern is remarked upon by Millar [*HV* IV, 4/435].) But this acknowledgment of density is not just a recognition of a local development, because it also reflects the general phenomenon that the first congregations of people (cities) were located either on the coast or on navigable rivers. This location meant they could engage in trade; the Phoenicians and Carthaginians in the Mediterranean and the Egyptians and Bengalis with the hinterland of the Nile and Ganges (*WN* I.iii.4–7/34–5).

This last argument is worth an excursus that will link up with the claim in Chapter 2 that 'commercial republics' were distinct from the commercial society of the fourth stage. As mentioned in that chapter, Robertson wrote what was effectively a history of commerce as part of his Introduction to his *History of America*.[16] Dunbar has, probably not coincidentally, a similar account (*EHM* 299–305). Robertson holds that there must be considerable 'improvement', principally in navigation, before commerce becomes 'an object of great importance' (*HAm* 727). Its development was sporadic but in due course 'the advantages derived from navigation and commerce' spread with the Phoenicians leading the way. Their location meant that commerce was 'the only source from which they could derive opulence or power' and, Robertson declares, 'the spirit of their laws were entirely commercial. They were a people of merchants'. The Phoenician legacy was taken up by the Carthaginians and in both peoples commerce generated 'its usual effects' – curiosity, enlarged ideas and an incitement to 'bold enterprises' (*HAm* 728–9). The Greeks and the Romans followed but slowly and fitfully. Eventually 'several of the Grecian commonwealths' became significant maritime powers as commerce was undertaken with 'ardour and success' (*HAm* 730). The Romans, as Robertson portrays them, were for a long time strangers to commerce and naval affairs, leaving those enterprises to slaves and citizens of the lowest class (a point also made by Smith [*WN* IV.ix.47/683], while Dunbar says their 'aspiring genius was not formed for the commercial arts' [*EHM* 304]). It was only with exposure to Eastern luxuries that navigation played a role as they sought to trade (*HAm* 732). Eventually, of course, Rome fell to barbarous conquerors, returning Europe to a 'second infancy' (*HAm* 734). As discussed in Chapter 2 it was the 'peculiar causes' of the Crusades and development of free towns that began the slow development to the maturity of an age of commerce through eroding the power base of the great proprietors.

Smith, for his part, gives a potted history of ancient (principally Greek and Roman) history (Hont 2009: 155–66). He charts the growth from a herding 'economy', at the time depicted by Homer, to the establishment of fortified towns, wherein the 'arts and sciences' were cultivated (*LJB* 31–3/409). Alongside this improvement of arts and opulence they experienced 'refinement' (*LJB* 37/411) and Smith does refer, in passing, to the Greek city-states as 'civilized' (*WN* V.i.a.35/703) (Robertson says they advanced to a 'state of greater civilization', with sciences and arts carried to a 'high pitch of improvement [*HAm* 730]). Smith, however, remarks that they 'honoured agriculture more than manufactures and foreign trade' (*WN* IV.ix.47/683). These ancient city-states were distinctive. Three criteria can be identified. First, for Smith the 'antient republicks of Greece and Italy' derived their revenue principally from the produce or rent of the 'publick lands', whereas 'there is not at present in Europe any civilized state which derives the greater part of its publick revenue from the rent of lands which are the property of the state' (*WN* V.ii.a.13/821; V.ii.a.18/823–4). Wallace, though the lesson he draws is different, also remarks that while the ancients did not neglect trade (it was more confined – citing the standard examples of Phoenicians and Carthaginians – than the moderns) they focused more on agriculture (*DNM* 97–9). A second key difference pertains to defence and is part of a long argument in Smith on the historical role of militias. Whereas in 'antient times the opulent and civilized found it difficult to defend themselves against the poor and barbarous' in 'modern times' the reverse is true. The explanation for this difference is the 'natural progress of improvement', which in this case refers to the establishment of a professional army and superior weaponry (both we can infer exhibiting the benefits of the division of labour) (*WN* V.i.a.43, 44/708). Ferguson takes a different view (see *ECS* 270) as we will discuss in Chapter 6.

The third case is perhaps the most revealing because it is the most obviously loaded.[17] The ancient republics differed from those of Renaissance Italy (let alone from contemporary Europe) because they relied on slavery (*LJB* 34/410). Even if the label 'civilised' was attached to Athens it was, as Hume, Smith, Millar and others recognised, underpinned by slavery. Although in the Scots' writings there is no explicit definition or even delineation of what constitutes 'civilisation' (a new term),[18] nevertheless there was a definitive difference between Athens and Edinburgh (the so-called 'Athens of the North'). The latter was civilised and free. The Scots are clear that their own (and similar)

society is civilised. Hume identifies 'humanity' as 'the chief characteristic which distinguishes a civilized age from times of barbarity and
ignorance' (and in the next paragraph he describes the 'old Romans as
'uncivilized' (*E-RA* 274–5). 'Humanity' however is linked with 'industry' and 'knowledge' as a component in an 'indissoluble chain' that is
'peculiar to the more polished and [. . .] [luxurious] ages (*E-RA* 271)
(see Chapters 4 and 5).

   The presence of this chain is what makes contemporary society both
civilised (free) and commercial.[19] But just as the Scots do not give an
unambiguous declaration of the meaning of 'civilisation' so they are
scarcely more precise with the term 'commercial'. Hume, however, does
make a tellingly key observation. Referring to 'ancient authors' he comments that for them commerce relates to the exchange of commodities
and nowhere (that he can recall) do they ascribe the growth of city to
the 'establishment of a manufacture' (*E-PAN* 418).[20] We can exploit
that observation to identify a distinction between commerce as the
practice of trade (as undertaken by Carthage and other maritime 'commercial republics' – see Chapter 2) and commerce as a type of society (a
'fourth stage' product of the natural progress of improvement), where
the inter-dependency – both sociological and technological – implicit in
manufacture is embedded (see below).

   What effectively ('properly') makes a society 'commercial' is, as
Smith said, where 'everyman is a merchant' (*WN* I.iv.1/37). It is that
inclusivity that is vital and it derives from the extent of the division of
labour, of the market and of stock accumulation. In an early discussion,
Smith was clear that the 'compleat division of labour [. . .] is posterior
to the invention of even agriculture' (*FA* 4/584). Following Hume's
distinction, a commercial society is necessarily one that includes
manufacture and industry. Hence despite Robertson's description of
the Phoenicians as a 'people of merchants' they did not constitute a
commercial society (which is also an arguable implication of Wallace's
view). The same may be said of Venice which Robertson calls a 'commercial state' (*India* 1118). Although Venice did 'manufacture' ships
(using an extensive division of labour) none of the Scots picks up
on that. Venice is a trading republic as was Palmyra ('a commercial
city' [*India* 1096]), strategically placed on the route from India to the
Mediterranean. The link between commercial, that is, trading cities
and 'republican' governance was a commonplace. This association
we noted in Chapter 2 (p. 26) and we will meet again, and is present
here in Smith's reference to 'antient republicks' and Robertson's to
'Grecian commonwealths'. The adoption of the more inclusive reading
of commerce as a post-feudal 'society' of 'universal opulence' is what

differentiates the Scots' idea of a commercial society. I return to this in Chapter 7.

A society where tasks like pin-making (presumably embodying 'completion') are minutely divided must necessarily be complex. (Recall here from Chapter 2 the trajectory assumed by the Scots' natural history; the progress from simple to complex.) The members of a commercial society are deeply interdependent; this lies at the heart of the sociological dimension of the division of labour. Smith illustrates this with the example of a coarse woollen coat as worn by a day-labourer. Even this humble product, he remarks, is 'the produce of the joint labour of a great number of multitude of workmen'. After listing nine trades he firstly tacks on the phrase 'with many others' then goes on to note all those employed in transporting the materials, then those in manufacturing the transport, which is not to include those involved in making the tools used to make the coat (and so on). This leads to the inevitable conclusion that 'many thousands' are involved in the manufacture of this relatively simple garment (*WN* I.i.11/22–3). What this example of a deliberately unsophisticated product demonstrates is the fact of interdependence in a commercial society. Every individual, in what he here refers to as a 'civilized society', 'stands at all times in need of the co-operation and assistance of great multitudes' (*WN* I.ii.2/26). It is because of this that Smith is led to make the remark that is the leitmotif of this book, that 'everyman thus lives by exchanging or becomes in some measure a merchant'. I return to this also in Chapter 7.

One sense in which this is a 'proper' characterisation is that it marks the depth of penetration, or inclusivity, of exchange relations. The agricultural sector is admitted to be more resistant to this penetration. It is a running motif in Smith (and others such as Millar *HV* IV, 4/735) that agriculture is less susceptible to specialisation. Even in the context of pin-making Smith contrasts the relative productive powers of agriculture and manufacture. The former does not keep pace with improvements in the latter, since while the 'spinner is almost always a distinct person from the weaver' the 'ploughman, the harrower, the sower of seed, and the reaper of the corn are often the same' (*WN* I.i.4/16). However, this is a matter of degree and will diminish. The process of improvement results in better quality agricultural tools and the application of fertilisers, requiring more technological expertise and specialisation (industry and knowledge are indissolubly linked), so that agriculture is woven into a web of market relations. Also, of course, land itself – despite the obstructive legacy of entails – is a thoroughly marketable commodity. We can add here that there is another sense in which the woollen coat exemplifies the difference between commercial and earlier societies. The fact of interdependence that it represents also bears significantly on the blessing of liberty and, as such, it will be developed in Chapter 4.

## THE MISERY OF POVERTY

The obverse of the blessing of opulence is the misery of poverty. Historically that contrast is not self-evident. It is a central plank in the idea of a commercial society – a key ingredient in its normative vindication – that it marks a shift in values. This is, of course, a wider cultural shift than the work of the Scottish Enlightenment but its members are, nonetheless, important contributors. Again this contribution is two-sided. There is a critique of the view that poverty is in some sense noble or redemptive and a defence of the view that wealth, opulence and indeed luxury are positive societal features. This chapter takes up the critique and leaves the defence until later chapters. Both however share the same perspective that the basic conditions of material life matter and are a matter of morality.

By being 'blessed' by opulence the members of a commercial society are able to enjoy a far better standard of living than those in earlier ages. In material terms the three basic needs of food, shelter and clothing identified by Plato and reiterated throughout ever since are better and more adequately met. Smith is explicit (*WN* I.viii.36/96) and Kames who, as we shall see, criticises many aspects of commerce, comments disparagingly how, before the Europeans arrived, the Canadians were thinly clothed in a bitterly cold climate (*SHM* I, 363). Smith advertises what is at stake in the rhetorically powerful Introduction to the *Wealth of Nations*. There he contrasts the 'savage nations of hunters and fishers' with 'civilized and thriving nations'. The latter, as we have seen, enjoy abundance whereas the former are 'miserably poor'. As a consequence of this poverty these hunters 'are frequently reduced or, at least, think themselves reduced, to the necessity sometimes of directly destroying and sometimes abandoning their infants, their old people and those afflicted with lingering diseases, to perish with hunger or to be devoured by wild beasts' (*WN* Introd/10). Millar closely follows Smith. He too notes the link between the 'misery' of the savage and the practice of abandoning children to 'perish by hunger or to be devoured by wild beasts' (*OR* 230; cf. 236).[21] By contrast in 'those European nations which have made the greatest improvements in commerce and manufactures' children are subjected to their father no farther 'than seems necessary for their advantage' (*OR* 243). As Smith reports in the body of the *Wealth of Nations*, the 'lower ranks' among the Chinese are so impoverished that not only do they commit the 'horrid practice' of infanticide but the actual task is itself a means of subsistence for those who execute it. In an implicit contrast with European standards, he also observes how the Chinese regard as wholesome food the 'putrid and stinking' garbage which the European ships have discarded (*WN* I.viii.24/90). There is another dimension to Smith's use of China, to which I shall return, but he brings this 'message' closer to home. While the Scottish Highlanders might not deliberately practise infanticide, such is their poverty that of the twenty children that a 'half-starved Highland woman' not unusually bears only two might survive (*WN* I.viii.37–8/96–7).

In an uncomplicated way these costs imposed by indigence are high. Poverty produces pain both in a directly material way, as in starvation and having no adequate protection from the environment, but also indirectly as in witnessing the death of one's children. Pain is bad: this is a Newtonian 'ultimate' in the science of man. By extension poverty, when a cause of it, is also bad. This is a powerful and important argument. Contrary to Stoic and republican 'frugality' or Christian asceticism, that is, contrary to two deeply influential doctrines, Smith is firmly repudiating any notion that poverty is ennobling or redemptive. And since the abundance that commerce brings is indeed a blessing then Smith's and others' repudiation of the nobility of poverty is a key factor in the vindication of a commercial society.

Before developing some further aspects of the material advantages of commercial society, I wish to elaborate on this critique of poverty as an 'ideal'. In this idealised portrayal, 'poverty', like its contextual close relations 'simplicity', 'austerity' and 'severity', belongs within a particular moralised vocabulary. They are all expressions of the estimable practice (virtues) of temperance and continence. To live the simple life of poverty in this sense is to be in control of oneself and thus of one's actions; it is to know the true and proper value of things and to be in a position of forswearing temptations, that is, things of illusory value. Thus understood poverty is a product of choice or will or reason and this makes it possible to draw a conceptual distinction between poverty as a self-imposed voluntary state and being impoverished (or necessitous, that is, having no choice).

This idea of self-control, of poverty as a voluntary state, was expressed by Stoic philosophers like Seneca and Epictetus and played an important role in Christian teaching and practice (I discuss this in Chapter 5). In part this was negative. As St Thomas Aquinas expressed it, poverty is commendable because it frees a man from 'worldly solicitude' (1928: III.2.133/141–2). The more positive aspect, as also articulated by Aquinas, was that those who embraced voluntary poverty did so to follow Christ and 'be useful to their community' (1928: III.2.135/148). Part of that utility was to relieve the poor (and that 'mission' was central to monastic orders like the Benedictines or of friars like the Dominicans, of whom Aquinas was a member). This command seemingly acknowledges that for some poverty was not a voluntary state.

The canon lawyer Huguccio (of Pisa) (d.1210) elaborated upon this distinction between voluntary and involuntary poverty. In his commentary (1188) on Gratian's *Decretum* (1140), the primary canon law text, Huguccio divided the poor into three categories. There were those who while born poor willingly endured it as an expression of their love of God, and also there were those who deliberately surrendered their possessions that they might live a virtuous Christian life. Both of these exemplified voluntary poverty. The third category, however, comprised those who were destitute and liable to be inhibited from achieving the higher moral values. This was involuntary poverty. However, the thrust here is on the involuntary poor being inhibited; as the first category intimates, the dominant sensibility was that poverty was not of itself an evil to be extirpated. Indeed, Stoic echoes can still be heard in Huguccio's explicit identification of this third category with those who are poor because they are filled with the 'voracity of cupidity' (quoted in Tierney [1959: 11]).

The theologians of the Reformation, as well as advocating a return to a more austere theology, also fostered a view of salvation that associated it with industry or work in conjunction with a worldly asceticism. A corollary of this was to associate indolence with lack of virtue. While this applied to the 'idle', consumption-orientated, rich (Booth 1993: 162) it also encompassed 'beggars and vagabonds' whose poverty became presumptive evidence of their wickedness (Hill 1968: 215). Voluntary poverty now takes on a negative character, a 'popish conceit' as William Perkins called it (1609: 148). Nonetheless Perkins still held that poverty should be seen as providential and even those whose 'calling' requires the performance of 'poore and base duties' will not be base in the sight of God, if they undertake those duties in obedient faith to His glory (1612: 757–8).

Hume set himself against this idealisation of poverty (Berry 2008). His explicit target is 'men of severe morals' (*E-RA* 269). These men, citing the example of ancient Rome, associate poverty and virtue (*E-RA* 275). Hume dissociates them. He remarks, in what we can see as a direct rebuttal of Perkins, that 'poverty and hard labour debase the minds of the common people and render them unfit for any science or ingenious professions' (*E-NC* 198). While this particular remark is made in passing, he carries out a sweeping critique of this debasement. Hume associates poverty with a pre-existing sense of destitution,[22] linked traditionally to the plight of orphans, widows, the aged and so on, who were the proper recipients of alms. This is a compassionate, not a severe, morality.[23] Hume can also be seen to dissociate '(hard) labour' that the poor experience from industry. The former debases because it is a miserable condition, injurious to well-being, the latter, in the guise of 'action' (see Chapter 6), is a component of human happiness. Hume is here shifting the emphasis in the established position that industry is a virtue by detaching it from both its biblical penitential moorings and from 'the perpetual cant of the Stoics and Cynics' (*M* 6, 21/*SBNM* 242), as they enjoin 'suffering and self-denial' as a mark of the severe or austere demands exacted by reason in order to control appetites (*M* 9, 15/*SBNM* 279). Smith similarly upbraids those 'whining and melancholy moralists [. . .] who regard as impious the natural joy of prosperity' and who, moreover, do not consider those 'many wretches [. . .] labouring under all sorts of calamities, in the languor of poverty, in the agony of disease [. . .]) (*TMS* III.3.9/139). Smith too has principally in mind the 'ancient Stoics' (*TMS* III.3.11/140) (I return to Smith and Stoicism in Chapter 5, where the further significance of this passage is addressed). But this positive evaluation of frugality or poverty was not the sole preserve of the ancients since it remained a stock ingredient of civic republicans, such as Algernon Sidney who, in his *Discourses concerning Government* (1698), in a typical expression of that perspective, declared that poverty is 'the mother and nurse of [. . .] virtue' (1990: 254). (For another example see Mackenzie quoted below p. 140.)

The thinkers who uphold the virtue of poverty typically contrast it with the vice of luxury. Hume, as we will see in Chapter 6, subverted this contrast. Here it is sufficient to note that on his argument luxury nourishes commerce and this both reduces destitution and augments the resources available for amelioration. This improvement is manifest in a commercial society. Those who live in non-opulent states will be 'miserable'; they will be poor in the sense of being painfully impoverished. If poverty is bad then there is a prima facie obligation to alleviate. But for that to be effective more than exhortation is required. The Scots bring their social science to bear. Of course private benevolence is appropriate and morally enjoined but that leaves unconsidered the 'causes' of poverty. Some of these are physical (features of the environment) but others are moral. However, these should not be regarded as oppositional fixed categories, for as Dunbar argued (in Baconian language) the 'natural history of the terraqueous globe varies with the civil history of nations' (*EHM* 354–5). Environmental factors, like soil and climate, are susceptible of improvement and that correlates 'in a high degree with the progress of civil arts' (*EHM* 360). In short, Dunbar argues that 'the series of events, once begun, is governed more perhaps by moral than physical causes' (*EHM* 239).[24]

On the more specific question of poverty the essential answer the Scots supply is that it is the development of commerce that raises the poor out of destitution. Smith is indelibly associated with the argument that the operation of the principle of natural liberty in a well-regulated society will achieve that aim. The next chapter will explore that argument but here we can pick up on one its corollaries. If 'liberty' is the solution then removing obstacles to it is an integral element of poverty alleviation. These obstacles are thus subject to criticism. There are two related points of attack – on the politics and policy of the Poor Law and a rebuttal of the objections to the payment of high wages.

The Elizabethan 'Poor Law' (Settlement Act) (1601) (which for Perkins was an 'excellent statute' and 'in substance the very law of God' [1612: 755]) charged each parish with the responsibility to support its own poor. Smith put its origin down to Henry VIII's dissolution of the monasteries, which had previously been the major source of charitable relief for the impoverished and destitute (*WN* I.x.c.46/152). This law was revisited over the years. The Act of Settlement of 1662 enabled parishes to eject immigrant paupers. Smith judged the removal of a 'man who has committed no misdemeanour from the parish where he chuses to reside an evident violation of natural liberty'. Although the parish-based localism of the English system was distinctive, restriction of labour was, as Smith observes, common throughout Europe. It is the restrictiveness of mobility that draws Smith's ire. The Poor Law was 'ill-contrived' and its effect was such that 'there is scarce a poor man in England of forty years of age' who has not been 'most cruelly oppressed' by it (*WN* I.x.c.59/157). He later includes its repeal as one of a series of laws that prevent the 'natural liberty of workers from 'exercising what species of industry they please'; they should if 'thrown out of employment' in one place be able 'without the fear of a prosecution' to seek it elsewhere (*WN* IV.ii.42/470). The effect of this law by penalising mobility is to entrench poverty. It is an example of an 'impertinent obstruction' to the 'natural effort of every individual to better his own condition' which is powerful enough to lead 'society to wealth and prosperity' (*WN* IV.v.b.43/540). The removal of the law removes a major human (moral) cause of poverty.

The other Scot who writes on the subject of Poor Law is Kames, who devoted a whole Sketch to this issue. His interpretation is part of

his more general ambivalence toward a commercial society. He, like
Smith, recognises that regulations for the poor 'make a considerable
branch of public police' (*SHM* II, 37).[25] Also like Smith he judges the
Elizabethan law 'oppressive' and 'grossly unjust' as well as ineffective
(*SHM* II, 40). What especially exercises Kames about this law is that it
was a form of compulsory charity (*SHM* II, 57). Charity should rather
be voluntary and he believes that in 'a well-regulated government' that
promotes 'industry and virtue' there will be little need for it (*SHM* II,
56). However, Kames does differ significantly from Smith. He follows
the original Poor Law (and its supporters like Perkins), in distinguishing between the deserving poor who worked and the undeserving
who were dependent on 'public largesse', such as paupers and sturdy
beggars (*SHM* II, 67). With a faint echo of Perkins, for Kames, the latter
are a particular concern because they are a symptom of the 'disease of
poverty' (*SHM* II, 37). Wallace is another Scot who remarks on the
number of beggars (*DNM* 89; *CGB* 117) but it was a recurrent theme
in the literature of the times. Kames advocates a more interventionist
solution than Smith's confidence in the socially ameliorative effects of
the liberty to better one's condition. This divergence reflects a difference in how a commercial society should operate (see Chapter 1 above
and Chapter 4 below). Kames' remedy is a combination of tax and
voluntary contribution from gentlemen who would oversee the use of
the funds to separate the profligate from the innocent poor (*SHM* II,
60–1).

However, the biggest divergence between Smith and Kames is their
view of wages and incentives. For Kames a major fault of the compulsory charity of the Poor Law is that if some support is guaranteed then
the recipient will sink into idleness, because, he holds, for the labouring
poor, 'fear of want' is the only effective motive to make them work.
Although he allows that 'high wages at first promote industry', their
'remote consequences' produce a 'dismal scene' (*SHM* I, 83), such that,
in the Sketch on the Poor, he is able to declare that 'extravagant wages'
are a 'deplorable evil' (*SHM* II, 43; cf. Horne 1990: 108). Kames is
here subscribing to what has been called the 'utility of poverty' (Furniss
1920: Chap. 6, a still valuable source for the 'history' of this argument). Mandeville is a typically artful exponent; the poor are to be
'well-managed', so that while they should not starve yet they 'should
receive nothing worth saving' (1988: I, 193).[26] This argument was
firmly rejected by Smith. Nathan Rosenberg regards Smith's argument
as 'novel' (1975: 379; cf. Himmelfarb 1984: 51), though, as ever, precedents can be found, including Hume (*E-Com* 265)[27] and Daniel Baugh
(1983: 86) rather reads the *Wealth of Nations* as having 'clinched

victory for a revisionist argument that had been gaining influence over four decades'.

In explicit contrast to Kames, Smith argues that 'the liberal reward of labour [...] increases the industry of the common people'. High wages, not 'want' is the spur to activity; they supply encouragement to that desire to better one's condition (*WN* I.viii.44/99). For Hume, the desire to live better than one's predecessors 'rouses men from indolence' (*E-Com* 264). Steuart says something very similar (*PPE* I, 157), while for Smith, the evidence is that 'liberal reward' is both 'the necessary effect' and 'natural symptom of increasing national wealth' (*WN* I.viii.27/91). Wages are highest in the most thriving countries (*WN* I.viii.22/87) because the same cause that raises wages also increases productive powers (*WN* I.viii.57/104). Indeed the high price of labour 'constitutes the essence of public opulence' (*ED* 12/567). Since in an 'opulent and commercial society labour becomes dear and work cheap' (*ED* 11/567) then what matters is not the money price of labour but 'the real quantity of the necessaries and conveniencies of life' the wages can procure (*WN* I.viii.35/95). Wallace had similarly argued that 'the most substantial riches consist in the abundance of those things that are necessary for the support and comfort of life' and 'industry, indeed is the great source of wealth' (*CGB* 96, 110).

The argument is more than 'economic'. As pointed out above, when individuals' basic needs are better provided then this is a 'good' state of affairs. Deprivation is a privation, a 'bad' set of circumstances; while to treat asceticism as some form of ideal is as Hume disparagingly said a 'monkish virtue' rejected everywhere by 'men of sense' (*M* 9, 3/*SBNM* 270). Moreover, as Smith declared, it is a matter of 'equity' that those who provide for the basic needs of society should themselves be 'tolerably well-fed, cloathed and lodged'. Moreover, bearing in mind the joy that prosperity brings then 'no society can be flourishing and happy of which the greater part are poor and miserable' (*WN* I.viii.36/96). Hume, too, while making passing acknowledgment of the standard mercantilist argument that a high price of labour has some disadvantage for foreign trade, nevertheless declares that this consideration is insignificant in the face of the 'happiness of many millions' (*E-Com* 265). Happiness, joy, material comforts are the stuff of modern morality and are to be found, accordingly, in a modern commercial society. The moralised vocabulary of severe or austere poverty, as enjoined in 'ancient republics', has been thoroughly overturned.

Hume also in this context observes that 'poverty of the common people is a natural, if not infallible, effect of absolute monarchy' just as with equal fallibility riches are the 'result of liberty' (*E-Com* 265

[Wallace quotes this, *CGB* 66n]). This underlines that the misery of poverty is indeed an alterable moral cause. One of Smith's remarks about China exemplifies this argument. Though, as we noted earlier, he comments on their poverty he also says China has reached the 'full complement of its riches' consistent with its laws and institutions (and its physical environment). If, however, these laws were changed then it could leave its 'stationary state'. In addition to allowing foreign commerce what it should do is remove 'the pretence of justice', under which guise the poor and 'owners of small capitals' are 'pillaged and plundered' (*WN* I.ix.15/122). In other words, provide security for all by the operation of the rule of law. That provision is a central component of the idea of a commercial society and is the subject of the next chapter.

## NOTES

1. Scott (1966: 237). In fact the passage in question from the *System* (2005: I, 287–9) is not a sustained discussion, being illustrative of the necessity of a social life. Mandeville's references, too, are made in passing (1988: II, 142, 284). He employs the familiar example of a watch (see also Martin's *Considerations* (1701) [1952: 591]) of which the probable source is Petty's *Another Essay in Political Arithmetic* (1683) (1899: II, 473) but again the observation is not pursued. It is Smith's systematic exploitation of these possible precedents that distinguishes him and what matters.

2. This is a well-established distinction. What I have labelled 'technological', Groenewegen (1977: 162), for example, calls 'industrial', and Fiori and Pescarelli (1999: 101) refer to as 'technical'.

3. On the general role of persuasion in Smith see Kelly (2011: 119–28) and McKenna (2006: 134), who emphasises the 'centrality of persuasion as a means of achieving cooperation necessary in a civil society'.

4. Tony Aspromourgos (2009: 62) cites the 'propensity to exchange' along with 'self-regard' and 'desire for material self-betterment' as the three 'fundamental "drivers" of human economic behaviour' but, analytically as opposed to textually (which is all Aspromourgos can be judged reasonably to be saying), it is not self-evident that its motivating power (so to speak) is on par with the other two.

5. Compare Josiah Tucker, 'self-love is the great mover in human nature' and is 'implanted in Mankind much more strongly than the Love of Benevolence' (1755: 9, 7). Even Kames, who is a severe critic of aspects of a commercial society, says 'every man has more power, knowledge and opportunity to promote his own good than that of others; by which more good is actually produced than if we were entirely surrendered to benevolence' (*PE* 32). The 'history' of self-love is complex, I will return to this issue in Chapter 5.

6. North, *Discourse on Trade* 1691 (1952: 516): 'Trade is nothing else but a Commutation of Superfluities; for instance: I give of mine, what I can spare for somewhat of yours, which I want, and you can spare.'

7. 'Necessity' (or need) was commonly invoked. See for example Abbé Goguet , '*la necessité*' is the source of commerce, the desire to acquire goods that one lacks (1758: I, 570), Mirabeau, commerce is '*la rapport utile et nècessaire de tout Etre sociable avec son sembables*' (1759: II,7) or Quesnay simply, '*l'échange rend le superflu nècessaire*' (1764: I,8). In Scotland see Adam Ferguson (*PMPS* II, 424). The point goes back at least as far as Aristotle who identified *chreia* (need) as the basis of barter (1944: 1257a).

8. 'How selfish soever a man may be supposed, there are evidently some principles in his nature, which interest him in the fortune of others and render their happiness necessary to him, though he derives nothing from it except the pleasure of seeing it' (*TMS* I.i.1.1/9). It echoes the opening sentence of Hutcheson's *An Inquiry concerning Moral Good and Evil* (1725) where he defines 'moral goodness' as 'our idea of some quality apprehended in actions which procures approbation and love toward the actor, from those who receive no advantage by the action' (*PW* 67).

9. Compare Joan Robinson's (1962: 53) gloss on the 'butcher baker' passage that there is often a 'note of gentlemanly distaste' in Smith's tone.

10. Vernon Foley's (1976: 140, 141, 151) claim that Smith's account is close to Plato (or closer than it is to Mandeville) is vitiated by lack of appreciation of Plato's underlying metaphysic. On one reading Plato is far more radical – since it is 'nature', which is a question of fitness to task, that is the relevant factor then gender differences are irrelevant.

11. See his *Réflexions* (1760 – first published 1719) which argued for the influence of what he called 'air' as a physical cause as more explanatory than moral causes to account, for example, for the absence of history painting in England. He was criticised by Turnbull in his essay on *Painting* (1740: 109) and Hume cites him several times.

12. For passing comment on Smith and Helvetius and others see West (1964: 290). Not surprisingly, given his emphasis on education, Helvetius is critical of Dubos' argument (1845: 305f).

13. The key source is Alexander Delaire's [sic] entry *Epingle* in volume 5 of *Encyclopédie* (1755) (one of the volumes bought by Smith for Glasgow University Library). This is an essentially descriptive entry, devoting a paragraph to each of the eighteen tasks (with references to illustrative plates) thus exemplifying the full title of the work as *Dictionnnaire raisonnée des sciences, des arts et des métiers* (his name is customarily spelt Deleyre [cf. Lough 1971: 48]). Earlier Ephraim Chambers in his *Cyclopedia or an Universal Dictionary of Arts and Sciences* (1728) – and one of the inspirations behind Diderot's similarly titled enterprise – had remarked that pin manufacture was a commodity that involved twenty-five workers successively in their production.

14. Cf. Dunbar *EHM* 423; Ferguson *PMPS* II, 424, *MSS* 143; Millar *HV* IV, 154/736. Steuart also uses the example (*PPE* I, 158) and though this pre-dates *WN* Smith had used the pin example in the 'Early Draft' of the early 1760s (*ED* 6/564).

15. Petty in a typical passing comment in *Political Arithmetic* observed that 'those who live in Solitary places must be their own Soldiers, Divines, Physicians and Lawyers' (1899: I, 255–6).

16. A somewhat similar account is given in his *Disquisition* on India, where he explicitly says he is has furnished a 'general history of commerce' (*India* 1124).

17. See J. G. A. Pocock's (1999: 328) observation that Smith engaged in 'a critique of city-state civilisation' which was 'unable to sustain itself [. . .] under the imperatives of an agrarian economy worked by slavery and lacking an internal market'. He further points out the contextual vindication here of modern commercial societies against the neo-republican challenge. I will discuss that challenge in Chapter 6.

18. Jean Starobinski (1993: 3) in a thorough (if French focused) discussion attributes the first use of the word (in a non-juridical sense) to Mirabeau in 1756. The OED quotes Boswell in 1772 recording that Dr Johnson would not admit the word into his *Dictionary* and he, in demurral, saying he thought it a better word than 'civility' in the sense of opposed to 'barbarity'. This is the frequent Scottish context and Starobinski further observes (1993: 5) that the establishment of this antithesis was 'the crucial point'. See also Marshall and Williams (1982: 177) on the changing criteria of 'civility'.

19. Ferguson makes a point of denying the terms 'commercial' and 'civilised' are conterminous. He cites the Romans, calling them 'very accomplished' while (nearly) peasants. He also cites the Spartans, although that is in virtue of their commitment to public service rather than 'literary genius and the fine arts' but, as an illustration of the imprecision of the term 'civilisation', he also remarks they 'dispensed with the laws of nature and humanity, as to devote, in the capacity of slaves, a particular race of men to perform the labours necessary for the maintenance of the people' (*PMPS* I, 252).

20. 'Commerce' as a subject of enquiry became common in the seventeenth century as markets and foreign trade became established. Robertson, in a work published in 1791, remarks that it is only now that 'modern ideas with respect to the importance of commerce' have begun to unfold (*India* 1115; cf. 1124). Margaret Schabas (2005: 2) argues that prior to the nineteenth century 'commerce' connoted 'civil transactions between individual merchants and consumers and was not by and large used in the aggregate sense'. This is part of her argument that the 'economy' as a distinct entity needed to be 'de-naturalised'. Something she claims Smith did not achieve.

21. It is very likely that Millar is following Smith's account in the *Moral Sentiments* where the 'extreme indigence' of the savage results in abandoning children 'to wild beasts' (*TMS* V.2.15/210; cf. *LJA* iii.78/172).

22. See further his characterisation, 'when a poor man appears, the disagreeable images of want, penury, hard labour, dirty furniture, coarse or ragged cloathes, nauseous meats and distasteful liquor, immediately strike our fancy' (Hume M 6, 33/SBNM 248). The references to apparel, furnishing and food recall the focus on the three basic (bodily) needs.

23. See Hume's sardonic reference to Epictetus, who 'scarcely ever mentioned the sentiment of humanity and compassion but in order to put his disciples on their guard against it' (M App.4, 14/SBNM 319).

24. See Robertson's comment that climate produces greater effects on 'rude nations' than in 'societies more improved'. 'Civilized men' are, through their 'ingenuity and inventions', able to 'supply the defects and guard against the inconveniences of any climate' (HAm 850). The relative sway of moral and physical causes is in this way an index of development. See also Chapter 2.

25. Smith defined 'police' as 'whatever regulations are made with respect to the trade, commerce, agriculture, manufactures of the country' (LJA i.2/5). This was not atypical.

26. In related fashion he criticises charity-schools as pernicious, it is 'requisite' that the labouring poor should be ignorant (Mandeville 1988: I, 288). Kames echoes this in his assertion that knowledge is dangerous for the labouring poor and charity-schools are more hurtful than beneficial (SHM II, 53–4).

27. There has been some debate over this. The text most quoted as indicating Hume was an advocate of low wages is his report in 'Of Taxes' that ''tis always observed in years of scarcity, if it be not extreme, that the poor labour more and really live better than in years of great plenty' (E-v 635). This is cited by Johnson who treats Hume as 'partially' accepting low wages as incentive (1937: 287), by Gertrude Himmelfarb (1984: 51) and by Edward Furniss (1920: 122). However Furniss later identifies Hume as urging the utility of increasing real wages so that the standard of living might rise (1920: 189). According to Coats (1958), Hume presents both sides but the main weight of his case was against restrictions on the expansion of labourer's wants and improvement of their living standards. Coats (1992: I, 90) elsewhere is more emphatic in aligning Hume with the view that a rising standard of living was a good for all. The passage from 'Of Taxes' was omitted from the 1768 and subsequent editions of the *Essays* (note also the conditional clause) but see Hume HE II, 259 where 'necessity' is cited as required to shake people from 'habits of indolence'. Hume is non-committal about the Elizabethan Poor Law; it is, however, consistent with his stress on action and the virtue of industry that labourers are more deserving than sturdy beggars (though he is contemptuous of Elizabeth's declaration of martial law to rid London of 'idle vagabonds' (HE II, 583). Elsewhere, Hume also remarks in a discussion of benevolence that 'giving alms to common beggars is naturally praised; because it seems to carry relief to the distressed and indigent: But when we observe

the encouragement thence arising to idleness and debauchery, we regard that species of charity rather as a weakness than a virtue' (*M* II, 18/*SBNM* 180). Conceivably this remark is more reportage of a widely held view to illustrate his argument about the effective role of utility in assessments of virtue rather than a judgment of his own; not of course that these are mutually exclusive.

# 4. *Markets, Law and Politics*

There is more to a commercial society than a better material standard of living, than simply the blessing of opulence (vitally important and significant though that is). This type of society also enjoys the blessing of liberty. That second blessing is the focus of Chapter 5, although admitting the division is somewhat artificial, this chapter considers the framework (so to speak) that facilitates liberty as well as other commercial virtues. At the heart of the 'idea' of a commercial society is a series of connected conceptual relations. This chapter explores these and comes in three parts. The first examines the relation between the impersonality of commercial exchange and law. Markets deal in impersonal transactions (commercial life is seen as comprising a 'society of strangers') and the rule of law means that it is 'no respecter of persons'. The second part investigates the complementary conceptual relation that pertains between commercial inter-dependence and legal/political independence from the authority of specified individuals. These connected relations explain why justice has such a central, if not in all respects convergent, place in the Scots' writings. The chapter concludes with a discussion of how/why the implementation of justice is seen as a key task of a government and what, in the light of the earlier discussion, can be said about the politics of a commercial society.

## MARKETS AND THE RULE OF LAW

To explore the relation between markets and law, I start by summarising the underlying conceptual linkages. Commerce requires consistency and security and in order to sustain a society where everyman is a merchant this requirement needs to be assured. There are two reasons for that; first because commerce rests on a set of expectations and beliefs and, secondly, because, in a commercial society the butcher, baker or brewer are routinely not going to be related, by ties of kin, marriage or friendship, to their customers. The intangibility of expectation and the impersonality of exchange among strangers both reflect the 'abstract' character of a commercial society, in contrast to the more 'concrete' relations in earlier ages, whether the tangibility of an actual posses-sion or the face-to-face contact of the barter between the hunter and bow-maker. The apt source of the requisite assurance has likewise to be abstract and takes the form of the rule of law rather than the con-crete or substantive edict of a ruler directing the actions of particular individuals.[1]

These simplified summative statements clearly require elaboration. As the rudimentary example of hunter and bow-maker implies there had to be some form of constancy even in their environment. For the bow-maker, the hunter had to be part of the same tribe or settlement so that he would return with his venison to 'repay' him for his labours (Smith assumes these are male occupations). For the hunter, in an inse-cure environment a known and relatively permanent source of good-quality bows is at a premium. In line with some contemporary work, a pattern of reciprocity builds up trust thus reinforcing their shared mem-bership (Ostrom 1998; Paganelli 2013). Trust matters because there will only be an exchange if the bow-maker spends time now making a bow (thus incurring the 'opportunity cost' of not hunting) and trusts the hunter to supply him with meat, while the hunter is in the field trust-ing the bow-maker is 'at home' making more weapons.[2] Of course, the small-scale face-to-face nature of their settlement means this trust is less of an issue and 'policing' it is largely a matter of group-sanction (such as shame or banishment). Omitting for the moment the intermediate stages, in a commercial society, by contrast, most people do not know each other and the informal sanctions of the first stage will not operate in the relative anonymity of a society of strangers. This means a reli-able alternative has to be found. This is found in law but, as we would expect, the Scots are sensitive not only to its operation but also to how it emerged. It is bad social science simply to assert law is necessary.

It is evidentially clear that the sphere of security and stability expe-rienced by the bow-maker and the hunter in the first stage is very circumscribed. The environment, both natural and human, is hostile (inter-tribe warfare is endemic [Hume *E-OG* 40]). One consequence of this is that there may be little opportunity for the hunter and bow-maker to build up reciprocal relations given the likelihood that at least one of them may not survive to repeat the transaction. Smith himself declares that in the 'rude state of society' exchanges are 'seldom made' (*WN* II.Intr.1/276). This rarity, combined with the general precariousness of life, explains to a large degree the 'universal poverty' experienced in that stage (*WN* V.i.b.7/712). In the virtual absence of the division of labour there will be no specialisation which, as we recall from Chapter 3, is the cause of improvement of the productive powers and consequent economic growth to commercial opulence. Moreover, the circumstances of hunter-gatherer life are so confined that there is no market beyond the venison/bow level of exchange (barter) and, again, we can recall from Chapter 3 that the intensity of the division of labour correlates with the extent of the market. There is a further considera-tion. In line with the developmental assumptions of natural history (see Chapter 2), these 'savages' are 'scarce capable of forming any arrange-ment for futurity' (Dunbar *EHM* 15). This judgment implies that even the hunter/bow-maker arrangement reflects some progress beyond the world of 'immediacy'. In the *Early Draft*, Smith refers (on the authority of Peter Kolben) to the Hottentots as having some division of labour and that they have thus developed beyond the North Americans, while they are not as advanced as the herders (*ED* 4/583–4).

Using the four stages as an ideal-typical template some progress can be expected in the worlds of herders and farmers. However, although relations have lost the immediacy of the first stage and ideas are enlarged, so that there is now a conception of property, yet security and stability remain fragile. The core of this fragility is that power is still localised and is exercised capriciously. We can appreciate why this is the case by picking up the discussion of subordination from Chapter 2. The guiding 'rule of thumb' is Robertson's declaration that 'upon discovering in what state property was at any particular period we may determine with precision [. . .] the degree of power possessed' (*VP* 375). And as Millar argued it was, in the second stage, with 'invention of taming and pasturing cattle' that the 'opportunity' for differential ownership arose and with that came 'a permanent distinction of ranks' (*OR* 203–4).

This permanency stems from the owners of the herds being in a posi-tion to create a 'train of dependence' because those without ownership of their own animals have to look to the chiefs or khans to 'afford them subsistence' (Millar *OR* 250). This differential ownership is maintained or underwritten by forms of social control. This 'control' serves to fore-close alternatives by making ownership acceptable. But it would be a mistake to attribute this control simply to fear. As Smith remarks of the Tartar chief he has a 'natural authority over all the inferior shepherds and herdsmen of his horde or clan' (*WN* V.i.a.11/714). This is 'natural' in Smith's often used sense of what can be normally be expected to follow in a given circumstance.[3] That is to say it conforms to the principles of natural history. But, also in line with those principles, it is distinguishable from the 'natural' personal qualities of strength whereby the leader of a tribe of hunters enjoys his eminence. Those qualities were 'palpable'; the Tartar chieftainship relies, we recall from Chapter 2, on the less immediately tangible 'causes' of fortune and birth.

Smith allows this Tartar chief to be 'some sort of judicial authority' in the sense that when these dependants suffer 'injuries' they look to their chief to interpose himself. They do this because they acknowledge not simply his power to rectify but also recognise that in virtue of this power the offenders are more likely to acquiesce to his decisions than to any counter-action on their part. It follows that the Tartar chief is not accurately considered as a Hobbesian sovereign who keeps peace through terror. This exemplifies an important strain in the Scots' social theory. For the Scots 'legitimacy', like other social facts, is to be explained by addressing the facts of social life and not by invoking an extra-societal notion of a state of nature. In sharp contrast to the ahistoricity of a state of nature, human social experience is temporally structured. This temporalisation is a necessary condition in the forma-tion of habits and it is this that is crucial to Smith's 'natural authority'.

Hume's analysis led the way. In his account, in line with 'princi-ples of human nature', and the soft determinism of moral causation (see p. 72 above; cf. Livingston 1984: 271), men 'once accustomed to obedience never think of departing from that path in which they and their ancestors have constantly trod' (*E-OG* 39).[4] More pointedly, it is 'time and custom' that make 'legal and obligatory' what was 'founded only on injury and violence' (*T* 3.2.10.19/*SBNT* 566). It is only this acquired habit that can explain the prima facie puzzling fact that a few rule so easily over the many, especially since strength (of numbers) must always lie with the latter. Drawing on some earlier usage, Hume invokes the role of 'opinion' (*E-FPG* 32–3; cf. *E-BG* 51, *E-OG* 40, *HE* III, 395)[5] and more particularly the 'opinion of right', of which his chief example is attachment to 'ancient government', since 'antiquity always begets the opinion of right'. Smith echoes this in his *Lectures* when he professes 'everything by custom appears right (*LJA* v.132/322). In pastoral societies this is particularly evident. Millar observes that 'gene-alogy and descent' is a matter of 'exact knowledge' among the Tartars (*OR* 250) and, according to Smith, it is the case that 'men more easily submit to a family to whom they and their ancestors have always sub-mitted' (*WN* v.i.b.8/713).

The reason why this is such a prominent feature of pastoral societies is because in that 'state of society' there is no outlet for wealth other than in the maintenance of dependants (*WN* V.i.b.7/712). This situation persists into the third stage, with landlords replacing khans, but decisively changes with the advent of 'diamond buckles' portending the revolutionary change to a commercial society (see Chapter 2). The effect of this retention of wealth in the hands of the few is to establish the stability necessary for the development of customary beliefs. Millar provides a particularly clear example of this chain of reasoning, 'thus the son, who inherits the state of his father, is enabled to maintain an equal rank [. . .] which is daily augmented by the power of habit and becomes more considerable as it passes from one generation to another' (*OR* 250).[6]

This 'natural' habituated authority is thus a powerful social force. It does not, however, have a monopoly. In his *Lectures* Smith identified 'utility' alongside 'authority' as another 'principle' (*LJB* 12/401). It is this that makes the poorest accede to a ruler (their chief) as the best available means to obtain some possible redress for their injuries received from the wealthiest. This accession went along with an implicit utilitarian calculation, since the undoubted 'irregularities' in any response from rulers were accepted in order 'to avoid greater evils' (*LJB* 14/402). As so often, Millar follows his teacher. He too distinguishes authority and utility as principles (*HV* IV, 7/796) but he is inclined to give greater emphasis to utility. Whereas Smith had argued that in many cases 'the principle of authority is the foundation of that of utility or common interest' ( *LJA* v.132/322), Millar remarks that general utility of government is 'more satisfactory than that of mere authority' (*HV* IV, 7/799). However, what is of current moment is his observation that 'in every rude nation' those with authority are likely to indulge in 'arbitrary proceedings' with impunity (*HV* IV, 1/694). Although through the softly determining effects of long custom these 'irregular acts' pass without punishment, he affirms (here with particular reference to Ireland), the 'great interests of society' will in time prevail thanks to the 'general advancement of commerce and manufactures' (*HV* IV, 1/695).

The message of this discussion of authority is that it is in the second stage of property in herds that 'some degree of [. . .] civil government' is introduced (*WN* V.i.b.12/715). This introduction is a self-interested move on the part of the rich (the owners of the herds). They require government to preserve 'that order of things which can alone secure them in the possession of their own advantages'. As we noted in Chapter 2 (see quotations p. 48) any idea that this rule could be impartial is misplaced. Millar comments generally that, 'in every rude nation, persons invested with authority are apt to lay hold of opportunities of indulging themselves in arbitrary proceedings' (*HV* IV, 1/694). Smith makes the same point more specifically, 'the authority of an Arabian scherif is very great; that of a Tartar khan altogether despotical' (*WN* V.i.b.7/713). Hence rule and what passes for 'law' in the second stage is inherently capricious – it depends on the khan's whim and certainly will lack generality or inclusivity, since it will not apply to him or his entourage.

Exactly the same can be said of rule/law in the third stage. Here the local base of rule is even more pronounced. In Smith's account of the 'revolution' that brought about the age of commerce, discussed in Chapter 2, he observes that the feudal lords were 'judges in peace' as well as 'leaders in war'. The eventual separation of these roles, which happened 'by chance' as the offspring of social growth and attendant multiplication of business, Smith judges to be 'the great advantage' of 'modern times [. . .] and the foundation of that greater Security which we now enjoy' (*LRBL* ii.203/176). Prior to this separation, the writ of the 'great proprietors' ran but only within their territory. Hence they levied, as they saw fit, taxes on travellers through their lands and any traders who remained within their demesnes were in an effectively 'servile' condition (*WN* III.iii.2/397–8). The corollary of this was that these proprietors had no authority or clout beyond their boundaries. One consequence of this localisation of power was that there could be no consistency of decision between localities or any 'external' guarantee of consistency within a 'jurisdiction'. Steuart makes the point eloquently when he refers to 'the ambulatory will of any man or set of men', so that the 'laws' were liable to changed 'through favour or prejudice to particular persons or particular classes' (*PPE* I, 206). Lack of consistency meant lack of security. We know from the historical story told in Chapter 2 that the king was not an exception to this localism; he was too weak, outside his own personal lands, to be able to protect his subjects from the oppression of the great lords (*WN* III.iii.8/401). We also drew attention to how in England after the 'commercial revolution' (as we might term it) the (Tudor) monarchs obtained non-localised power before, in turn, being curtailed by the rise of the Commons (see p. 57 above). This curtailment ushers in the age of commerce.

We can infer what will be different about the fourth stage. Steuart immediately follows his comment about unpredictability (the 'ambulatory will') and particularity by making the explicit contrast to a situation where people are 'governed by general laws', which are 'established so as not to be changed but in regular and uniform way' (*PPE* I, 206). And, in an argument to be pursued in Chapter 5, this regularity is institutionalised as the rule of law, whereby in Hume's (*E-OG* 41) characterisation the administration of government 'must act by general laws, that are previously known to all the members' and when that obtains the government is free. This connection between liberty and the absence of capricious will by those in power was commonly made and, of course, was not the prerogative of the Scots.[7] Among the Scots, in addition to Steuart and Hume, the same link is made, for example, by Hutcheson (*SIMP* 258), by Wallace (*CGB* 215), by Kames (1732: 20, *PE* 268) and by Ferguson, who as we shall discuss in Chapter 6, while he endorses an 'activist' view of liberty, is nonetheless firm that it is dangerous to allow discretion in the exercise of law (*PMPS* II, 477).

We already know a commercial society will be blessed by opulence and liberty. As we indicated in Chapter 3 these two blessings are linked. Smith is clear,

> commerce and manufactures gradually introduced order and good government and with them the liberty and security of individuals among the inhabitants of the country who had before lived almost in a continual state of war with their neighbours and of servile dependency upon their superiors. (*WN* III.iv.4/412)

And, as Hume said more particularly, tradesmen and merchants 'covet equal laws, which may secure their property and preserve them from monarchical as well as aristocratical tyranny' (*E-RA* 278).

How is this supposed to work? The argument relies on a series of causal connections: stability from a framework of law causes security and security is a causal precondition for the development of a market and extension of contracts and exchange. This goes to the heart of the idea of a commercial society. We observed above that even the primitive bow-maker/hunter relation implied some current commitment for future return. Until that commitment can be assured, and relationships are not prey to capricious power, then a society wherein every man is a merchant cannot operate. As Smith observes, in 'unfortunate countries' (he refers to 'most governments of Asia' and the feudal era), where 'men are continually afraid of the violence of their superiors' then they do not use 'their stock' but have it 'always to hand' in case they need to escape. Whereas 'where there is tolerable security' men will use their stock either for 'present enjoyment or future profit' (*WN* II.i.30/285).

Stock, as we noted in Chapter 3, is required to enable a weaver to have both the material with which to manufacture, as well as the wherewithal to live, before he can sell his woven cloth. And of course he will have no-one to sell it to unless there is a market whereat he can purchase the products of (say) a shoe-maker. Given what was involved in Smith's example of the simple woollen coat then the web of interdependence is immense and, as we would expect from the trajectory of 'natural history', the society where this occurs will be not only complex but abstract. I want to pursue what is involved in this notion of 'abstraction' because this will uncover the conceptual connection between market transactions and the rule of law.

It is one of the Scots' contribution to the history of the social sciences that they effectively write a history of belief; the history of what Hume himself calls 'the minds of men' (*HE* III, 12) and Robertson the 'history of the human mind' (*HAm* 811). This, I think, is best interpreted as a (Lockean) natural historical sociology of knowledge, and, *pace* Mary Poovey (1998: 224), this 'history' does not imply some Aristotelian entelechy. Mark Salber Philips (2000: 49–51) is on the right track when he associates that phrase of Hume's with his treatment of 'opinion' (see above). Hume's 'opinion' can be construed as a form of belief. Hume gives 'belief' a wide-ranging role. It is an 'act of mind arising from custom' (*T* I.3.9.13/*SBNT* 114) and custom is at the heart of his analysis of causation. In his famous billiard ball example we are 'determined by custom' (that is by repeated occurrence) to believe that the movement of a previously stationary ball was caused by the impact upon it of a moving ball (*A* 15, 17/*SBNT* 649–50). On this basis, customary belief is the 'guide of life' and, as such, the 'standard of our future judgments' (*A* 16, 25/*SBNT* 652, 656). While the belief that the future will resemble the past is, for Hume, of universal application it is a particular application to an aspect of commerce that I here want to exploit.

In a simplified version, and in line with the 'logic of exchange' outlined in Chapter 3 (p. 70), a manufacturer spends time now producing a particular product on the expectation that others will want it and that belief about their desire is itself premised on the belief that others are producing different products. That 'belief' is an experiential acquisition, which is extended to the qualitatively different level of probabilistic knowledge with the development of towns and trade wherein markets are formed and the participants act in expectation of future return. Hume captures this:

> The poorest artificer, who labours alone, *expects* at least the protection of the magistrate, to ensure him the enjoyment of the fruits of his labour. He also *expects* that when he carries his goods to market and offers them at a reasonable price, he shall find purchasers and shall be able, by the money he acquires, to engage others to supply him with those commodities which are requisite for his subsistence. In proportion as men extend their dealings and render their intercourse with others more complicated, they always comprehend in their schemes of life a greater variety of voluntary actions which they *expect*, from the proper motives, to co-operate with their own. In all these conclusions they take their measures from past experience. (*U* 8.17/ *SBNU* 89 – my emphases)

Although he prefaces this observation with the declaration that 'the mutual dependence of men is so great in all societies', it is clear that Hume is here presuming a commercial context (note the reference to 'more complicated' – see Stewart quoted above p. 32). What is required to underwrite this interdependency is predictability or confidence. Where the magistrate is absent or fickle (and thus affords no protection), with the consequence that the actions of others are not predictable, then it is better (more prudent) to be independent and self-sufficient (cf. Smith *WN* II.Intr.1/276). But, of course, since this is generalisable then the blessing of the opulence is lost because there is effectively no market and hence to all intents and purposes no division of labour and thus miserable poverty.

Of course not all beliefs/expectations are on a par; some are more certain than others. Indeed in the context of markets uncertainty might appear to be the default condition. There are inherent risks in specialising. This uncertainty at the centre of a system that seems to depend on predictability was thought by many to identify a fundamental flaw in a commercial society; it seemingly rests on nothing solid, merely on a flimsy tissue of beliefs. I will explore this question at length in Chapter 6 but here observe that Hume's example of the artificer is intended to demonstrate predictable solidity, appearing as it does in his discussion of liberty and necessity and the constancy and universality of human nature.

The comparative complication of a commercial society reposes not simply on a series of (abstract) beliefs about the actions of complete strangers (and I will come back to that in Chapter 5) but also on its basic operating principles. These are most obviously manifest in the institutions of money and credit. I will discuss the latter and its perceived dangers in more detail in Chapter 6, but I want to use the former to illustrate the abstractness I am imputing to a commercial society (cf. Simmel 1990: 120, 142, 214). I should stress the illustrative intent, I refrain deliberately from participation either in the debate on money that surrounds Hume in particular[8] or in the broader question of what might be called the financial dimension ( banks, interest rates, taxation and so on) of commercial society.

Hume defines money as 'nothing but the representation of labour and commodities' (*E-Mon* 285). This definition indicates its inherent 'abstract quality'; it is what it stands for, not its concrete form that counts. Indeed its value is 'fictitious' (*E-Int* 297). It is an artificial (the product of convention [*T* 3.2.2.10/*SBNT* 490]), 'instrument to facilitate exchange'; the 'oil which renders the wheels of trade to run more smoothly (*E-Mon* 281; Kames repeated this imagery *SHM* I, 82). It performs this task of facilitation by serving as the 'method of rating or estimating' the labour and commodities that it represents (*E-Mon* 285). Given this instrumental role it follows that there is little need for money until there is an extension of exchange beyond barter (the bow-maker and hunter can function without it) (*E-Mon* 291). It is only when property transference (one of Hume's three 'laws of nature' – see below) goes beyond the particular and present to the general and absent (*T* 3.2.5.8/*SBNT* 520) that the need arises for the 'representation' that money provides.

Hume does not discuss the evolution of money, simply presuming that after barter it initially takes the form of coin then paper money (what Steuart calls – helpfully for our purposes – 'symbolical money' [*PPE* II, 407]). Kames is more forthcoming on the development of coin. In the 'first stage' savages have few wants so barter 'in its rudest form' suffices. However, as soon as 'wants multiplied' then barter became inefficient and so there arose the need for 'some commodity in general estimation that will be gladly accepted in exchange for every other'. This commodity had to meet the three negative criteria of being not too bulky, not too expensive to keep and not 'consumable by time', and these are met by gold and silver (*SHM* I, 70–2). Where they are absent then the prime function of establishing a 'standard of value' is performed by animal skins or shells (*SHM* I, 79; Smith gives a long list of such commodities [*WN* I.iv.3/38]).

Smith is most instructive on the further step to paper money. Like Hume and Kames (and others too of course), in commercial society money is 'the great wheel of circulation, the great instrument of commerce' (*WN* II.ii.23/291; I.iv.11/44; *LJA* vi.127/377). Paper money is an expedient contrivance to increase the amount of stock in circulation (*LJA* vi.130/378). The substitution of paper for gold and silver increases opulence because it enhances productivity (converts dead into active stock [*WN* II.ii.86/321]) and thus increases the number and quality of goods. Hume, if more cautiously and within a specific time-frame, said the same (*E-BT* 317n). Paper money originated as an arrangement between merchants (*LJA* vi.132/379) and this led to the establishment of banks (*LJB* 248/504), which, with explicit reference to Scotland, Smith judges have 'contributed a good deal' to the increase in trade and industry (*WN* II.ii.41/297). Generically the paper constitutes a set of promissory notes (*WN* II.ii.28/292). The term itself is instructive; as Hume declares, a 'promise always regards some future time' (*T* 3.2.5.3/*SBNT* 516). The note is only able to function because it is believed to have value. That belief needs to be underwritten. Smith counsels that abstraction embodied in paper money needs to be secured in gold and silver.[9] Moreover for paper money to carry out its beneficial function there has to be confidence in banks as the issuing agents (*WN* II.ii.28/292) and even prior to their development it was necessary to trust in the honesty and fidelity of fellow merchants (*LJB* 248/504) (see further in Chapter 6). Hume put it crisply, 'the freedom and extent of human commerce depend entirely on a fidelity with regard to promises' (*T* 3.2.8.7/*SBNT* 546) (Schabas 1994; Wennerlind 2001).

Steuart points out that 'paper money is but a species of credit' so that 'he who pays in paper puts his creditor in possession only of an obligation to make that value good to him' (*PPE* II, 406–7). In effect this is a contract. We saw in Chapter 2 [p. 45] how the history of contracts exemplified the natural historical progress from concrete to abstract and that the pervasiveness of contracts is a distinctive feature of a commercial society. It is now appropriate to honour the pledge there made to develop the assumptions behind Smith's comment that the obligatoriness of contract arises 'entirely from the expectation and dependence which was excited in him to whom the contract was made' (*LJA* ii.56/92).

We have already elaborated upon the place of 'expectation' in this quotation, however, we now have to outline what lies behind the bindingness of contracts. This brings us back to stability. What underpins the obligation to keep a promise/contract, and what sustains the co-operation that the contracts embody, is what Smith calls the 'regular administration of justice' (*WN* V.iii.7/910), or what Hume calls the 'universal and perfectly inflexible' [laws of justice] (*T* 3.2.6.9/ *SBNT* 532). Before proceeding to detailed examination we can lay out in general terms the key point. A system of justice is an impersonal abstract order that operates through general rules and is the antithesis of the personal particular rule of the tribal chiefs or local landlords. At the heart of this system is the principle of the rule of law and, as Millar remarks, in 'opulent and polished nations' the 'impartial administration of justice is looked upon almost as a matter of course' (*HV* I, 8/131). It is only through living under the rule of law that individuals will have 'confidence' in the 'faith of contracts' and 'payment of debts' (Smith, *WN* V.iii.7/910). It is only in 'commercial countries' that the 'authority of the law [. . .] [is] perfectly sufficient to protect the meanest man in the state' (Smith, *TMS* Vi.ii.1.13/223).

Behind this lies the commonplace that no-one will sow if they cannot reap. What the authority of law provides is security of property for all. With the confidence that accompanies this, I will expend effort that, with luck and my apt industry, will bring me a return. My 'right' to my proceeds will be enforced inflexibly. As we have seen, the inherent abstractness entailed by a conception of a 'right' only comes to fruition with that very authority of the law to which Smith here refers. Similarly, the property to which a right is attached can be correspondingly abstract as in a credit note or patent (Smith *LJA* i.20/11; *LJB* 175/472). Indeed only in a commercial society does the notion of an intellectual property right become an intelligible proposition.[10]

## JUSTICE

Justice is a key principle in a commercial society. It is testament to its centrality that it was the subject of extensive analysis. Of these analyses Hume's in the *Treatise* is rightly famous and while in many respects the functionality (as we might term it) he attributes to justice is shared by most of his compatriots the structure of the analysis is distinctive.[11] While a detailed exploration of that distinctiveness is not here apt I will address it alongside the broader argument of the role allotted to justice.

Hume distinctively argues that justice is an artificial virtue. From Plato through to the great systems of Natural Law of Grotius and Pufendorf, justice had been thought 'natural' – it was part of human nature to act justly. But being acutely aware of the ambiguity in the term 'natural', Hume is at pains to establish exactly his own position. In outline his argument is that justice is a convention generated from the concurrence of (what he takes to be) two facts: it is a uniform fact of human nature that humans have only a 'limited' or 'confin'd generosity' and that, in fact, 'external objects' are scarce relative to the desire for them (*T* 3.2.2.16/SBNT 494–5). The constancy and ineluctability of this concurrence means that the artifice of justice arises 'necessarily' from them. Hume is emphatic: 'without justice society must immediately dissolve' (*T* 3.2.2.22/SBNT 497; cf. M 3, 38/SBNM 199). This functional necessity is what is echoed by other Scots, (though Cicero [1913: 209/II.40] by linking *iustitia* with *negotiis* had established an influential precedent). Hence we find Smith's equally uncompromising verdict: ' justice is the main pillar that upholds the whole edifice. If it is removed, the great, the immense fabric of human society [. . .] must in a moment crumble into atoms' (*TMS* II.ii.3.4/86). Kames, too, is unambiguous: '[justice] being so necessary to the support of society' (*PMNR* 33).

For Hume justice upholds society by means of rules that have been self-imposed by humans; they have agreed to regulate or restrain themselves. Justice is artificial because it is the product of this agreement. Hume gives a careful account of how these rules/agreements/ conventions arise so that it does not fall foul of the criticisms he makes of

Contract theory (*T* 3.2.5.1/*SBNT* 516, *E-OG*).[12] Because these rules are so necessary to society's cohesion then it is not, he says, 'improper to call them Laws of Nature'; they are, therefore, 'natural' in conformity to one standard meaning of 'nature', namely, what is 'common to' or 'inseparable from the species' (*T* 3.2.1.19/*SBNT* 484).

This last phrase is indicative. Hume's explanation of why these artificial rules are necessary lies at the heart of his philosophical anthropology (Berry 2003b). He opens his chapter on the 'origin of justice and property' by comparing the situation of humans to that of other animals and notes, from observation, that the 'numberless wants and necessities' of the former are not naturally 'compensated' for (*T* 3.2.2.2/ *SBNT* 484). Compared to lions, sheep and oxen, humans experience 'in its greatest perfection' an 'unnatural conjunction of infirmity and necessity' (*T* 3.2.2.2/*SBNT* 485). This incommodiousness of 'outward circumstances' is compounded by the 'circumstances of human nature', in particular the confined generosity in 'our natural temper'. Put together, in contrast to the stable 'natural order' experienced by other species, where needs and the means of satisfying them are in balance, human group life is naturally unstable, for which the only remedy is an artificially or conventionally induced stability. This is what justice provides.

Hume identifies three laws of nature or rules of justice – stability of possession, its transfer by consent and promise-keeping (*T* 3.2.6.1/ *SBNT* 526).These rules have two important characteristics – generality and inflexibility. General rules are formed on the basis of expecting past occurrences to continue (*T* 1.3.15.6/*SBNT* 173; *T* 2.2.5.13/*SBNT* 362). They are indispensable; indeed Hume regards it as a truth about human nature that we 'are mightily addicted to general rules' (*T* 3.2.9.3/*SBNT* 551). This is an echo of his analysis of causation as the 'guide of life' (the 'cement of the universe' [*A* 35/*SBNA* 662]), whereby the very coherence of the world depended upon extending through habit the experience of one case to another. These three rules restrain or regulate behaviour precisely because, and only in so far as, they are impersonal (abstract and general) being 'unchangeable by spite and favour, and by particular views of private or public interest' (*T* 3.2.6.9/*SBNT* 532). It is indeed the hallmark of the 'best civil constitution' that therein 'every man is restrained by the most rigid laws' (*E-PSc* 31). This rigidity or inflexibility is the second characteristic and is necessary to underwrite the ability of individuals to act 'in expectation that others are to perform the like' (*T* 3.2.2.10/*SBNT* 498). Such expectations, built up through 'repeated experience', are self-supporting because this accumulated experience 'assures us still more that the sense of interest has become common to all our fellows and gives us a *confidence* of the *future regularity* of their conduct. And 'tis only on the *expectation* of this, that our moderation and abstinence are founded' (*T* 3.2.2.10/*SBNT* 490 – my emphases).

Given our earlier discussion, these references to 'expectation' and 'confidence' reveal that it is a picture of commercial society that lies behind Hume's analysis. This is consolidated by his selection of those three particular rules of justice. In his identification of the human predicament, Hume distinguishes three species of human 'goods' – 'internal satisfaction of our mind, the external advantages of our body and the enjoyment of such possessions as we have acquir'd by our industry and good fortune'. But without any elaboration he proceeds to assert that only the last are 'both expos'd to the violence of others and may be transferr'd without suffering any loss or alteration' (*T* 3.2.2.7/*SBNT* 487). From which assertions it follows, for Hume, that improvement in the condition or status of this last category of goods is 'the chief advantage of society'. This advantage reposes crucially on stabilising possession and, as we have already seen, that is the function of the artifice of justice.

Stability of possession is the key convention upon which, in the form of the transfer of these stabilised possessions by consent, a second is contrived. This contrivance is natural in Hume's sense of inseparability since it accords with the conjunction of two further facts; first that 'different parts of the earth produce different commodities' and, second, with the fact that given men 'are fitted by nature for different employments' then specialisation of endeavour produces 'greater perfection'.[13] This conjunction thus requires 'a mutual exchange and commerce' (*T* 3.2.5.1/*SBNT* 514). This second rule, transfer by consent, in turn, requires the third, promise-keeping. This is required because of the combination of the natural limits to human generosity with the fact that, in the (natural) way of things, this exchange cannot typically be simultaneous. Together these inhibit the effective operation of the first two rules, stable possession and its transfer (*T* 3.2.5.8/*SBNT* 519). The convention of promise-giving (and -keeping) remedies that inhibition because, on Hume's account, it permits 'interested commerce'. A promise is a commitment or resolution to act in a particular way at some future date (*T* 3.2.5.3/*SBNT* 516) on the 'penalty of never being trusted again in case of failure' (*T* 3.2.5.10/*SBNT* 522). While externally enforced sanctions are necessary, the fact that this is mutually interested commerce has its own internal momentum, namely, that 'I foresee that he will return my service in *expectation* of another of the same kind and in order to maintain the same correspondence of good offices with me or others' (*T* 3.2.5.9/*SBNT* 521 – my emphasis). This recognition of mutual advantage Russell Hardin (2007: 149) calls

Hume's 'central political principle'. Again its appositeness to a commercial society is easily discernible (we will return to the role of 'trust' in Chapter 6).

One of the commonest complaints of Hume's account of justice is that he confines it too narrowly to questions of property (for a typical assessment see Harrison 1981). The explanation for the role played by property takes us back to the inflexibility of the rules of justice and the key functional role played by that attribute. Justice has to be inflexible because the temptation to relax the rules is strong. There are two types of temptation. The first lies in human passions. The 'infirmity' of the human condition means humans are naturally moved by their passions to the preclusion of their satisfaction. However, by artifice they restrain these passions by establishing the rules of justice so that they may be satisfied. This explains the convention of property. Although there is an indelible 'heedless and impetuous' passion to acquire goods for ourselves (family and friends) (*T* 3.2.2.9/*SBNT* 489), experience makes it 'evident' that this 'passion is much better satisfy'd by its restraint than by its liberty' (*T* 3.2.2.13/*SBNT* 492). Property is an artifice invented to establish stability of possession since it is 'nothing but those goods whose constant possession is establish'd by the laws of society; that is the laws of justice' (*T* 3.2.2.11/*SBNT* 491). Similarly, humans create the artificial institution of magistracy to counter what Rachel Cohon (2008: 219) felicitously terms 'temporal myopia', that is, the 'dangerous' quality of human nature to prefer trivial 'present advantage' to the 'remote' maintenance of justice (*T* 3.2.7.3/*SBNT* 535; *E-OG* 38). This Hobbesian point (1991: 129) views the issue in what Hume calls in the 'Origin of Government' an 'abstract light', and while the myopia rests on an 'incurable' weakness in human nature yet, in evidential practice, government's origin is casual and non-purposive (*E-OG* 38–9).

The second temptation lies in the application of 'natural morality'. Hume claims our 'natural uncultivated ideas of morality' consolidate rather than counter our 'partiality' and thus provide no stability. This inconstancy of our natural morality can be seen in Hume's example of the miser who justly receives a great fortune. The 'natural moralist' may well judge the money should go to someone more deserving rather than to someone who has no need of it.[14] Hume duly admits that a 'single act' of justice like this may 'in itself be prejudicial to society' (the money could have done more good elsewhere) but, nonetheless, affirms that the 'whole plan or scheme' is 'absolutely requisite' (*T* 3.2.2.22/*SBNT* 497; cf. *T* 3.3.1.12/*SBNT* 579). If an exception is made in one case, if the rules are made flexible or made to forfeit their generality, then justice in the form of expectations that 'everyone will perform the like' will break down.

There is a polemical dimension to Hume's analysis. If property is conceived of as a 'natural right', as 'antecedent and independent' of justice, as another ingredient of a 'natural morality' then, for Hume, it would 'produce an infinite confusion in human society' (*T* 3.2.6.9/*SBNT* 532).[15] To follow 'the common principles of human nature' (*T* 3.2.6.9/ *SBNT* 533) is no solution, since they are inherently flexible in favouring most patently our nearest and dearest. Similarly, the Natural Law/ Lockean account of property as a natural right is flawed because it effectively makes justice flexible through its ever-present potential to induce variability in fixed determinations of ownership. In virtue of this posited authority to 'trump' any particular distribution or positive regulation it thereby destroys the 'public utility' of justice, its ability to ensure stability 'through strict and regular observance' (*T* 3.2.6.8/*SBNT* 530; *M* 3, 12/*SBNM* 188). To adopt a more expansive definition of justice is to make it, in effect, the code of conduct suffusing all human relationships. While existing alongside a narrow or strict (Grotius' 'expletive justice' for example)[16] this broader sense was a central presence in not only Greek (such as Aristotle's 'universal justice' which includes all virtue)[17] but also Christian and Natural Law ethics. Hutcheson appositely exemplifies Hume's target. In Hutcheson's account of the 'public interest' an individual can 'be deprived of his acquisitions' when such a deprivation is deemed appropriate by the 'moral sense', the determinant for Hutcheson of 'natural morality'.[18] But this reliance on natural morality, as we have noted, is conducive to indeterminacy. Once, therefore, we stray beyond the narrow understanding of justice with its restricted focus on property and give it a broader, or 'thicker' (Boyd 2004: 130), meaning then we get lost in the intractable, and effectively pointless, debates over first principles (cf. Krause 2004).

Hume's resolute denaturing of justice was not accepted by his fellow Scots. Kames, who follows, though not uncritically, Shaftesbury and Hutcheson, in attributing a 'moral sense' to humans, makes Hume an explicit target. Justice is independent of convention and 'belongs to man as such' and is founded upon an 'innate sense' (*PMNR* 35, 83). Although he seemingly agrees with Hume that justice is the virtue that 'guards' property, yet far from property being the creation of the artifice of justice, it too is founded on a 'natural sense independent altogether of agreement or convention'; indeed man 'by his nature is a hoarding animal' (*PMNR* 47, 49; cf. *SHM* I, 113). As part of his supporting argument Kames observes that 'violation of property is attended with remorse' (*PMNR* 47) and, while he is also critical of

Smith's moral philosophy (*PMNR* 70–3), this chimes with Smith's own divergence from Hume.

Smith, like Kames, talks of 'remorse': of all the 'sentiments which can enter the human breast it is the most dreadful' (*TMS* II.ii.2.3/85). Smith roots (so to speak) his account of justice in natural sentiments. His chief objection to Hume's 'utilitarian' account of justice is a subset of a more general argument that 'utility' or functionality is often of less moment in human behaviour than a concern with the way the end is realised (so a watch that loses two minutes a day is discarded by 'one curious in watches' in favour of one that loses a minute in a fortnight while being no more punctual in the business of daily life) (*TMS* IV.i.5/180). When applied to justice it is a concern with individuals rather than, as with Hume, a concern with a society's well-being that is its effective source. Smith does not deny utility a role, only that it is the 'first or principal source' (*TMS* IV.2.3/188).[19] We are, he claims, 'animated' by injustice without needing to reflect on its consequential destructiveness to the main pillar of the social edifice. Moreover, the 'injustice' that animates 'us' is suffered by individuals and it is their particular 'fortune and happiness' that concerns us rather than a more general concern for society. Indeed on Smith's reading of human nature, humans 'delight' in seeing the unjust punished, without paying any 'regard to the preservation of society' (*TMS* II.22.3.9–10/89). This delight itself is but an effusive expression of the basic human disposition to resent injustice, of which punishment is the 'natural consequence' (*TMS* II.ii.1.5/79; cf. Vi.ii. intro.2/218).[20] Smith speculates that the sense of resentment 'seems to have been given us by nature for defence' since it 'prompts us to beat off mischief' or 'retaliate that which is already done' (*TMS* II.ii.1.5/79). What makes this an appropriate response is that this retaliation would be approved of by the 'impartial spectator' (see Chap. 5).

The role given to resentment here was well-established. Kames (*HLT* 4) places it, as a 'fierce passion', at the head of his discussion of criminal law, while for Turnbull (*MCL* 293; cf. Reid [*Active Powers*] 1846: 655) resentment is a 'principle' possessed by man, the purpose of which to is 'to fill us with indignation against injury'. Less theoretical acceptance of this role was given by Robertson. He gives a historical account of the development of justice from its source in the 'natural' desire to 'repel injuries and to revenge wrongs' (*VP* 321). On this account from being at first concerned (concretely) with wrongs done to individuals personally (or those to whom they are connected) this 'desire' develops over time, with the progress of civilisation, to express itself in regular (and abstract) procedure. Smith also imparts, like Kames and indeed Hume,[21] a temporal dimension to the operation of justice. He concludes the *Moral Sentiments* by contrasting the circumstances where the 'rudeness and barbarism of the people' make the system of justice irregular with those in a 'more civilized nations' where the 'natural sentiments of justice' arrive at 'accuracy and precision' (*TMS* VII.iv.36/341).

The last phrase here alludes to the role of rules in Smith's account and where he now shares much with Hume. A crucial dimension to the well-established distinction between justice and other virtues such as benevolence (see Chap. 5 below) was that it was, as Hume expressed it, more a question of restraint (not acting) than acting. It is in accord with this line of reasoning that Smith refers to justice as a negative virtue. It is negative because it requires forbearance, not hurting another, so that indeed 'we often fulfil all the rules of justice by sitting still and doing nothing' (*TMS* II.i.1.9/82).

Smith likens these rules of justice to the rules of grammar since both possess the qualities of precision, accuracy and indispensability (*TMS* III.6.11/175). This precision makes both grammar and justice amenable to instruction. Hence in the same way that we can be taught how to conjugate verbs correctly so we 'may be taught to act justly'. This has two significant consequences. First it reiterates Hume's message of inflexibility. Just as it is inaccurate (is not a discretionary rule) to employ 'seeked' as the past tense of 'seek' so 'the rules of justice are accurate in the highest degree and admit of no exceptions of modifications' (*TMS* III.6.10/175). The second consequence is that justice is inclusively in the reach of all or at least 'the coarse clay of the bulk of mankind'. (The significance of this inclusivity will be brought out in conjunction with Smith's account of liberty in Chap. 5.) This is the case because,

> there is scarce any man [. . .] who by discipline, education, and example, may not be so impressed with a regard to general rules, as to act upon almost every occasion with tolerable decency, and through the whole of his life to avoid any considerable degree of blame. (*TMS* III.5.1/163)

The effect of this process of instruction (or socialisation) is to establish certainty and predictability, for 'without this sacred regard to general rules there is no man whose conduct can be much depended upon' (*TMS* III.5.2/163). Again we can detect the linkage between justice as rule-following and living in a society where every man is a merchant, that is to say, involved, like Hume's 'artificer', in a web of inter-dependent relations that repose on the confidence that expectations will be met.

Millar follows Smith closely. He too explicitly associates justice with 'general rules' that are capable of 'accuracy and precision' (*HV* IV,7/787).[22] In Millar the institutional context is the focus. It is the 'advancement of commerce and civilization' that has tended to 'promote the virtue of strict justice'. This promotion was part and parcel of the cultivation of the science of law (*HV* IV, 7/787). Millar also follows Hume. He echoes Hume's view of the addictiveness of general rules, by arguing that the introduction of a general rule, and its extension by 'habit and analogy', originates in a 'propensity natural to all mankind'. Notwithstanding this foundation, it is the 'utility' of these rules that counts. This utility is two-fold. It enables every person to 'simplify his transactions' and it checks 'the partiality of judges' (*HV* IV, 7/793). In broadly similar fashion, and equally picking up the depersonalisation of rule, Robertson traces the development of the system of judicial procedure from its original dependence upon 'private persons', and thus liable to 'capricious and unequal' execution, to the establishment of a more 'regular course' (*VP* 321).

At the heart of this 'regularity' is the gradual effacement of the principle of revenge to settle internal disputes. The significance of ceding this right to the chief (who originally dealt with external affairs [Kames *HLT* 35, 283; Ferguson *ECS* 100]) was picked up by Stuart (*VSE* 37; cf. *HD* 90) and, especially, by Robertson who refers to it in several of his writings (see *HAm* 828; *VP* 322; *HSc* 97). Millar is not exempt. He puts this process down to the 'progress of government' (*HV* I, 6/107). Perhaps the most decisive development was the separation and independency of the judiciary for it is that which ensures the impartiality of administration that imparts security to all (Smith *WN* V.i.b.25/723; *LRBL* ii.203/176; Kames *HLT* 285/6).

## COMMERCIAL POLITICS

To enable a commercial society to function the rule of law and the impartial regular administration of justice are necessary. From the foregoing we know this enablement is specifically a 'fourth stage' task. Earlier governments were marked by partiality, by acting in the interests of 'the leaders' (khans and landlords). In a well-known enumeration by Smith, government in a commercial society has three duties: protection from external foes, maintenance of public works and 'an exact administration of justice' (*WN* IV.ix.51/687). I will say more about the second of these in Chapter 6 but here it is the third that it is of paramount importance. This duty befits a commercial or 'civilized and thriving' society. Before heeding the significance of 'civilisation' here we need to elaborate on what this 'administration' entails, what it excludes and includes as the job of government.

In Smith there is a clear polemical element. The three duties are prefaced as 'according to the system of natural liberty', in terms of which 'everyman, as long as he does not violate the laws of justice is left perfectly free to pursue his own interest his own way'. Government polices any such violations but is 'completely discharged from a duty [. . .] of superintending the industry of private people and of directing it towards the employments most suitable to the interest of society' (*WN* IV.ix.51/687). The prime target is the policy of the mercantilists, although the Physiocratic preference for agriculture is similarly suspect (Medema and Samuels 2009: 307). The mercantilist endeavour to force trade into a particular channel (*WN* IV.v.a.3,24/506, 516) is judged 'mean and malignant' (*WN* V.vii.c.56/610). Not only is the outcome of that endeavour less advantageous than if the trade had been left to find its own course, but it is also contrary to the principle of impartiality by favouring some industries over others. Moreover, this mercantilist aim is delusional because such forced steering is 'a performance of which no human wisdom or knowledge could ever be sufficient' (*WN* IV.ix.51/687). Even Ferguson in the *Essay*, which, as we will see in the following chapters, strongly emphasises political engagement, remarks that 'when the refined politician would lend an active hand, he only multiplies interruptions and grounds of complaint' (*ECS* 144). For Smith, the principle of government non-involvement has a wider remit than commerce, as when he scornfully dismisses sumptuary laws as 'the highest impertinence and presumption' whereby 'kings and minister [. . .] pretend to watch over the economy of private people and to restrain their expense' (*WN* II.iii.36/346). Hume is equally dismissive of such legislation (*HE* I, 535; cf. *HE* II, 231; *HE* II, 602). For him government has 'no other object or purpose but the distribution of justice' (*E-OG* 37).[23] Indeed this restrictiveness is advantageous. In the context of Henry VII, he generalises that compared to the 'long experience and deep reflection' required to implement the 'complicated' 'principles of commerce', the administration of internal justice is relatively simple and thus implicitly less prone to error and easier to execute (*HE* II, 51).

While this anti-mercantilist polemic is undoubtedly a powerful presence in the *Wealth of Nations*, Smith's argument seen in the round is more complicated. There are three complicating factors: a role for government in removing obstacles to liberty; a more positive role – even independent of the specified task of maintaining public goods; and a sober recognition of the tenacity of vested interests. I will take these in turn, each more complicated than its predecessor.

We have already touched on examples of the first of these factors when we noted Smith's opposition to entails, and his attack on the Poor Law, to which can be added his advocacy of the repeal of the statute of apprenticeships and conviction that the exclusive privileges of corporations should be ended (*WN* IV.ii.42/470). The argument here is that the government should withdraw from certain tasks. In effect the legislation should be repealed thus relieving government from the obligation to administer. As we also noted, Smith was not alone in this argument for political retrenchment. Hume supported the removal of hindrances to the exercise of economic liberty. Hence he too opposed the 'absurd limitations' on industry imposed by corporations (*HE* II, 56–7) and the 'absurd' seven year apprenticeship in the cloth industry (*HE* II, 323) as well as the fixing of wages by statute (*HE* II, 231); while deviating somewhat from Smith he judged usury laws 'unreasonable and iniquitous' and regarded as 'pernicious' the consequences of granting patent monopolies (*HE* II, 573; cf. II, 595; III, 83–4n).[24]

The case for directly positive government action within a commercial society (the second factor) is less straightforward. In addition to advocating the removal of hindrances, Hume argued for consistent, non-arbitrary taxation (*E-Tax* 345) and free trade, speaking forcefully against the 'narrow and malignant' policies of prohibition (*E-JT* 328; cf. *E-BT*). Smith's default position is that it is the principled and proper role for government to provide security thus allowing individuals the liberty to pursue their own goals and thereby bring about prosperity, that is, enhanced universal material well-being (see Chap. 3 p. 78 above). This is seemingly the message of the 'invisible hand', wherein it is not only ineffectual to attempt deliberately to direct industry in the name of the public good but also is dangerous to trust public authority with that task (*WN* IV.ii.9–10/456).[25] Smith is followed by Millar (*HV* IV, 3/717) and Ferguson (*PMPS* II, 425) but it runs counter to Hutcheson's view that 'it must be the business of legislators to promote by all just and effectual methods, true principles of virtue, such as shall lead men to piety to God and all just, peaceable and kind disposition towards their fellows' (*SMP* II, 310). Yet caution is needed. In his usual circumspect way Smith hedges this evocation of the invisible hand with qualifications. Hence it is not 'always the worse for the society' that the 'publick interest' is 'frequently' the unintended outcome of individual's pursuing their own interests. This cautious wording reveals that this is indeed a 'default' that may be over-ridden and not some absolute rule. And Smith does countenance exceptions (Skinner 1996: 1, 86ff who acknowledges Viner 1927), though not in a Hutchesonian direction.

Jeffrey Young (2005: 92, 106), in an informed and informative analysis, while identifying a 'fundamental tension' in Smith's treatment of the state, goes so far as to attribute to him a 'theory of interventions'. These interventions generally make some sort of appeal to the 'national interest' or security.[26] Hence invoking, implicitly, government's first task, its responsibility for defence, 'the act of navigation very properly' gives British shipping a monopoly of their own trade (*WN* IV.ii.24/463). It is an appropriate component of the 'administrative' task to effect apt regulation (this is not solely a matter of 'police' – regulations that promote opulence once the task of securing internal peace has been achieved [*LJA* i.2/5]). For example, on the same principle that building fire walls to prevent the spread of a blaze is a justified infringement of the natural liberty of builders, so is regulation of the issuing of notes by banks (*WN* II.ii.94/324). Similarly Smith – here deviating from Hume – justifies a legal rate of interest in order that capital is put 'visibly' in the hands of those who will make more productive use of it (*WN* II.iv.15/357). It can also be appropriate to deviate from the principles of 'free trade' in order to 'lay some burden upon foreign for the encouragement of domestick industry' (*WN* IV.ii.23/463). Finally, though without making any positive recommendation, and reflecting what we call in Chapter 5 his version of a 'moralised economy', he remarks that regulation in favour of workmen is 'always just and equitable' (the same cannot be said of that which favours 'the masters') (*WN* I.x.c.61/158).

We now come to the third complicating factor. Smith is acutely aware that an astute measure of judgment is needed to gauge the appropriateness of any deviation from the default position. However, he evinces doubts about the exercise of such judgment. These doubts are both pragmatic and more theoretical. Pragmatically, or practically, when he discusses the 'three great orders' of society he finds each judgmentally deficient when it comes to good governance. The order of those who 'live in profit' is disqualified because their interests and the general interest, as we have already seen, do not coincide. The interests of those who live by wages are 'strictly connected with the interest of society' but their circumstances mean they have no time to be informed thus making them 'unfit' (see also Chapter 7). The final order – the country gentlemen who live off rent – are the traditional mainstay of the political order, because, as Smith acknowledges, their own interests will not run counter to those of the nation, but they are indolent and incapable of the requisite 'application of mind [...] to foresee and understand the consequences of any publick regulation' (*WN* I.xi. p. 8–10/265–6). This scepticism of the link between landowning and political judgment, which we will meet again in Chapter 6, is complemented by the remark in his *Lectures* that in a 'polished' society authority reposes in 'superior mental capacity' (*LJB* 12/401).

On a more theoretical or abstract plane, Smith juxtaposes 'the science of a legislator', the deliberations of which ought to be governed by invariable 'general principles', to the skill of 'that insidious and crafty animal, vulgarly called a statesman or politician' which concerns itself with 'the momentary fluctuations of affairs' (*WN* IV.ii.39/468). Smith's terminology is loose. Hence he also refers at the beginning of Book IV to 'political oeconomy considered as a branch of the science of a statesman or legislator' [*WN* IV.Introd.1/428].[27] It is clear Smith is not advocating that some individual could play the role of 'legislator'.[28] Moreover, when he does consider the 'greatest statesmen and legislators' his assessment is cool. Even when they do possess merit they are prone to presumption and self-admiration (*TMS* VI.iii.28/250). Alexander and Caesar are classic examples but Smith brings it up-to-date citing, among others, Eugene of Savoy and Gustavus Adolphus as those whose immodest susceptibility to popular favour led to rash and ruinous 'adventures' (he allows that Marlborough is an exception) (*TMS* VI.iii.28/251).[29]

What is more significant is that this contrast between the 'legislator' and 'politician' echoes Smith's judgment, mentioned above, that it is a decisive advantage of the separation of the judiciary that it makes it 'scarce possible' justice can be sacrificed (even without any corrupt intent) to 'what is vulgarly called politics' (*WN* V.i.b.25/723). But this is little more than presumption. Smith presumes judges are not only exceptionally able (they possess that desiderated superior mental capacity) but also, because their emolument is 'very small', that they are motivated by the great honour of their office (*WN* V.i.b.18–20/718/19) so that the attendant public admiration is 'part of their reward' (*WN* I.x.b.24/123). (Millar adds that the independence of 'professional judges' was enhanced by appointment for life and also sees the jury system as a further buttress of the rule of law [*HV* IV, 2/707].) Beyond these presumptions it remains that, even with the security of a separate or independent judiciary, it is the 'vulgar politician' who determines the appropriateness of any deviations from the default. This raises the broad question of the 'politics' of commercial society.[30]

A few paragraphs after contrasting 'legislation' with 'politics' Smith observes that to expect free trade ever to be entirely restored in Britain is 'as absurd as to expect an Oceana or Utopia should ever be established in it'. The reason given for this is that such restoration is contrary to public 'prejudices' and what is 'much more unconquerable [. . .] the private interests of many individuals' (*WN* IV.ii.43/471). This assessment is echoed later when he remarks about his own scheme to deal with the crisis in the American colonies that it was fated to be a 'Utopia' because it ran counter to the 'private interests of many powerful individuals' (*WN* V.iii.68/934).[31] More broadly, as Jerry Muller (1995: 79) observes, the *Wealth of Nations* contains a compendium of examples of how individuals and groups attempt to promote their interests at the expense of the public. This recognition of the power of 'interests' jells with Smith's unflattering depiction of merchants as hypocrites who complain, for example, of high wages while being silent on the 'pernicious effects' of high profits (*WN* I.ix/24115); as conspirators as they contrive to raise prices (*WN* I.x.c.27/145); and who 'generally have an interest to deceive, and even to oppress the publick' (*WN* I.xi.p.10/267). Moreover, these interests (in monopoly) are supported by members of parliament (largely the mentally indolent landowners) since this gives them 'the reputation for understanding trade' and, crucially, 'great popularity and influence with an order of men whose numbers and wealth render them of great importance' (*WN* IV.ii.43/471). Of a piece with this, Smith entertains no illusions about those who participate 'in the management of publick affairs' since they do so 'chiefly on account of the importance it gives them'. They do not participate as an expression of their commitment to public virtue (see Chapter 6). A similar implicit undermining of the link between 'virtue' and 'politics' is detectable in Hume; everyone (rulers included) in 'politics' is to be presumed prudentially a 'knave', even if few actually are (*E-IP* 42).[32]

In the face of this 'disenchantment' (Lindgren 1973: 78), Smith places some reliance (or perhaps hopes) on the effort of individual self-betterment potentially to surmount the 'impertinent obstructions with which the folly of human laws too often incumbers its operations' (*WN* IV.v.b.43/540; cf. *WN* II.iii.36/345). This optimistic gloss does, of course, presuppose that the administration is already sufficiently exact to provide individuals with enough security to risk action to better their condition. Despite some comments in his *Lectures* (*LJA* v.10–12/273–4) that the English enjoy more security than the Scots because their suffrage is more extensive, he does not pursue that line in his published work. It is not that Smith envisages an Engels-like division between the 'administration of things' that with the coming of 'the revolution' will replace the 'government of men', but this approach does appear to 'de-politicise' a commercial society (and something like a concept of 'civil society' can be detected – or, perhaps better, constructed – within Smith's and others' thinking [Berry 2010; Boyd 2013]). More soberly, it is the case that the practical place of politics in commercial society is under-considered.[33] Smith is not alone here. It must be admitted that this inattention is a relative matter. There is a real sense that much of the critique of commerce to be examined in Chapter 6 is from a 'political' perspective, expressing 'republican' concerns about the corruption of political virtue that wealth, luxury and thence commerce pose. Nor as we shall see is this a simple black-and-white affair, since defenders of commerce are alert to these concerns. Allowing for this, it remains the case that the Scots had no notion to write a *Leviathan* or *Treatises on Government* (Hume's *Treatise* might be judged to have some affinity to the former of these in scope and ambition but he never repeated the enterprise).

Three factors can be suggested for this underplaying. First, in the background is the Scots' own anti-Jacobite sensitivities; they are anxious to be seen as good Hanoverians (see Chapter 1). They are full of praise for the British constitution. Second, in part reflecting this, there is little overt, 'engaged' political speculation. Aside from Hume's early essays, when he comments on, and participates in, aspects of contemporary debate,[34] and Millar's late commentary on developments in the English constitution (see below), the possible exceptions to this are the 'militia' question (see Chapter 6) and the American colonies (see Berry 1997: 107–9). Third, as social theorists, they see commercial society as a complex whole within which politics is but one ingredient and not necessarily a pivotal one.

Given this, and in the current context, there are two questions that can be pursued for the light they shed on the Scots' idea of commercial society. The first, echoing the final factor identified in the previous paragraph, is the non-pivotal place of constitutional thinking. The second focuses on Scottish policy – what in fact they thought it appropriate to do, and where, unlike their adherence to the house of Hanover, differences can be detected.

Ever since Plato, and perhaps more significantly Aristotle, discussion of government was in terms of type of constitutions (see Chapter 1). None of the Scots entirely jettisons this talk and some continue to use this language more than others. Moreover, there was always what we might term a 'sociological' element in 'classical theory', as in Aristotle's conception of oligarchy and democracy as rule by the rich and poor for example. In addition, as we also noted in Chapter 1, Montesquieu had reformulated the classification, regarding aristocracy and democracy as subsets of 'republic' and distinguishing monarchy from despotism.

As Duncan Forbes (1975b: 188) observed this last distinction resurfaced in Hume who distinguished between a civilised and an absolute monarchy. It is the former term that is indicative of the Scots' approach. Hume declares 'it may now be affirmed of civilized monarchies what was formerly said in praise of republics alone, that they are a government of laws and men' (*E-CL* 94; cf. *E-AS* 125, *HE* II, 15) (cf. Vlachos 1955: 169, McArthur 2007: 12). This has the significant consequence of permitting a temporal distinction to be drawn between commercial society and mercantile republican governance. Since the weight falls on the qualifier 'civilised' rather than the substantive 'monarchy' then it enables constitutional form to be historicised. This is clear in Smith. He contrasts contemporary 'civilised' to 'ancient monarchies' (*WN* V.11.a/822). The latter were martial states and in them the administration of justice was a source of revenue not expense. In the former revenue is collected by tax.[35] The degree of civilisation (or, conversely, the 'gradation of despotism' [Smith *WN* V.i.g.19/799]) is the key criterion rather than outward constitutional form when it comes to assessing whether the 'general principles' of government are adhered to and its three tasks are carried out. (Of course the British/Hanoverian mixed constitution is supremely 'civilised'.)[36]

This line of argument also applies to Millar's *An Historical View of the English Government* (to give it its full main title). As we have already seen, and as will be confirmed as we proceed, for Millar 'government' is always situated in what we might call a sociological context. Hence the criterion for the three 'political system[s]' into which he divides English history, namely, 'feudal aristocracy' (pre-1066), 'feudal monarchy' (William I to the Stuarts) and 'commercial government', is 'the distribution of property' (*HV* Introd/11). This is not to deny that there is a 'political' dimension to Millar's disagreement with aspects of Hume's *History*. But that, too, should be put into perspective against the full-blooded assaults on Hume offered by, for example, Daniel McQueen and Catherine Macaulay.[37] Millar's more overtly 'political' concerns are clearly expressed in one of the essays added posthumously to the *View*, where he charts critically 'the secret influence of the crown' as one of the two great changes since the Restoration (the other is the countervailing rise of commerce and liberty) (*HV* IV, 2/707).[38]

The argument between Millar and Hume we could say is 'academic' but there were disputes with a more practical policy focus. We noted in Chapter 1 that it was deliberate policy after the '45 to 'civilise' the Highlands. On the back of legislation this meant prosecuting particular policies. These were premised on the association of commercial society with civilisation and provide an illustration of how the 'politics' of a commercial society might be supposed to 'work' when it comes to questions of policy. On this issue we can detect, to employ Young's term, a tension between the 'exactness' of the administration and the requirements and practicalities of policy implementation. A key case in point is the plans 'for civilizing the Highlands' which we noted in Chapter 1.

There were historical precedents. In Chapter 1 we noted also Robertson's comment on the policy of James I/VI regarding the

Highlands that the 'principle' was right but its implementation was thwarted. Hume picked up on James' 'civilising' policy toward Ireland. The objective of this policy was to reconcile the Irish to 'laws and industry', thus making their subjection 'durable and useful to the crown of England'. In order to achieve that end it was necessary to 'abolish Irish customs which supplied the place of laws and which were calculated to keep that people for ever in a state of barbarism and disorder'. In particular, those customs which hindered 'the enjoyment of fixed property in land' (without which there is no incentive 'to enclose, to cultivate, to improve') were to be replaced (*HE* III, 33, 34; cf. Millar *HV* IV, 1/684). Hume's position with respect to contemporary Scottish Highlanders is elliptical. In the loaded context of defending Archibald Stewart, the Lord Provost of Edinburgh, for his conduct in the '45, he calls them 'barbarous' and imbued with (an ill-disciplined) 'martial spirit'.[39] However, the formulation of 'general principles' (*E-Com* 254) that he sets forth in the *Political Discourses* of 1752 do not descend to local particulars, which means only interpretative inferences can be made (Emerson 2008a; Caffentzis 2001). The Irish reforms were essentially to the legal system but James' introduction of 'humanity and justice' would have required 'ages of perseverance and attention' to take full effect (*HE* III, 35). By extension, given the enactment of legal changes, Hume's emphasis on manners and customs as causal agents (Berry 2006b) makes it reasonable to impute to him a counsel of caution against a quick external economic 'fix' of the 'Highland question'.

Some of the civilising measures planned for the Highlands were infrastructural, such as the building of roads and bridges, and could fall under the remit of the duty to supply public works identified by Smith as one of the three proper tasks of government. But other measures were more directly purposive and, we can identify, the commitment to improve and civilise the Highlands through deliberate 'interventionist' policies as the fault-line. The liberty under law (on which see Chapter 5) that is a central feature of a commercial society devolves to government, as have seen, the task of ensuring a supportive framework within which individuals pursue their own interests. This means that government is not properly in the business of making people make pins. Moreover, should it involve itself in ensuring pins are made it will reproduce the follies of mercantilism; its aim to aggrandise the 'state' is bought at the cost of the well-being of the individuals within it. The Scots are not doctrinaire; certainly their idea of a commercial society does not exclude in principle a role for government that goes beyond the provision of a framework. We will come across this issue again in Chapter 6 but in the current context we can explore a little further the fault-line.

This exploration is best conducted via the issue of 'bounties'. Like Hume, Smith's analysis is conducted at a general level (as the full title reveals he is enquiring into the 'nature and causes' of the wealth of nations). Nonetheless the book contains 'Digressions' on particular topics and the question of 'bounties' is one such. What is pertinent here is that Smith added comments to the third edition of the *Wealth of Nations* (1784) that clearly reveal the presence of the Highlands debate. The broad context is the bounty on corn and Smith remarks, regarding exportation of a home-made commodity, that it exhibited the basic failing of the mercantile system by 'forcing some part of the industry of the country into a channel less advantageous than that in which it would run of its own accord' (WN IV.v.a.24/516). Typically Smith is not against bounties tout court, as when they contribute to defence. But in the particular context of the bounty on herring fishing, where Scotland is explicitly mentioned, Smith's verdict is that 'the legislature has been very grossly imposed upon' (WN IV.v.a.28/518).[40]

One of the critics of Smith's analysis of corn bounty was James Anderson (the editors note that in the third edition of the *Wealth of Nations* Smith amended a detail in his argument in the light of this).[41] Anderson, like Smith a founding member of the Royal Society of Edinburgh, wrote a substantial work with the indicative title *Observations on the Means of Exciting a Spirit of National Industry; Chiefly Intended to Promote the Agriculture, Commerce, Manufactures and Fisheries of Scotland* . This book bears some hallmarks of the general Scottish Enlightenment perspective, referring, for example, in the Preface to 'every stage in the progress of civil society' (1777: v, xi, xiv). As its title implies he is animated by the conviction of the need to 'keep alive a spirit of disinterested patriotism' (1777: xvii). As part of this intent he discusses the herring industry. There is a strong Smithian flavour to his discussion. He decries 'regulating politicians', declaring it 'safer to entrust a man with the management of his own affairs than to subject him to the controul of another', and paraphrases Smith on the unproductiveness of slaves and talks of the 'natural progress of improvements' (1777: 445, 465, 467, 475). However, he believes that if 'properly attended to' the herring industry could flourish and advocates a 'small bounty' on every barrel of cured herrings and a 'moderate premium' to encourage equipping larger vessels (1777: 466, 474).

This interchange between Smith and Anderson illustrates at one level the presence of debate that could be unexceptionally expected to take place on policy questions within a commercial society. While Anderson is more optimistic than Smith both exhibit a distrust or wariness about what we can call the politics of policy making. In part this is the lesson of experience – both Smith (*WN* IV.v.a.28/518) implicitly and Anderson (1777: 468n) explicitly remark adversely on legislation enacted (Geo II c.24). Nonetheless, it would be contrary to the non-perfectionist quality of the Scots' thought (Millar *HV* IV, 2/703) if they thought commercial society would run without let or hindrance from the passions of politics.

## NOTES

1. This consonance between law and a money economy was emphasised by Simmel (1990: 354, 427, 442). The 'logic' that Simmel is concerned to expound was (largely implicitly) present in the Scots (Simmel refers in the manner of the Scots to the parallels between a child and a primitive man and refers on the same page to pin manufacture [301]).

2. It might be thought the hunter is less future-dependent, since he *now* has a better bow than a self-made one, but he too has to consider where his next 'quality' bow will come from.

3. On the meaning(s) of 'nature' in Smith see the helpful discussion in Aspromourgos (2009: 43–8).

4. Despite Hume's wording this is not to be understood as a 'thought-less' process. Annette Baier (1991: 79, 97) draws attention to what she calls the 'epistemic force' of habit in his thought. Craig Smith (2006: 61) brings out more generally that for the Scots habit and custom were 'forms of experienced-based knowledge'. For an extended discussion of the role of the habit and custom in the Scots see Berry (2003a).

5. See, especially, Sir William Temple, *An Essay upon the Original and Nature of Government* (1672) included in his *Miscellanea* (London: 1680) p. 54. Hume knew Temple's writings and judged him a 'considerable writer' (*HE* III, 782). My thanks to Ryu Susato for alerting me to this judgment.

6. Compare Ferguson (*ECS* 100), 'the multitude who admire the parent are ready to extend their esteem to his offspring'.

7. John Locke (1965: 409), for one, gave it eloquent expression in his Second *Treatise* (1689–90) declaring that the legislative power is 'to govern by promulgated and establish'd Laws, not to be varied in particular Cases. But to have one Rule for rich and Poor, for the Favourite at Court and the country Man at Plough'.

8. See for example Wennerlind, Schabas and Caffentzis (in Wennerlind and Schabas (eds) (2008), Duke (1979); Gatch (1996); Wennerlind (2005), Vickers (1960: Chap. 11).

9. In a fanciful metaphor commerce is more secure when it rests on 'the solid ground' of gold and silver than when it is 'suspended upon the Daedalian wings of paper money' (*WN* II.ii.86/321). That metaphor has provided

the title for two discussions of Smith's view of money – Paganelli 2006 and Rockoff 2011; for Smith's views on money see also Vickers 1975. The metaphor's likely source is Swift's poem on the Bubble (1721), with its reference to the 'Rashness of the Cretan Youth' who 'On Paper Wings he takes his Flight'. See Wennerlind 2011: 237.

10. Smith refers to authors of new books as being entitled to a 'temporary monopoly' (*WN* V.i.e.30/754). See Rahmatian (2006: 188, 200) for a discussion of intellectual property right with particular reference to Kames, who made clear his legal opposition to any idea of perpetual copyright. Patents have been seen to be a crucial factor in Britain's economic development. Eric Robinson (1964: 209) for example declares that 'the granting of an extension to James Watt's patent [1775] for an improved steam-engine might be considered the most important single event in the Industrial Revolution'. For comment on contemporary dispute and modern scholarship on this question see Mokyr 2009: 403–6.

11. I have given a fuller treatment in Berry 2009b (on which I draw here). For a painstaking analytical examination see Harrison 1981 and among recent treatments Hardin 2007 and Harris 2010.

12. The conventions of justice are the effect of mutual agreement which when known to the participants 'produce[s] a suitable resolution and behaviour'. For example, 'two men who pull the oars of a boat do it by agreement or convention though they have never given promises to each other'. And it is through the operation of this same principle that 'gradually' and 'by slow progression' languages are formed and gold becomes the measure of exchange (*T* 3.2.2.10/*SBNT* 490).

13. In line with the non-Platonic consensus discussed in Chapter 3, by 'nature' here Hume is utilising another of its standard meanings as the opposite of 'unusual' (*T* 3.1.2.8/*SBNT* 475). As in the limited nativism to which Smith subscribes, it is a common observation that some individuals are more adept at some tasks (bow-making) than others.

14. Kames contests this (*PE* 19). On his account of natural morality, it will also insist on inflexibility: ' a man in low circumstances by denying a debt he owes to a miser saves himself and his family from ruin [. . .] but the moral sense admits no balancing between good and ill and gives no quarter to injustice whatever benefit it may produce'.

15. This same language and argument are retraced in his analysis of allegiance in the *Treatise*. The way to avoid confusion in both property and allegiance is to 'proceed by general rules' (*T* 3.2.10.3/*SBNT* 555) and these are the work of artifice not nature.

16. Grotius, Bk 1, Chap. 1, sect. 8 (2005: 142). Harris judges Hume's account of justice is best understood in the Grotian tradition (Harris 2010: 26; cf. Teichgraeber 1986: 101). For helpful comments on Hume and Grotius see Buckle 1991.

17. Aristotle 1894: 1129b. Smith cites Grotius' comments on Aristotle in his version of the distinction between strict, narrow or negative justice and

justice as 'comprehending all the social virtues' or, as attributed to Plato, as 'the perfection of every sort of virtue' (*TMS* VII.ii.1.10/270).

18. Hutcheson *SMP* I, 254. On 'moral sense' see Hutcheson *SIMP* Bk 1, Chap. 4. The moral sense approves the 'generosity of a worthy man' above the 'parsimony of a miser' (*PW* 72). Compare Pufendorf who observes that 'the assignment of legacies' looks 'not to distributive but to universal justice', where, in Pufendorf's gloss, the latter refers to 'imperfect rights', that is, those that are left to 'each person's sense of decency and conscience' (1934: Bk 1, Chap. 7, paras 9, 7). Hutcheson (SMP I, 258) followed suit; Grotius (2005: 142) himself had made the link.

19. That 'utility' plays a crucial (though not foundational) role in Smith is emphasised by Campbell (1971) and Rosen (2000).

20. Smith does allow that breaches of discipline (cases of what Hutcheson terms 'small guilt' [*SMP* II, 354]) are punished and severely (as of a sentinel who falls asleep on duty) 'merely from a view to the general interest of society' (*TMS* II.ii.3.11/90). That public utility can outweigh justice to prevent general mischief is upheld by Kames (*PE* 267). Smith's objection to Hume is that he generalises the exception, but once rooted in natural sentiments Smith is able to accept that it is 'undoubtedly true' that we 'confirm our natural sense of the fitness of punishment' on broadly 'utilitarian' lines (*TMS* II.ii.3.7/88). For Smith on punishment see, for example, Miller 1996 (who contests Norrie 1989), Stalley 2012 and in a comparative context Simon 2013.

21. Although justice must on Hume's account be co-eval with society (it is present in the family) these 'first rudiments of justice must every day be improv'd as the society enlarges' (*T* 3.2.2.14/*SBNT* 493); there is a 'natural progress of human sentiments' whereby there is experienced a 'gradual enlargement of our regards to justice' (*M* 3, 21/*SBNM* 192).

22. Kames notwithstanding his insistence on justice as a primary and benevolence as a secondary virtue (*PMNR* 37; cf. *PE* 20) – see further Chap. 5 – argues that the latter in certain circumstances (such as parent/child) 'is susceptible in many cases of a precise rule' (*PMNR* 59, 61).

23. As Richard Teichgraeber (1986: 10) argues Hume and Smith 'de-moralize politics', just as they 'de-politicize morality.'

24. The case for Hume as a 'liberal' is well-made in Stewart 1992 and he is followed by McArthur 2007. It is an important counter to the reading of Hume as a 'conservative' (I discuss that reading, and the extensive literature it has generated, in Berry 2011).

25. Smith's use of the term 'invisible hand' has been the subject of considerable commentary. I am sympathetic to the argument of Rothschild (2002: Chap. 5) and Kennedy (2011) that it has been over-interpreted. The best account of 'unintended consequences' (of which the 'invisible hand' is a sub-set) is in Smith 2006.

26. With interpretive licence it could be held that there is another overarching principle by citing from *TMS* his comment that 'all constitutions of

government' are to be valued 'only in proportion as they tend to promote the happiness of those live under them' (*TMS* IV.i.11/185). The difference in context between the two texts makes me reluctant to give this equal weight as a principle.

27. The term 'statesman' is perhaps loaded. Steuart used the term stipulatively 'to signify the legislature and supreme power, according to the form of government' (*PPE* I, 16). Steuart allocates to this figure the 'business' of judging the 'expediency of different schemes of oeconomy' and modelling ' by degrees the minds of his subjects so as to induce them, from the allurement of private interest to concur in the execution of his plan' (*PPE* I, 17; cf. 'I constantly suppose a statesmen at the head of government, systematically conducting every part of it [political oeconomy] so as to prevent the vicissitudes of manners and innovations by their natural and immediate effects or consequences from hurting any interest within the commonwealth', *PPE* I, 122). As this wording suggests this runs counter to the thrust of Smith's argument. In a well-known letter Smith is dismissive of the *Principles* predicting (in *WN*) that 'every false principle in it will meet a clear and distinct confutation' (*Corr* 132/164). This is notwithstanding, and as we have had occasion to note in earlier chapters, that a number of Steuart's positions are not out of kilter with those of Smith (not surprising given Steuart's own acknowledgment of his debt to Hume, see *PPE* II, 343).

28. His references to Solon (*TMS* VI.ii.2.16/233; *WN* IV.v.b.53/543) are not indicative of a viable role for such a law-giver. Moreover, Smith famously warns against the 'man of system', who enamoured of his 'ideal plan of government' treats society as 'chess-board' oblivious to the fact that the 'pieces' have a 'principle of motion of their own' with the outcome of 'the highest degree of disorder' (*TMS* VI.ii.2.17/234).

29. Smith could be said to acknowledge the Platonic dilemma, where those who can clearly see the sun of truth are reluctant to return to the murky cavern of opinion. That most admirable specimen of humanity (the 'wise and virtuous man') is ill-equipped to 'lead'; he and his like are too conscious of their own imperfections (McNally thus errs when he argues that Smith looked to 'public-spirited action by individuals to preserve the moral integrity of governments' [1988: 191]). Smith's examples pointedly are artists and philosophers – they live their lives by the standards of 'exact propriety and perfection' and are to be contrasted to the 'legislator' who adheres to the less exacting standard of what 'is commonly attained in the world' (*TMS* VI.iii.23–6/247–9). Not, of course, that Smith divided humanity for everyone can appreciate the more exacting standard. For a discussion of the 'wise and virtuous' see Fricke 2013, Hanley 2013.

30. I have been stimulated to pursue this line of enquiry by Yoshiya Ichinose.

31. This policy occupied a sizable portion of the text to the extent that he was criticised for delaying publication of it in order to accommodate developing events (the best-known such complaint is from Blair [see *Corr*

151/188]). For a general discussion see Skinner 1996: Chap. 9; Winch 1978: Chap. 7; Pitts 2005: Chap. 2.

32. Hume is more complacent than Smith. Even when he admits that governors may 'often' be 'led astray by private passions' he still claims they have a 'visible interest in the impartial administration of justice' (*E-OG* 39). This admission itself qualifies the argument in the *Treatise*, where he attributed the observance of justice to the 'immediate interest' of a few who, being 'satisfy'd with their present condition' and thus being 'indifferent to the greatest part of society', could act equitably (*T* 3.2.7.7/*SBNT* 537).

33. See Pulkkinen (2003: 19, 121) for a detailed exploration. It is the thrust of her overtly conceptual/linguistic analysis that the Scots look upon politics as a 'philosophical phenomenon' and not as an activity (politicking).

34. See especially LP, FPG, IP, BG, PG, PGB in the 1741 edition of his *Essays*. Hume did retain these essays in later editions but they were subject to considerable amendments, which is indicative of their initial status as pièces d'occasion, as he himself acknowledged in the Advertisement to the first edition of the collection about its contents (1875: III, 41). Moreover in the 1758 edition of the *Essays* he appended a note stating that he had retracted some of his views in the light of his work in the *History* (*E-PGB* 72n). That note itself reflects Hume's concern to treat 'politics' in the broad social and historical context, while the early Advertisement admitted to his intended 'moderation and impartiality in handling political subjects'. Similarly he opens the *Political Discourses* (1752) with a declaration that in these essays he was engaging in 'abstruse' thinking, rather than 'coffee house conversation' (*E-Com* 253–4). Emerson (2008a: 11) does point out that *Letter to a Gentleman* (1748) and *Bellman's Petition* (1751) were efforts to 'affect the course of political events'.

35. The principles of taxation conform to the primacy of rules and consistency that are the hallmarks of a commercial society. Hence the second of Smith's four maxims on taxation is that what an individual should pay 'ought to be certain and not arbitrary', with the timing, manner and amount to be paid 'clear and plain to the contributor and to every other person' (*WN* V.ii.b.4/825).

36. This debate is a running commentary on the French. Hume sees their government as 'absolute' (*E-LP* 10; *E-CL* 92) but although such a monarchy, he continues, is given 'in high political rant' the name 'tyranny' in fact, by its 'just and prudent administration' and provision of 'security to the people', it 'meets most of the ends of political society'. Somewhat similarly Smith regards the French as despotic even if of a 'gentle and mild' variety when compared in the 'gradation' to Constantinople (*WN* V.i.g.19/799). Forbes judged that the 'unity and continuity' in Hume's thought lay in what labels 'scientific whiggism' (1975a: 139; cf. Forbes 1977: 41). This view questioned such 'holy cows of the Whigs' as the justification of the 1688 Revolution, the 'ancient constitution', the wickedness of Stuart kings

and (pertinent here) the contrast between English 'liberty' and French 'slavery'. Forbes (1954) had used the label with reference to Smith and Millar and in 'Sceptical Whiggism' (1975b) applied it to Smith again.

37. McQueen was the author of *Letters on Mr Hume's History of Great Britain* and he detects therein not only 'irreligious sneers' but an 'apology for the 'principles of arbitrary power' (1756: 327, 254). Macaulay's *History of England* was intended to do justice to those who set up 'banners of liberty' against the 'pretensions of the Stewarts' with Hume identified as one of their defenders (1769: I, ix; III, 84).

38. See Tomkins (2009) for a general interpretation of Millar as deeply concerned with the threats to liberty in the growth of the power of the Crown in the contemporary British constitution. Millar was a strong Whig, dedicating the *Historical View* to Fox, and used his legal expertise to defend those 'in danger of being subject to punishments more than adequate to their offences' (Craig 1990: lxxxix). He is the disputed author of two (late) political tracts – *Letters of Crito* (1796) and *Letters of Sydney* (1796).

39. *A True Account of the Behaviour and Conduct of Archibald Stewart* (1748) p. 7.

40. In his correspondence Smith is more forthright. In an undated fragment he declares, 'I could write a volume upon the folly and the bad effects of all the legal encouragements that have been given either to the linen manufacture or to the fisheries' (*Corr* 299/327). Regarding the former of these Smith was at odds with Kames whose pamphlet on Flax had strongly advocated support for linen (just as Lindsay had done in the 1730s). Regarding the latter there is indirect evidence from William Wilberforce that Smith rebuffed his scheme to develop fishing villages (quoted in Ross 2010: 403). That same letter of Wilberforce is quoted by Rashid (2009: 225) in his critique of Smith's account of economic development. He also asserts, at odds with the evidence here presented, that Smith 'was virtually unconcerned with Scotland as a distinct problem'.

41. Smith, in 1780, in a letter to Andreas Holt judged Anderson 'a very diligent, laborious, honest Man' who had picked up on what Smith acknowledges to have been a passage wherein he expressed himself in manner 'certainly too strong'. However, Smith also judges that Anderson had used that slip to launch a more general attack but thinks his own amendment in the second edition has taken away the foundation of Anderson's whole argument (*Corr* 208/251). Anderson while complimentary of Smith and his book judged a corn bounty the 'wisest and best political institution' (1777: 370). Anderson is discussed at length in Youngson 1972.

# 5. Liberty and the Virtues of Commerce

This chapter takes up the postponed topic of liberty. Smith, as we have seen, called it a 'blessing' and the same accolade had previously been bestowed by Hume (*E-CP* 494), Kames (1766: 5),Wallace (*CGB* 117) as well as Turnbull in his commentary on Heineccius (*MCL* 245). George Berkeley, in his *Essay towards Preventing the Ruin of Great Britain* (1721, 1752) is another who employs it to characterise the greatest possession of a 'virtuous man' and 'good Christian'. He then proceeds to say that in 'the present age', 'injudicious patrons of liberty' have not distinguished between it and licentiousness (1953: VI, 70). This statement indicates that the meaning of 'liberty' is not straightforward. As a term, and perhaps also as a concept, it is subject to a variety of meanings and it is part of the task here to tease these out within the broad context of commercial society.

How commercial society functions – its operating principles and motivations – is the backdrop to the Scots' moral philosophy. That commerce appeared to 'work' on the assumption of self-love (as Smith said of consumers' dealings with the butcher) did not mean that it operated in an 'ethics-free' zone. Aside from the recognition that human interactions in a commercial society were not confined to buying sausages (as it were), a distinctive set of what can be called 'commercial virtues' was identified. This represents a shift in the schedule of virtues (plotted via the 'natural history' outlined in Chapter 2). The examination of that shift is the other key theme of this chapter.

When Smith refers to the twin blessings of liberty and opulence in the *Lectures* the context, in both versions, is slavery. In a seemingly counter-intuitive way he says that the condition of slaves is worse the more a society is 'improved' because they are better treated in 'rude periods of mankind' (Wallace makes a similar point [*DNM* 91]). His explanation for this is that the less inequality there is the more the masters live in similar manner to their slaves. He contrasts the North American planter, who often works alongside his slaves, with the 'rich and proud West Indian', who being far above the slaves 'gives him the hardest usage' (*LJA* iii.110/184–5; *LJB* 137/453). Smith makes it immediately clear he is not condoning slavery – 'it is almost needless to prove that slavery is a bad institution' (*LJB* 138/453).

This is without exception the position of the Scots and the rest of the Enlightenment. While it is not absent, the Scots do not exhibit great moral outrage. Hence Smith's emphasis is on the fact that slavery was economically unproductive; the judgment on the 'badness' of slavery is immediately illustrated by the fact that a free man works better than a slave (an argument reiterated in *WN* [III.ii.9/387; IV.ix.47/684]); as we noted in Chapter 3, he argues that wealth is increased by diligent workers and diligence is enhanced by the 'liberal reward for labour' [p. 84 above]). Kames was a member of the bench in the famous case of Wedderburn vs Knight (1778) and he voted with the majority for the latter on the grounds that what might be law in Jamaica has no bearing in Scotland because slavery 'is repugnant to the first principles of morality and justice' (quoted in Ross 1972: 144).[1]

Millar implicitly rebukes Smith for omitting the position of women within his argument that slaves are better treated in rude nations. He argues that 'in ages the most remote from improvement' women are held in low esteem and are treated as the servants or slaves of the men' (*OR* 193). This argument was adopted by Robertson who remarks of the Amerinds that so 'humiliating and miserable' is the condition of women that they were bought and sold (*HAm* 822); a consequence Millar had himself judged to be 'natural' (that is, in accord with 'natural history', predictable given human nature and circumstances) (*OR* 195). Kames is another who makes this point (*SHM* I, 303f), as does Hume who observed luridly that in barbarous nations men exhibit their superiority by 'reducing their females to the most abject slavery; by confining them, by beating them, by selling them, by killing them' (*E-AS* 133).[2] Implicit here is a point we will later make explicit about how the manners and virtues of commercial society make such behaviours inapplicable. Indeed Hume's choice of language deliberately points up that contrast.

## ANCIENT AND MODERN LIBERTY

While the contrast between liberty and slavery is relatively clear there is another, which though also chronological, is subtler. This latter contrast is between ancient and modern liberty. Though famously identified by Benjamin Constant in 1819 (1988), it is clear that the Scots point-edly make that distinction (cf. Castiglione 2000). One explicit mani-festation of this is Smith's observation (quoted in Chapter 2) that it is the presence of a choice of occupation, along with the ability to have one's children inherit and to dispose of one's property by testament, that makes individuals 'free in our present sense of the word Freedom' (and its absence is a principal attribute of 'villanage and slavery') (*WN* III.iii.5/400). This is almost an aside but its self-consciousness reveals an appreciation that there is something novel abroad. He is, of course, not alone. Hume on at least two occasions in his *History* referred to a 'new plan of liberty' that the 'manners of the age' had produced (*HE* II, 602; III, 99).

The crux of this novelty is the idea of liberty under the rule of law, the procedural operation of general laws known previously to all, or strict administration of justice, that we discussed in Chapter 4. Ancient liberty is that characteristic of classical Greece and republican Rome. We can identify two strains. There is the pre-eminently Stoic view where liberty is a state of tranquillity, where bodily desires are firmly controlled by the rational will. There is also the 'civic' or republican view of Livy, Cicero and others where liberty consists of activity in the political world to realise the public good. The two views are of course related. Behind both lies Aristotle and both inveigh against corruption. While the division is somewhat artificial, we will deal with the latter strain in detail in Chapter 6 and only allude to it here, where the former is the focus.

I should acknowledge at the outset that the discussion that follows is cursory and indulges in some brazen generalisation. Additionally, in the Scots there is a spectrum. They all accept, aside from the almost wilfully perverse Monboddo, what we can call the 'early modern consensus', so there is a rejection of Aristotle's physics and Stoic cosmology. Though, as we shall see, there was some divergence when it came to ethics.

Epictetus is a helpful exemplar. The compilation that comprises his *Encheiridion* or *Manual* opens by contrasting what is under our control and what isn't. The former are 'by nature free' and are exemplified by 'conception, choice, desire (*orexis*), aversion'. The latter are 'naturally slavish' and are exemplified by 'our body, our property, reputation, office' (1928: 483). To live according to nature (*kata phusin* or *secun-dum naturam*) is to heed the distinction. The 'natural life' is the free life. To live a naturally free life is, as Zeno (the founder of Stoicism) declared, to live a life of virtue according to reason. Conversely to invest the 'unfree' with value is a harmful mistake; it is to be literally 'pathological', prey to *pathê* (passions as irrational and unnatural [*alogos kai para phusin*] disturbances of the soul) (Diogenes Laertius 1925: par. 110) (cf. Rist 1969: 27).

Two general points can be derived from this analysis. First that 'desire' is controllable, second that the body (*soma*) is included in the naturally slavish category. The 'control' is an exercise of the rational will and it is a persistent strain in Stoicism that the body needs controlling; in particular it is the desire (*epithumia*)[3] for somatic pleasures that must be limited to its proper end. Seneca, for example, pointed out that since the 'end' of food is to assuage hunger (and fuel the body), it follows that to eat when not hungry is to be unfree, to manifest 'imperfection'; stale bread is as functional as fresh, since Nature demands the belly be filled not flattered (*delectari*) (1932a: no. 119). Those who maintain control are living life as it should be led; living in accordance with what is definitive of us as humans, our reason (Aristotle 1894: 1177a-b). This life is devoted to the contemplation of the immutable First Cause or the eternal perfection of God. This tranquil, ascetic or Stoical apathetic life stands in marked contrast to the mutable mundane life which is unceasingly at the beck and call of the demands of bodily desires (hunger, thirst, sex and the like). Although this Epictetean binary is sharp, it is not that there was no room for 'things indifferent' (*adiaphora*); wealth and health for example can be put to 'proper' use, albeit they are prone to improper exploitation as exemplified by the pursuit of luxury.[4]

As we will see in Chapter 6 the status of 'luxury' prompted different stances among the Scots, and thence, on a broad front, differing assessments of Stoicism. There is, however, a consensus that the 'power' allotted to 'reason' in this account is unsustainable. This judgment is a key factor in the 'modern' (post-Aristotelian) perspective. Reason's motivating force is rejected in favour of passions or desires (or instinct). The Scots accept broadly John Locke's empirical version of this, that is, they follow his rejection of the Cartesian strand of modern rationalism. They also demur from the starkest exposition of the modern position in the work of Thomas Hobbes. That demurral, though, was based on a rejection of the egocentric implications of Hobbes' argument rather than of his basic proposition that humans are motivated by the passions (their appetites and aversions) so that reason's role is subordinately instrumental. Hence Smith, for example, comments unequivocally that 'pleasure and pain are the great objects of desire and aversion' with the added observation that it is not reason that distinguishes those objects (*TMS* VII.iii.2.8/320; cf. Hume *T* 3.1.1.12/SBNT 455).[5]

In Locke's account, 'desire' was 'an uneasiness of the mind fixed on some absent good': either negative, as in endurance of pain, or positive, as in enjoyment of pleasure. This uneasiness is the 'spur to human industry and action' and it is the case, he declares, that 'we are seldom at ease and free enough from the solicitation of our natural and adopted desires, but a constant succession of uneasinesses out of that stock, which natural wants or acquired habits have heaped up, take the will in their turns: and no sooner is one action dispatched [. . .] but another uneasiness is ready to set us to work' (1854: I, 378, 353, 388). The echoes of this are obviously audible in Smith's judgement (*WN* II.iii.28/341) that everyone has, from the womb to the grave, a ceaseless desire to better their condition. The Lockean vocabulary of 'unease' is directly adopted by Hutcheson (*PW* 81). If for Hume reason is inactive (*T* 3.1.1.10/*SBNT* 458) it is still for Hutcheson, 'too slow, too full of doubt and hesitation' to direct our actions (*PW* 109). The curtailment of reason's scope is most evident in their moral philosophy. For Hume "tis impossible that the distinction between moral good and evil can be made by reason' (*T* 3.1.1.16/*SBNT* 462) and for Smith 'it is altogether absurd and unintelligible to suppose that the first perceptions of right and wrong can be derived from reason' (*TMS* VII.iii.2.7/320). Kames is equally forthright (*PMNR* 69).

The implications of this rejection of the pre-modern view bear on the understanding of modern liberty in the following way. One consequence of rejecting the normative superiority of the eternally immutable was the acceptance of the worth of the mundanely mutable. The commercial life – the organising framework for the provision of the wherewithal for living – is of itself valuable. The prosecution of that life is thus moral. As we will proceed to outline, life in a commercial society is governed by moral norms such as justice, humanity, probity and law-abidingness. These underwrite the actual operation of the rule of law, the guarantor of the blessing that is liberty. Modern liberty is enjoyed by all, as Smith said 'everyman', consistent with acting justly, is, to be 'left perfectly free to pursue his own interest his own way' (*WN* IV.ix.51/687). This inclusiveness demarcates it sharply from 'ancient liberty', a point to be developed in Chapter 6 when the second, civic, strain is discussed. It is a further consequence of this that the sovereign's interest lies not in the specific content of these 'interests' (desires) only in the likelihood of their peaceful co-existence; not in the particular choice of music but the volume at which it is played; not in the particular religious ritual performed but in its confinement to those who have chosen to practise it; not in the particular nature of the business enterprised but in its conformity to the principles of fair competition and so on.

This modern liberty of choice, exercised within a general framework of universally applicable law, goes both to the heart not only of human motivation but also of a commercial society. What links these is the idea of 'self-love'. This is an idea with a complicated history (Brooke 2012 is particularly valuable; see also Myers 1983, Hutchinson 1988, Force 2003). However, an examination of that history is beyond my remit, although I shall have to make some reference to it.

## JUSTICE AND BENEVOLENCE

As noted in Chapter 4, Smith, like Hume and Kames among others, declared justice to be indispensable. He chose quite deliberately to illustrate this indispensability by the fact that it makes a society of different merchants possible, that is, one where 'mutual love and affection' are absent (*TMS* II.ii.3.2/86; cf. Hutcheson *SIMP* 270). From this it follows that, 'beneficence is less essential to the existence of society than justice' (*TMS* II.ii.3.3/86). And since in commercial society 'everyman is a merchant' then its coherence does not depend on love and affection. You can co-exist socially with those to whom you are emotionally indifferent.

In line with my claim that commercial society embodies ethical relationships, nothing in this means that Smith is denying the virtuousness of benevolence or implying that a commercial society is inimical to virtue and morality. The premium to act justly in a commercial society, the concern 'not to hurt our neighbour', constitutes a correspondingly just character, that of the 'perfectly innocent and just man'. And such a character, he continues, can 'scarce ever fail to be accompanied with many other virtues, with great feeling for other people, with great humanity and great benevolence' (*TMS* VI.ii.intro.2/218). Members of a commercial society can thus be both just and benevolent. Hence it is a mistake to regard the narrowness or strictness of the Scots' concept of justice as indicative of an indifference to 'morality'.[6]

However, the very complexity of commercial society means, on the one hand, that any individual needs the assistance of many others (this was the message of the coarse woollen coat [see above p. 77]) but, on the other, only enjoys 'the friendship of a few persons' (*WN* I.ii.2/26). In a commercial society we live predominantly among 'an assembly of strangers' (*TMS* I.i.4.9/23; cf. Ignatieff 1984: 119; Paganelli 2010). Relationships of mutual love and affection or friendship are correspondingly relatively scarce. Since the bulk of our dealings are impersonal then they must thus be conducted on the basis of adhering to the complementary impersonal (abstract) rules of justice. In a complex society a shopkeeper is unlikely to be also your friend; to you he provides something you want, to him you are a customer. This pattern of relationships lies behind Smith's famous passage, partially quoted in Chapter 3,

> it is not from the benevolence of the butcher, the brewer or the baker that we expect our dinner, but from their regard to their own interest. We address ourselves not to their humanity but to their self-love and never talk to them of our own necessities but of their advantages. Nobody but a beggar chuses to depend chiefly upon the benevolence of his fellow-citizens. (*WN* I.ii.2/26–7)

Again Smith is not denying the presence (nor a fortiori the virtuousness) of benevolence but its scope.[7] Indeed, in the *Moral Sentiments* he is careful to say that a society of merchants would be 'less happy and agreeable' than one where beneficence was practised. Moreover, since just 'action' is 'inaction' (restraining from injury) then one who is 'merely' just is entitled to 'very little gratitude' and, possessing 'very little positive merit', will be treated without affection (*TMS* II.ii.1.9/82).

That justice was distinct from other virtues such as benevolence was not Smith's argument alone. In fact the distinctiveness has a long pedigree. In early modern thought it was often expressed as the difference between perfect and imperfect rights, where the performance of the former can be compelled (Hutcheson *SIMP* 113; *SMP* I, 257). In the *Moral Sentiments* Smith alludes (as the editors note) to Kames' *Principles of Morals and Natural Religion* for support for the view that we are under a stricter obligation to be just than we are to be generous (*TMS* II.ii.1.5/80n). Kames had said that 'benevolence and generosity are more beautiful and more attractive of love and esteem than justice' but that they are 'virtuous actions beyond what is strictly our duty' (*PMNR* 33; cf. Forbes 1982: 199). A somewhat different 'take' on the distinction is made by Millar. He distinguishes justice from the other virtues because it is amenable to precision and reducibility to accurate general rules (see above p. 107), whereas the exercise of the others (generosity and other benevolent affections) is so variable and dependent on the particularities of circumstances that 'there seldom occur two instances altogether alike' (*HV* IV, 7/787/8; cf. IV, 7/795).

## A MODERN MORALISED ECONOMY

While it is clear that the Scots do not consider commercial society an 'ethics-free zone' they are aware that this society can be construed to appear to rely to a reprehensible extent on 'self' or 'private', rather than, 'social' or 'public' interest. What made them apparently vulnerable was that having dismissed arguments that make morality a matter of objective rational judgment they were left in the subjective realm of sentiment. This was an intellectually, or argumentatively, dangerous terrain because it seemed to be occupied by Hobbes, according to whom all human action was determined by the interests of the actor. It was necessary that they put some conceptual distance between their position and that of Hobbes and its later deliberately polemical expression in Mandeville. All the Scots, whatever their internal differences, set themselves against the 'selfish system', as Hume generically termed it (*M* App.2, 4/*SBNM* 297). This is the common theme and guiding thread in their moral philosophy. A detailed exposition of that philosophy in its various forms is not here necessary; I will thus be selective. My principle or criterion of selection is how their moral philosophy supports what may be called the 'moralised economy' of a commercial society.[8]

In line with post-Aristotelian 'modernity' the material fact that all humans enjoy pleasure and avoid pain underwrote the predictability and certainty inherent in human behaviour (a regularity that was integral to the establishment of what we would today call the 'social sciences'). The most palpable evidence of such constancy is the 'fact' of the salience of self-interest in human nature (recall Tucker from Chapter 3 [quoted p. 85n]). 'Salience', of course, does not mean 'exclusive'. Humans have manifold motivations, even in 'Smithian economics', as Amartya Sen has emphasised (2011; cf. Sen and Rothschild 2006). The Hobbesian/Mandevillean version was contradicted by experience. This was the central theme of Hutcheson's philosophy.

While Hutcheson criticises rationalist moral philosophers his chief targets are the egoistic systems, especially of Mandeville (one of his earliest works [1726] is a systematic dismantling of Mandeville's *Observations on the Fable of the Bees*). The whole thrust of Hutcheson's argument is that the principle of self-interest does not represent 'human nature as it is' (*PW* 129) and that defect means it fails to explain the reality of morality. Of course, he recognises that humans are motivated by self-love. Indeed at one point he declares that 'the preservation of the system [of universal benevolence] requires everyone to be innocently solicitous about himself' (*PW* 89). Although Hutcheson does not here explicitly make the connection, this requirement is in line with what Smith identifies as the argument of the Stoic founder Zeno, according to whom 'every animal was by nature recommended to its own care and was endowed with the principle of self-love' (*TMS* VII.ii.1.14 /272). Leonidas Montes (2004: 8) claims, I think exaggeratedly, that Smith 'relies heavily' on the Stoic principle of *oikeiosis*.[9] But it is the case that that principle, especially its re-presentation by Cicero in *De Finibus* (1931: V, 9 – *Omne animal se ipsum diligit*), was commonly invoked.

One particularly notable invocation was by Rousseau, who carefully distinguished the notion of *amour de soi* from the negatively-charged *amour-propre*.[10] (I will return to Rousseau in Chapter 6.) While indeed allowing that humans have self-interested motives, it is Hutcheson's recurrent theme that the facts of benevolence; the desire for the public good, the exercise of generosity and other virtues are inexplicable on the assumption that humans are solely motivated by a sense of their own advantage. This is scarcely unique. Turnbull for example says the same (*MCL* 256).

Hutcheson framed his argument as an 'Inquiry'. Its aim was to discover the 'general foundation there is in Nature' for moral goodness (and moral evil) (*PW* 67). The outcome of the investigation is the location of this foundation in the possession by all humans of a moral sense.[11] On this basis he erects an account of morality that culminates in the principle of benevolence which he held to be the summit of moral goodness (cf. *PW* 88–9, 100). His Scottish successors accepted his evidential basis for morality (see the opening sentence of Smith's *Moral Sentiments* quoted in Chapter 3 [8n]). Where Hutcheson's successors differed was over the need to invoke a distinct moral sense to justify that reality as well as over the privileged position he allotted to benevolence. This is clear in Hume and Smith and although Kames, in his critique of Hume and Smith, gives a foundational role to moral sense he also distances himself from Hutcheson's reduction of morality to benevolence to the detriment of an adequate account of why we *have to* be just (*PMNR* 31; cf. *PE* 30–2).

Though Hutcheson had used the term 'sympathy' this comes to the fore in Hume and Smith (especially). Following Hutcheson, Hume does *not* accept Hobbes' argument that humans are *only* self-interested and in many passages he stresses human sociality and its importance (for example, *T* 2.2.4.4/*SBNT* 353; *T* 2.2.5.15/*SBNT* 363). The support for this is 'common experience' since if that is consulted then the finding is that 'kind affections' outweigh the selfish (*T* 3.2.2.5/*SBNT* 487). Such kind affections as meekness, beneficence, charity, generosity, clemency and the like are both *natural* and social virtues (*T* 3.3.1.11/ *SBNT* 578; cf. *M* 5, 3/ *SBNM* 214, *E-OC* 479). The undeniable evidence of their existence means that Hume is forthright in dismissing the Hobbesian/ Mandevillean view that *all* moral distinctions are the product of the 'artifice of politicians' (*M* 5, 3/*SBNM* 214; cf. *T* 3.2.2.25/*SBNT* 500, *T* 3.3.1.11/*SBNT* 578). Yet, and here is the clear break from Hutcheson, since even these social virtues cannot sustain society then, as we outlined in Chapter 4, for that task justice and other artifices are needed. Having established that justice is useful Hume still has to explain why it is also 'virtuous'. This explanation is all the more necessary because, as he admits, it was established out of self-interest (*T* 3.2.2.24/*SBNT* 499). From our perspective this can be read as Hume's attempt to underwrite a morality suitable for a commercial society.

To establish a link between virtue and self-interest he calls upon the principle of 'sympathy'. This principle takes us 'out of ourselves' (*T* 3.3.1.11/*SBNT* 579). Its pivot is a process whereby my 'idea' of a stranger's 'unease' (such as suffering an injustice) is 'converted into the very impressions' so that I too feel the uneasiness (*T* 2.1.11.7/*SBNT* 319). Now given that 'every thing which gives uneasiness in human actions upon the general survey is call'd Vice' (*T* 3.2.2.24/*SBNT* 499) then, though I am materially unaffected by that particular act of injustice, I nonetheless condemn it. In this way sympathy 'produces our sentiment of morals' in all the artificial virtues (*T* 3.3.1.10/*SBNT* 577). Sympathy is not itself a moral principle yet neither do we require, like Hutcheson, a direct moral sense to identify the virtue of justice.

The very technicality (cf. Mercer 1972: 44) of Hume's account rendered it vulnerable. Kames, for example, in direct rebuttal thinks it inadequate for the task Hume as allotted to it (*PMNR* 32, 19). In part recognition of this, Hume in his later discussion of justice drops the references to an 'abstruse' system of sympathy and declares that it is sufficient to accept as a fact the presence in human nature of 'humanity or fellow-feeling' so that no-one is indifferent to the happiness or misery of others (*M* 5,18n/*SBNM* 219–20n). This later vocabulary was commonplace. Ferguson, for example, in the one chapter in the *Essay* ('Of Moral Sentiment') explicitly devoted to 'moral questions', sees in the 'amicable disposition' the foundation of our moral nature whereby our 'sense of a right' is extended by a 'movement of humanity' to our fellow-creatures (*ECS* 35, 37). In the later systematic *Principles* he states that 'humanity' is the name given to a 'principle of sympathy and indiscriminate concern in the condition of a fellow creature' (*PMPS* I, 125). Virtually Millar's only reference to moral issues in his published work is his remark that it is 'feelings of humanity' that dispose mankind to abstain from injustice (*HV* IV, 4/773).[12] We will come back to 'humanity'.

Smith's account of sympathy is by far the most extensive and one that he continued to refine through the various editions of the *Moral Sentiments*. There exists considerable scholarship on this issue[13] and in accordance with my professed selective approach I will confine myself to one aspect. He admits that each individual has a 'natural preference [. . .] for his own happiness above that of other people' (*TMS* II.ii.2.1/82). It is, however, he believes a weakness of the Hobbesian/

Mandevillean view that it cannot accommodate the fact that the inter-actions of social life 'humble the arrogance of self-love' so that no-one 'dares to look mankind in the face' and admit he acts according to the principle of self-preference (*TMS* II.ii.2.1/83). This ocular language is a key motif. Humans are social beings and living in society is like looking in a mirror (*TMS* III.i.3.3/110; cf. Hume *T* 2.2.5.21/*SBNT* 365, *M* 9, 10/*SBNM* 276). Just as the mirror allows us to see our own appearance so life in society enables us to see the impact of our behaviour on others. A crucial effect of this exposure to the social gaze is that 'a human creature' will observe that others approve of some of his actions and disapprove of others with the consequence, for Smith, that he 'will be elevated in the one case, and cast down in the other'. The explanation for this response lies in his account of the dynamics of sympathy.

For Smith it is a fact about human nature that 'nothing pleases more than to observe in other men a fellow-feeling with all the emotions of our own breast' (*TMS* I.i.2.1/13). (This pleasure, he notes, following Hutcheson, cannot be explained by those who would derive all our sentiments from self-love.) This is all the more significant since it is this fellow-feeling that is the root of moral judgment. If we, as spectators, through an act of imagination, replicate through sympathy the passions emoted by others in their situation then we sympathise and, in so doing, approve of the response (*TMS* I.i.3.1/16). It is a given fact of human nature that a spectator's sympathetic emotions are less intense than those of the party observed (the actor). It is equally a fact, given that humans are social beings, that the actor wishes the spectator's sympa-thy. In response to these facts the actor in order to induce 'harmony and concord' between his emotions and those of the spectator 'lowers his passion to that pitch in which the spectators are capable of going along with him' (*TMS* I.i.4.7/22). It is this responsiveness to others – pleasure in their approval, pain in their disapproval – that Smith used to explain why the rich parade their wealth while the poor hide their poverty. The rich value their possessions more for the esteem they bring than any utility (*TMS* II.iii.2.1/51) and it is this disposition to 'go along with the passions of the rich and powerful' that establishes the foundation for rank distinctions (*TMS* II.iii.2.3/52). Furthermore, and now one of the links to a commercial society becomes more evident, it is this desire for esteem that constitutes the key explanation of that incentive to better our condition mentioned above (*TMS* II.iii.2.1/50; cf. IV.i.10/183).

Accordingly, for Smith, it is 'the vanity, not the ease or the pleas-ure that interests us' and 'vanity is always founded upon the belief of our being the object of attention and approbation' (*TMS* I.iii.2.1/50). This is not some superseded pre-commercial aristocratic or feudal

phenomenon but part of what it means to live in society. This is reinforced by Smith's observation, and one that marks his distance from
Hobbes' narrowly conceived account of motivation, in his *Lectures*
that 'the whole industry of human life is employed not in procuring
the supply of the three humble necessities, food, cloaths and lodging,
but in procuring the conveniences of it according to the nicety and
delicacy of our taste' (*LJB* 209/488). Of course, in line with the trajectory of natural history, this 'procurement' develops. This clearly bears
on commercial society. The society described, or implied, by Hume,
Smith and others is one where its members are status conscious. The
characteristic modern (commercial) form that this self-awareness takes
expresses itself in 'taste', which is tangibly exhibited through possessions. For example, much of Hume's discussion of the passions in Book
II of the *Treatise*, with its elaborate discussion of pride is a recognition
of this fact of 'common life'.[14] As we will discuss in Chapter 6, this can
become a cause for concern but there is a positive dimension since the
jostle for (even) 'prestige goods' produces, as Smith, observed industry.
Moreover, this form of competition is less destructive in commercial
society than in earlier times when the constraints of justice were looser
and where the 'great proprietors' made war 'almost continually upon
one another' (*WN* III.iv.9/418; cf. Hume *E-RA* 277) and where status
accrues to success in that field. As we will bring out, bellicosity and
attendant martial virtues come to be displaced by gentler, peaceful commercial virtues.

We can initially pursue this by seeing how this socio-moral interaction has direct bearing on Smith's analysis of commercial society.
As mentioned above, the very complexity of that society meant that
the bulk of inter-personal dealings were with strangers. According to
Smith's theory, an actor can expect less sympathy from a stranger than
from a friend.[15] This follows because Smith supposes, in an argument
reminiscent of Hume, that in earlier simpler ages, where dealings with
family and friends dominate, plenty of sympathy will be forthcoming. Given this then less effort is needed to 'tone down' the emotions.
Strangers, however, are less obliging (*TMS* I.i.4.9/23) and much greater
effort is required.

There are two related consequences of habitually living among strangers. The first is that individuals identify themselves (almost) with the
'impartial spectator' (*TMS* III.3.25/147; cf. III.3.38/153). This spectator
is an internalised standard of rectitude and plays the role traditionally
associated with conscience – he is 'the man within the breast, the great
judge and arbiter' (*TMS* III.2.32/130). This standard is anchored in
another of the facts that Smith attributes to human nature, namely, that

humans wish 'not only to be loved but to be lovely [. . .] not only praise but praiseworthiness' (*TMS* III.2.1/113–14). The result of this is that we are still pleased with having acted in a praiseworthy manner even if nobody praises us. We do not, therefore, in our conduct rely on actual praise or blame but seek to act in such a way that an 'impartial specta-tor' would approve of our conduct (*TMS* III.2.5/116). It is 'only by con-sulting this judge' that we can ever get a proper evaluative distance on our actions (*TMS* III.3.1/134). Everyman, he says later, is able to form gradually from his own 'observations upon the character and conduct of both himself and other people' an idea of 'exact propriety and perfec-tion' (*TMS* VI.iii.25/247). In other words, we can all potentially (since shortfall is always possible) establish an ideal or benchmark. By apply-ing to others as well as ourselves this benchmark in principle enables us to obtain a distance on social practices. Individuals and institutions can be judged as, for example, too heavily swayed by praise and insuf-ficiently attentive to the praiseworthiness of their endeavours. Hence Smith's criticism of the court of Louis XIV for lauding that monarch's mediocre talents and conversely for causing 'knowledge, industry, valour and beneficence' to lose respect (*TMS* I.iii.2.4/54).

The second consequence of the habitual effect of living among strangers is that the greater effort that is required to acquire sympathy serves to strengthen character. This enables the actor to attain a greater degree of moderation and exhibit more consistently the virtue of self-command in a commercial society than is possible in more tribal or clannish times (*TMS* III.3.24/146). In this way individuals in a commer-cial society are (in general terms) able to act 'according to the dictates of prudence, justice and proper beneficence' (*TMS* VI.iii.11/241). And not only is adherence to the 'sacred rules of justice' – the foundation of a commercial society – made possible but also adherence to the 'gentler exertions of self-command' gives 'lustre' to the distinctively commercial virtues of 'industry and frugality' (*TMS* VI.iii.13/242) (see below).

The reference here to self-command takes us back to the 'control' mandated by the Stoics, like Epictetus. The claim that Smith sub-scribes to Stoic tenets is often made (a classic statement is Macfie and Raphael's [1982] Introduction to the Glasgow Edition of *TMS* but they are hardly alone).[16] It would not be surprising if he did subscribe since that was a common stance. Ferguson, for example, openly admitted in the Introduction to his *Principles* that he 'may be thought partial to the Stoic philosophy' (*PMPS* I, 7).

However, there are good grounds to doubt Smith's affiliation. He flatly declares that, 'the plan and system which Nature has sketched out for our conduct seems to be *altogether different* from that of the Stoical philosophy' (*TMS* VII.ii.1/292; my emphasis). But more significantly these grounds can be seen to stem from his account of commercial society. Some of them will become apparent in Chapter 6 but we can here appositely recall from Chapter 3 (p. 81) Smith's affirmation of the 'joy of prosperity' as a striking example of his anti-Stoical position.[17] Another telling factor in distancing Smith from Stoicism is that the basis of his moral theory lies in the dynamics of social life. The thrust of the passage that likens society to a mirror is that morality is a matter of socialisation. Social intercourse teaches individuals what behaviour is acceptable and, in due course, these social judgments are internalised as conscience. Smith knows full well this is contrary to classical Stoicism with its depiction of a 'sage', who in the expression of his complete independence truly knows what is in his control. We can recall from Epictetus' account that the 'free man' is indifferent to his 'reputation', to the opinions (*doxai*) of others. In sharp contrast Smith declares that 'the sentiments of other people is the *sole* principle which, upon most occasions, overawes all those mutinous and turbulent passions' (*TMS* VI.concl.2 /263; my emphasis). For the Stoics the virtue of self-command derives from the rational will; in Smith its source is social interaction. Moreover, the exercise of this virtue, as we noted above, improves as the requirements of living among strangers, the inter-dependency characteristic of a commercial society, assist sympathetic concord (cf. *TMS* V.2.8–10/205–06; I.i.4.7/22). This inter-dependence is the decisive factor that distinguishes Smith from Rousseau and we will pick up that argument in Chapter 6.

But there is one passage in particular that is frequently cited in support of Smith's Stoic credentials. This is when he contrasts, on the one hand, the deceptive satisfaction afforded by the palaces of the rich and the 'pleasures of wealth and greatness' that 'strike the imagination as something grand, beautiful and noble' with, on the other, 'real happiness' – understood as 'ease of body and peace of mind', a condition that can be possessed by all ranks, even beggars (*TMS* IV.1.9.10/183, 185). (Epictetus was a slave while the other major late Stoic, Aurelius, was an emperor.) However, his argument is more subtle than a piece of Stoic moralising. The full import of this passage is positive (Hundert 1994: 222; Berry 1997: 44–5). While individuals may be deceived in thinking wealth brings happiness, the pursuit of that deception does nonetheless produce the blessing of opulence. Hence, *in this same passage*, Smith proceeds to identify these benefits. This deception 'raises and keeps in continual motion the industry of mankind' and it is through these means that the earth has been transformed, cities founded, population increased and provided for and 'all the sciences and arts which ennoble and embellish human life' have been invented (*TMS* IV.1.10/183). The implication is that if Stoic (or Rousseauan) precepts had been adhered to, that is, had mankind confined themselves to 'real' satisfactions, then human life would have been miserably poor (and unhappy). Indeed Smith later calls the cultivation of land, the advancement of manufactures and increase of commerce (opulence) 'real improvements' through which 'mankind are benefited' and 'human nature ennobled' (*TMS* VI.ii.2.3/229). This last phrase has a particular further significance. It underlines the distance between Smith's position and an anti-Stoic neo-Augustinian moral psychology, despite claims, themselves evidentially strained even via Mandeville, that have been made that his argument is especially indebted to it.[18]

This discussion in Book IV of the *Moral Sentiments* is where Smith makes his only reference in that book to the 'invisible hand' (*TMS* IV.1.10/184). It too has been read to reflect a neo-Stoic Providentialist account of nature and society[19] but it is more plausibly a particular expression (a metaphorical flourish) of the more general phenomenon of 'unintended consequences'. It is true Smith does here invoke Providence but it is hard to give this much substance,[20] especially since he does not see all cases of unintended consequences as benign – the growth of national debt and stultifying effects of the division of labour being two notably malign cases that we will discuss in Chapter 6.

Leaving Hume to one side,[21] it is indubitably the case that Providence is frequently invoked by the Scots. David Allan (1993: 207–17) has argued that the recognition of 'unintended consequences' is part of their Presbyterian Calvinist legacy, though he is sparing in specifics (but we can recall Halyburton's use of the phrase 'invisible hand' [p. 30n]).[22] Kames frequently evokes Providence and the fact that thinkers like Reid, Blair and Robertson were professional clerics (and Ferguson had been ordained) is not merely incidental. What 'Providence' generally betokens is the view, supported by 'science', that Nature comprises a systematic order or Design. Ferguson expresses the common view that 'it is proofs of design from which we infer the existence of God' (*ECS* 6). This was easily coupled with the idea of benign superintending Providence. The geometric properties of honeycombs were for Reid the work of the 'great Geometrician' who designed the bee rather than the bee itself (1846: 546–7; Ferguson too cites the bee to the same point in *ECS* 182; it had been the subject of a paper by Maclaurin as Reid acknowledges). And Kames' writings abound with references to 'beautiful final causes'. Smith too on occasion employs that vocabulary (see *TMS* II.ii.3.5/87) and it is seemingly redolent of a latent Aristotelianism. Some commentators, while making a number of caveats, have attempted to align Smith with that outlook but like the Stoic alignment this too seems strained.[23]

## COMMERCIAL VIRTUES

Like all other 'states of society' the age of commerce generates certain ways of acting, a distinctive set of manners and norms (a *Sittlichkeit*). Directly echoing Smith's remark that everyman is a sort of merchant, Millar declares that the 'mercantile spirit is not confined to tradesmen or merchants; from a similarity of situation it pervades in some degree all orders and ranks and by the influence of habit and example it is communicated, more or less, to every member of the community' (*HV* IV, 6/777). The references here to 'habit and example' reveal the soft determinism to which he, and his fellow natural historians, subscribe (see p. 72 above); a point underwritten by his next sentence, 'individuals form their notions of propriety according to a general standard, and fashion their morals in conformity to the prevailing taste of the times' (see similarly Smith *TMS* V.2.7/204).

What are 'the morals' fashioned by commerce? What are the distinctively 'commercial virtues'? A little earlier in his text Millar had observed that as social intercourse extends (that is, as society gets more complex) it 'requires more and more a mutual trust and confidence, which cannot be maintained without the uniform profession and rigid practice of honesty and fair-dealing' (*HV* IV, 6 /773). Ferguson, in an aside, refers to 'punctuality and fair-dealing' as the 'system of manners' of merchants (*ECS* 189; cf. identically *IMP* 39). Once again a Smithian precedent is identifiable. In his Glasgow lectures Smith observed that 'when the greater part of the people are merchants they always bring probity and punctuality into fashion' so that these are 'the principal virtues of a commercial nation' (*LJB* 328/539). That these virtues are pre-eminent is a direct reflection of the need for predictability and confidence in future-oriented 'market' dealings. This is 'diametrically opposite' to 'rude nations' so that, as we have noted, 'barbarians are but seldom acquainted with the rules of justice [and] [. . .] have seldom any regard to their promises' (Millar *HV* IV, 6/774). This contrast opens the way for a progressive history of 'civilisation'.

Hume's essays of the 1750s can be instructively read from this perspective. From his essay 'Of Refinement of Arts' we can pick up again his statement that 'industry, knowledge and humanity are linked together by an indissoluble chain and are found [. . .] to be peculiar to the more refined and, what are commonly denominated, the more luxurious ages' (*E-RA* 271). This trio stands in marked (and almost symmetrical) contrast to the 'ignorance, sloth and barbarism' employed slightly later (1758) (*E-JT* 328). The indissolubility here signals the shared position of the Scots that societies form synchronic wholes, which we will explore in Chapter 7.

We have already met 'industry', the first component in the initial trio, in Smith's account of how the earth has been transformed. The governing presumption is that humans are indolent. Robertson described the 'efforts' of those in 'the early ages of society' as 'few and languid' (*HAm* 819). This description was also typically applied to the Highlanders. Thomas Pennant his *Tour* of 1769 judged them 'indolent to a high degree, unless roused to war and as 'idle and lazy except when employed in the chace' (though he admits the women are 'more industrious') (1979: 193, 117). Smith observes that 'our ancestors were idle' but he proceeds to attribute this not to some supposed 'natural attribute' but to 'want of a sufficient encouragement to industry' (*WN* II.iii.12/335). In Hume, and in line with the 'revolution' that ushered in commerce, that encouragement is a 'desire for a more splendid way of life than what their ancestors enjoyed' (*E-Com* 264).

Hume typically associates, though not exclusively, industry with 'frugality' (*M* 6, 21/*SBNM* 243; *M* 9, 12/*SBNM* 277; *M* App, 4, 2/ *SBNM* 313). This association reflects a shift. *Frugalitas* meant living simply, in accordance with the requirements of natural needs (see, for example, Seneca 1932a: no. 5). Similarly, neo-Stoics, like Sir George Mackenzie in 1691, enjoined 'us [to] embrace ancient Frugality, under whose empire Vice was of old curbed with great success and which by freeing us from Poverty, secures us against all Snares which it occasions' (1711: 292) and, even more recently, it had been lauded by Berkeley in his *Essay* (1953: VI, 74). In this line of reasoning, frugality, along with austerity and poverty, was a component of what Hume calls 'severe' morality (*E-RA* 269), that exemplified a worthy (*honestum*) life. This stood in contrast, as characterised by Cicero (1913: I, 106/109), to a life devoted to luxury, softness and effeminacy (see Chapter 3 for this view of poverty and Chapter 6 for discussion of this contrast). Hume's context is different (and opposed). He employs the term against the background of the collapse of Smith's great proprietors and his own account of the emergence of commerce. Where there is nothing but 'a landed interest' he declares there will be 'little frugality' because landlords are 'prodigal' (*E-Int* 298–9; cf. Wallace *CGB* 125). But with the development of commerce we get an increase in industry. This he declares 'encreases frugality' because it gives rise to merchants ('one of the most useful races of men' [*E-Int* 300]) whose passion is love of gain.[24] They are not inclined to dissipate this on pleasure but 'beget industry' as they distribute resources through society. This sets in train a process whereby competition among traders reduces profits which causes a willing acceptance of low interest rates that makes commodities cheaper thus encouraging consumption and thereby 'heightening the industry' (*E-Int* 302–3). We know from earlier discussion that, since merchants 'covet equal laws', the concomitant of this is that commerce begets liberty.

As we quoted above, Smith, too, links frugality with industry and, like Hume, says it is directed at the 'acquisition of fortune' (*TMS* IV.2.8/190). Not only is this again contrary to Stoic teaching but also contrary to the prescriptions of thinkers like William Davenant, who, in 1698, issued the imperative that 'ancient frugality must be restored' (1771: IV, 424). Whereas Hume had aligned frugality with merchants, Smith thinks the 'principle of frugality' predominates in 'the greater part of men' over their lifetimes (*WN* II.iii.28/342). In his discussion, following classical precedent (cf. Cicero 1927: III, 8/245), Smith links frugality with the virtue of prudence.

Of all the virtues prudence is the one most useful to ourselves (*TMS* IV.2.6/189); its 'proper business' is care for one's health, fortune, rank and reputation (*TMS* VI.1.5/213). It is in 'the steadiness of his industry and frugality', in sacrificing present advantage for greater return later, that the prudent man's conduct is approved by the impartial spectator (*TMS* VI.1.11/215). Although it is not the 'most ennobling of virtues' it fits the circumstances of a society of merchants. The dispositions of this prudent man of commerce, because he does not agitate to involve himself in public service or in the pursuit of 'solid glory' (*TMS* VI.1.13/216), represent, as we will see in Chapter 6, for Ferguson, a danger in commercial society. For Smith, commercial society hinges, as we have seen, on justice and, importantly, adhering to that virtue does not rely on noble characters merely on prudent ones.[25] Moreover, the tempering of conduct that an assembly of strangers induces, means this (commercial) society can be harmonious; it can experience 'concord' (which is 'all that is wanted and required') if not 'unison' (*TMS* I.i.4.7/22). Though Smith does not make the point, it is difficult to see how the inherent pluralism of a society marked by the individually identified desires that stimulate the pursuit and enjoyment of natural liberty could comport with one marked by the singularity of purpose that seemingly constitutes 'unison'.

But given Hume's imagery of the indissoluble chain, industry (frugality and prudence) does not operate in isolation; developments in one component of the trio affect and are affected by developments in the other two. Hence 'industry is much promoted by the knowledge inseparable from ages of art and refinement', while reason 'refines' itself 'by exercise and by an application to the more vulgar arts, at least, of commerce and manufacture' (*E-RA* 273). Moreover, 'industry' and 'refinements in the mechanical arts' go along with 'refinements' in the liberal, so 'we cannot reasonably expect that a piece of woollen cloth will be wrought to perfection in a nation which is ignorant of astronomy or where ethics are neglected' (*E-RA* 270–1). (Note again the synchronicity assumed here.) That uncivilised nations are ignorant, and as a consequence superstitious, is an enduring theme across the Enlightenment. A significant indicator of a commercial society is that its citizens no longer live distantly from one another (a characteristic peculiar to 'ignorant and barbarous nations'), but flock into cities. Aptly enough 'civility' becomes a valued modality (Boyd 2008). As Robertson pointed out cities gave rise to 'polished manners' (*VP* 319). One example of this, that Hume picks up, is that in cities both sexes meet in an 'easy and sociable manner'. This is part and parcel of a distinctively commercial way of life; its manners and virtues. As we remarked at the beginning of this chapter, one manifestation of this is the advance in the status of women. It is a consequence of this advance, as Hume remarks, that together with the 'improvements' in knowledge and liberal arts, both sexes 'must feel an encrease of humanity' (*E-RA* 271).

Humanity, the third link in the chain, we have also already met as Hume's replacement for the role played by sympathy in the *Treatise*. The term carries a lot of historical baggage[26] but its membership of this trio indicates a significant and wider-ranging set of associations. As we indicated in Chapter 4 there is a distinctively modern twist to humanity. Once men are 'less oppressed with their own wants' then they are 'at more liberty to cultivate the feelings of humanity' (Millar *OR* 176). Hume had developed the implicit link here with sentiment. He associates humanity with the softening of 'tempers' or emotional dispositions (*E-RA* 274) and contrasts this to the severity of ancient moralists like Epictetus. Smith ties these humane sentiments to a heightened sensitivity to the feelings of others, 'a humane and polished people [. . .] have more sensibility to the passion of others' (*TMS* V.2.10/207). In a comment, the full force of which will become apparent in Chapter 6, he at one point identifies 'humanity' as 'the virtue of a woman' (*TMS* IV.2.10/190). Against the sensitivity of the humane he contrasts the 'hardiness demanded of savages', as manifest in their resistance to and infliction of torture. But this behaviour 'diminishes their humanity' (*TMS* V.2.11, 13/209).

While this hardiness might look like an exemplary exhibition of the virtue of self-command this is misleading. I differ here from Maureen

Harkin's (2002: 29) reading that this betrays Smith's 'extremely' 'ambivalent account of modernity'. As I interpret it, this savage (Stoic) self-command, when compared to that exercised by civilised peoples is more a matter of repression (Berry 1997: 139). Its putative exemplary status is further undermined because it is rather the civilised than the savage man who exhibits 'the most exquisite humanity [and] is naturally the most capable of acquiring the highest degree of self-command' (*TMS* III.3.36/152). The savage's behaviour is all the more unedifying given its association with 'falsehood and dissimulation' once again compared to the 'frank, open and sincere' habits of a 'polished people' (*TMS* V.2.11/208; cf. Hume on treachery as the 'usual concomitant of ignorance and barbarism' [*E-NC* 211]). The virtuous humanity of a commercial people (along with their truthfulness and justice) is rewarded with the 'confidence, the esteem and love' of their fellows (*TMS* III.5.8/166). And since, as we sketched out above, Smith's moral theory hinges on responsiveness to others then these virtues will establish themselves and individuals will act accordingly. In addition, because the 'good opinion' of others is always desired then it will produce 'regular conduct' (*TMS* I.iii.3.5/63) or, in other words, the rule-governed, predictable behaviour necessary to the functioning of a commercial society.

Ferguson too remarks on the salience of humanity. In the manner of Hume (see p. 76 above) he identifies it as the 'principal characteristic' of civilisation that the 'laws of war' have been 'softened', while Millar declares that killing one's enemies is 'disgusting to humanity' (*HV* IV, 6/754). In that same passage Ferguson further observes that glory consists in protecting the vanquished not destroying them (*ECS* 199–200). Nonetheless he fears that commercial states tend to exhibit a 'contempt for glory' (*ECS* 258). Glory is 'won' on the battlefield by exhibiting courage, the definitive martial virtue. I will return to that virtue in Chapter 6 but here it is apt to examine how that virtue, in particular its association with bellicosity, sits uneasily with the commercial virtues. Smith, Hume and Millar all throw doubt on the propriety of courage (or fortitude) in the modern world.

Millar stipulatively distinguishes between courage and fortitude. The former is active, the latter is passive. He thinks the latter is practised in the 'infancy of society' because it is 'the want of humanity' that makes it apt (*HV* IV, 6/747–8). By contrast, the 'lively sensibility and exquisite fellow-feeling which in opulent and polished nations take place among individuals are [. . .] peculiarly unfavourable to fortitude'. This fellow-feeling is the product of the commercial 'mode of life', which comprises 'regular government', 'tranquillity' and a 'secure and comfortable situation' which with the establishment of more 'intimate conversation' has 'softened' manners' (*HV* IV, 6/751). Millar draws implicitly on his historical and ethnographical sources (on which see Fauré 1997) to declare that 'savage nations [. . .] in all parts of the world are said to be cowardly and treacherous' (*HV* IV, 6/749) thus courage is exhibited when a sense of chivalry and honour is developed (he mentions duels) (*HV* IV, 6/748; cf. Hume *E-RA* 274). However, it too has been altered by the 'improvement of commerce and manufactures' so that 'the customs of chivalry' and 'punctilios of military honour' are 'plainly contrary to the manners of a commercial people' (*HV* IV, 6/750, 752).

Smith does not include courage in his dedicated section on virtue in the *Moral Sentiments*. Since this was one of the four classical cardinal virtues (along with justice, temperance and prudence, which he does consider) this omission is significant but in the light of this discussion unsurprising (pace Raphael 2007: 73). Smith does not question that command of fear is virtuous (see Chapter 6 on the deleterious effects of the division of labour) but observes that 'the most intrepid valour may be employed in the cause of the greatest injustice' and because it can be used to equal effect to good or bad ends then it can be 'excessively dangerous' (*TMS* VI.iii.12/241; cf VI.concl.7/264). Hume too acknowledges that courage and love of glory are species of heroic virtue and are on the face of it 'much admir'd' but those of 'cool reflection' are inclined to regard heroism as mischievous and a 'suppos'd virtue' (*T* 3.3.3.13–15/ *SBNT* 599–601; cf Baier 1991: 210). The time for heroes has passed; they cause disorder and they would be out of place in a society where order is premised on predictability. He gives this view a clear historical perspective – 'it is indeed observable that among all uncultivated nations who have not as yet had full experience of the advantages attending beneficence, justice and the social virtues, courage is the predominant excellence' (*M* 7, 15/*SBNM* 255). In his *History* he remarks, referring to sixteenth-century Scotland, that when 'arms' prevail over 'laws' then 'courage preferably to equity or justice was the virtue most valued and respected' (*HE* II, 81; cf. I, 115 on the Anglo-Saxons).

It is accepted that courage has only a limited role in a commercial society. The frequent approbative references to 'softness', that we have already come across, are indicative of the line of thought that is captured in the expression, '*doux commerce*' (Hirschman 1977: 60). The expression occurs in Montesquieu. In Book 20 of *De l'Esprit des Lois* he states that commerce polishes and softens barbarous manners (*adoucit les moeurs barbares*) and that its natural consequence is to induce peace (*porter à la paix*) (1961: II, 8). As Hirschman points out

Montesquieu's wording was closely followed by Robertson. Indeed he provides one of the clearest expositions of this position:

> commerce tends to wear off those prejudices which maintain distinction and animosity between nations. It softens and polishes the manners of men. It unites them by one of the strongest of all ties, the desire of supplying their mutual wants. It disposes them to peace [. . .] (*VP* 333)

This picture, alongside what Montesquieu called '*un certain sentiment de justice exacte*' (1961: II, 9), effectively captures a core factor in what distinguishes a commercial society. Like all forms of society it develops its own set of norms of virtues or puts its own twist upon their expression in earlier forms. But for all the broad endorsement of the commercial way of life this was not given unquestioningly. Indeed, among the Scots and indeed across the Enlightenment, it was the subject of intense debate, as the next chapter will reveal.

## NOTES

1. Kames incorporated reference to this case in the 3rd edition of his *Principles of Equity* (1778). That a form of slavery was present vestigially in contemporary Scotland in the circumstances of colliers and salters, who were bound to work for life in those occupations, was regretfully acknowledged by Millar. This 'pernicious' practice he believes is manifestly to the detriment of the proprietor and likely to be imminently abolished (*OR* 319) (this occurred in 1799 after an unsuccessful attempt in 1774).

2. Stuart, typically, is an exception to this consensus. He carries his disputes with Robertson, Kames and Millar into denying that women were in an abject state of servility before property (*VSE* 11). Stuart's interpretation is discussed in Sebastiani (2005).

3. This term is employed (by Zeno for example [Diogenes Laertius 1925: 110]) as a form of excessive impulse *(hormê)* and more specifically as an irrational mode of *orexis* [Diogenes Laertius 1925: 113]. It was thus a negatively loaded term and distinct from 'desire' qua *orexis* as employed by Epictetus (see text above). For the difference between the terms see Inwood (1985: 167) and Nussbaum (1986: 275). *Epithumia* was typically employed when discussing the 'body' and can be translated often as 'appetite' and was taken over by Christian theologians.

4. The evident element of relaxation here mirrors the development of Stoicism, especially in its Roman form. Seneca despite his generally censorious tone was himself a rich man who wrote an essay *De Vita Beata* that contained a defence of wealth (1932b: pars 21–6). This development was also affected by the Stoics' need, as by now a mainstream position, to distinguish their position from the notoriety of the Cynics, who took 'living according to nature' to extremes (popularly captured by the image

of Diogenes living in a barrel [Zeller 1885: 317]) as well as by a reformulation of the role of the 'sage' or *sapiens* from judge to therapist (Griffin 1976: 170). Epictetus, though chronologically a late Stoic, represents a throwback to the earlier austere formulation, hence, in part, the starkness of his teaching, though despite some favourable references to Diogenes he retained the antipathy to the Cynics (see *Discourses* [1928: 4, 11]). For a discussion of this relation see Schofield 2007.

5. That Smith is to be firmly located in this 'early modern consensus' is the key theme in Joseph Cropsey's (2001) interpretation of his thought first published in 1957.

6. John Salter (1994: 312) contends in a critique of Hont and Ignatieff (1983) that Smith's view of justice did not require him to attend to the needs of the poor, even if his view of humanity did, but even then he was unprepared to make unrealistic claims that 'extreme inequality and oppression' would be compensated for. This, of course, is distinct from denying that Smith disavows the applicability of moral criteria to commercial society.

7. That, when properly construed, self-love and benevolence were not in conflict was a major theme of Butler's *Sermons* (1964), whose writings were influential among the Scots; indeed Hutcheson's later thought has been characterised as 'Butlerised' (Filonowicz 2008: 236), though Moore (2000: 250), for one, doubts Butler is decisive. For Smith and Butler see Raphael 2007 and Forman-Barzilai 2010.

8. This is distinct from that associated with E. P. Thompson. He used it to refer to the legitimating function of traditional rights and customs, which he contrasted to the 'new political economy', whereby the economy was 'disinfected of moral imperatives' and of which Smith is identified as an exponent (Thompson 1991a: 201ff). For a critique of this see Hont and Ignatieff 1983 and also Thompson's reply in which he denies he was arguing that Smith was operating in a moral vacuum (Thompson 1991b: 271, 268–9).

9. See Forman-Barzilai for a measured assessment of Smith's 'cautious appropriation' (2010: 7; cf. Chap. 4). For the Stoics themselves see Annas (1993: 262f), she translates *oikeiosis* as 'familiarisation'.

10. Rousseau makes this distinction (though it does originate with him) in his *Discours de l'ineqalité parmi les hommes* (1755) (1962: 118), reviewed by Smith in the *Edinburgh Review* (*Letter* 11–17/250–4). In that essay Rousseau referred to Mandeville and Smith picked up on that in his review. Mandeville for his part had distinguished between 'self-love' and 'self-liking' (1988: II, 129). For a subtle investigation of Smith's usage see Heath 2013.

11. Although Shaftesbury had used the term 'moral sense' Hutcheson's usage reflected his adoption of Locke's empiricism (despite some qualms on the consequences that can be drawn from the rejection of innate ideas [*PW* 35]). This divergence from Shaftesbury put him firmly in the 'modernist

camp'. This is captured by William Leechman (contemporary Professor of Divinity [1743–61] at Glasgow) who in his 'Account' of Hutcheson's life, observed that Hutcheson had seen how 'natural philosophy had been carried to a greater degree of perfection than ever it was before' and was convinced that 'only by pursuing the same method' could 'a more exact theory of morals' be formed (see his link between benevolence and gravitation, p. 22 above). In addition, by basing this moral sense in universal human experience, Hutcheson, as Daniel Carey (2006: 100) puts it, 'democratised the moral sense'. This further served to differentiate his argument from Shaftesbury's version, which presupposed a level of aristocratic detachment and sensibility (as well as a Deist disposition that went against Hutcheson's deep Presbyterian commitments). That Hutcheson's 'universalism' fails because the natural theology on which it is dependent is based on the Lockean empiricism is argued by Elton (2008), developing an interpretation put forward by MacIntyre (1998: 289).

12. In his Glasgow lectures Millar as part of his duties covered Ethics and its relation to Jurisprudence – see 'Notes on Lectures on *Institutes of Justinian according to Heineccius* (1789) in Glasgow University Library (MS Gen 812). The influence of Smith is apparent.

13. For example, Griswold 1999, Broadie 2006, Otteson 2002, Forman-Barzilai 2010, Frazer 2010.

14. See Christopher J. Finlay's comment that Hume provides a 'sophisticated account of the kinds of social bonds that were both required and reinforced by the interactions of consumers on commercial societies' (2007: 42 and see Chapters 6 and 7 for an insightful elaboration of this position). See also James Harris (2010: 35) who remarks, of *Treatise* Book II, that according to Hume humans are 'pre-eminently concerned with social status and with the things that confer such status, including material possessions, rank and reputation'.

15. Griswold (1999: 142 and throughout) refers to 'circles of sympathy' (a term that Forman-Barzilai incorporated into the title of her book [2010]). Otteson (2002: Chap. 5) somewhat similarly refers to the 'familiarity principle'.

16. See, for example (and notwithstanding differences between them) Force 2003, Turco 2003, Fitzgibbon 1995, Muller 1995, Waszek 1984.

17. See also his observation that the 'condition of human nature' would be 'peculiarly hard' if the affections which naturally affect our conduct could 'upon no occasion appear virtuous' (*TMS* VII.ii.3.18/305). For commentary on human nature in Smith see Berry 2012.

18. The work of Pierre Nicole (1625–95) is particularly invoked in this context but, even leaving aside that there is no room for 'ennoblement' in his Augustinian view of human nature, any direct impact is at best inferential. He had read and was influenced by Hobbes (Malcolm 2002: 509). Nicole himself argued, as part of his Jansenist critique of the Stoics, that '*un amour-propre éclairé*' could 'outwardly'(*au-dehors*) replicate

a society '*trés réglée*', although 'inwardly' (*au-dedans*) and in the sight of God this might be corrupt (1999: 408). That is to say, although self-love is intrinsically pride-full, greedy and envious yet this nature has to be hidden or disguised when dealing with others, including conducting the business of commerce (1999: 384; cf. 213) and in the generation of *civilité* (1999: 182). This interaction indeed produces (we might say) a sort of self-deception (cf.1999: 409). Mandeville in Brooke's (2012: 155) phrase gave a 'secularizing twist' to this account in his own critique of the Stoics. (That Mandeville was in fact a sincere Augustinian is argued by Burtt [1992: Chap. 7].) Phillipson (2010: 61) claims that Mandeville and Smith 'must have known' Nicole's work but regarding Smith this 'necessity' is not based on any direct textual evidence. Forman-Barzilai (2010: 38n, 40) concedes Smith's familiarity with Nicole 'appears to be mostly secondary' but that Mandeville 'doubtless' drew on him, noting that Mandeville does refer to him in a later writing (*Free Thoughts on Religion*, 1729), which Smith is presumed to have 'likely' encountered. However, Mandeville's particular references there do not speak to the matter at hand. Forman-Barzilai also judges that Butler employed 'concepts and categories strikingly similar to Nicole' and that Smith was 'influenced by the Nicole-Butler orientation to "enlightened or "reasonable self-love"' (2010: 40, 42). Muller (1995: 51) quotes the usual passages from Nicole (plus also from another Augustinian, Jean Domat, who borrowed from Nicole) but makes no express claim for influence. Domat (from the English translation [1722] of his *Lois Civiles* [1689]) is also quoted identically by Hutchinson [1988: 101–2] to whom, along with more significantly Nicole, Mandeville was 'importantly indebted'. Hutchinson also claims Nicole 'anticipate[d] precisely' Smith's comment on the butcher, baker and brewer but such precision is elusive, while Wootton (1986: 75) holds Nicole 'provided in embryo the key arguments of the opening chapters of Adam Smith's *Wealth of Nations*' and even that it is to Nicole 'that we owe the first clear formulation of the new philosophy of commercial society'. Almost all of this is presumptive and the whole Jansenist connection should be treated with great scepticism.

19. See Force 2003: 74; Macfie 1967: 107; Murphy 1993: 193ff; Otteson 2002: 245ff; Young 1997; Alvey 2003: 267; Forman-Barzilai 2010. Not that these thinkers adopt a uniform position or are in necessary agreement with each other. For an explicitly historical overview see Vivenza 2001.
20. Smith's own beliefs are hard to discern. Ian Ross (2010: 432) confined himself to saying 'there is no great evidence that Smith set stock in an after-life'. Some commentators do see in his thought a principled theistic or Deistic commitment (see for example Evensky 2005, especially Chap. 4 but throughout, Hanley 2009a, Otteson 2002, Young 1997). For a subtle account of a duality between theological presupposition and secular empiricism in Smith see Tanaka 2003 and also Campbell 1971. For a thorough biographical account of Smith and religion see Kennedy 2013.

21. Hume's common reputation was as an infidel, even though in deference to his friends he arranged for his most subversive work (*Dialogues concerning Natural Religion*) to be published posthumously.
22. Anand Chitnis (1976: 254), as part of his argument that the Enlightenment themes of improvement and reform were stirring before the eighteenth century, also invokes the Calvinist legacy. See also Emerson 1989.
23. For example, Calkins and Werhane (1998: 50) claim that on a practical level Smith's and Aristotle's notion of human flourishing differ 'very little', though they immediately say 'Smith's scheme lacks Aristotle's focus on the telos or universal and final end of happiness'. Hanley (2007: 20, 19) charts similarities in Smith's and Aristotle's substantive accounts, as well as their conceptions of methods and ends of ethics, but admits there are 'crucial differences' between Smith and Aristotle that 'may be insurmountable'. Fleischacker (1999: 120, 140) considers Smith as close to Aristotle while yet being crucially different.
24. This distinguishes Hume's view from Montesquieu's (1961: I, 52) portrayal of frugality in democracies. Though *l'esprit de commerce* brings with it inter alia *frugalité* and *travail* yet within *une république commerçante* (such as Athens) it serves to limit the *désir d'avoir* (1961: I, 47). In these republics frugality remains a severe virtue; it exemplifies a negative view of avarice (or Hume's love of gain). This affinity between frugality and this 'spirit' make it distinct from Hume's modern account of incentives and helps distinguish a commercial society from a mercantile republic. As we will also see in Chapter 6 Hume links virtue with luxury and does not oppose them, as is the case in these republics.
25. This is not to say Smith dismisses 'nobility' or the merits of 'superior prudence' but in the ordinary context of social (commercial) life their 'perfection' makes them extra-ordinary (commercial society functions effectively without heroes or sages). See Hanley (2009a: 43, 69) for a forceful (if perhaps at times a shade forced) argument that it is 'central' to Smith's moral philosophy that he distinguishes 'genuine transcendent virtue' from 'mere social propriety', with nobility a key example of the former and the 'recovery' of which was, on his interpretation, one of Smith's goals. Recall Smith's own references to 'ennoblement' (text above) are made in the context of material improvement.
26. We have already noted its role in jurisprudence, where it is the object of an imperfect right (see Reid 1990: 147) and, as a synonym for 'benevolence' it was distinguished from the perfect obligation to be just (see Chapter 5, p. 129). The Roman moralists gave it a broad meaning encompassing learning and culture as well as kindness and forgiveness (see Ferguson 1958: 116). The former of these passed into the Renaissance in the form of *studia humanitatis*, so that the professor of Humanity in the Scottish universities in the eighteenth century taught Latin.

# 6. *The Dangers of Commerce*

James Moore has remarked that the 'distinguishing feature' of the Scottish Enlightenment was 'intellectual disagreement' (2009: 180). While this point is well-taken it is something of an overstatement. That the Scots did not always see eye to eye is nowhere more apparent than in their shared realisation that commercial society had its drawbacks or flaws. The character and remediability of those deficiencies produced lively debate and is the chief focus of this chapter.

We can start by picking up the claim made in Chapter 5 that two strains in ancient liberty could be identified. One discussed in that chapter dealt with liberty as a state of tranquillity, where unruly desires were under the control of reason, the other to be discussed here dealt with liberty as a civic or political activity. To be free on this latter understanding meant positively acting as a citizen, participating in the *res publica*, with the significant negative corollary that a commercial life was less 'free' and must be confined to an appropriately limited sphere.

The roots of this twin-pronged argument lie in Aristotle. Man, he says famously, is by nature a creature of the *polis*.[1] Since for Aristotle humans only realise themselves when they act according to their nature, then being political, that is to say doing politics, is a fulfilment of their end (*telos*). 'Doing politics' meant participating in the public realm of the *polis*. Those who participated were *polites* or, using the Roman vocabulary, citizens. Citizens are active. As actors they enjoy a moral equality one with another and possess an educated ethical disposition to maintain the public good. Implicit in this characterisation is that citizens are also free or independent – Aristotle indeed defined the *polis* as 'a community of free men' (Aristotle 1944: 1279a23). Within this community, a citizen was the head of a household. The household looked after the instrumental business of mere living – it was the unfree

realm of women, slaves and animals. With his needs taken care of the
male head of the household had 'leisure' (*skole*) to devote himself to the
'good life', to intrinsically worthwhile activity, of which doing politics
was a central feature. This vision of active citizenship was rearticulated
by Roman political moralists. For them the citizen was one who devoted
his activity to the public affairs (*rei publicae*), whence the association
of this vision with 'republicanism'. Republican thought re-emerged in
the independent city-states of Renaissance Italy (with Machiavelli a
key figure) and from there it was transported into seventeenth-century
English thought (with Harrington a major exponent) and then into the
eighteenth century. This strain can be aptly called 'republican' liberty
(Goldsmith 1994: 197).

Alongside this account of the meaning of citizenship was an urgent
concern with what threatened it. The source of the particular threat
might differ but the threat itself retained the same structure. Again
its roots are Aristotelian. The intrinsically worthwhile public task of
politics should not be confused with the instrumental private purpose
of the household, and its governance (*oikonomikê*). Nor should that
be confused with the task of money-making (*chrêmatistikê*) (Aristotle
1944: 1256a). The household's function is to gather such goods as are
necessary to its function (meeting limited needs). This may be extended
to exchange, so a coat may be exchanged for some earthenware, as long
as the recipient uses it for its proper or natural purpose (*kata phusin*),
that is, the coat should not be produced for the sake of exchange but to
be worn, to meet the need for warmth and money can play a legitimate
role in facilitating this process. The danger is that this instrumental role
becomes perversely an end in itself. This was the nub of the enduring
threat, namely, that private interests would subvert the public good.
'Economics' and money-making (exchange) were cases in point.[2] By
extension both the desire for private aggrandisement (ambition), rather
than for public benefit, and the desire for goods for private consumption (avarice), rather than for the public treasury, corrupt the moral
framework that should govern the republic. In sum a worthwhile
human life is debased if it is spent slavishly pursuing private ends,
which were defined essentially by seeking the satisfaction of appetite
and desire (*epithumia*).

This negative reference to desire indicates the link to the first strain
of ancient liberty. This linkage is exemplified in the (negative) role allotted to luxury and the (positive) role played by poverty. We can see this
conjunction and its role in the second strain of ancient liberty in the
strategically placed Preface to Book 1 of Livy's history of Rome (*Ab
Urbs Conditur*):

No republic was ever greater, none purer [*sanctior*] or richer in good examples, none into which luxury and avarice entered so late or where poverty and parsimony were so honoured. It is true that the less wealth there was so there was less desire [*cupiditatis*]. More recently riches have imported avarice and excessive pleasures [*voluptates*] with a craving for luxury and licence [*desiderium per luxum atque libidinem*] to the ruination of ourselves and all things. (1919: I, pars 11–12 – translation amended)

This helped to set an influential template. Rome from a circumstance where poverty was honoured and virtue paramount succumbed to luxury and fell into decline. The causality at work here assumed a conception of 'virtue' as 'character'. Virtue (*arête*) is a form of practice that is attained through training or habituation whereby a natural disposition is developed and expresses itself in action; for Aristotle overseeing this is a proper task of 'legislators' (*nomothetai*) (1894: 1103b). From these premises it followed that a weak environment would produce a weak character.

A society where wealth is valued will produce a generation that is 'prey to luxury, avarice and pride' (Sallust 1921: par. 12). This society, it follows, will devote itself to private ends and men will be unwilling to act for the public good, where crucially central to such action is a willingness to fight. Once poisoned by luxury (Sallust 1921: par 11) they invest life itself with value and become afraid of death (Seneca 1932a: no. 124), with the consequence that the society will be militarily weak – a nation of cowards (those with a soft character) will easily succumb. While Sallust's account is strong on rhetoric (these passages are setting up his account of the Catilinean conspiracy), he is drawing upon a set of conventions that he reinforced. For example, Florus (second century AD) in his own history of Rome describes how Antiochus of Syria after having conquered some Greek islands then relaxed and spent his time in *otia* and *luxus* so that when he faced the Romans he was easily defeated (1943: I, 24). The only way a luxurious, soft nation or, not coincidentally, one devoted to trade could meet its military commitments was by hiring others to play that role. This established an important and long-lasting association between luxury, wealth (commerce) and mercenary armies, which was a mark of civic unfreedom. A free state depended on virtuous (free) men devoted to the public good for which they were willing to fight (and die). This encapsulates the civic strain of ancient liberty and this persisted from Aristotle's identification of bearing arms as a criterion of citizenship to the eighteenth-century republican constitution of Jefferson and his compatriots.

This is a complex legacy and that complexity itself fuels the debate. Defenders of trade and commerce from the seventeenth century onwards had to disarm its negative association with luxury and mercenaries. The former had to be demoralised (Berry 1994: Chap. 5) and the latter re-evaluated. On both fronts the classical notion of 'virtue' required a recalibration. We discussed an aspect of this in Chapter 5 but need now to develop the argument.

This initially will unfold in three stages. The first subsection looks again at the difference between the modern liberty as subscription to disinterested regulation (the rule of law) and this participatory strain of republican liberty before, secondly, proceeding to examine how the Scots debated the issues around the demoralisation of luxury and then, the final subsection, turning to their disagreements over the relative merits of a citizen militia as against a professional army. This discussion will lead on to the two final parts.

I

## PRIVATE AND PUBLIC LIBERTY

One way to capture the debate over liberty in a commercial society is to typify this as a dispute over whether liberty is centrally or predominantly a matter of public engagement or centrally and predominantly a matter of private choice. This is a question of balance; neither argument denies that the other has merit.

The thinker among the Scots who has been most identified with the former position is Adam Ferguson, especially in the *Essay*. Because his argument is the most telling example it is worth considering at some length. The declaration that 'man is not made for repose' (*ECS* 210; cf. 7, *PMPS* II, 508), that humans are naturally active, has been justifiably seen as a key leitmotif in Ferguson's thought (Smith 2008; Oz-Salzburger 2008). What is crucial is the arena in which this action should properly display itself. This can be appreciated if we contrast his position with that of Hume (see Finlay 2006: 44, though my point is rather different). Hume considers 'action' a key component in human happiness (*E-RA* 269–70). Hume here emphasises action in the form of 'industry'. This is itself a source of pleasure but consequentially is, as we saw in Chapter 5, the source of improvement – the development of the 'arts', both mechanical and liberal, and the concomitant growth of knowledge and humanity as the other components of the indissoluble chain (see p. 139 above). In an argument that we will develop in the next section, industry is prompted by 'avarice' and 'luxury' (*E-Com* 263–4). Hume is careful to argue that the 'public' benefits from this as well as individuals. But public benefit is measured by the progress

of the arts across the board, including the enhancement of liberty
(*E-RA* 277). The relevant current message from this is that Cicero's
*negotiis publicis*, the involvement in public or political affairs, is not
the direct focus of action, which, rather, lies in the private endeavour
of industry. The Ciceronic view captures the civic republican strain in
ancient liberty, in contrast, and for Cicero himself in preference to the
Epictetean strain, manifest in those who withdraw from the forum and
in their 'leisure' (*otium*) look for a tranquil, contemplative life (1913: I,
20–1).

Ferguson is in the Ciceronic mould. He believes that 'action' should
be exercised by citizens as members of 'the public' (*ECS* 214) and it is
misdirected when they focus on their 'private engagements' (*ECS* 255)
or aim to preserve their own separate 'gain' without 'any attention to
the commonwealth' (*ECS* 222). This last phrase signals Ferguson's
sympathy with the 'classical' position that 'politics' is what free men
do in contrast to 'economics' (the organisation and conduct of the
household) which is, in varying degrees, as we have already observed,
the necessitous or unfree sphere of women, slaves and animals. And to
devote oneself to trade or commerce was to involve oneself in 'private'
matters with the corollary, in this Aristotelian tradition, that compared
to a citizen in the full sense, that is, one who dedicated his life to the
public good, a merchant lived a less fulfilling, less humanly worthwhile,
life.[3]

That Ferguson has sympathy with this 'republican' position does
not mean he is wholeheartedly committed to it. Contrary to Lisa Hill
(1999: 44) and with Marco Guena (2002: 183), Ferguson is not nos-
talgic for a pre-commercial socio-economic order. He clearly rules out
slavery (*ECS* 161, 185; *PMPS* II, 472), on which social foundation he
recognises, like Hume and Smith, the classical republics reposed. While
he is thus far from denying the advantages and advances that a commercial society brings,[4] he is perturbed, in particular, by the implicit
devaluing of an active public life in that society; this for him is a significant danger. His concerns focus on the issue of liberty. He accepts
the 'modern' position that links liberty and the rule of law; 'we must
be contented' to get liberty and justice from the 'limits which are set to
the powers of the magistrate and to rely for the protection on the laws
which are made to secure the estate and the person of the subject' (*ECS*
161; cf. 261, *PMPS* II, 459–61). Yet even in this passage there is an
intimation that this is second best to a situation where, rather than law,
'virtue' is an 'object of state'. At the heart of Ferguson's misgivings is
his antipathy to the passivity that he sees this 'modern' view of liberty
engendering.

From Ferguson's perspective this is not an incidental flaw but intrinsic to the operation of the rule of law, the key principle of commercial society. Liberty, he declares, is 'never in greater danger than it is when we measure national felicity [. . .] by the mere tranquillity which may attend on equitable administration' (*ECS* 270). While tranquillity might be an individual 'ideal' to be attained by the Stoic sage, as a societal attribute it does not enjoy that honorific status in the civic republican strain of ancient liberty. What that means, and what Ferguson is lamenting, is that individual citizens are happy to allow the 'administration' to get on with its public task of enforcing the general rules of justice while they get on with their own private business. And from their individual point of view the less the administration interferes in the 'commercial and lucrative arts' the better. This is, of course, precisely what Smith thinks is desirable; government administers justice strictly and individuals enjoy their natural liberty to follow their own interests in their own way. But, for Ferguson, the effect of this 'indifference to objects of a public nature' (*ECS* 256) is precisely to endanger liberty itself, even to the extent, he proclaims in a rhetorical flourish, of producing a situation that is 'more akin to despotism than we are apt to imagine' (*ECS* 269).

By inculcating or permitting passivity modern liberty fails to protect the true values of liberty, a task at which ancient liberty was much more effective. Following the Livian tradition, Ferguson litters the *Essay* with examples from Roman history and was sufficiently convinced of the value of the 'lessons' of Rome that he wrote a multi-volume history of the republic. In that work he tells the familiar story of its decline from virtue into imperial corruption, with, as he announces in his Dedication, a focus on 'the latter times of the Republic'. His treatment of the relation between Rome and Carthage is appositely instructive. Their constitutions were 'in respect to mere form [. . .] nearly alike' (*Rom* I, 108) but, for Ferguson, that simply demonstrates the inadequacy of heeding formal structures. What really matters is the animating spirit. In Carthage that was one of 'rapacity' because in order to be great in that city one had to be rich, whereas among the Romans 'riches were of no account in constituting rank', because what counted there was 'rendering signal service to their country' (*Rom* I, 110, 122). Though Carthage was superior to Rome in commerce, this superiority was bought at the price of stifling 'the military character of their own citizens' which meant they had to have 'perpetual recourse to foreigners whom they trusted with their arms' (*Rom* I, 10). In contrast, the Romans' superiority lay in their 'national character' and 'public virtue' (*Rom* I, 108). This 'virtue' expressed itself in 'military spirit' (*Rom* I, 126), with the decisive consequence that in the ensuing struggle the citizen-soldiers of Rome were victorious over the Carthaginian mercenaries. Throughout the *History*, Ferguson conjoins 'military and political spirit' seeing therein the 'strength and security of states' (*Rom* I, 333, also inter alia III, 304; V, 396). Alas, by the time of Caesar and Pompey that 'austere virtue which confined the public esteem to acts of public utility' had become ineffectual 'antiquated notions' as the corruption attendant on 'extravagance and luxury' took hold (*Rom* III, 79, 98).

The lesson spelt out over these volumes reinforced Ferguson's diagnosis of the dangers that commercial society faced. Aside from Rome, Ferguson's other key model was Sparta. It was, indeed, Sparta that Ferguson depicted as the state whose 'sole object was virtue' and where also the preservation of 'civil liberty' resided in the 'dispositions' and in 'the hearts of its members' (*ECS* 158). Of course, he is under no illusions about the fundamental deficiencies of Sparta (not least because of its slavery) but it is those 'dispositions' that make it exemplary;[5] it is they that reveal the true value of liberty. Being a citizen, being a free man, requires active involvement in the running of the 'republic'. This should not be confused with 'democracy' as now understood. Ferguson's position, as outlined in the *Principles*, is that the number who participate is an important factor when evaluating government but there is a qualification: there should be 'diffusion of political deliberation and function to the greatest extent that is consistent with the wisdom of its administration' (*PMPS* II, 509). This qualification is put to polemical use in his pamphlet directed against Richard Price's own pamphlet on civil liberty, prompted by the dispute with the American colonies. In that publication, Ferguson identified the 'essence of political liberty' to be 'an establishment as gives power to the wise and safety to all' (*Remarks* 8–9). He follows up this identification with the declaration that 'the Liberty of every class and order is not proportioned to the power they enjoy but to the security they have for the protection of their rights' (*Remarks* 11; cf. 3, 7). Rome is still invoked since its history demonstrates that the 'power of the people is not the good of the people' (*Remarks* 52, cf. 5).

While the references to safety and security are hallmarks of 'modern liberty', it remains the case that Ferguson is dissatisfied with the role that liberty plays in commercial societies. This is apparent in the *Principles* (a work the tone of which is distinct from the more engaged character of the *Essay* and his pamphlets) where he comments that it is in 'the exercises of freedom' that 'the interests of human nature' consist (*PMPS* II, 508). Commercial society requires no such exercise, all that it requires is forbearance from injustice and abiding by the rules. While, as we have seen, not disputing the cardinal provision of security, he differs from those, like Smith. Instead of seeing in this rule-following the 'seeming perfection' of government, he sees political apathy (Medick and Batscha 1988: 79). On Ferguson's reading this apathy not only runs counter to a basic agonistic trait in human nature (*ECS* 20), but also reduces politics to running an administrative machine (cf. *ECS* 225), a reduction that can 'weaken the bands of society' (*ECS* 191).[6] The implicit linkage here is that political inactivity insidiously introduces insouciance. Through being too busy on private affairs the 'political spirit' is laid to rest and by chaining up the 'active virtues', commercial nations become 'unworthy of the freedom they possess' (*ECS* 221).[7]

The value of liberty is only realised when 'national institutions' call upon the citizen 'to act for himself and to maintain his rights' (*ECS* 191). The meaning of 'rights' here requires some untangling. We have seen that Ferguson adopts what we can call the standard modern jurisprudentialist position that 'liberty is the security of rights' (*APMP* 53), where these are understood negatively as restraining others from invading (cf. *IMP* Pt 5). Alongside this he also proclaims, as we have just noted, that liberty is a 'right which every individual must be ready to vindicate for himself' (*ECS* 266). The maintenance of rights cannot be delegated to 'political establishments' because 'the influence of laws where they have any real effect in the preservation of liberty is not any magic power descending from the shelves that are loaded with books but is in reality the influence of men resolved to be free' (*ECS* 263). The requisite vindication stems from a 'firm and resolute spirit' possessed by 'the liberal mind' (*ECS* 266). This last phrase echoes his earlier reference to the 'rights of the mind' (*ECS* 167). This is not some evocation of free will but of the will to be free. These rights are the expression of political freedom (*ECS* 167) that itself betokens a virtuous character (cf. *ECS* 247).

Ferguson's recurrent references to 'vigour' or 'spirit' evoke the root meaning of 'virtue' (masculine virility). One passage in the *Essay* captures this association, 'nations consist of men; and a nation consisting of degenerate and cowardly men is weak; a nation consisting of vigorous, public-spirited and resolute men is strong [. . .] Virtue is a necessary constituent of national strength' (*ECS* 225). In the republican lexicon virtue is counterposed to 'corruption'. Ferguson's, at least partial, subscription to this vocabulary is evident in the later Parts, especially, of the *Essay*.[8] As when he says, for example, that the rules of despotism (which as we saw he feared modern liberty approaches) are 'made for the government of corrupted men' (*ECS* 240). A key source of this corruption was 'luxury' but before turning to that topic, the significance of Ferguson's argument on the dangers of commercial society for its neglect of politics needs to be underscored. This can be most readily accomplished by revisiting Smith.

Smith's adoption of 'modern' liberty means he severs the Fergusonian (qualified republican) linkage between the virtue of political action and the promotion of the public good. For Smith the public good in a commercial society is the good of the public, which is manifest in the universal enjoyment by those individuals who comprise it of material well-being (the blessing of opulence). This well-being is the product of the division of labour as individuals mutually interact in the pursuit of their own private interests, within the confines of the rule of law (the blessing of liberty). Thus understood the public good no longer requires purposefully directed *political* action. Moreover, this is no loss. As we saw in Chapter 4 those who do participate do so not as an expression of their commitment to public virtue but because it gives them 'importance'.

## THE LUXURY DEBATE

One of the clearest intersections between the two strains of ancient liberty is their antipathy to luxury. We saw in the opening part of this chapter how it was invoked as a causal force in Roman history and in Chapter 5 how it was decried by the Stoics. Their conjunction stems from the identification of luxury with effeminacy; luxury emasculates (*virilem effeminat*) (Sallust 1921: par 11; Mackenzie 1711: 355). The gendered language is not coincidental. The root of 'virtue' is *vir* (man) and its governing meaning was courage (the same is true in Greek). Hence the significance (in part) of Smith's linking humanity with the 'virtue' of women (see p. 142).

For the moral strain this meant that men were unable to withstand the seductive delights of bodily pleasures; like women they craved sumptuous apparel, soft furnishings, delicate food and hot baths. For the civic strain, as we have already seen, this meant manly virtues were corrupted since to pursue or value luxury was to promote private (over public) interests, to favour 'economics' (over politics) and to pay others to fight your battles; in sum this was to blur the roles of men and women, citizens and non-citizens.

While the classical disparagement of those who live an instrumental life, one that is deemed less worthy than the free one of a citizen,[9] did abate with the spread of commerce, this sharpened two other concerns. Because commerce rests on nothing more tangible than belief, opinion and expectation or 'credit' then it seemed clearly too insubstantial to support a social order. This concern we will discuss in Part III below. The second concern is that commerce constituted a danger to the defence of the realm. This we will discuss in the next section. However before these discussions we need to examine how the defence of modern liberty required a re-evaluation of luxury.

The initial engagement in the seventeenth century was in pamphlets defending 'trade'. These were often 'local' in character, making a particular case for a particular interest (such as the East India Company) but couching that in terms of the national interest, as by – to give just one example – John Houghton in his *England's Great Happiness* (1677). The literature was originally apologetic. For example, one of best known early forays, Thomas Mun's *England's Treasure by Forreign Trade* (published 1664 but probably written earlier), defends the noble profession of the merchant, whose private endeavours will, when properly conducted, accompany the public good, but he also refers to 'Piping, Potting, Feasting, Fashions and mis-spending our time in Idleness and Pleasure [. . .] hath made us effeminate [. . .] declined in our Valour' (Mun 1952: 122, 193) thus revealing the hold of the luxury critique (as we can term it). That hold weakened as seen in 1690 in Nicholas Barbon's defence of fashion and desire ('wants of the mind') for those goods that 'can gratifie his Senses, adorn his Body and promote the Ease, pleasure and Pomp of Life' (1905: 14). By the time of Mandeville a more open defence of luxury emerges, though even in his polemics it does not feature prominently (I will refer to his argument shortly). However, his notoriety ensured that the luxury critique did not wither. Indeed rather than waning it waxed.

Paul Langford has commented that

> a history of luxury and attitudes to luxury would come very close to being a history of the eighteenth century [. . .] there is a sense in which the politics in this period [1727–83] is about the distribution and representation of this luxury, religion about the attempt to control it, public polemic about generating and regulating it and social policy about confining it to those who did not produce it. (1989: 3–4)

Though Langford is here referring to England, Maxine Berg and Elisabeth Eger similarly declare more expansively that 'luxury was the defining issue of the early modern period' (2003: 70). We can generalise that a key factor in the explanation of this pervasiveness is the emergence of a commercial society and the anxieties generated by the pace and extent of social change together with the availability in the luxury critique of a ready-made critical repertoire. These lurking fears produced a large literature, much of it a lament against the 'character of the times' as manifesting 'a vain, luxurious and selfish effeminacy' in a phrase of John Brown's immensely popular *An Estimate of the Manners and Principles of the Times* (1758: I, 29, 67, 129). This book went through six editions in its year of publication (1757) and its popularity suggests it hit some contemporary nerve, despite (or perhaps because of) its unsubtle argumentation.

On a more sophisticated plane the issues raised by 'luxury' were debated across Europe, including Scotland, and although there were different 'contexts that themselves evolved' the contours remained much the same.[10] On the one hand, luxury encourages population and the well-being of states by circulating money, it serves to replace savage with polite civilised manners, to advance progress and the cultivation of the fine arts and to increase the happiness of individuals and the power of nations. On the other, according to the luxury critique, it sustains inequality in wealth, it ruins the countryside by encouraging city-living, it leads to depopulation, stifles patriotism and weakens courage.[11]

In Scotland most of the literati participated, though there was a generally shared approach. This can be detected in Hume's contribution. We have already hinted at his position but, as the most sophisticated Scottish argument, we can now examine it in some detail, before in a more cursory fashion noting the position of others along a spectrum.

Hume opens his essay 'Of Refinement of Arts' by stating that 'luxury' is a word of 'uncertain signification' (*E-RA* 268) (so much so perhaps that he changed the original 1752 title 'Of Luxury' to 'Of Refinement of Arts' for the 1760 edition). He is not alone in this detection of uncertainty. Other Scots adopted a similar position, as did Diderot after and Melon before him.[12] In line with his general strategy in the *Political Discourses*, he is seeking to dispel shallow thinking, aiming to penetrate beneath the over-wrought extremes of the debate. His motivation is not merely irenic; he is also pushing an agendum in favour of a modern commercial society. Hence while he opens by contrasting the position of those 'severe moralists' (as he calls them – Sallust is named as an example) for whom 'luxury' is a vice with Mandeville's (though he is unnamed) defence it is clear that it is the former that is chiefly in his sights.

In his essays, 'Of Refinement of Arts' and 'Of Commerce', Hume defends what I have called 'superfluous value' (see Berry 2008 for a full account).[13] What for severe moralists would be an oxymoron is rather for Hume an expression of his repudiation of that outlook. We have already seen that he rejects the philosophical anthropology that privileges reason and that he displaces the ethic of poverty by equating being poor with being necessitous – painfully lacking the material basics of life. What commerce holds out is the way to alleviate impoverishment, and integral to that alleviation is giving value to the production of luxury goods. There are two aspects to this positive assessment.

The first follows from his own definition: luxury is 'great refinement in the gratification of senses' (*E-RA* 268). Its role as a counter to the 'severe' position is made apparent by his generalising remark that 'ages of refinement' are 'both the happiest and most virtuous' (*E-RA* 269). In a clear break from the luxury critique Hume is coupling luxury/ refinement with happiness/virtue *not* opposing them. Luxury goods, while seemingly superfluous, represent a source of pleasure or enjoyment that is intrinsically valuable in its own right.

The second aspect recognises the instrumental benefits that flow from the production of luxuries as consumption goods, and their participation in a system of commerce; benefits that redound to the general advantage. Hume here signals his subscription to the 'modernist' perspective (see Chapter 5) that desire drives humans. The Spartan regime, where everyone has a 'passion for the public good', is contrary to the 'natural bent of the mind' (*E-Com* 262–3; cf. Moore 1977: 820). Indeed to govern men along Spartan lines would require a 'miraculous transformation of mankind' (*E-RA* 280). The effective human, all-too-human, motivations are 'avarice and industry, art and luxury' (*E-Com* 263). 'Avarice', which Hume depicts as both an 'obstinate' and a 'universal passion', was uniformly condemned by the civic and severe moralists alike, as we saw above in Livy and Sallust. But picking up the point made earlier, for Hume, it is commendably 'the spur of industry' (*E-CL* 93; *E-AS* 113). This spur is central to the benefits that flow from the recognition of superfluous value because when industry abounds then individuals will be not only opulent but happy as (to requote from Chapter 5) they 'reap the benefit of [. . .] commodities so far as they gratify the senses and appetite' (*E-Com* 263).

Furthermore, the inhabitants of 'industrious and civilized' nations will 'desire to have every commodity in the utmost perfection' (*E-JT* 329) as they 'desire [. . .] a more splendid form of life than what their ancestors enjoyed' (*E-Com* 264). This splendour is the essence of 'refinement', the recognition of qualitative differences. The 'severe' view treats all departures from functionality as superfluous (recall Seneca's comment from Chapter 5 [p. 127] on the moral failing of valuing the quality of bread). Hume aptly compares the gluttonous Tartars, who feast on dead horses, to the 'refinements of cookery' experienced in the contemporary courts of Europe (*E-RA* 272). To develop refinement, as manifest both in the presence of qualitatively differentiated goods and in the ability to appreciate both the skill and the beauty of a fine meal or splendid apparel, is not to indulge in excess. Excess, as exhibited by the Tartars, is mere quantitative increase beyond some fixed sum but, as such, it is conceptually distinct from qualitative refinement. To recognise that goods possess superfluous value is to recognise and endorse that distinction. This separation of luxury from excess was followed by others.

Nonetheless, this positive argument in favour of civilised commercial society might still fall foul of the luxury critique's claim as exemplified by Mackenzie's declaration that 'frugality hardened Men into the Temper of being soldiers' (1711: 303–4). Hardiness is vital to national greatness, as measured by military strength. It is, accordingly, important to the argumentative success of Hume's defence of a commercial society that this view of 'greatness' and its associated virtues is undermined. In this defence he appeals to the evidence (a ploy also adopted by Mandeville (1988: I, 122–3). The supposed causal link between luxury and military weakness fails the test of constant conjunction, as manifest by the cases of France and England, that is, the two most powerful *because* most polished and commercial societies (*E-RA* 275; cf. *HE* II, 598–9).

Hume elaborates on this latter causal link. It is for him 'according to the most natural course of things' that 'industry and arts and trade encrease the power of the sovereign' *and* do so without impoverishing the people (*E-Com* 260). This combination is made possible by the very 'superfluity' that industry in the pursuit of luxury has created. In times of peace this superfluity goes to the maintenance of manufactures and the 'improvers of liberal arts' (hallmarks of civilisation), but when an army is needed the sovereign levies a tax, the effect of which is to reduce expenditure on luxuries. This frees up, for the military, those who were previously employed in luxury-good production; they constitute a sort of 'storehouse' of labour (*E-Com* 261–2; *E-RA* 272). Nor does it follow that these will be inferior troops. On the contrary, recalling the 'indissoluble chain' that links industry, knowledge and humanity, these fighters will benefit not only from the technology that a commercial society can command but also from the overall higher level of intellectual competence.[14] All that the 'ignorant and unskilful' soldiers of rude nations can achieve are 'sudden and violent conquests' (*E-Com* 261; cf. Hume *HE* I, 627). As Culloden testified, they are ineffective against trained troops armed with sophisticated weaponry.[15] This bears on the debate surrounding militias to be considered in subsection 'Defence' below.

Picking up an argument from Chapter 5, we can now appreciate how Hume, by calling the luxurious ages the 'most virtuous', is implicitly declaring that the quintessentially male virtue of courage is now passé. Once the military virtues are downgraded then the accusations of effeminacy and feeble commitment to the public good levelled at merchants can be dismissed as untenable. Hence his judgment quoted above [p. 140] that 'merchants are one of the most useful races of men' because not only are they the 'best and firmest basis of public liberty' but also they 'beget industry'. Industry is thus advanced to the benefit of all. But 'delicacy' is also stimulated by the pleasures of luxury and, as we have seen, desires for a more splendid way of living ensue. Delicacy and industry come together as men are roused from 'their indolence' to obtain commodities ('objects of luxury': *E-Com* 264). There is an implicit dynamism here. Hume recognises, as did Melon (1735: 123) and Mandeville (1988: I, 169–72), that one-time luxuries become necessities, which implies that the relation between them is relative. There is not some fixed intrinsic natural criterion (need) to distinguish them as implied by the luxury critique.[16] There is not some immutable or given norm in terms of which appropriate limits can be established. Rather the 'value' humans attach to 'any particular pleasure depends on comparison and experience' (*E-RA* 276; cf. *T* 2.1.6.2/*SBNT* 290).

As we have seen, this desire to enjoy a more splendid form of life, compared to that of an earlier generation, promotes employment and industry, as well as all-around national strength. This results in an improvement in the conditions of the poor, who can not only possess the necessaries but also 'many of the conveniencies' of life (*E-Com* 256). Hume explicitly states that in ages of refinement 'many' can now 'enjoy' the 'finer arts'; such pleasures are not the prerogative of the (few) rich. This enjoyment adds more to the happiness of the poor than it diminishes that of the rich. As we noted in Chapter 4, for Hume, restrictions on consumption, as purposed by sumptuary legislation, are more than ineffectual; they also diminish human happiness, the enjoyment of material things (Hume is here exemplifying what Werner Sombart [1913: 122], in his study of Luxury, terms *Versachlichung*).

The by-product of this defence of luxury is that it still enables Hume to allow that it can be 'vicious' as well as innocent (virtuous). What he means by vicious is non-beneficial or without advantage to the public (*E-RA* 269, 278).[17] His argument permits him to dismiss Mandeville's position as casuistry – he sees no need to deny (implicitly invoking Sallust) that pernicious luxury is poisonous (*E-RA* 279). Neither does he need to accuse of hypocrisy those who decry luxury.[18] In effect, 'vicious luxury' for Hume describes an individual who, by confining gratification to himself, is unable to execute those 'acts of duty and generosity' that his station and fortune require. Even here the thrust is that the virtue of relieving the poor (*E-RA* 279) disperses gratifications more widely to public advantage. This is a utilitarian calculation. While he allows that luxury 'when excessive' can generate both private and public ills, it is still, nevertheless, better to accept it than attempt vainly to eradicate it (*E-RA* 279–80). It is a trade-off. Without the spur to industry that luxury supplies, individuals (and thence their society) will fall into sloth and idleness. The social and individual cost of such outcomes outweighs any benefits that might conceivably accrue from proscribing luxury – a circumstance, he holds, the historical record bears out.[19]

Although Hume's discussion was loaded against the Sallustian (Brownian) critique, the trade-off or 'on balance' utilitarian dimension was taken up by the other Scots. There is both a positive and negative dimension to luxury in relation to commercial society. Some, in contrast to Hume, emphasise the latter. Given Hutcheson's fundamental antipathy to Mandeville then it is no surprise to see him contesting the merits of luxury. In his direct critique of Mandeville, he defines 'luxury' as 'using more curious and expensive habitation, dress, table, equipage than the person's wealth will bear' (1989: 80), which is tantamount to what Hume was to characterise as vicious luxury. However, Hutcheson later takes exception to the Mandevellian/Humean view that luxury is necessary or useful in order to 'encourage arts and manufactures' and, in the voice of a severe moralist, he proclaims 'luxury' a 'plague' (*SIMP* 269).

Given its ready-to-hand quality, it is not surprising to find passing references to the luxury critique across the literati. Stuart, for example, exploits it in his polemical histories (*HD* 36; cf. 95; *VSE* 2, 105; *OPL* 119). The one Scot who sticks most closely to the luxury critique is Kames. Although he acknowledges with Hume that luxury is an elusive and relative term (*SHM* I, 363–4) yet his text is littered with Brownian laments on the indulgence of 'soft pillows and easy seats' and the 'luxurious indolence' of riding in carriages (*SHM* I, 368–9) before he issues the general indictment that the 'epidemic distempers of luxury and selfishness are spreading wide in Britain' (*SHM* I, 477). Since Britain had reached the age of commerce then this represents a danger. Rather than the Smithian gloss, Kames holds that opulence 'begets luxury', which, as well as 'invigorating sensual pleasure', fosters selfishness (*SHM* I, 230–1; I, 195). Yet, in a clear echo of Hutcheson, he holds that 'refinement of dress, of the table, of equipage, of habitation' is not a luxury for those who can afford them. Indeed, here exhibiting the presence (albeit etiolated) of the 'on-balance' posture, 'the public gains' by 'the encouragement that is given to arts, manufacture and commerce' (*SHM* I, 373). He allows that commerce is 'immediately' advantageous as it bestows wealth and power but by introducing luxury it is 'ultimately harmful' (*SHM* I, 474) and 'pernicious' (*SHM* I, 373). He fears the tranquillity engendered by 'strict and regular government' makes a 'warlike people effeminate and cowardly' (*SHM* I, 459), since it eradicates both manhood (*SHM* I, 487) and patriotism (*SHM* I, 474).

That there is some sort of consensus along a spectrum is borne out by Ferguson. He does think with Kames that in a peaceful environment, where there is a 'respite from public dangers', the commercial arts by facilitating the pursuit of 'private advantages' may induce the individual to become 'effeminate, mercenary and sensual' (*ECS* 250). However, like Hume (and earlier Turnbull [*PMP* 360]), he thinks the meaning of 'luxury' is imprecise and in his chapter on Luxury he openly adopts the balance-sheet approach; there are grounds for censure and for praise. On the former side luxury is the source of corruption and national ruin, on the latter it is the 'parent of arts, the support of commerce and the minister of national greatness' (*ECS* 244). Dunbar's cursory treatment echoes this. Luxury can be salutary (as a motive for industry it is 'productive of the noblest effects') or it can be destructive (once the 'ingenious arts, and fruits of industry have been obtained) (*EHM* 368–9).

The most systematic attempt at a 'balanced approach' is given by Steuart. He separates a 'moral' from a 'political' sense of the term. According to the latter, luxury 'necessarily must produce good effects' (*PPE* I, 265), whereas according to the 'doctrine of morals' it conveys ideas of 'abuse, sensuality or excess' (*PPE* I, 44n). Steuart attempts to resolve this issue by focusing on the question of excess. He argues, implicitly following Hume, that while the political sense is 'inseparable' from our ideas of luxury, 'vicious excess' is separable (cf. Dunbar *EHM* 368). This intellectual manoeuvre now permits him to argue that 'luxury consists in providing the objects, in so far as they are superfluous. Sensuality consists in the actual enjoyment and excess implies an abuse of enjoyment' (*PPE* I, 268). In providing those 'objects' luxury has beneficial consequences that can be assessed independently of the 'doctrine of morals'. In effect this is the 'utilitarian' strategy that we identified in Hume.

Given the prominent place of population in the luxury debate we can expect Wallace to be a participant. He does not disappoint: 'modern cities and modern times have more powerful sources of depopulation within themselves because of those numerous instruments of luxury with which they are more abundantly supplied than ancient cities or ancient times' (*DNM* 334). Yet Wallace's overall position is not accurately captured as Kamesian. This is evident in the *Characteristics* where he engages in a running critique of Brown's *Estimate* (especially in Part 5). He also takes issue with Hume's *Political Discourses* but it is notable that he does not select 'Of Commerce' or 'Refinement of Arts' for criticism but focuses rather on Hume's view of banks and credit (see below).

Wallace allows that 'a certain portion of licentiousness' goes along with liberty (*CGB* 65) and there is an echo of this in Millar. As we discussed in Chapter 2 he endorses the connection between commerce and liberty but the latter, Millar allows, can stray into licentiousness, especially as it affects women. Compared to 'simpler ages', in 'opulent and luxurious nations' the 'free intercourse of the sexes ' gives rise to 'licentious and dissolute manners' that serve to 'diminish the rank and dignity of women' (*OR* 225).[20] Millar indeed made more of this between the first (1771) and third (1779) editions of the *Ranks*. In his later elaborations he cites the familiar example of Juvenal's Sixth Satire and draws on the example of Rome (cf. *HV* IV, 4/769) in its 'voluptuous ages' to observe that 'similar consequences' may be discerned in some of the 'modern European nations' (*OR* 228). He cites France and Italy because (as Smith similarly had done [*TMS* V.2.10/207]) that is where the 'fine arts' and 'a taste for refined and elegant amusements has been generally diffused' (*OR* 225 [also in *Obs* 75–6]).[21] Throughout this discussion Millar is trading on some common associations from the luxury critique. This should not be exaggerated. It is part of the Scottish spectrum on this issue and is not, I think, attributable to any potent 'republican' sympathies on his part.[22] There is, for example, minimal reference here to the corruption of virtue (but see *OR* 223, added from the first edition) or lack of public zeal. Millar, however, clearly recognises dangers in commercial improvement, as we shall see again in Part III below.

Another reason for doubting any strong adherence to republicanism in Millar is his silence over sumptuary legislation. Hume, as we have observed, regards these laws with disdain and this was the basic position of the Scots. Sumptuary laws were a recurrent feature of the Roman republic and empire (Arena 2011, Berry 1994: Chap. 3) and a persistent one of medieval and early-modern Europe; almost no-one was excluded from their reach.[23] The underlying philosophy was Stoic. The laws sought to police desires in the light of a supposedly rational, objectively valid, account of the 'good life' or the constituents of 'good and politic order'.[24] In practical or realistic terms they were attempts to control political corruption (particularly in Rome) and, later, to sustain some rank order by regulating permissible apparel by social status. These laws failed and they gradually atrophied, even if at different rates.

We have already noted Smith's contemptuous dismissal of sumptuary laws [p. 109] and this is the best indication of his attitude to the 'luxury critique'. This attitude can be best characterised as 'indifference'; Neil de Marchi (1999: 18) calls him 'sceptical' but this is more about his own personal fastidiousness than any moral position. He has no truck with Kames' perspective but neither does he take up the polemical posture of Hume. Of course, one can find examples of the established association between luxury and effeminacy (*LJA* iii.121/189) and dissolution of manners (*TMS* I.ii.3.4/35) but these are very few – indeed in a book on moral sentiments this sparseness is all the more telling. He gives the most historically significant version of the conversion of 'luxury' into 'necessity' by adopting a societally relative account of the latter and defining the former formally as what does not fall under the latter (*WN* V.ii.k.3/ 870).[25] This informs his account of taxation but his most common references to luxury goods are in the context of the collapse of feudalism that we discussed in Chapter 2. There he is interested in causality and not in judgment. The one place where Smith does seem to venture a critique is in a passage in his *Lectures*, where he remarks that the 'bulk of the people [. . .] by having their minds constantly employed on the arts of luxury, they grow effeminate and dastardly' (*LJB* 330/540). This occurs in the context of an enumeration of three 'inconveniencies' arising from a 'commercial spirit' (*LJB* 328/539). However, this enumeration, which reappears in an altered form in the *Wealth of Nations*, cannot be straightforwardly read as a critique. This will become apparent as we proceed. The third of these inconveniences pertains to the tendency of commerce 'to extinguish martial spirit'. This leads to the next section.

## DEFENCE

The gendered juxtaposition between soft feminine luxury and hard masculine virtue manifested itself most obviously in military matters. The danger facing commercial societies was their defensive vulnerability given that *le doux commerce* disposes societies to peace so that martial capacity is not prioritised. More pointedly, fighting is made a commercial enterprise, paying either mercenaries to do battle on your behalf or using tax revenues to pay for a standing army. Both of these ran foul of the republican emphasis on citizens, as part of their commitment to the public good, being themselves prepared to bear arms. As influentially propounded by Machiavelli, the virtuous alternative to mercenaries or a standing army was a citizen militia. Again Rome provided a supposedly apt historical 'message'; corrupted by a soft life of luxury it was in due course no match militarily for the belligerently nomadic Vandals and Goths.

As ever, recourse to Roman history was not some arcane dead historical question but a proxy for a live political issue in Britain. The Seven Years War (1756–63) raised military questions and concomitant ones of finance. (Britain had to import, at considerable expense troops from Hanover and Hesse to supplement its own forces [Raynor 2008: 65].) A Militia Bill was raised in 1756 and passed in the Commons but despite defeat in the Lords it became legislation. This had the effect of bringing large numbers into military service, though, given its unpopularity among those conscripted, how effective as an actual fighting force this could be was questioned (Langford 1989: 334). In post-Jacobite Scotland there was, separately, a movement to establish a locally raised and based militia. In both cases, though not identically, the machinations of contemporary 'politics' were the driving factors. Nevertheless the political positions adopted still needed defending and articulating. Hence the Tory defence of militias, led as they were by country gentlemen, called on the resources of an 'ideology' that emphasised the integral link between land ownership (independence) and public duty, over against (as they saw it) the weaker Whig commitment to national defence, attributable to their involvement in trade. The broadly Whig consensus among the Scottish literati did not prevent them in their arguments over a militia drawing on the language of virtue and threats posed to it by the increasing commercialisation of their society.

In the light of earlier discussion it is no surprise to find both that Ferguson was a leading advocate of a militia and that Smith defended the merits of standing armies. Again, their relative positions should not be polarised; both arguments are nuanced. This 'debate' was also one in which other Scots participated. The underlying issue is how a society wherein everyman is a merchant defends itself. The danger is that for systemic reasons this might be executed ineffectually. Here lies one of the crucial underlying concerns that was at stake in the luxury debate covered in the last section.

In the *Moral Sentiments* Smith says a good citizen should promote the welfare of his fellows as well as respecting and obeying the laws. He notes, however, that in 'peaceable and quiet times' these two principles coincide – 'support of the established government seems evidently the best expedient for maintaining the safe, respectable and happy situation of our fellow citizens' (*TMS* VI.ii.2.12/231). These requisite 'times' are, as a general rule, provided by a commercial society. It is this association of commerce with 'peace and quiet' that alarms Ferguson. The key danger he detects is that if the 'pretensions to equal justice and freedom should terminate in rendering every class equally servile and merce- nary we make a nation of helots and have no free citizens' (*ECS* 186). Citizens should be 'willing to sustain in their own persons the burden of government and of national defence' and not leave it to others (*ECS* 266).

In matters military the sociological division of labour, what Ferguson calls the 'separation of professions', is dangerously inappropriate. In an echo of the gendered language of the luxury critique, he says to make the 'art of war' a profession is to render citizens and soldiers as distin- guishable 'as women and men' (*ECS* 231). He allows that the techno- logical specialisation of the clothier and tanner gives us better clothes and shoes but – and this is the nub – to 'separate the arts which form the citizen and the statesman, the arts of policy and war, is an attempt to dismember the human character' (*ECS* 230). Commerce not only threatens to tie up the 'active virtues' but also erodes the 'social spirit of society' by extending specialisation so as to make the art of war a technical profession. I will return to Ferguson's view of the division of labour in the next Part but the current issue is how he sees this danger being met.

The answer lies within the resources of the tradition of ancient liberty, namely, the citizen militia. The advantage of a militia was that 'in the higher ranks' it kept together the 'talents for the council and the field', while at the same time it gave the 'body of the people' that 'zeal for their country, and that military character, which enable them to take a share in defending its rights' (*ECS* 227; cf. 266). To rely on mer- cenaries is to play fast and loose with those rights; as commercial actors mercenaries will fight where the pay is best not where the cause is just. Similarly to rely on a professional 'standing' army will also threaten those rights, since this army can be used not only against an external foe but also, in the classical fear of republicans (citing Sulla, Pompey and Caesar) against any perceived 'enemy within' (cf. *ECS* 227, Millar *OR* 286, Kames *SHM* II, 12, 37).

Ferguson's concerns expressed themselves practically. He wrote a pamphlet as a contribution to the debate over the Militia Bill (he refers in its opening pages to 'this Occasion' [*Reflections* 5]). (The pamphlet itself adumbrates many points that occur in the *Essay*.)[26] He argues, citing some recent successes, that the proposal to institute a militia is 'not impracticable' (*Reflections* 5). To sustain the success of any militia his recommendations are to revive in the 'people' familiarity with arms (*Reflections* 20) and to (re)connect honour with public service for 'gentlemen' (*Reflections* 38). These recommendations relate to the damage commerce has done to manners. However, this means their implementation is not susceptible to a 'quick fix'. It is on this basis that Ferguson identifies his own contribution to the debate – more attention should be paid to the preconditions for the successful establishment of regiments and less on their formation (*Reflections* 48).[27]

Ferguson was one of the leaders of a campaign to establish a militia in Scotland. He was a member of the 'Poker Club', indeed according to Alexander Carlyle (1910: 439) he came up with the name. Instituted in 1762 to coincide with the scheduled renewal of the English Act, it included Hume, Blair, Robertson, Dalrymple and Smith among the literati, although the majority of members were nobles and gentlemen (Robertson 1985: 189–91). Typical of such associations the Club had a 'social' dimension (though Carlyle remarks on its frugality and moderation [1910: 440]), as well as a public purpose.[28] At least part of its support was attributable to it being a marker of Scottish acceptability, that post-Culloden the Scots were loyal Hanoverians so that they could be trusted with arms.

Kames was another member of the Poker Club (Ross 1972: 180) and he along with Ferguson is the Scot who paid most attention to this issue, devoting an entire Sketch to 'The Army' (*SHM* II, Sk. 9). Predictably he judges 'our people' have become 'effeminate, terrified at the very sight of a hostile weapon' (*SHM* II, 9) but the remedy of a standing army is a precarious one (*SHM* II, 10). Yet he was aware of the problems surrounding a militia. He refers to the inadequacies of Harrington's 'republican' scheme as well as that of Fletcher of Salton [sic], Harrington's Scottish successor (*SHM* II, 12–13).[29] Kames accepts that classical militias are injurious to manufactures and commerce, which he acknowledges are now the source of power. Sensible of that fact he developed his own elaborate plan. According his scheme there would be periodic conscription so that everyone was bound to serve in the army. This would revive 'in our people of rank some military spirit' (the officers are the most important element) (*SHM* II, 19), while for 'private men' the periodicity of service means the 'spirit of industry' can be united with that of 'war' (*SHM* II, 24). Admitting with uncharacteristic modesty the plan's imperfections he offers it as an attempt, by making a standing army a matter of rotation, to 'discipline multitudes for peace as well as war' (*SHM* II, 37).

Kames' recurrent references to military spirit recur in Smith but although Smith was a member of the Poker his views on the militia differ from Ferguson, as the latter acknowledged.[30] For Smith, as professed in his Glasgow classroom, militias are outmoded; standing armies 'must be introduced' (*LJB* 337/543). In a society where everyman is a merchant then there is no incongruity in being paid to be a soldier. On a more practical level, with improvement (the development of arts and luxury), the 'better sort' are disinclined to serve in war and the 'better sort of mechanicks' cannot get sufficient compensation for the time they would have to spend in a militia with the consequence that it is the 'very meanest' who have to be 'formed into a standing army' (*LJA* iv.169/265–6). In addition, in modern warfare artillery is a decisive factor (cf. Hume *HE* I, 498) and its development is itself the product of technological advance. The effect of this is to reduce drastically reliance on individual dexterity with weapons. What now counts is 'regularity, order and prompt obedience to command', something more appropriately achieved by professional soldiers than by a contingently collected group of uneducated amateurs (*WN* V.i.a.22/699).[31]

On these criteria a standing army is superior to a militia. There are other factors that weaken the 'militia case'. In an 'industrious and wealthy nation', to 'enforce the practice of military exercises' would require 'a very vigorous police' in the face of the 'interest, genius and inclinations of the people' (*WN* V.i.a.17/698). And in a later context he refers again to the 'continual and painful attention of government' that would be needed to maintain a militia (*WN* V.i.f.60/787). Millar put the point succinctly when he noted that the difficulty of enforcing militias was 'sufficient evidence that they are adverse to the spirit of the times' (*HV* IV, 189). Militarily they are not suited to a long campaign, a point also made by Hume (*E-Com* 261). For Smith in 'an opulent and civilized nation' a professional army is the means to preserve civilisation against invasion from a 'poor and barbarous nation'. Not only does this mean that the fate of earlier 'civilised' peoples as they were overrun by barbarians can be avoided but also it has local recent purchase as seen in his comment in his *Lectures* that had the few thousand 'naked unarmed Highlanders' in 1745 not been opposed by a standing army they would have seized the throne 'with little difficulty' (*LJB* 331–2/540–1; cf. Millar *HV* IV, 4/757).

The fear of a professional or standing army, as we noted above, was that it could be used to suppress domestic liberties. Smith addresses this fear directly. In explicit repudiation of the position of 'men of republican principles', he claims this army can 'in some cases be favourable to liberty' (*WN* V.i.a.41/706). The claim is evidently qualified. It only applies in those circumstances where the chief officers in the army are drawn from the 'principal nobility and gentry', who have, in consequence, the 'greatest interest in the support of the civil authority' (*WN* V.i.a.41/706).[32] Also in later discussion, Smith admits that if 'every citizen had the spirit of a soldier' then a smaller (less expensive) standing army would suffice. This same 'spirit' would also diminish those supposed dangers to liberty posed by standing armies (*WN* V.i.f.59/787). While Edward Harpham (1984: 765, 769) judges Smith is here exhibiting his distance from civic humanism, Leonidas Montes hears, in these qualifications, 'a republican consciousness', which if listened to is saying that 'economic progress does not eradicate the moral foundations of classical republicanism' (Montes 2009: 328). Montes' argument (and that of others who see civic republicanism in Smith) is best considered in the light of another danger that a commercial society is seen to face.

## II

## DIVISION OF LABOUR (AGAIN)

In Smith's account, one of the advantages of a smaller standing army, consequent upon the presence of a military spirit, is that it would reduce costs. This is not an incidental factor. His discussion of this issue occurs in that section of the *Wealth of Nations* devoted to 'Of the Expence of Publick Works and Publick Institutions'. That context is crucial to understanding why Smith returns to the division of labour in Book 5. That this also involved these issues of military organisation and spirit additionally throws decisive light on Ferguson's discussion of the division of labour.

What really exercises Ferguson about the division of labour is its sociological dimension (see Chapter 3): it compartmentalises society such that none of its various separated elements is 'animated with the spirit of society itself' (*ECS* 218). Ferguson's preoccupation, as his militia concerns reveal, is with the loss of public spirit when this compartmentalisation affects the 'higher departments of policy and war' (*ECS* 181). He is alarmed about the impact of commercialisation on the 'higher orders of men' who cease to possess 'courage and elevation of mind' and who languish, in the 'absence of every manly occupation'. This languor is a more serious matter than the circumstances experienced by 'the poor' (*ECS* 259–60). David Kettler (1977: 451) is one of the few commentators to have taken on board that Ferguson's focus is the 'political class' (but see also Hill 2007: 353 and Guena 2002: 189).

This focus crucially conditions the two paragraphs in the *Essay* that have been the subject of some hyperbolic commentary.[33] He observes that 'manufactures [. . .] prosper most where the mind is least consulted and where the workshop [. . .] may be considered as an engine the parts of which are men' and contrasts the opportunity afforded to the workshop's 'master' to cultivate an 'enlargement of thought' to the lot of the 'inferior workman' (*ECS* 183; cf. *PMPS* I, 251). However, rather than overload these passages with retrospectively gained significance they should be put in context; they comprise neither a stand-alone nor emphatic treatment of an issue now deemed important. Ferguson's observations are illustrative rather than substantive. They are an exemplification of his alertness to Providential unintended consequences. The 'artifices of the beaver, the ant and the bee' are attributed to the 'wisdom of nature'. 'Human affairs', he declares, are no different. By linking this topic to Providential superintendence then it is a reasonable presumption that we not going to find here sustained moral condemnation. His pivotal point is that there is no direct correlation between social and individual development. Accordingly and illustratively, manufacture can prosper where individuals' reason is not exercised and the workshop can be likened to the 'parts of an engine' that 'concur to a purpose without any concert of their own'. Thus understood, the master/workman distinction instantiates the complicated, unforeseen, character of a developed society, not 'class analysis'. Moreover, in the context of his argument, this particular instantiation serves stylistically to set up the topic of the next chapter on subordination.

The opulence produced by the division of labour was also for Smith an unintended consequence but that was not the only one; there were other less benign manifestations. As we will see there is some similarity with Ferguson's observations about the mechanical arts inducing ignorance, but without the latter's Providential gloss. These non-benign consequences of the division of labour are discussed in Book 5. This later discussion has prompted much commentary,[34] generally focusing on its consistency with the discussion in Book 1 (that we analysed in Chapter 3). That commentary tends to overlook the fact that the later discussion is driven by Smith's aim to outline the reasons why and where government intervention and thence expense is required. The topic of the division of labour reappears because Smith does indeed detect ailments to which this intervention, in the form of public works (one of the three duties of government – see Chapter 4), seeks to remedy.

We noted above that passage in his *Lectures* where Smith identifies three inconveniences that arise from 'a commercial spirit'. The third refers, as we have seen, to the 'martial spirit', the first two refer to the division of labour (*LJB* 328–9/539–40). While not exactly corresponding, in Book 5 of the *Wealth of Nations* he observes, in summary, that the dexterity of the specialised operative (read pin-maker) is bought at the cost of his 'intellectual, social and martial virtues' (*WN* V.i.f.50/782). In order to alleviate this condition into which the 'labouring poor' in a 'civilized society', that is, the great body of the people', will 'necessarily fall', revenue is needed. The monies raised will subsidise government intervention.

In what way does Smith think the division of labour undermines these three virtues? The 'intellectual' virtues are eroded by the fact that the 'pin-maker' has 'no occasion to exert his understanding or to exercise his invention' and, in line with the principles of moral causation, he loses the 'habit of exertion' and with that loss becomes 'as stupid and ignorant as it is possible for a human creature to become. The torpor of his mind renders him [. . .] incapable of relishing or bearing a part in any rational conversation' (*WN* V.i.f.50/782).[35] This torpidity was fastened onto by others. Dunbar patently follows Smith when, after citing pin-making, he refers to the 'torpor of intellect' suffered by the artisan (*EHM* 423). Millar is similarly indebted. He observes that workmen in the mechanical arts, confined to a 'single manual operation', are 'apt to acquire an habitual vacancy of thought' so that they are enveloped in a 'cloud of ignorance and prejudice' (*HV* IV, 4/732, 737. Indeed they become 'like machines' (*HV* IV, 4/732). This image recalls Ferguson of the *Essay* where in his contrast between the master and the workman he noted that the latter's 'genius [. . .] lies waste'.[36] Kames is another who uses the familiar language. Concentration 'on a single object' excludes 'thought and invention' so that the operator 'becomes dull and stupid' like 'a beast of burden' (*SHM* I, 110).

The effect of the division of labour on the 'social virtues' follows from the impact on the intellectual because Smith in the same sentence that refers to mental torpor continues to say of the pin-maker that his confined occupation makes him incapable of 'conceiving any generous, noble or tender sentiment, and consequently of forming any just judgment concerning many even of the ordinary duties of private life' (*WN* V.i.f.50/782). We know that Smith's moral philosophy hinges on the principle of sympathy, whereby our actions are judged through reciprocal social interaction and which judgments are in time internalised, through the habitual recognition of heeding the injunctions of the impartial spectator, to constitute conscience. With an allusion to the urbanisation that accompanies the commercialisation of society, he contrasts the circumstances 'in a country village', where conduct is 'attended to' by himself and others, with that of a 'man of low condition' when he comes into a 'great city'. In the latter environment he is 'sunk in obscurity and darkness'. He lacks the 'light' necessary for the mirror of society to function (*TMS* III.i.3/110 – see above p. 134). In that confined unilluminated situation he is apt to 'abandon himself to every sort of low profligacy and vice' (*WN* V.i.g.12/795). The only way he can gain attention is by joining a small religious sect. Here he finds his mirror. In consequence his conduct becomes 'remarkably regular and orderly' but, in another unintended consequence, the austerity of these sects tends to make their 'morals' frequently 'disagreeably rigorous and unsocial' (*WN* V.i.g.13/796).

The reference here to 'unsocial' should not be misunderstood. Smith is not in this discussion addressing an argument that makes commercial society or its 'spirit' anti-social, as inducing an egoistic attitude and fostering self-seeking behaviour. A number of commentators (e.g. Dwyer 1987; Dickey 1986; Tegos 2013), picking up especially on the post 1776 amendments to the *Moral Sentiments*, have sought to detect a deeper concern with the danger to virtue (the 'corruption of sentiments', as a new chapter in the sixth edition of 1790 calls it). In as much as these pertain to an assessment of commercial society specifically, this concern has been linked to the impact of Rousseau stemming from Smith's (1755) review of his *Discours sur l'inegalité* (1755). Pierre Force (2003) interprets, not entirely successfully (see Berry 2004), the *Wealth of Nations* as an attempt to reconcile Hume's defence and Rousseau's critique of a commercial society. Ryan Hanley (2008b especially, but also 2008a) and Denis Rasmussen (2008, also 2013 with a good bibliography) have subsequently used Smith's review as an entrée into his account of commercial society. Both judge Rousseau's critique powerful and that Smith was indebted to it. I think this is an exaggeration on both fronts. As we have seen, Smith is scarcely oblivious to detrimental effects but he is not to be saddled with the possession of some profound disquiet about the soul of modern man. More firmly than Force, both Hanley and Rasmussen recognise that, in the final analysis, for Smith commercial society is 'unequivocally preferable' (Rasmussen 2008: 9) and that he is a 'true friend of commercial society' (Hanley 2009a: 8).[37]

Millar does voice concerns about the pursuit of wealth in what he terms 'mercantile nations'. This pursuit 'becomes a scramble in which the hand of every man is against every others' as 'innumerable competitions and rivalships [. . .] contract the heart' (*HV* IV, 6/778–9). But this remains at some distance from the putative depths of Rousseau's indictment. Indeed, elsewhere he is close to Smith. He notes that these 'pin-makers' when they are not actually working will draw little improvement from the company of companions similarly afflicted and what interaction there is will take the form of 'drinking and dissipation' (*HV* IV, 4/732) (this could also be held to be true of Smith's man of 'low condition' [Weinstein 2006: 109]). He also, somewhat apocalyptically, worries that a gap will emerge in society between those with virtue and intelligence and those lacking them – a situation that might recreate the Europe of the Dark Ages (*HV* IV, 4/737).[38] Kames simply links together in the same phrase the ignorance and unsociableness of the 'operator' confined to 'a single object' (*SHM* II, 111).

What of the decline in martial virtue? Smith's sentiments on this issue are perhaps the major ground for interpreting him as a (sort of ) civic republican, as we saw exemplified by Montes.[39] Certainly Smith's language is strong. The uniformity of the pin-maker's life 'corrupts the courage of his mind' (*WN* V.i.f.50/782), that is to say, it instils coward-ice, which involves a 'sort of mental mutilation, deformity and wretch-edness' (*WN* V.i.f.60/787); a circumstance that will clearly weaken the state's defensive abilities by 'extinguishing the martial spirit' (*LJB* 331/540), although of course the professionalisation of the military (as a mode of the sociological division of labour) will help make this less crucial. The direct connection between the division of labour and mili-tary weakness is not so openly made by the others. Dunbar does link the mental torpor with 'the absence or annihilation of every manly virtue' (of which we can reasonably suppose 'courage' is a key component) and judges that martial virtues were most respected in rude ages (with minimal division of labour) (*EHM* 424, 389; cf. Smith *LJB* 300/527). As we saw in the discussion of the merits, or otherwise, of militias there was a common view that there has been, in Millar's words, a 'decay of the military spirit in the modern commercial nations'(*HV* IV, 6/753). But neither he nor Kames and Ferguson single out the 'pin-makers' from this pervasive decadence.

Smith's purpose in identifying these threats to these virtues, these deficiencies or ailments of commercial society, is programmatic. This purpose, it should be noted, distinguishes the discussion from the listing of deficiencies in the *Lectures*, where these are set up in contrast to the virtues of a commercial society (like probity and punctuality – see p. 139 above). This contextual point has eluded commentators like Hirschman (1977) who mistake this listing in the *Lectures* as Smith's own view. In the *Wealth of Nations*, the point is to identify where government action, and the public purse, is called for in order to remedy the deficiencies.

Although Smith himself does not proceed in this manner, we can locate three remedies corresponding to the three ailments. The remedy for torpid intellectual virtues is, not surprisingly, education and it is to this he gives most attention (see broadly Weinstein 2006 and Skinner 1995 among others). In the *Lectures* the second of the three deficien-cies in commercial society is said to be the great neglect of education (*LJB* 329/539). It is one of the proper tasks of government to end or prevent that neglect. Recall that it is a duty of government to erect and maintain public institutions that cannot be sustained by individuals (*WN* IV.ix.51/687–8) and, later, he specifies as falling under this remit

that which facilitates commerce and that which promotes 'the instruction of the people' (WN V.i.c.2/723). Given that the ailment affects
(representatively) 'pin-makers' then this remedy does not apply to all
'the people'. Those of 'rank and fortune' are declared to have the leisure
and inclination to fend for themselves while the 'common people' have
neither of these (WN V.i.f.52–3/784). It properly falls to the 'publick'
to establish, as in Scotland, a local school where, as another example of
the social division of labour, children can be taught for a fee set at such
a level that 'even a common labourer may afford it' (WN V.i.f.55/785).
The public purse will pay the residue of the teacher's salary.[40]

Smith also makes some recommendations as to what is to be taught.
The essentials should be covered. This means the ability to 'read, write
and account' plus, instead of the 'little smattering of Latin' they are
sometimes taught and which is of little use to them, the 'elementary
parts of geometry and mechanicks'. Smith explicitly states this is sufficient for this 'rank of people' (WN V.i.f.55/785). The public can
reinforce this duty by giving 'small premiums and little badges of distinction' to those who excel and by 'obliging' those who wish to set up
trade or attain membership of a corporation to 'undergo an examination or probation' in these essentials (WN V.i.f.56–7/786). Not all of
Smith's prescriptions are restricted to the common people. The state
can impose on members of the 'middling or more than middling rank
and fortune' a study of 'science and philosophy' before they can enter
'any liberal profession' or 'honourable office of trust or profit' (WN
V.i.g.14/796). As we will see this has bearing on how to remedy the
defective social virtues of the 'pin-makers'.

Smith clearly adopts a functional view of education. The state derives
'advantage' from subsidising the 'instruction of the inferior ranks of
the people'. It benefits because a less ignorant people is less prone to
'enthusiasm and superstition', the 'delusions' of which are 'frequently
the occasion of the most dreadful disorders' (WN V.i.f.61/788). (I will
return to this.) It is possible, as an act of interpretive charity, to over-
emphasise this functionality and read this as a form of social control
(cf. Winch 1978: 120), since as well as pointing out these advantages
he also says that even in their absence education deserves the state's
attention. And while Latin may be of minimal utility he opines that his
preferred curriculum of geometry and mechanics learnt by the common
people is a 'necessary introduction to the most sublime as well as most
useful sciences' (WN V.i.f.55/786).

Smith's educational solution to deficient intellectual virtues was
taken up by others. For Millar 'it ought to be the great aim of the
public' to counter the obstacles to mental improvement confronting

'the common people' by instituting 'schools and seminaries of education to communicate as far as possible to the most useful but humble class of citizens that knowledge which their way of life has in some degree prevented from acquiring'. Again Scotland's parish schools are cited as an example (*HV* IV, 4/738). Dunbar says the ill-effects of the pin-maker's occupation require 'some expedient of government' to counteract them and, though not specified, education would seem to be what he has here in mind (*EHM* 423–4).

With respect to the shortfall in the 'pin-maker's' social virtues it is initially apt to note Smith's reference to the duties of government in the *Moral Sentiments*. He there says the law-giver 'may prescribe rules [. . .] that command mutual offices to a certain degree' and that discourage 'vice and impropriety'. But the mood is subjunctive not imperative and he counsels that it requires 'the greatest delicacy and reserve' to execute these rules (*TMS* II.ii.8/81; cf. *TMS* IV.2.1/187). This cautious modal language precludes reading this as a mandate for moral reform, even though it is, in principle, an endorsement of the propriety of public attention to social virtue, yet to say, as Ralph Lindgren (1973: 72) does, that this is to enforce morals is to overstep even the principle. Moreover, in practice, it is telling that when he comes to consider, in the *Wealth of Nations*, the execution of this high-flown task the prescriptions are modest. Aside from some passing remarks about the use of the tax system to reduce the number of alehouses and levy a higher rate on spirits than beer (*WN* V.ii.g.4/853; V.ii.k.50/891),[41] the deficiencies in the exercise of the social virtues are offset in two ways.

The first looks to education again, but indirectly. One of the symptoms of anti- or unsocial behaviour is unruliness; as we saw above enthusiasm can lead to disorder. In resounding Enlightenment language, Smith declaims that science is the 'great antidote to the poison of enthusiasm and superstition' and the imposition upon the higher social ranks of study of science will reduce the exposure of the 'inferior ranks' to those socially disruptive poisons (*WN* V.i.g.14/796). The operant presumption here is (has to be) that the mirror now reflects back to these ranks a view of society wide enough to encompass those in a superior position, who now exposed to 'science' will exhibit wisdom and virtue rather than (we can suppose) fashionable profligacy (*TMS* I.iii.3.4/62–3).[42]

The second remedy to a weakening of social virtue gives the state a more direct role, even if still obliquely. It concerns the role of the austere sects. These associations while socialising the pin-maker are, nonetheless, prone to instil socially disruptive zealotry. To counter this, Smith judges that the state can encourage 'publick diversions', such as drama, poetry, music, dancing and the like. By 'encourage' he means give 'entire liberty' to those who would 'for their own interest' put on these diversions provided this was done 'without scandal or indecency' (*WN* V.i.g.15/796). This policy of 'toleration' not only conforms to Smith's normative espousal of natural liberty but also could be read as a case of the 'delicacy and reserve' that accompanies the obligation laid down in the *Moral Sentiments*.[43] The effect of these diversions is to lift the 'melancholy and gloomy humour' that Smith associates with the 'disagreeably rigorous and unsocial' character of those sects (*WN* V.i.g.12/796). Kames also makes the link between 'public spectacles' and support for the social affections. He believes these spectacles and amusements, by being available to all ranks, help counteract the divisiveness of the 'separation of men into different classes by birth, office or occupation' (*EC* II, 443).

When it comes to addressing the erosion of martial virtues, Smith's recommendations are not specific. We know that instituting citizen militias is no solution. He refers to the military exercises that the Greeks and Romans made the citizens perform and judges they were a better instrument for maintaining 'the martial spirit' than the modern militias (*WN* V.i.f.60/787), which can simply be read as a further illustration of the outmodedness of the latter. These exercises were a compulsory part of their education (*WN* V.i.a.12/696 – referring to the Greeks). (Kames observes that the Roman army was 'invincible' because its citizens were 'trained to arms from their infancy' [*SHM* II, 20].) But engaging in those exercises will decay with the progress of improvement 'unless government takes proper pains to support' that engagement (*WN* V.i.f.59/786). More than that, as noted above, any such exercises would require intense regulation in the face of the inclinations of the people. John Robertson (1985: 216) and Andrew Skinner (1996: 194) interpret Smith to be claiming that nonetheless they should be made a compulsory part of contemporary public education. Ferguson for his part, in an unpublished piece on the 'separation of departments', did advocate that 'military tactics and manual exercises' should, suitably, be included in the 'Rudiments of Education' (*MSS* 148). Turnbull too thought that 'exercises' were necessary to 'maintain a masculine, hardy, martial spirit' but, apart from a reference to 'rightly model'd education', he gives no details (he also observes that these exercises should be limited so as to preclude becoming a 'nation of mere soldiers') (*PMP* 362, 361). Smith is equally unforthcoming on details. He does not say (pace Robertson and Skinner) the exercises should be compulsory but what those 'proper pains' or 'serious attention of government' (*WN* V.i.f.60/787) would amount to is left unspecified (cf. Sher 1989: 255).

The best guess is that the close textual recurrence of the phrase 'pre-miums and badges of distinction' (*WN* V.i.f.56 and V.i.f.58/786) with respect both to parish schools and the Greek and Roman republics sug-gests that these exercises might constitute a government-backed incen-tive structure to encourage participation in activities that would help counteract the decline of the martial spirit. But even that speculative solution seems ill-equipped to deal with a deficiency that he likens to a contagious disease (*WN* V.i.f.60/788).

Whether the indication of the seriousness of the ailment and the seeming inadequacy, or difficulty, of locating a remedy represents, in Montes' phrase 'the nuanced twilight of civic humanism' is moot (2009: 328). It runs the risk of over-stating this particular aspect by presuming that Smith significantly subscribed to the civic 'case' in the first place. There is some further reason to doubt his subscription when the final danger that besets a commercial society is examined. This last threat is posed by the system of credit and the effects of public debt.

## III

### PUBLIC CREDIT

What Craig Muldrew (1998: Chap. 10) termed the 'culture of credit' slowly formed from the sixteenth century. Starting with local networks relying on a personal reputation for trust it gradually extended to become what he calls a 'contractual society'. In this process credit had to be institutionalised (Ito 2011). The key to this process was extending the ability of credit to circulate. Integral to this was the development of banking, culminating in the founding of the Bank of England in 1696 and the so-called 'financial revolution', with the opportunity to invest in the government and thus for it to incur debt. These developments were not made without resistance. The fundamental concern was that trust was no longer anchored in known personal relations but was being left to float in a world of uncertainty and opinion – as Nicholas Barbon, who we have already met, declared, 'Credit is a Value raised by Opinion' (1905: 19). For Barbon this was not a negative develop-ment. Those who defended a system of credit pointed to its necessity to military success (the Bank of England was founded in the middle of the war with France), which rested on credit's ability to stimulate manufacture and trade. Indeed the extent of actual hostilities and the ever-present threat of international conflict, especially if not exclusively generated by colonial expansion, was a permanent backdrop (Dickson 1967: 7).

It was recognised that this reliance on credit put a still greater premium on behaving creditably (Hoppit 1990: 320) and all the more so since the development of credit instruments opened the way to exploitation. Charles Davenant, for example, in a frequently quoted passage, captured what was at stake – 'of all things that have existence only in the minds of men [cf. Barbon's 'wants of the mind' quoted p. 159], nothing is more fantastical and nice than Credit [. . .] it hangs upon Opinion' (1771: I, 151). This world of intangibles enabled speculators and 'stock-jobbers' to flourish, that is, individuals who Davenant characterises as supporters of 'projects, remote funds of credit and running the nation into yet a further debt (1771: IV, 212). For Davenant a viable credit system, which he desiderates, requires that 'the immorality and irreligion' of the age be corrected, something that the institution of sumptuary laws would facilitate (1771: I, 167; I, 347; V, 379). Of course, as Carl Wennerlind (2011: Chap. 4) has argued, it was recognised that to sustain a credit system in practice required more than exhortation and putative edicts on consumption; the condign enforcement of the law was also needed.

Davenant's concerns were reinvigorated by the spectacular financial collapses of the early eighteenth century (infamously the South Sea Bubble in England, but that was not an isolated occurrence). The luxury critique, as we have seen, developed a corresponding momentum, and the insubstantiality of credit was a further illustration of the superficiality of luxury. The primacy of desire, as manifest in the ephemerality and contagiousness of fashion, matched the irrationality and inconstancy that typified an economy of speculation, where 'projectors' and stock-jobbers flourish. This fitted the gendered language of the critique; women desired to be fashionable thus demonstrating their proverbial fickleness and unreliability. These feminine qualities were all attached censoriously to a credit-based economy. By contrast in one based on land, the landowner was the bastion of what Edmund Burke identified as 'the great and masculine virtues, constancy, gravity, magnanimity, fortitude, fidelity and firmness' (1889: 427).[44]

Just as the proponents of a commercial society were challenged by the luxury critique so were they by the critics of the culture of credit. The latter challenge was potentially more profound. The abstract and belief-dependent character of a commercial society meant this danger was all the more insidious. Uncertainty or risk are intrinsic to commerce, there is no guarantee that you will be able to sell the goods that are the fruit of your decision to specialise. As we brought out in Chapter 4, the extent of the division of labour (and thence of societal opulence) depends on having confidence in the future. The credit system equally depends on confidence; Steuart indeed defines it as 'reasonable expectation' (*PPE* II, 440). Funds are advanced (to buy the stock needed to begin manufacture) on the expectation they will be repaid, and there needs to be confidence that money deposited (that can then be lent to others) is secure and that it may be withdrawn on demand. The funding of government expenditure was no exception. It required monies now to meet current (and foreseeable) costs, especially those generated by war, so it borrowed (incurred debt) on the strength of a reliable future revenue stream from taxation. Millar, glossing the policies of William III but claiming they apply generally, identifies three causes of contracting national debt: from 'the dissipation and extravagance that are the usual effects of wealth and luxury'; from 'ambition' incurring costs in excess of revenue; and 'above all' from the 'facility of borrowing, occasioned by the circulation of capitals which is the natural consequence of extensive trade and manufacture' (*HV* III, 7/657). But the dangers of credit were not historical. The collapse of the Ayr bank that we mentioned in Chapter 1 indicates that these are not trivial matters and had not gone away. It also means that the status of credit and (related issue) of public debt constituted clear and present dangers to the idea of a commercial society. Even those supportive of commerce, such as Hume, were acutely aware of this threat and doubtful about how to meet it successfully.

Hume devoted an essay ('Of Public Credit') to the topic. This was included in the 1752 *Political Discourses* but within that collection it has more in common with the essay 'Of the Balance of Power' than it does with 'Of Commerce'. The main, though not sole, focus of 'Of Public Credit' is that public debt leads to the erosion of defensive capabilities and, significantly, as he explicitly says, to lack of attention to the balance of power (*E-PC* 365). His account thus jells with the dangers outlined in the final subsection of Part I above. It is true that he does consider the effect of public debt on 'domestic management'. On that front he judges that on balance the disadvantages of debt finance outweigh its supposed advantages for commerce and industry (which of course means admitting there are some positives). Nevertheless these disadvantages are 'trivial' compared to the damage the debt does to the 'state considered as a body politic' (*E-PC* 355).

It is the contemporary salience and pervasiveness of war and national defence that supplies Hume's perspective (his first sentence refers to 'peace, 'war', 'conquest' and 'defence' [*E-PC* 349]). The essay's opening gambit is a contrast between 'the common practice of antiquity' and the 'modern expedient'. The former meant hoarding treasure, the latter borrowing (contracting public debt). The hoarding is done in peacetime in order to conquer or defend in time of war. The context for the borrowing is not made explicit in 'Of Public Credit' but in 'Of the Balance of Power' the link with war is made (*E-BP* 340). Bereft of hoarded treasure, modern regimes in order to raise funds mortgage public revenues trusting that 'posterity' will redeem the debt. But, of course, the next generation will simply adopt the same policy and pass the debt on to their successors and they to theirs. The upshot is that the debt thus accumulated will lead, 'beyond all controversy' to eventual ruin; it will 'almost infallibly' produce 'poverty, impotence and subjection to foreign powers' (*E-PC* 350–1). This reveals the particular 'political' thrust of this essay. Though the ancient practice was also subject to abuses yet 'in this respect' it is more prudent than the modern version (*E-PC* 350). There are some 'internal' dangers (as we might term them) to commerce, such as the high price of labour, from unsupported debt, chiefly in the form of an ever-growing requirement for more tax revenue to service it. And he reiterates his doubts about paper money (in 'Of Money' [*E-Mon* 284]) since public securities or stocks function as a kind of money (*E-PC* 355, 356). But the 'external' dangers are catastrophic. Hence the rhetorical flourishes that characterise 'Of Public Credit' – 'either the nation must destroy public credit or public credit will destroy the nation' (*E-PC* 360–1).

He outlines two paths to destruction. Overburdened with taxes and having exhausted all sources of new revenue, a government when confronted with an emergency will act like an absolute ruler (cf. *E-CL* 96) and seize the monies earmarked for interest repayment. Though it will swear to replace them, this abrogation of 'public faith' will destroy the confidence on which a modern economy depends and thus bring the 'tottering fabric' to the ground. This scenario Hume calls 'the natural death of public credit' (*E-PC* 363). But an even worse scenario is possible. This recourse to voluntary bankruptcy runs too much against the grain of 'popular government' (cf. *E-CL* 96) with the result that, with no resources left, the nation is too feeble to resist an external conqueror. This is the 'violent death of our public credit' (*E-PC* 365). This brings the essay full circle, unlike the ancient practice of hoarding in order to be ready for war the modern practice of borrowing has eroded that capability.

His final words in the essay appear to verge on the bathetic. There is no resounding advocacy in the manner of Davenant to restore ancient frugality (1771: IV, 424) (indeed as we saw he ruled that out) but instead a plea to escape from the 'influence of popular madness and delusion'. This echoes 'Of the Balance of Power' where it is the 'most fatal delusion' to mortgage revenues for a war (of the Austrian Succession) that was of only incidental concern (*E-BP* 340). As Duncan Forbes (1975a: 174) pointed out it is this international dimension (especially vis-à-vis France) that is the central message of Hume's Credit essay.[45] This is not to say that Hume, especially in the iterations of the essay in later editions (Hont 2005: 340), did not air Davenant-like concerns on the dangers of commerce. In this mode he declares that an indebted over-taxed society is 'unnatural' and therein only 'stockholders' have any revenue (beyond that immediately gained through industry). But these individuals have no 'connexions to the state'; they can enjoy their revenue anywhere.[46] Hume declares they will be city-dwellers who will 'sink into the lethargy of stupid and pampered luxury' (*E-PC* 357), where again the real problem is sloth not sensual gratification. Moreover, the fluidity of these funds prohibits their solidification into hereditary authority. This removes a traditional bastion of good governance, a 'middle power' of independent magistracy between 'king and people' (*E-PC* 358).[47] Presumably this 'power' acts as a counter-force to 'popular madness' and the 'delusions' of an unrestrained ruler.

Other Scots beside Hume commented on the danger of debt. A contemporary Edinburgh-published pamphlet refers to Hume but judges he has been too decorous. The authorship of this pamphlet is uncertain[48] but it pulls no punches – 'the public debt [. . .] is a gangrene in the commonwealth and will submit to nothing but amputation' (elsewhere it is likened to leeches and vermin, is productive of immorality and a spirit of gaming [Anon. 1753: 1, 2, 6, 12, 13]). However, Wallace takes issue with Hume. Credit is necessary to commerce and Hume's objections to 'paper-credit' are misplaced (*CGB* 27). Similarly he emphasises the advantages of pubic debts in encouraging commerce that Hume had allowed but had judged to be overweighed by disadvantages (*CGB* 49). Wallace indeed declares that 'a nation may be opulent and flourishing at the same time that public debts are high' (*CGB* 95). He turns the tables on the argument that stock-jobbers are idle and useless since that description can equally apply to their chief critics, the 'landed men' (*CGB* 50). He concedes that it is not easy to fix limits to the extent of borrowing (*CGB* 50), a conclusion shared by Ferguson. More than Wallace and closer to Hume, Ferguson thinks the expedient of contracting debt, rather than 'suspend[ing] private industry', in order to execute a 'great national project' has advantages yet it is 'extremely dangerous' and, with an allusion to the Dutch, can lead to ruin (*ECS* 234–5). In his *Principles* he emphasises the dangers of 'temptation' that debt funding induces in both the lender and the borrower. The more the debt increases the more, here echoing an analogy made by the author of that anonymous pamphlet and by Smith (*LJB* 326/538), 'it resembles the vicissitudes of a gaming table' (*PMPS* II, 450–1) (lottery schemes both private and state sponsored were a feature of the late seventeenth century [Murphy 2009: 34–5]). In the end for Ferguson, as for Wallace, the danger is not the practice of public credit but keeping it within bounds *PMPS* II, 455).

Steuart does not refer to Hume by name but an enumeration of 'consequences' echoes Hume's concerns in 'Of Public Credit'. However, he thinks it impossible to 'foretell' their likelihood (*PPE* II, 601).[49] Steuart believes that 'past experience' indicates that the problem has been manageable but now where creditors are dominant then 'I suppose the case may be different' (*PPE* II, 636). And in a manner further reminiscent of Hume he adverts to war, emanating from ambition, as the cause of debt increase (*PPE* II, 637). However, he demurs from the Humean consequence that bankruptcy is unavoidable (*PPE* II, 647) and sees the restoration of confidence in the hands of his 'statesman' as the means to pay off debts (*PPE* II, 656).

Steuart declares that public credit is 'established upon the confidence reposed in a State or body politic' (*PPE* II, 472). That confidence or trust was key was accepted by both Wallace (*CGB* 47) and Ferguson (*PMPS* II, 449). This in itself unremarkable point was central to Smith. For him the established maxim, adopted by Wallace as we saw [p. 166 above], that with liberty comes its abuse is exemplified by a system of public credit. Free actions have 'unintended consequences'.

Like Hume, Smith contrasts ancient and modern practice. In commercial nations the availability and attractive quality of luxury goods means that in peace funds are spent, not hoarded. As a result, in time of war in order to meet the extra costs there is a need to borrow revenue and contract debt (*WN* V.iii.4/909). But the operation of the 'moral cause' that produces this need also produces the means to meet it, that is, the presence of merchants and manufacturers with the wherewithal to lend (*WN* V.iii.5, 6/910; cf. Steuart *PPE* I, 182). In this context Smith makes one of his strongest declarations of the importance of the regular administration of justice. This regularity that commercial societies enjoy gives these merchants sufficient trust and confidence in the government to give credit (*WN* V.iii.7/910). Since the government is in dire straits then the terms of the loan will be attractive to lenders (*LJB* 321/536). But since the government can now foresee a source of revenues, Smith declares, it 'dispenses itself from the duty of saving' (*WN* V.iii.8/911). Smith gives no explanation for this – not even the implicit recourse to scientific regularity upon which Hume drew. Since his discussion continues with a historical narrative (as Steuart's had done) then this declaration comes across as descriptive.

Once government foregoes saving then a chain of events is set in motion that produces those 'enormous debts which at present oppress and will in the long run probably ruin all the great nations of Europe' (*WN* V.iii.10/911). Smith proceeds at some length to itemise the various methods that have been employed to fund the debt. However, as with the entrenchment of supposedly temporarily raised taxes and the 'ruinous expedient of perpetual funding', these have exacerbated the situation (*WN* V.iii.39, 41/920–1). Despite the ingenuity thereby shown, bankruptcy, when the revenues are insufficient to pay off the interest, let alone the capital, on past loans, is the ultimate consequence. This, Smith notes, is often 'disguised' by 'raising the denomination of the coin' (*WN* V.iii.60/929). (Hume had noted this in one of the passages that he excised in later editions 'Of Public Credit' [*E-v* 638].) This 'juggling trick' only aggravates the situation and extends the 'calamity' to more innocent people (*WN* V.iii.60/930). Smith thinks it 'vain to expect' the public debt ever to be paid back (*WN* V.iii.66/933).

This language avoids the rhetorically apocalyptic tone of Hume. In principle, there are solutions: the debt can be reduced by increasing public revenues (including tax from the colonies) and/or reducing public expenditure (*WN* V.iii.66/933). In practice, Smith's circumscribed view of 'politics' (Teichgraeber 1986: 18) means he has no illusions that effecting these solutions would be easy. That said, he is more inclined to regard indebtedness as a fact of commercial life, even if it is one that we would ideally be better off without. This illustrates how the unintended consequences of the emergence of commercial markets are not only beneficial in destroying feudal power and instigating the rule of law but also harmful in threatening via debt the ruin of the society that emerged in that manner. Commercial society is not the best of all possible worlds. What this tells us about the Scots' idea of a commercial society, along with an assessment of the idea's significance, is the subject of the concluding chapter.

## NOTES

1. '*anthrôpos phusei politikon zoon*' (Aristotle 1944: 1253a10–11). Despite the generic *anthrôpos* here (reflecting Aristotle's view that humans were not uniquely 'political'), his argument, and that which follows him, was gendered; males participate in politics (women manage the *oikos* and a 'modest silence' on their part regarding the *polis* as such is fitting [1944: 260a31]).

2. Just as the first strain of ancient liberty saw no limit to desire once the limits of need satisfaction had been met, so Aristotle saw no limit to the

pursuit of riches that are generated by the art of wealth getting (1944: 1257b17–18).

3. Smith (*LJB* 301–2/527) refers to merchants being despised, indeed remarks that this prejudice has not yet been entirely extinguished and has 'greatly obstructed the progress of commerce'.

4. David Kettler (1965: 236) while acknowledging Ferguson's 'grave doubts' nonetheless concludes that 'in the final analysis [. . .] Ferguson's position eventuated in a vindication of commercial society'. This conclusion is followed by a long quotation from the *Principles* (*PMPS* I, 249–50).

5. This recourse to Sparta put Ferguson at odds with Hume, who had a deeply critical view of the Spartan regime (see text below). He acknowledged this divergence in a letter (see *CorrF* I, 76). That Ferguson regarded Sparta as his 'ideal polity' is claimed by Jack (1989: 151).

6. This agonism has prompted much commentary, especially because of its link with 'unintended consequences' – see Lehmann (1930: 98–106) for a pioneering discussion in English, see Hill (2006: Chap. 7) for a recent treatment. In Ferguson the benefits of 'conflict' are (not unexpectedly) manifest in the struggle between the patricians and plebians in Rome (*Rom* I, 85–6). This Livian trope was a mainstay of the civic republican tradition, especially as regenerated by Machiavelli's *Discorsi* on the opening ten books of Livy's history.

7. When discussing the final events of the Roman Republic Ferguson remarks that Cato, Cicero, Brutus and others acted with a 'commendable zeal for liberty' to support their fellow citizens when, in fact, they were unworthy of it (*Rom* V, 71). More generally it is a recurrent theme in his *History* that with the relaxation of military and political virtues 'human nature fell into a retrograde motion' (*Rom* V, 397).

8. Pocock called the *Essay* 'perhaps the most Machiavellian of the Scottish disquisitions on this theme [corruption]' (1975: 429). Cf. McDowell (1983: 545): 'Ferguson's understanding of virtue was Machiavellian.' See also Medick and Batscha (1988: 69).

9. Aristotle declared generically that the 'best polis' (*beltistê polis*) will not treat 'workers' (*banausoi*), that is those who have to work for their living, as citizens (1944: 1278a8); Plato had established a connection between *hoi kapeloi* (traders) and bodily weakness making them naturally unfit for military tasks (1902: 371c, 374a). Xenophon links these together – *banausikai* (instrumental 'unfree' or 'illiberal' activity) softens the body, weakens the mind so its practitioners are bad defenders of the polis (1923: IV, 3).

10. Hont 2006 provides a survey of the first half of the century though confined to Britain and France. There is a large literature on the French debate; the most thorough is Shovlin 2006. The debate elsewhere is not well covered but for Italy there is a dedicated study (Wahnbaeck 2004); for passing comment on Spain see Herr 1958. Steuart was influential in 'Germany', the Cameralist notion of *Polizei* incorporated the regulation of luxury.

11. I draw these lists from St Lambert's (1757) article 'Luxe' in the Encylopédie (volume IX). As we will see the former list closely resembles Hume's argument and reflects his considerable influence in France – see Charles 2008.

12. Melon declares *'le terme luxe est un vain nom'* that conveys *'les idées vagues, confuses, fausses'* and advises it be banished when considering *'de police et de commerce'* (1735: 130). (Melon's *Essai* was influential – Hume was familiar with it.) Diderot cites *'luxe'* as an example where its application to an infinity of objects means it escapes exact definition (article, *'Encyclopédie'* ([1755: V 636r]).

13. For other discussions of Hume on luxury see Cunningham 2005, Susato 2006 and my own earlier treatment, Berry 1994: 144–9.

14. In his *History* Hume implicitly connects the development of artillery with humanity (the third link in the chain) when he observes that, though 'contrived for the destruction of mankind', it has 'rendered battles less bloody and has given greater stability to civil societies' (*HE* I, 498).

15. Not that Hume was under any illusions about the competence of contemporary military conduct. He witnessed first-hand the disastrous 1746 campaign in Brittany of General St Clair (Mossner 1980: Chap. 15).

16. Fénelon, the most influential critic of luxury in early eighteenth-century France, contrasted *les arts superflus* to *les vrais besoins* that were imposed by nature (1962: 453–4). For discussion of Fénelon see Bonolas 1987 and Hont 2006.

17. Hume had called luxury (along with prodigality, irresolution and uncertainty) 'vicious' in the *Treatise*, the fault being that these characteristics 'incapacitate us for business and action' (*T* 3.3.4.7/*SBNT* 611). In line with Hume's later account in 'Of Refinement in the Arts' this fault lies in them not being advantageous in the conduct of life, rather than in lying in some intrinsic defect. I am grateful to Carl Wennerlind for originally drawing my attention to this passage.

18. Mandeville's characterisation of the 'main Design' of the *Fable* was that it was impossible simultaneously to enjoy, as is evidently the case, 'all the most elegant Comforts of Life' (as found in 'an industrious, wealthy and powerful Nation') while judging that the benchmark of proper conduct is to be 'bless'd with all the Virtue and Innocence that can be wish'd for in a Golden Age' (1988: I, 6).

19. See his account of England under Elizabeth when the 'nobility were by degrees acquiring a taste for elegant luxury'; though this led to the decay of 'glorious hospitality' yet it is 'more reasonable to think that this new turn of expense promoted arts and industry, while the ancient hospitality was the source of vice, disorder, sedition and idleness' (*HE* II, 601).

20. Hume observes that in polite ages libertine love is more frequent (*E-RA* 272). For Kames 'chastity becomes a mere name' (*SHM* I, 338).

21. Though even in 1779 this is less applicable to England and Germany where the emphasis on the 'more necessary and useful arts' has retarded this development (but England is included in the corresponding passage in

the *View* [HV IV, 4/770]). The emphasis in this short section is on fine or elegant arts, as stated in the new title of the relevant section in the third edition. Millar refers to limits (*OR* 225; *Obs* 77), and this is redolent of a long-standing trope that such arts have a term after which they enter into decline.

22. Michael Ignatieff sees in Millar's treatment of sexual licentiousness the 'civic republican strain in his thought', though judges him 'ambivalent' about modern individualism and this as indicative of his position as a theorist caught between the 'two languages' of civic humanist moralism and political economy' (1983: 340, 336, 341). Whether he is so 'caught' of course depends on the facility for bilingualism. Knud Haakonssen sees an 'argumentative triumph' here in the way Millar distinguishes matters of justice from moralising about virtue (1996: 169). Catherine Moran (2003: 79,71) detects anxiety on Millar's part but reads him, pace Ignatieff, as adopting 'an unchanging womanhood' against which to measure the 'desires and sentiments of men'.

23. Cf. Muzzarelli 2009 and Hunt 1996. There are a number of studies of particular 'national' ordinances.

24. Preamble to the English Act of Apparel of 1533 as quoted in Harte (1976: 39).

25. Smith observes that a day-labourer would be ashamed to appear in public without a linen shirt (its non-possession, indeed, would indicate a 'disgraceful degree of poverty') when the Greeks and Romans of an earlier age lived very comfortably without such a garment (*WN* V.ii.k.3/870). On Smith's influence on this score see Roberts 1998 and on a wider footing Berry 1994: Chaps 7 and 8).

26. For example, 'we have indeed suffered Repose to steal upon our Minds'. Other examples include his acknowledgment that the state of commerce 'at which we have arrived' has affected our manners to remove an earlier 'contempt of lucrative arts' and produce a decline in the status of 'profession of arms' because 'its profits are trivial'; Britain will become a nation of manufacturers each confined to own branch and will have allowed public service to become a livelihood (*Reflections* 14, 8–9, 12, 43).

27. Regarding the major contention as to whether joining the militia should be voluntary or compulsory his stance is oblique – while an Act might make take the form of compulsion yet 'chearful and ready compliance', with little need for coercion, would occur if manners were changed (*Reflections* 49). Raynor (2008: 70, 72) reads the pamphlet as in favour of a voluntary arrangement, arguing that it appears to have been written to oppose the case for compulsion.

28. Robertson (1985: 186) tends to emphasise the former aspect, Sher the latter (1989: 259n).

29. A militia was a central component of Harrington's plan for Oceana (1656) – see Note 30 below. In a *Discourse* (1698) devoted to the topic, Fletcher praised militias as the 'true badges of liberty' and as constituting a 'school

of virtue' (1979: 19, 24). That Fletcher was an important formative influence is put forward by Davie (1981; cf. Pocock 1985: 230) but there is negligible evidence to support that proposition. Kames' is one of the few references to his work.

30. Ferguson wrote to Smith after reading the *Wealth of Nations* and said that he supported him in much but opposed him over the militia (*CorrF* I, 193–4). The relationship between Smith and Ferguson on this issue is discussed by Sher who concludes they disagreed 'fundamentally' (1989: 208). See also Mizuta 1981. Just as Smith's membership of the Poker does not translate into support for militias nor does it for Hume. But David Raynor, as part of his argument that the pamphlet *Sister Peg* (1760) was written by Hume (Ferguson is more frequently identified), refers to Hume's 'zealous advocacy of citizen militias' (1982: 26). Others (for example, Robertson 1986: 70ff; cf. also 1983 and Forbes 1975a: 212) who attribute antipathy to standing armies and support for militias as evidence that Hume was a form of civic republican rely heavily on his essay 'Idea of a Perfect Commonwealth', although this was explicitly designed as an imaginary exercise with Harrington's identified as the 'only valuable model' (*E-IPC* 514). I incline to Richard Teichgraeber's (1986: 117) nice description of this essay as 'playful irony'.

31. Although true of modern armies this general message applies in earlier times (see above p. 75). Smith picks up the example of Rome and Carthage, of which as we saw Ferguson made much, but makes the point that both armies due to the prolonged nature of the conflicts took on the character of a professional army. The Romans defeated the militias of Greece, Syria and Egypt who put up 'but a feeble resistance' (*WN* V.i.a.32–5/702–3). Ferguson judged this same development a sign of Roman corruption.

32. This echoes his view (identified in Chapter 4 p. 111) that the gentry's interest and that of the public coincide. It coheres less obviously with his view that they were mentally ill-equipped to make political judgments, unless of course effective military leadership is deemed to depend less on intelligence.

33. This was perhaps begun, or at least prompted, by Marx quoting this passage in *Capital* (1967: I, 361 – he also refers to Ferguson at other points regarding him, thanks to the priority of the *Essay* to the *Wealth of Nations*, as Smith's teacher [I, 123n, 354]). These references when coupled with the 'discovery' of the 'young Marx' and his analysis of 'alienation' or 'estrangement' (*Entäusserung, Entfremdung*) has led to claims that Ferguson foreshadows Marx, in sketching 'a vivid scene of class oppression' (McDowell 1983: 543) or that he is 'among the most acute critics of capitalism' (Blaney and Inayatullah 2010: 106). That this passage (and Ferguson's thought in the *Essay* more widely) portends a wider critique of 'enterprise culture' (Benton 1990) and 'the market' (Varty 1997: 38; Ehrenberg 1999: 96) has also been promulgated. Duncan Forbes (1967: 46) declares that in Ferguson can be discerned 'the first

clear announcement of one of the most explosive themes in the history of
modern thought; the idea of alienation' and David Kettler (1965: 9–10)
that his 'concerns clearly foreshadow the problems of over-rationalisation,
dehumanisation, atomisation, alienation and bureaucratisation'.

34. See, for example, West (1964, 1969) who later debates (1975) with Lamb
(1973), and also Rosenberg (1965) and Werhane (1991). Again Marxist
alienation sets a frame in much, if not all, of this; on that perspective see,
for example, Winch (1978), Hill (2007) and MacRae (1969: 24) who sar-
donically commented when this question surfaced that much of the discussion of alienation seemed to him 'void'.

35. This is reinforced in even stronger language a little later, the 'inferior
ranks' in a 'civilized society' suffer from 'gross ignorance and stupidity'
and nothing is more contemptible than ' a man without the proper use of
the intellectual faculties (*WN* V.i.f.61/788).

36. In his later work, where he shows his indebtedness to Smith, Ferguson
remarks, in an unpublished essay (1806) in the context of pin-making, on
the 'torpor' of those whose task is 'mere movement of the hand or foot'
(*MSS* 15/145). The *Principles* while talking at length about the division of
labour make no reference to its effects on the virtues (*PMPS* II, 42–30).

37. One of the earliest as well as most perceptive explorations of the Smith/
Rousseau relation can be found in Ignatieff (1984: Chap. 4). See also more
recently Griswold (2010) for a philosophical exploration of that relation
that picks up the deep significance of interdependency in Smith.

38. Hans Medick and Annette Leppert-Fögen (1974: 31) interpret this division in Marxist terms as symptomatic of other components in Millar's
thought that reveals an '*Zweiklassentheorie*'. For them, as the title of their
piece states, Millar is a theorist of the petty-bourgeoisie whose thought is
riven by 'contradiction' (1974: 34, 47 and throughout).

39. Others who detect civic humanism in Smith include (in a qualified way)
Robertson (1983) and McNally (1988), Hirschman (1977), Evensky
(2005), Tanaka (2007). Winch (1978) influenced by Pocock casts much of
his exposition in these terms but in later essays (1983, 1988) makes clear
the limits of this interpretation.

40. Smith is against wholly public funding because it will encourage the teacher
to 'neglect his business' (*WN* V.i.f.55/785); a maxim Smith extended to
university education (*WN* V.i.f.7–8/760–1) comparing, implicitly, Scottish
practice favourably with, explicitly, the Oxford system (see also *Corr*
178).

41. Smith says explicitly of the latter measure that this policy has been adopted
to discourage consumption of spirits 'on account of their supposed tendency to ruin the health and to corrupt the morals of the common people'.
He reports this but sees no grounds to contest its propriety and defends the
tax differentials against Davenant (*WN* V.ii.k.51/891).

42. It is moot whether Smith's concerns here in this chapter (added in the 6th
edition [1790]) pertain to commercial accumulation rather than to landed

rents and an aristocratic environment. See Tegos 2013 for an insightful exploration.

43. This same principle of 'toleration' covers Smith's view that these 'sects' are only troublesome when they are few in number and a multitude of sects would diffuse that aspect. He further thinks that fissiparity would follow if the government 'let them alone', while obliging them to respect others (*WN* V.i.g.9/794). He even claims that the very fact of multiplicity might indeed induce 'that pure and rational religion, free from every mixture of absurdity, imposture or fanaticism' (*WN* V.i.g.8/793) (see Boyd 2004: 137 for an argument that Smith 'envisions a pluralistic world'). This is distinct from the state's role where there is an established religion. Here the issue is the government's first duty, its provision of security, not public works. In order to prevent clerics from conspiring against the sovereign's authority it is necessary, for the sake of 'publick tranquillity', that the state should exercise a 'considerable degree' of influence over the 'greater part of the teachers of religion'. This 'influence' will be principally by means of some control of the career structure; it is 'not the proper department' of a temporal sovereign to involve itself in the actual 'articles of faith' (*WN* V.i.g.18/798).

44. This gendered vocabulary contrasted virtue (virility) with the female goddess Fortuna, whose 'goods' (wealth, fame) are ephemeral. This juxtaposition was common in the Renaissance (famously in Machiavelli's *Il Principe* [especially Chap. 25]) but had been evoked by Roman moralists like Sallust who emphasised Fortuna's capriciousness (*ex lubidine*) (hence the sway of luxury and rise of Catiline) (1921: para 8). See Pocock (1975: Chap. 2) for discussion of the role of this vocabulary and for its relation to credit (1975: 452ff). He later cautions against presuming an antithesis between land and credit, while highlighting that the 'morality of the trading man' was at odds with the virtue of the citizen (1975: 449, 445; cf. 466).

45. Forbes' undeveloped observation was followed up more thoroughly by Hont (2005) who in effect is defending Forbes against Pocock's (1985: 132) interpretation where Hume is seen as condemning public credit as the agent of a commercial society's self-destruction. Hideo Tanaka (2007: 43) neatly captures the issue in his remark that Hume's 'ambivalence is not of a vision of commercial society but of the relation of commercial society and international power politics'.

46. Compare Bolingbroke's image that 'moneyed men' are 'no more than passengers [in the political vessel]' (1754: III, 174). Smith too expressed this sentiment (*WN* V.ii.f.6/848; cf. III.iv.24/426) but it is not invested with any severe censure.

47. In the late 'Of the Origin of Government' Hume had identified as one mark of a free government that it possessed a 'partition of power among several members' (*E-OG* 41). Contextually in 'Of Public Credit' this middle power appears to comprise the landed gentry (Bolingbroke

contrasted money men as 'passengers' with 'landed men as the true owners of our political vessel' [1754: III, 174]). However, this sits uncomfortably alongside the argument in 'Of Refinement of Arts' that the tradesman and merchants appear to be that 'middling rank of men' who are the best basis of public liberty (*E-RA* 377 – see p. 56 above). On a difference between 'power' and rank' see Giarrizzo (1962: 52, 68n).

48. The British Library attributes it to Lord Elibank but the National Library of Scotland attributes it to Lord Eglinton. Elibank was a friend of Hume's, a focal member of the literati, he belonged to the Select Society and was a militia supporter (Carlyle [1910: 63, 279] speaks highly of his abilities). Eglinton, an 'improver', was also known to Hume and moved in higher political circles in London.

49. Hume admits it is 'difficult to foretel' but still refers to 'natural consequences' and a 'natural progress of things' (*E-PC* 357, 360). These appear to be based on certain predictable constancies in behaviour (he refers to the 'nature of men and ministers' and to 'mankind in all ages' being 'caught by the same baits' [*E-PC* 360, 363]). Notwithstanding this his rhetorically heightened prognostications are presented as a reasonable 'guess' (*E-PC* 360).

# 7. The Idea of a
# Commercial Society

My aim in this concluding chapter is to identify what the Scots understand by 'commercial society' and what is distinctive about it. This
exercise will also serve to highlight particular episodes in the story told
in the preceding chapters.

The core of the idea of a commercial society is that it is a 'society',
not a polity or a clan, even though it contains governments and families.
These latter two are component parts of the interlocking set of institutions, behaviours and values that constitute a 'society'. This integration
is as true of the Iroquois, the Tartars, feudal Europe and city-states of
the ancient and Renaissance world as it is of commercial societies. The
world of commerce has its own distinctive set and this distinctiveness
is the work of history. To reiterate my earlier formulation (p. 49), in
the work of the Scots, commercial society has both a synchronic and
diachronic dimension.

We can piece together some key features of a commercial society
from the earlier discussion. From Chapter 3 we learnt that commercial
societies were prosperous in virtue of the systemic employment of the
division of labour. We also know that this prosperity was diffused;
all participants in the market, even the relatively poor, were better
off absolutely than in any other period. This diffusion of 'universal
opulence' further differentiated a modern commercial society from
life in trading cities like Venice, which were rigorously policed to
keep the ruling oligarchy in their pre-eminent position and even more
from the slave-based classical republics. The common good in a commercial society was judged in terms of what promoted the material
well-being of the many not the few, something sumptuary laws, like
those in Venice, thwarted and was precluded in Athens and Rome. We
saw in Chapter 4, that once 'triggered', modern prosperity developed
pari passu with the rule of law and the strict administration of justice;

this institutionalisation of equity again being contrary to the legally enforced hierarchy of sumptuary law and slavery. It was only through the operation of a secure and equitable system of law, with its embedment of constancy and predictability, that there could be the confidence required for future-oriented market behaviour. These behaviours inherently involved interacting with large numbers of people. But the difference was as much qualitative as quantitative. The majority of these interactions would be indirect and anonymous and even when direct most would be with strangers, so that the mode of interaction was predominantly impersonal and discretely functional rather than personal and valued for its own sake. Living in a society where the rule of law was operant gave a particular modern form to liberty; the freedom, as Chapter 5 brought out, to pursue one's own interests in one's own way. A society that underwrites those diverse pursuits will be pluralistic. Whether or not these pursuits are commercial they will be undertaken within a peaceful environment or at least one where lawlessness is not endemic.

Despite these positive factors, commercial society also had its negative dimensions. Yet these, as covered in Chapter 6, also inform, in relief, what marks out a commercial society. There are not just more consumable goods but they can also be of a high quality, manifesting taste and refinement (luxury). A commercial society regards the sphere of politics, just like military affairs, as an area of specialisation; it is a society of banks and credit and one where public resources are appropriately utilised to general social benefit. Integral to these features are patterns of behaviour and conduct. The wealth created through its reliance on self-interest enables more scope for beneficence; the weak and the vulnerable can be tended to and not left to perish. Commercial societies are polite, women are treated with respect, and individuals deal honestly with each other and treat even enemies humanely.

Importantly, these features are not randomly co-existent; they exhibit an inner coherence, though, as we will take care to confirm, this does not mean this coherence is undifferentiated, without tensions and anomalies. This coherence can be illustrated by a brief examination of two institutions and norms not hitherto considered – religion and the fine arts. Commercial societies as societies are more enlightened. The beliefs of their members reflect that. This should be qualified to acknowledge that this is not the case uniformly or universally (I will return to that qualification as an instance of the differentiation within the coherence). Possessing greater knowledge, the educated are able to appreciate that such is the order that the Universe exhibits that it bespeaks a Design that must emanate from an informing, superintending Intelligence.

This meant that, unlike the nineteenth-century confrontations between 'science' and 'religion', in the Enlightenment increases in scientific knowledge and understanding were thought to demonstrate the perfection of the Design ever more clearly and conclusively. Hutton's epoch-making *Theory of the Earth* exemplifies this – 'we live in a world where order everywhere prevails; and where final causes are as well-known, at least, as those which are efficient' (Hutton 1795: 545; cf. 566). Good scientists were true believers, as Newton himself demonstrated beyond any shadow of doubt (cf. Gregory 1788: 248). This 'pure rational' religion, as Smith termed it (p. 192n above), or Deism, was distinct from particular forms of religious practice; in particular it was distinct from superstition.

Just as the Scots wrote a natural history of property – its move from concrete possession to increasingly abstract forms – so they wrote a natural history of religion. Hume published a lengthy essay with that title in 1757, the explicit aim of which was to enquire into the origin of religion in human nature. But Hume was not alone. One of Kames' *Sketches* had the same intent and in an embryonic form such a history is present in Smith (Berry 2000). Despite differences the shared narrative was that religious beliefs developed from superstition to reason, from concrete worship of many gods, who intervene in human affairs and need to be placated or beseeched, to the abstract appreciation of a Divine order. This is equally a growth from ignorance to knowledge but that itself is embedded in a history of 'society'. Polytheists are ignorant of the connections between causes and effects (cf. Kames *SHM* II, 389) and that is attributable to their circumstances. Pressed by 'numerous wants and passions' (Hume *NHR* I, 6/35), they lack leisure and that shortcoming means they have no opportunity to acquire instruction. 'Free' time is required to enable humans to begin the process of tracing causal links (cf. Smith *HA* III.3/50; Wallace *Prospects* 19, 52n). As societies develop so humans become civilised and so 'science and literature' as the 'natural fruit of leisure, tranquillity and affluence' grow (Millar *HV* III, 3/507; *OR* 176).

This consonance between the history of property and religion should be no surprise given the Scots' ambition to write a 'natural history of mankind' (as, among several others, Millar explicitly announced [*OR* 180]). In the same vein there can be a 'history of literature' (the title of a chapter in Ferguson's *Essay*). Language progresses from poetry, abounding with vivid metaphoric imagery, to prose, with its emphasis on clarity (see Smith *LRBL* ii.115–16/137; cf. Amrozowicz 2013). As the 'quality' of religious belief improves so too does that of literature. It is not denied that Homer (and Ossian) produced literature that we still read but its value reposes on the principle, as declared by Blackwell in his book on Homer (1735), that 'every kind of writing, but especially the Poetick depends upon the Manners of the Age' (1972: 68–9). But, of course, these 'manners' are not solely evidenced by literature, they are societally pervasive.

To hold that literature 'improves' is to hold that there are criteria by which this can be assessed. Hence the ubiquitous Enlightenment discussions of the 'standard of taste' to which many Scots contributed (Berry 1997: 174–80). The recurrent theme of these discussions was that it was a universal trait of human nature to 'reconcile' the 'various sentiments of men', to criticise according to standards and the source of that 'standard' was human nature itself (Hume *E-ST* 229; Kames *EC* II, 437–8; and others). Again just as the morality and religion of 'savages' was inferior to the practices and beliefs of a commercial society so, as Blair (1838: 21) puts it, taste had 'no materials on which to operate' in 'rude and uncivilized nations'; accordingly when making artistic judgments, it is the 'sentiments of mankind in polished and flourishing nations' that establish the criteria. The 'uncivilized' would have standards, since aesthetic considerations are a truly universal aspect of human nature, but what they do value is crude and, by definition, lacking in refined taste, so 'mortifications' and self-mutilation are practised in order to appear formidable before enemies (Dunbar *EHM* 389) or to conform to religious rite (Kames *SHM* II, 436).

The synchronic picture of a commercial society that emerges can be diachronically contrasted with the picture of a first-stage hunter-gatherer one. Hence summarily, a society of hunter gatherers will have little in the way of personal possessions, nothing to speak of in the form of governmental machinery, few status distinctions except the inferiority of women, and will live in a world populated with a multiplicity of gods whose actions make their feelings plain. These savages would also respond to these events in a speech abounding in vivid and animated imagery and would likely variously bedaub or scarify themselves and represent their gods in idols. In contrast, a commercial society will treat intangibles like promissory notes as property, its members will live under a rule of law administered impersonally by a government dedicated to that task, and in that regard enjoy an equality regardless of social status, the relations between the sexes will also approach some sort of equality, they will be monotheists, tasteful and measured in word and deed and will be scrupulous in business and generous in both private and public. This contrast conforms to the trajectory of natural history from concrete to abstract, from simple to complex and from rude to cultivated. This development to complexity can be seen as the Scots' version of the various nineteenth-century schema of the move from status to contract (Maine), *Gemeinschaft* to *Gesellschaft* (Tönnies); from mechanical to organic solidarity (Durkheim) or homo- to heterogeneity (Spencer).

Of course these are two ideal-types, yet so constructed they enable further questions to be raised. I want to pursue three: what might be said to be distinctively Scottish about their idea of a commercial society as a fourth stage; how, and with what assumptions, the Scots themselves view the superiority of this fourth stage over the preceding social formations; and what the implications are of this superiority and how it might be interpreted.

## DISTINCTIVENESS OF THE SCOTTISH IDEA OF A COMMERCIAL SOCIETY

We saw in Chapter 2 that stadial theory was common in the Enlightenment, although explicit references to commerce as a distinct (fourth) stage was not. The enumeration of itself is not decisive. Hume, for example, does not avail himself of a stadial approach to social change, though it is a subject to which he devotes much attention, just as he does to most components of the ideal type of a commercial society. These various components can also be found across a range of Enlightenment thinkers. Hence (randomly) Condillac links credit and confidence, and argues free commerce results in abundance (1847: 296, 339), Goguet points out that in a regulated society the objects of commerce multiply and diversify (1758: I, 573), Turgot observes that shepherds have a better idea of property than hunters and that as humans progress beyond barbarism they become more humane (1973: 66, 79), Genovesi remarks that everyone has a natural propensity to distinguish themselves from others (1765: 145) and so on. What comes out in the Scots is their appreciation that commerce does constitute a distinct type of society.

Some brief comparisons will help reinforce that claim. Cantillon, Galiani, Turgot and Condillac, for example, all write analytically about 'commerce' (discussing money, interest, taxation and the like) and, in that regard, the *Political Discourses* and the *Wealth of Nations* are not distinctive. But the work of Hume and Smith as a whole does differentiate them. Even though Condillac, like Hume, wrote an important 'philosophical' text (*Essai sur l'origine des connaissances humaines* [1746]) and a 'history' (*Histoire ancienne, histoire moderne* [1758–67]), Hume stands apart. The *Treatise* especially, but not only Book III, as we have seen, is integrally concerned with the operation of a 'modern' society and his *History of England* is centrally a story of the emergence of this modern world of liberty and commerce (see Danford 1990 or Capaldi and Livingston 1990). The sheer scale and ambition of the *Wealth of Nations* obviously make it stand out, as its subsequent renown testifies. But when coupled with a fully-articulated moral theory in the *Moral Sentiments* then Smith is offering more than agenda-setting 'economics'. At the heart of this thought is an appreciation that the contemporary world has seen the emergence of a distinctively different social system. We now live in a commercial society definitively characterised by an all-pervasive inter-dependency. Montesquieu (1961: I, 52), Helvetius (1843: 272) and Turgot (1973: 73) might all refer to '*l'esprit de commerce*' but they restrict its application to small-scale republics that are no longer extant.

This same conclusion can be drawn even when an ostensibly more significant usage is examined. Quesnay and Mirabeau (1764: II, 19) refer to *les sociétés marchandes*. However, they view them not as a new type but a derivative addition (*seconde et postiches*). In line with their Physiocratic principles, this 'society' is not foundational or self-sustaining (indeed it is unstable). In a fanciful but revealing piece of imagery, agriculture is the roots of a state, the trunk is population, the branches are industry and the leaves are commerce, which, though the most brilliant part of the tree, are less solid and more liable to be blown away in a storm (Mirabeau 1759: II, 12) (he employs the same basic image again in his work with Quesnay [1764: III, 1]). Though agriculture and commerce are closely tied together, it ever remains that *une société marchande* is dependent on the former (1764: II, 24). And in a manner similar to Montesquieu and others, Quesnay and Mirabeau continue to follow the standard line and associate commercial societies with trading republics (1764: II, 20).

In Chapter 2, we suggested it was the focus in the Scots' historical analysis on the emergence of the commercial age from the distinctly different social formation of feudal Europe that gave to their conception of a commercial society a distinctiveness not prefigured by mercantile city-states. Smith's potted history in the *Wealth of Nations* alongside the fuller treatments in, especially, Robertson, Millar and Hume provide a deep context in which to locate the emergence of commerce as a modern phenomenon. Hence although Voltaire's histories, such as his *Siècle de Louis XIV* (1751) and *Essai sur les Moeurs* (1756), do refer to commerce, in both cases these references are incorporated into a general survey without the topic receiving any sustained treatment and without any detailed account of its emergence.[1] Again, though both Genovesi and Danvila identify commerce as the fourth stage yet, as we also observed in Chapter 2 (p. 61n), neither writer explores or develops the notion that commerce is a distinct social formation nor, unlike in the Scots' enterprise, do they invest it with consequential portentous force.

That there is something qualitatively distinctive about commercial society is implicit in Smith's very definition. At the heart of a society where everyman is a merchant is the division of labour and that is more developed among 'artificers and manufacturers' than it is among agricultural workers (*WN* IV.ix.35/676). The greater development signals more than a quantitative extension. It ramifies to incorporate, as the ideal-type indicates, structures of belief, norms of conduct and a gamut of institutions. Hence for all Smith's acknowledgment of the superiority of the Physiocrats over the mercantilists the former do not articulate an idea of commercial society per se. Smith's recognition of the qualitative distinctiveness of a society based on commerce can reasonably be also said to be true of his compatriots. Collectively, as Hideo Tanaka (2007: 32) put it, they have 'brought a paradigmatic change into a theory of society'.

While making due allowance for fuzzy rather than sharp differentiation, that the Scots are distinctive raises the question as to why that might be the case. There is not going to be a definitive answer. Various explanations have been proffered. Typically they invoke the particular circumstances of Scotland in the mid-eighteenth century that I canvassed in the opening part of Chapter 1. In one unexceptional version, it is announced that 'it is no wonder' that they reflected on stages with a 'multiplicity of political, economic and social forms so close to hand' (Muller 1993: 23). I am chary about these invocations. The more they venture beyond the truism that 'everybody is a product of their times' the more difficult it becomes to explain how that particular aspect of the 'environment' accounted for that particular position or argument of that particular writer. It was also said in Chapter 1 that 'improvement' was a key Enlightenment motif. While in France that was effectively stymied (witness the failure of Turgot's attempted reforms), and the equally top-down efforts in Austria, Prussia and Russia lacked suitable social and economic roots (insecurity of property for example), it prospered more in Britain, where to use the terminology of Acemoglu and Robinson (2012), the institutions were relatively more 'inclusive' than 'extractive'. Again in contrast to France (as anglophiles like Montesquieu and Voltaire not disinterestedly proclaimed) as well as elsewhere, Britain's relative political liberty made the 'improving' project more viable. On a broad front it was recognised that progress (social amelioration and political clout) required commerce.

Though this is true of both England and Scotland, their circumstances were different. For a variety of reasons, as adumbrated in the opening chapter, Scotland had some catching up to do. I suggest, with all the circumspection thereby implied, that it is this perception that crucially informs the Scots' 'take' on improvement and commerce. This is reinforced by the fact that a central preoccupation of their history was Britain, how its story was the growth of modern independence and liberty from feudal dependency. This heightened the Scots' concern with improvement, with the transition in their own society of moving from a backward to an up-to-date cultivated society, the latter being encapsulated in an idea of 'commerce' as an across-the-board distinct type of social formation. For all John Robertson's (2005: 326, 379 and throughout) stimulating account of similarities, both in political and economic circumstances and in intellectual provenance, between Naples and Scotland, the sheer proximity to, and common state-hood with, England highlights the imputed significance of the Scottish 'perception'. And while both Neapolitans and Scots discussed political economy, it is out of the latter's discussion that the notion of a 'commercial society' emerges.[2] However, I emphasise the tentative and speculative nature of these conjectures. In the end I do not think for my enterprise that it matters hugely what the answer is to 'why' the Scots' had a more (rather than less) distinctive idea (this is not to say, of course, that others with different interests will not invest it with more importance).

## THE SUPERIORITY OF THE FOURTH STAGE

The contrast between the two ideal-types outlined above is clearly more than descriptive; it embodies an evaluative assessment. A commercial society, notwithstanding the dangers identified in Chapter 6, is superior to those that preceded it. The manifestations of this we have already covered; the task here is to look at the reasons the Scots themselves give, or imply, for this superiority.

According to its own presentation, everyone in a commercial society is freer (the law in principle applies equally to all) and conjointly healthier and wealthier than before. But commercial society, like its predecessors, still possesses rank differentials. These might be more fluid than in pastoral and agricultural societies because commercial wealth is less easily transmitted between generations (see Millar *OR* 291). They also differ in that social status is potentially more 'open', commercial wealth-based rank can be reasonably aspired to 'by the busy' (Ferguson *ECS* 237) – not an option for the herdsman or serf. But

they are still based on property/wealth and thus more securely established than the personal attributes that constitute differentiation in the
first stage. I mentioned at the beginning of this chapter that Deism, as
an abstract belief system, was consonant with the character of a commercial society. But I also suggested that evidentially this would only
be true of the relatively small numbers of enlightened members of that
society. To the same point, in a different context, Millar argues it would
be 'as vain' to look for liberty and independent spirit in 'uncultivated
parts of the world' as in an 'English waggoner' or 'persons of low rank
in the highlands of Scotland' (*OR* 295). The literati were all too aware
of that fact and this awareness, unlike the synchronic concerns raised
in Chapter 6, bears on their diachronic understanding of commercial
society as a temporal formation.

This understanding is encapsulated in their notion of the 'vulgar'. It
is most transparent in their discussions of taste but present elsewhere.
The vulgar in the Scots' accounts are not some historically removed
group; they are also present in commercial society.[3] Kames revealingly
in this context remarks that not only are savages unable to grasp the
conceptual distinction between property and possession, because it
is too abstract, but also 'to this day the vulgar can form no distinct
conception of property' (*HLT* 91). This similarity between the vulgar
of today and the savage in the past underlines the foundational status
of the principle of the constancy of human nature; there has been no
change in its 'principles and operations' (Hume quoted above p. 65n).
The similarity of past savage/current vulgar lies in the fact that they are
both relatively uninstructed, they are in that respect one and the same
(cf. Hume *E-AS* 111). On this same basis, they are both superstitious.
There is, though, a difference. Whereas in 'an age of superstition' men
of the 'greatest judgment are infected', in an 'enlightened age, superstition is confined among the vulgar' (Kames *SHM* II, 417; cf. Hume *NHR*
6, 4/53 and Smith *TMS* V.2.15/210 on Greek philosophers condoning
infanticide). Moreover, while generically the vulgar are those who go
by first appearances, in Kames' 'age of enlightenment' they can, as
Hume does, be contrasted with the 'wise' or 'philosophers' (Hume *U*
8.13/*SBNU* 86; *T* 1.3.13.12/*SBNT* 150). But this should not be over-
sold, since Hume also observes that 'in all the active parts of life' the
philosophers are 'in the main' governed by the same maxims as the
vulgar (*U* 9.5/*SBNU* 106).

Nonetheless, it is these philosophers who are the arbiters of taste.
The relative ignorance, definitive of the vulgar, means they are not
qualified to be arbiters (critics). Hume, in his essay on Taste, immediately after summarising what, as a matter of fact, are the desiderated

attributes of a critic, declares that they will be lacking in the 'generality of men' (*E-ST* 241). Blair expresses the key point. All humans possess the 'faculty' of taste but, while there may be some natural inequality in the extent of its possession, any such differences owe more to 'education and culture'. Hence that 'immense superiority which education and improvement give to the civilised above barbarous nations in refinement of taste' is repeated, within the 'same nation', in the superiority of those who have 'studied the liberal arts' above the 'rude and untaught vulgar' (Blair 1838: 12; cf. Kames *EC* II, 446; Gregory 1788: 132–3 and many others). This reinforces the earlier argument, exemplified by Smith's example of the philosopher and porter, that the crucial variable is sociological (moral causation). It is the presence (or not) of leisure and education that is decisive.

The underlying value judgment is that knowledge is better than ignorance but that universal value reflects another more basic universality, that of human nature itself. Contrary to the imputations or implications of some commentators, the Scots' idea of a distinctive commercial society does not prefigure some nineteenth-century historicist accounts whereby the savage is in some sense a different human being in virtue of living in a different 'culture' from that of a civilised society.[4] It is on the basis of that commitment to the universality of value that the Scots are able freely to criticise the non-civilised. Smith, for example, while recognising that infanticide has been locally authorised by 'uninterrupted custom', nonetheless condemns this 'horrible practice' as going against the grain of our sentiments; which are 'founded on the strongest and most vigorous passions of human nature; and though they may be somewhat warpt cannot be entirely perverted' (*TMS* V.2.16; V.2.1/211, 200).[5] The fact that there are different institutional expressions of a common human nature does not preclude evaluative judgments that one expression is better than another, so – to give an example of Hume's – while both monogamy and polygamy are humanly contrived institutions, the latter can be rightly judged 'odious' (*E-PD* 185). By the same token, the legal presence of slaves in modern societies can be criticised.

None of this is to say the Scots are unaware of cultural bias and the dangers of arrogant prejudicial judgment (see Pitts 2005: 26–7; Smith 2009). Dunbar thinks that the labels 'barbarous' and 'civilised' should be set aside as too general and more pointedly, that Europeans are prone to an opinion of 'superiority over other nations' (*EHM* 151–2; cf. 455). Similar sentiments are expressed by Ferguson: 'we are ourselves the supposed standards of politeness and civilisation; and where our own features do not appear, we apprehend that there is nothing which deserves to be known' (*ECS* 75; cf. 245 where it is casuistical to consider the practice of one's own age as 'the standard for mankind'). For Robertson, it is a 'copious error' to 'decide' about past 'institutions and manners' on the basis of ideas that now prevail (*VP* 417; cf. Kames *HLT* 82). Millar criticised the European mercantile companies for their oppression and plunder of the local inhabitants (*HV* IV, 6/785). And while Hume does not doubt the superiority of 'civilised Europeans' he deprecates the way this has led to the inhumane treatment of 'barbarous Indians' (*M* 3, 19/*SBNM* 191). Of course, as Hume's now notorious comments about 'blacks' in 'Of National Characters' seemingly illustrates,[6] nor should we deny that the 'civilised' superiority of the commercial societies was immune to prejudice.

## INTERPRETING THE IMPLICATIONS

It is undeniable that the Scots' idea of commercial society, with its self-conscious attribution of superiority to their society has the air of congratulatory self-justification. This is not too surprising since in theorising on commercial society they were theorising about their own society, indeed about themselves, as members of this Scottish elite (Emerson 2009: 239ff). However, as Chapter 6 aimed to establish, that did not mean the Scots were starry-eyed optimists, oblivious to the drawbacks of commercial society and the variety of dangers it might be thought to pose to social order and coherence.

Despite the occasional jeremiads the Scots are cautiously hopeful (cf. Broadie 2001: 38). Their hope emanates from their insight that social institutions are the locus of societal differences, and their social scientific account of social or moral causation made them aware that behaviour and values are largely a product of institutions. There is no road-block to institutional change. Humans are not perfect but that is no insuperable barrier. Although they are imperfect social beings, nonetheless they have found ways to co-operate; indeed, the very existence of their institutions is testament to that (a fact that for many was Providentially underwritten). The best way yet found to co-operate is in a commercial society. Any supposed alternative, like a virtuous Rousseauan republic, not only goes against the 'natural bent of the mind' (as Hume said implicitly of Sparta [*E-Com* 263], one of Rousseau's 'models' [Shklar 1969: 12–32]), but also will lack the material blessings of opulence and the moral blessings of individual liberty. Their caution also stems from their social science; since moral causation operates through habit then ameliorative change is a slow process. Millar encapsulated this perspective in his comment that 'how imperfect and defective' the institutions of country may seem yet they 'are only susceptible of those gentle improvements which proceed from a gradual reformation of the manners' (*Obs* v). 'Revolutions' that actually change things are sedately silent and insensibly gradual, not tumultuously noisy and dramatically sudden. Moreover, even gentle change remains vulnerable precisely because human nature itself has not fundamentally changed; its imperfections will not disappear. The anti-social aspects of self-love, avidity, pride or misalignment of priorities (preferring the contiguous to the remote, as Hume put it) are not always going to be corralled or successfully channelled by the institutional framework.

This is not, it seems to me, easily reducible to the prosecution of a class ideology, whether of agrarian capitalism (McNally 1988: 233), the petty-bourgeoisie (Medick 1973: 288–9; cf. Medick and Batscha 1988: 85) or 'embryonic industrialists' (Mizuta 1975: 115). Nor is enormous insight gained by interpreting their theoretical diachronic analysis as an account of the move from feudal to capitalist modes of production and attributing that analysis to their 'class-identified' environment (Pascal 1938; Meek 1967; Hobsbawm 1980). While to argue, as Marx himself did about Smith, that they hypostatise their own society as 'natural', is to read them in the light of their successors; an activity that simply throws a shadow over their own arguments.[7] What the Scots' idea seems to resemble is the outlines of a 'liberal' picture of society. Of course, that it arguably does so is further grist to the ideological mill. The 'liberal' reading is, moreover, prone to some of the same reductionism that characterises its ideological opponents. To a considerable extent this is owing to Smith's posthumous reputation as the (supposed) apostle of the free market and the enemy of state interference (or alternatively as the producer of an intellectual synthesis that 'reflects the growing maturity of the capitalist system' [Heller 2011: 149]).

Those resistant to the retrospective foisting of 'liberalism' onto the Scots typically emphasise the Scots as working through the legacy of republicanism. This is part of the explanation why the Rousseau/Smith relation has garnered such interest. As it was paraphrased by J. G. A. Pocock, this interpretation sees the Scots replacing the polis with politeness, that is, as developing a non-classical conception of liberty and seeing man in social, transactional rather than political terms. But, as Pocock also observes, this view has an alternative, where the Scots' social thought represents the evolution of the civil jurisprudential tradition where individuals are defined in terms of property relations. Pocock sees both co-existing and counsels against adopting an over-binary approach (1983: 240–50).

As a counsel that is obviously sensible but to see the Scots in either of these terms does not capture what is central to their idea of commercial society. Neither the virtuous citizen nor the possessor of personal rights is the focus of a society where everyman is merchant. A commercial society is defined in terms of neither politics nor law. Of course these are indispensable institutions, just as upright behaviour and respect for rights are requisite behaviour by individuals. The focal point of a commercial society is the inter-dependency of relations (something that escaped Rousseau, who saw only dependency in a community where the general will of independent citizens was not sovereign). What Andrew Skinner (1996: 177) claimed as the 'true measure' of Smith's contribution, namely, his grasp of the 'interdependence of economic phenomena', can be extended to the Scots in general and to their thought as a whole.[8] If any single image best encapsulates the Scots' idea it is Smith's 'humble woollen coat' (p. 77 above), with its incorporation of the efforts of many thousands in its manufacture. In Dugald Stewart's words this coat is emblematic of a 'state of things so wonderfully artificial and complicated' when set in contrast to the 'first simple 'efforts of uncultivated nature' (Smith *EPS*: 45/292; cf. p. 32 above).

What makes that image so focal is that, in addition to illustrating interdependency, it also exemplifies how, on the Scots' conception of it, a commercial society works with the grain of human nature. As a historical formation its institutions reflect the outcome of human passions. The division of labour, the key institution that makes that coat possible, is not, as Smith openly observed, the outcome of 'any human wisdom which foresees and intends that general opulence to which it gives occasion' (*WN* I.ii.1/25). It arose, as we examined in Chapter 3, from a propensity in human nature to truck. The Scots' adoption of a 'modernist' psychology means that they treat desire not reason as the mover of human action. Of course they do not deny that humans are rational but this expresses itself as a *Zweckrationalität*, the instrumental realisation of ends. Minimally each participant in a barter individually calculates (if only implicitly) how their own participation in that activity enables them the better to attain what they want. This is scaled up without requiring any motivational change. Each of the thousands involved in making the coat behaves similarly – working in co-ordination with others better enables individual desires to be realised (if only as the means to obtaining their next meal).

There are two other implications contained in the message of the coat. The same psychology that displaced the motivational force of reason also underpinned the process of moral judgment. The sentimentalist ethics adopted by the Scots made moral judgment a matter of feeling and imagination, not rational command. The process of coat manufacture, as one of human action, even if not design (to use Ferguson's language (*ECS* 122), does not occur in an amoral context. Merchants, that is, everyman (and woman – unlike Rousseau's resolutely masculine polity), are moral agents, exponents of, in the main, the gentle virtues. They are human, not superhuman. Commercial society has no need for heroes or sages and is the better for their absence. This commercial morality (as we might term it) informs the second implication.

Morality is one of the numerous background conditions that have to be in place for the coat to appear in the market-place. This is only to be expected once the interlocking character of society is borne in mind. The definitive interdependency is not the product of force (Wolin 1960: 291). There are formal institutions of coercion but it is not a task of the 'state' to compel people to make coats. Again in line with human nature, the thousands of implicated individuals in a 'free society' interact in the hope of some positive gain not in fear of retribution. The gain (more often than not) will be mutual, the envisaged pain (more often than not) would be personal. That mutuality is predicated on each participant seeing their own interest being furthered. In the right institutional environment (cf. Muller 1995), this provides as a secure a basis for predictability as does avoiding Leviathan's sword (cf. Cropsey 2001). Just as Hobbes thought he had pioneered 'civil philosophy' (political science) on the basis of his theory of the passions, so the Scots' systematically led the way in social science.[9]

The downplaying of coercion here is often linked to the notion of social order as 'spontaneous'.[10] This is not, I think, the happiest of terms. The paradigm of a spontaneous order is market co-ordination but although the Smithian distillation 'everyman a merchant' might suggest that economic factors or the market are the key ingredient in the Scots' idea this gives it an undue emphasis. The interdependency applies to all societal institutions. James Otteson (2002) has inventively applied spontaneity to Smith's moral philosophy but my point is wider. The decentring of law and politics is not replaced by the centrality of economic transactions, an error that lies at the heart of those who would make the Scots 'ideologues', whether 'Marxist' or 'liberal'. The Scots are institutionalists; any spontaneity occurs interstitially. Moreover, as here stressed, the Scots are aware that the world of commerce is a temporal formation and they are correspondingly attuned to the 'stickiness' of institutions (Berry 2003a).

The complex interlocking whole is not some perfect functioning system; as I summarily outlined above it is an 'ideal-type', a construction the purpose of which is to identify key features, not to offer an empirical description. As an imperfect whole it is misleading to regard 'commercial society' as falling of its own accord into a self-ordered structure. It will contain within it anomalous elements. The so-called 'law of unintended consequences', which Ferguson's action/design distinction, or Smith's 'invisible hand', supposedly illustrates is, as we have had occasion to note, not necessarily benign. The division of labour produces mental torpidity as well as opulence, credit stimulates industry while increasing defensive vulnerability, commerce improves the position of women while encouraging sexual laxity and it routinises the administration of justice while neglecting political commitment. The Scots' Baconianism has its point in the effort to amend or correct these. All of which efforts are made with the aid of social science but with that same science alerting them to the stickiness of the material with which they have to deal. As we have already affirmed in this Conclusion, the Scots' are well-aware of commercial society's imperfections just as they remain cautiously optimistic that these will be eroded by progress.

This, in conclusion, returns us to our beginning. The Scots' idea of commercial society is 'about' improvement. On that pivots the duality of the syn- and dia-chronic dimensions of the idea. A commercial society marks an advance on a society of landowners, as it does of pastoralists and hunter-gatherers. The former two cohere in virtue of the dependency of non-owners of property on its owners. The last have no property to speak of but live lives of precarious destitution and any social cohesion they possess is either in the form of kin or in contingent associations for the purpose of defence or attack. Within a commercial society the power of property is diffused by its focal characteristic of interdependency, the same feature that lifts its participants above a life of miserable poverty.

By its very nature, interdependency implicates not a few but many and that implication affects the range of social life and its institutional expression and serves to distinguish a 'properly' commercial society from a mercantile republic. It is in virtue of this synchrony, what James Fordyce (1776: 7) refers to as 'the great machine of society', that these institutions and behaviours by and large cohere. That this coherence is approximate provides scope for the enlightened work of improvement. What is important about this 'work' is not its extent and ambition (which may well be judged wanting) but that it is envisaged as occurring within the historically-formed set of institutions and behaviours (it will be informed by science not utopian aspiration). This delimitation is both the product and reinforcement of the insight that this rough-and-ready coherence, this set of self-implicating institutions, establishes that there is such a thing as a 'commercial society'. And although the word 'society' is not particularly selected for use (no more than 'people' or 'nation' for example)[11] yet Millar declares indicatively (or so I claim) à propos 'the revolutions [. . .] in the condition and manners of the sexes' that these have 'been derived from the progress of mankind in the common arts of life and therefore make a part in the general history of society' (*OR* 228). Commercial society is to be situated in that history and its own 'common arts of life' are practised and pursued on the basis that everyman is a merchant.

## NOTES

1. Robertson (*VP* 429) confessed that he had not used Voltaire's histories because of his failure to cite his sources. Voltaire's account of the development of European commerce after the Crusades makes but one chapter in a total of over one hundred in his *Essai* (2001: III, Chap. 82) and the partial subject matter of one chapter in *Louis XIV* (1929: Chap. 29) and other references are merely en passant.

2. Robertson's focus is on the period before 1760 which means, inter alia, that Hume is his key player (it was he who 'initiated Enlightenment in Scotland' [2005: 381]) and the *Wealth of Nations* is not analysed.

3. This qualifies the argument of Blaney and Inayatullah (2010: 45, but cf. 48 for their own qualification), in the context of their interpretation of Smith, that 'temporal walls' are erected between savage and civilised societies, as Smith 'barricades modern society within a temporal/ethical fortress'. Their broader argument (covering other Scots as well as other thinkers) that 'savage society' is a 'model' central to the vindication of commercial society (2010: 192, 47) echoes Meek (1976: 129–30).

4. This is implied by some commentators on Hume (see Berry 2007 for discussion). Nicholas Phillipson refers to Smith having 'historicised human nature' (2000: 84) and attributes to Robertson the recognition of 'different minds' and 'different selves' in different civilisations (1997: 59).

5. Compare Forman-Barzilai (2010: 248), 'Smith never allowed culture to trump justice; he never allowed diversity to trump "the strongest and most vigorous passions of human nature".' Although she also judges that 'ultimately' Smith was 'a radical localist and particularist' (2010: 194).

6. Hume added a Note to the essay for the 1753/4 edition of the *Essays* where he declares he is 'apt to suspect' that negroes are 'naturally inferior' to the whites since there 'never' was a 'civilised nation' or 'eminent' individual of that complexion. However, in the last edition of the *Essays* (published posthumously in 1777 [*E-NC* 208n]) Hume amended the Note. He struck out 'never' and replaced with 'scarcely ever' (*E-v* 62). This is a possible acceptance (and perhaps only here) of a criticism made by Beattie (1975: 310–11). See Immerwahr 1992 and in wider context Davis 1966.

7.  Of course this particular ideological reading has no monopoly. According to Trevor-Roper (1977: 375) the 'peculiar character of Scottish society' accounts for the Scots' emphasis on political economy and sociological history (cf. Horne 1990: 73).
8.  See Daniel Brühlmeier's (1996: 24) lapidary summary, 'Wir finden in der Schottischen Aufklärung ein gewaltig erstarkendes Bewußtsein soziale Interdependenz und Gegenseitigkeit.'
9.  This is not to say they were unprecedented. For William Letwin (1964: vi; cf. Appleby 1978: 184) the 'fundamental principles' of economics as a science were laid down at the end of the seventeenth century. It is, though, the breadth and systematic character of their analyses that distinguishes the Scots, hence in addition to the clichéd identification of Smith as the 'father of economics', MacRae (1969: 25) identifies Ferguson the 'first sociologist', Kames gets a chapter in a history of anthropology and Millar's *Ranks* has been fulsomely praised as a pioneering work on social stratification (Evans-Pritchard 1981). For Hobbes' claims about his priority see the dedicatory epistle to his *De Corpore* (1839: I, ix).
10. This notion is associated with Friedrich Hayek. He gave the Scots star billing as the expositors of what he regarded as the correct liberal tradition (1972: 57) (for systematic discussion of Hayek's relation to the Scots see Craig Smith 2006). Ronald Hamowy (1987: 3) openly acknowledges Hayek's impact in identifying the Scots' sociological significance as lying in the notion of 'spontaneous order'. The term, though, is found in Auguste Comte and Herbert Spencer, neither of whom fit Hayek's preferred genealogy. Again Craig Smith 2006 is an indispensable guide
11. The term 'society' in the sense of a space where people live in orderly community (cf. *OED*) is rare before the mid-eighteenth century. The same holds in French, see Gordon's (1994: 52ff) discussion of the 'semantic field'. Of course, the presence of 'Nations' in the title of Smith's magnum opus speaks to this imprecision.

# References

## PRIMARY: SCOTTISH

*Act Of Union, 1707,* www.rahbarnes.demon.co.uk/Union/UnionwithEngland Act.

Anderson, A. (1764), *A Historical and Chronological Deduction of the Origin of Commerce,* London.

Anderson, J. (1777), *Observations on the Means of Exciting a Spirit of National Industry; Chiefly Intended to Promote the Agriculture, Commerce, Manufactures and Fisheries of Scotland,* Edinburgh.

Anon. (1753), *An Inquiry into the Original and Consequences of the Public Debt,* Edinburgh.

Beattie, J. [1776] (1975), *Essay on the Nature and Immutability of Truth,* Hildesheim: Olms reprint.

Blackwell, T. [1735] (1972), *An Enquiry into the Life and Times of Homer,* Menston: Scolar Press reprint.

Blair, H. [1783] (1838), *Lectures on Rhetoric and Belles-Lettres,* in one volume, London.

— [1763] (1996), *A Critical Dissertation on the Poems of Ossian,* appended to *Poems of Ossian,* H. Gaskill (ed.), Edinburgh: Edinburgh University Press, pp. 343–408.

Carlyle, A. (1910), *The Autobiography of Dr Alexander Carlyle of Inveresk 1722–1805,* J. Burton (ed.), Edinburgh: Foulis.

Craig, J. [1806] (1990), *Account of the Life and Writings of John Millar,* J. Price (ed.), Bristol: Thoemmes.

Dalrymple, J. (1757), *Essay toward a General History of Feudal Property in Great Britain,* London.

— (1764), *Considerations upon the Policy of Entails in Great Britain,* Edinburgh.

Dunbar, J. (1781), *Essays on the History of Mankind in Rude and Cultivated Ages,* 2nd edn, London.

Ferguson, A. (1756), *Reflections Previous to the Establishment of a Militia,* London.

— (1766), *Analysis of Pneumatics and Moral Philosophy,* Edinburgh.

— (1776), *Remarks on a Pamphlet Lately Published by Dr Price*, London.

— [1783] (1813), *The History of the Progress and Termination of the Roman Republic*, 5 vols, Edinburgh.

— [1767] (1966), *An Essay on the History of Civil Society*, D. Forbes (ed.), Edinburgh: Edinburgh University Press.

— [1769] (1994), *Institutes of Moral Philosophy*, 3rd edn, London: Thoemmes reprint.

— [1792] (1995), *Principles of Moral and Political Science*, 2 vols, Hildesheim: G. Olms.

— (1995), *Correspondence*, 2 vols, V. Merolle (ed.), London: Pickering.

— (2006) *The Manuscripts of Adam Ferguson*, V. Merolle, R. Dix and E. Heath (eds), London: Pickering and Chatto.

Fletcher, A. [1698] (1979), *A Discourse of Government with Relation to Militias*, in D. Daiches (ed.), *Fletcher of Saltoun: Selected Writings*, Edinburgh: Scottish Academic Press, pp. 1–26.

Fordyce, J. (1776), *The Character and Conduct of the Female Sex*, 2nd edn, London.

Gregory, J. [1765] (1788), *A Comparative View of the State and Faculties of Man*, in *Works of the late John Gregory*, vol. 2, Edinburgh.

Halyburton, T. (1718), *Memoirs of the Life of the Reverend, learned and pious Mr. Thomas Halyburton*, London.

— [1714] (1798), *Natural Religion Insufficient; and Revealed Necessary to Man's Happiness in his Present State*, Montrose.

Home, F. (1756), *The Principles of Agriculture and Vegetation*, Edinburgh.

Hume, D. (1748), *A True Account of the Behaviour and Conduct of Archibald Stewart*, Edinburgh.

— (1875), *Philosophical Works*, T. Green and G. Grose (eds), London: Longmans.

— (1894), *History of England*, 3 vols, London: George Routledge.

— (1932), *The Letters of David Hume*, 2 vols, J. Greig (ed.), Oxford: Clarendon Press.

— (1975), *Enquiries concerning Human Understanding and concerning the Principles of Morals*, L. Selby-Bigge and P. Nidditch (eds), Oxford: Clarendon Press.

— [1739–40] (1978), *A Treatise of Human Nature*, L. Selby-Bigge and P. Nidditch (eds), Oxford: Clarendon Press.

— (1985), *Essays: Moral, Political and Literary*, E. Miller (ed.), Indianapolis: Liberty Press.

— [1751] (1998), *An Enquiry concerning the Principles of Morals*, T. Beauchamp (ed.), Oxford: Oxford University Press.

— [1748] (1999), *An Enquiry concerning Human Understanding*, T. Beauchamp (ed.), Oxford: Oxford University Press.

— [1739–40] (2002), *A Treatise of Human Nature*, D. and M. Norton (eds), Oxford: Oxford University Press.

— (2007), *A Dissertation on the Passions and the Natural History of Religion*, T. Beauchamp (ed.), Oxford: Oxford University Press.

Hutcheson, F. (1728), *An Inquiry concerning the Original of our Ideas of Virtue or Moral Good*, 3rd edn, London.

— [1726] (1989), *Observations on the Fable of the Bees*, Bristol: Thoemmes reprint.

— (1994), *Philosophical Writings*, R. Downie (ed.), London: Everyman.

— [1755] (2005), *System of Moral Philosophy*, 2 vols, London: Continuum.

— [1747] (2007), *A Short Introduction to Moral Philosophy*, L. Turco (ed.), Indianapolis: Liberty Press.

Hutton (1777), *Considerations on the Nature, Quality and Distinctions of Coal and Culm, with enquiries philosophical and political into the present state of laws and the questions now in agitation relative to the taxes upon these commodities*, Edinburgh.

— (1794), *An Investigation of the Principles of Knowledge and of the Progress of Reason*, 3 vols, Edinburgh.

— (1795), *Theory of the Earth, with Proofs and Illustrations*, Edinburgh.

Kames, H. Home, Lord (1732), *Essays upon Several Subjects in Law*, Edinburgh.

— (1747), *Essays upon several subjects concerning British Antiquities*, Edinburgh.

— (1758), *Essays on the Principles of Morality and Natural Religion,* 2nd edn, London.

— (1766), *Progress of Flax-Husbandry in Scotland*, Edinburgh.

— (1767), *Principles of Equity*, corrected 2nd edn, Edinburgh.

— [1774] (1779), *Sketches on the History of Man*, 3rd edn, 2 vols, Dublin.

— (1776), *The Gentleman Farmer: Being an Attempt to Improve Agriculture by Subjecting it to the Test of Rational Principles*, Edinburgh.

— (1777), *Elucidations respecting the Common and Statute Law of Scotland*, Edinburgh.

— (1779), *Historical Law Tracts*, 2nd edn, Edinburgh.

— [1779] (2005), *Essays on the Principles of Morality and Natural Religion*, 3rd edn, Indianapolis: Liberty Press.

— (1817), *The Elements of Criticism*, 9th edn, 2 vols, Edinburgh.

Leechman, W. (2005), 'An Account of the Life, Writings and Character of Francis Hutcheson', prefixed to Hutcheson, *A System of Moral Philosophy*, London: Continuum Classic Texts, pp. i–xlviii.

Lindsay, P. (1733), *The Interest of Scotland Considered*, London.

Mackenzie, G. [1691] (1711), *Moral History of Frugality*, London.

MacLaurin, C. (1750), *An Account of Sir Isaac Newton's Philosophical Discoveries,* 2nd edn, London.

McQueen, D. (1756), *Letters on Mr Hume's History of Great Britain*, Edinburgh.

Melvill, T. (1734), *The True Caledonian*, Edinburgh.

Millar, J. (1771), *Observations concerning the Distinction of Ranks of Society*, London.
— [1779] (1971), *The Origin of the Distinction of Ranks*, 3rd edn, in W. Lehmann (ed.), *John Millar of Glasgow*, Cambridge: Cambridge University Press, pp. 173–322.
— [1797/1803] (2006), *An Historical View of the English Government*, M. Salber Phillips and D. Smith (eds) in one volume, Indianapolis: Liberty Press.
Pennant, T. [1769] (1979), *A Tour in Scotland*, 3rd edn, Perth: Melven Press.
Ramsay, J. (1888), *Scotland and Scotsmen in the Eighteenth Century*, 2 vols, A. Allardyce (ed.), Edinburgh.
Reid, T. (1846), *Works*, in one volume, W. Hamilton (ed.), Edinburgh: Maclachan Stewart.
— (1990), *Practical Ethics*, K. Haakonssen (ed.), Princeton: Princeton University Press.
Robertson, W. (1840), *Works*, in one volume, D. Stewart (ed.), Edinburgh.
Sinclair, J. (ed.) (1973), *The Statistical Account of Scotland 1791–1799*, Wakefield: EP Publishing.
Smith, A. (1982), *Essays on Philosophical Subjects*, W. Wightman, J. Bryce and I. Ross (eds), Indianapolis: Liberty Press.
— (1982), *Lectures on Jurisprudence*, R. Meek, D. Raphael and P. Stein (eds), Indianapolis: Liberty Press.
— (1982), *The Theory of Moral Sentiments*, A. MacFie and D. Raphael (eds), Indianapolis: Liberty Press.
— (1982), *An Inquiry into the Nature and Causes of the Wealth of Nations*, R. Campbell and A. Skinner (eds), Indianapolis: Liberty Press.
— (1983), *Lectures on Rhetoric and Belles Lettres*, J. Bryce (ed.), Indianapolis: Liberty Press.
— (1987), *Correspondence of Adam Smith*, E. Mossner and I. Ross (eds), Indianapolis: Liberty Press.
Somerville, T. (1861), *My Own Life and Times 1741–1814*, Edinburgh: Edmonston.
Steuart, J. (1966), *An Inquiry into the Principles of Political Oeconomy*, 2 vols, A. Skinner (ed.), Chicago: University of Chicago Press.
Stewart, D. (1854), *Dissertation: Exhibiting the Progress of Metaphysical, Ethical and Political Philosophy since the Revival of Letters in Europe*, in W. Hamilton (ed.), *Works,* vol. 1, Edinburgh: Constable.
Stuart, G. (1768), *Historical Dissertation concerning the Antiquity of the English Constitution*, Edinburgh.
— (1779), *Observations concerning the Public Law and the Constitutional History of Scotland*, Edinburgh.
— [1792] (1995), *A View of Society in Europe in its Progress from Rudeness to Refinement*, 2nd edn, Bristol: Thoemmes reprint.
Turnbull, G. (1740), *Treatise on Ancient Painting*, London.
— (1741), *Discourse upon Moral and Civil Laws*, appended to his edition of Heineccius' *System of Universal Law*, Edinburgh.

— [1740] (2005), *The Principles of Moral Philosophy*, Indianapolis: Liberty Press.

Tytler, A. [1807] (1993), *Memoirs of the Life and Writings of the Honourable Henry Home of Kames*, 2 vols, Bristol: Thoemmes reprint.

Wallace, R. (1761), *Various Prospects of Mankind*, London.

— [1758] (1961), *Characteristics of the Present Political State of Great Britain*, New York: Kelley reprint.

— [1753 and 1809] (1969), *Dissertation on the Numbers of Mankind in Antient and Modern Times*, New York: Kelley reprint.

Wodrow, R. (1828), *Life of James Wodrow*, Edinburgh: Blackwood.

## PRIMARY: OTHER

Aquinas, St Thomas [1259–64] (1928), *Summa Contra Gentiles*, vol. 3, trans. English Dominican Fathers, London: Burns and Oates.

Aristotle (1894), *Ethica Nicomachea*, L. Bywater (ed.), Oxford: Oxford Classical Texts.

— (1944), *The Politics*, trans. H. Rackham with text, London: Loeb Library.

Bacon, F. (1740), *Works*, 4 vols, London.

— (1853), *The Physical and Metaphysical Works of Lord Bacon*, J. Devey (ed.), London: Bohn Library.

— (1868), *The Moral and Historical Works of Lord Bacon*, J. Devey (ed.), London: Bohn Library.

Barbon, N. [1690] (1905), *A Discourse of Trade*, J. Hollander (ed.), Baltimore: Johns Hopkins Press.

Beccaria, C. [1764] (1965), *Dei Delitti e delle Pene*, F. Venturi (ed.), Torino: Einaudi.

Berkeley, G. (1953), *Works*, A. Luce and T. Jessop (eds), 6 vols, Edinburgh: Nelson.

Bolingbroke, H. St John, Viscount (1754), *Works*, 5 vols, London.

Brown, J. (1758), *An Estimate of the Manners and Principles of the Times*, 7th edn, London.

Burke, E. [1774] (1889), *Speech on American Taxation*, in *Works*, vol. 1, London: Bohn.

Butler, J. [1726] (1964), *Fifteen Sermons Preached at the Rolls Chapel*, London: Bell.

Chambers, E. (1728), *Cyclopedia or an Universal Dictionary of Arts and Sciences*, London.

Cicero (1913), *The Offices*, trans. W. Miller with text, London: Loeb Library.

— (1927), *Tusculan Disputations*, trans. J. King with text, London: Loeb Library.

— (1931), *De Finibus*, trans. H. Rackham with text, 2nd edn, London: Loeb Library.

Condillac, E. [1776] (1847), *Le Commerce et le gouvernement*, in E. Daire and G. Molinari (eds), *Mélanges d'économie politique*, Paris: Guillaumin, pp. 247–443.

— [1746] (2001), *Essay on the Origin of Human Knowledge*, trans. H. Aarsleff (ed.), Cambridge: Cambridge University Press.

Condorcet, M. [1795] (1933), *Esquisse d'un tableau historique des progrès de l'esprit humain*, O. Prior (ed.), Paris: Boivin.

Constant, B. [1819] (1988), *The Liberty of the Ancients Compared with that of the Moderns*, trans. B. Fontana, Cambridge: Cambridge University Press.

d'Alembert, J. [1751] (1963), *Preliminary Discourse to the Encyclopedia*, trans. N. Schwab, Indianapolis: Bobbs Merrill.

Danvila y Villagrassa, B. [1779] (2008), *Lecciones de Economia Civil o del Comercio*, P. Ferri (ed.), Zaragoza: CISC.

Davenant, C. (1771), *Works*, 5 vols, C. Whitworth (ed.), London.

de la Condamine, C. (1745), *Relation abrégée d'un voyage fait dans l'intérieur de l'Amerique Méridionale*, Paris.

Deleyre, A. (1755), 'Epingle', in *Encyclopédie ou dictionnnaire raisonnée des sciences, des arts et des métiers*, vol. 5, Paris, pp. 804–6.

Descartes, R. [1637] (1912), *A Discourse on Method*, trans. J. Veitch, London: Everyman Library.

Diderot, D. (1755), 'Encyclopédie', in *Encyclopédie ou dictionnnaire raisonnée des sciences, des arts et des métiers*, vol. V, Paris, pp. 635–49.

Diogenes Laertius (1925), *Lives of Eminent Philosophers (Zeno)*, vol. 7, trans. R. Hicks, London: Loeb Library.

Domat, J. [1703] (1722), *The Civil Law in its Natural Order*, trans. W. Strahan, London.

Dubos J.-B. [1719] (1760), *Réflexions critiques sur la poésie, la peinture et la musique*, 2 vols, Paris.

Epictetus (1928), *The Manual and Discourses*, trans. W. Oldfather with text, London: Loeb Library.

Fénelon, F. [1699] (1962), *Les aventures de Télémaque*, J. Goré (ed.), Firenze: Sansoni.

Florus (1943), *Epitome of Roman History*, trans. E. Foster with text, London: Loeb Library.

Galiani, F. [1751] (1915), *Della Moneta*, F. Nicolini (ed.), Bari: Laterza.

Genovesi, A. (1765), *Delle Lezioni di Commercio o sia d'economia Civile da Leggesi*, Naples.

Godwin, W. [1798] (1976), *Enquiry concerning Political Justice*, I. Kramnick (ed.), Harmondsworth: Penguin Books.

Goguet, Y. (1758), *De l'Origine des Loix, des Arts et des Sciences et de leur Progrès chez les Anciens Peuples*, Paris.

— (1761), *The Origin of Laws, Arts and Sciences and their Progress among the most Ancient Peoples*, Edinburgh.

Grotius, H. [1625, trans. 1738] (2005), *The Rights of War and Peace*, R. Tuck (ed.), Indianapolis: Liberty Press.

Harrington, J. [1656] (1977), *Oceana*, in *Political Writings*, J. Pocock (ed.), Cambridge: Cambridge University Press, pp. 155–359.

Harris, J. (1757), *An Essay upon Money and Coins*, London.

Helvétius, C. [1758] (1843), *De l'Esprit*, P. Christian (ed.), Paris: Lavigne.

Hobbes, T. [1655] (1839), *Epistle Dedicatory* to *De Corpore*, in *Works*, vol. 1, W. Molesworth (ed.), London, pp. vi–xii.

— [1651] (1991), *Leviathan*, R. Tuck (ed.), Cambridge: Cambridge University Press.

Houghton, J. (1677), *England's Great Happiness*, London.

Johnson, S. [1773] (1791), *A Journey to the Western Islands of Scotland*, London.

Livy (1919), *From the Founding of the City*, vol. 1, trans. B. Foster with text, London: Loeb Library.

Locke, J. (1854), *Philosophical Works*, 2 vols, H. St John (ed.), London: Bohn Library.

— [1689] (1965), *Two Treatises of Government*, P. Laslett (ed.), New York: Mentor Books.

Macaulay, C. (1769), *History of England from the Accession of James I to the Elevation of the House of Hanover*, 3rd edn, London.

Machiavelli, N. [1532] (1998), *Il Principe*, in A. Capata (ed.), *Tutte le opere storiche, politiche e letterarie*, Rome: Newton, pp. 6–55.

Mandeville, B. (1729), *Free Thoughts on Religion*, 2nd edn, London.

— [1732] (1988), *The Fable of the Bees* , 2 vols, ed. F. Kaye, Indianapolis: Liberty Press.

Martin, H. [1701] (1952), 'Considerations on the East-India Trade', reprinted in J. McCulloch (ed.), *Early English Tracts on Commerce*, Cambridge: Economic History Society, pp. 541–630.

Marx, K. (1967), *Capital*, 3 vols, trans. S. Moore and S. Aveling, ed. F. Engels, New York: International Publishers.

Melon, J.-F. (1735), *Essai politique sur le commerce*, Amsterdam.

Mirabeau V. (1759), *L'Ami des hommes*, 6 vols, Amsterdam.

— (1760), *Tableau Oeconomique avec ses Explications*, Amsterdam.

Montesquieu, C. [1748] (1961), *De l'Esprit des Lois*, 2 vols, G. Truc (ed.), Paris: Garnier.

— (1989), *The Spirit of the Laws*, trans A. Cohler, B. Miller and H. Stone, Cambridge: Cambridge University Press.

Mun, T. [1664] (1952), *England's Treasure by Forreign Trade*, reprinted in J. McCulloch (ed.), *Early English Tracts on Commerce*, Cambridge: Economic History Society reprint, pp. 115–210.

Newton, I. (1953), *Newton's Philosophy of Nature: Selections from his Writings*, H. Thayer (ed.), New York: Hafner.

Nicole, P. (1999), *Essais de morale*, L. Thirouin (ed.), Paris: Presses Universitaires de France.

North, D. [1691] (1952), *Discourse on Trade*, reprinted in J. McCulloch (ed.), *Early English Tracts on Commerce*, Cambridge: Economic History Society reprint, pp. 505–40.

Perkins, W. (1609), *Three Books of Cases of Conscience*, in *Works*, vol. 2, Cambridge, pp. 1–176.

— [1597–1601] (1612), *Treatise of the Vocations*, in *Works*, vol. 1, Cambridge, pp. 747–79.

Petty, W. [1683] (1899), *The Economic Writings of Sir William Petty*, C. Hull (ed.), 2 vols, Cambridge: Cambridge University Press.

Plato (1902), *Politeia*, J. Burnett (ed.), Oxford: Clarendon Press.

Pufendorf, S. [1672] (1934), *On the Law of Nature and of Nations*, trans. C. and W. Oldfather, Oxford: Classics of International Law.

Quesnay, F. (1764), *Philosophie rurale ou économie générale et politique de l'agriculture*, Amsterdam.

Rousseau, J.-J. [1755] (1962), *Discours de l'ineqalité parmi les hommes*, Paris: Garnier.

St Lambert (1757), 'Luxe', in *Encyclopédie ou dictionnnaire raisonnée des sciences, des arts et des métiers*, vol. IX, Paris, pp. 763–71.

Sallust (1921), *The War with Catiline*, trans. J. Rolfe with text, London: Loeb Library.

Seneca (1932a), *Letters to Lucilius*, trans. R. Gummere with text, London: Loeb Library.

— (1932b), *Moral Essays*, vol. 2, trans. J. Basore with text, London: Loeb Library.

Sidney, A. [1698] (1990), *Discourses concerning Government*, T. West (ed.), Indianapolis: Liberty Press.

Sprat, T. (1702), *The History of the Royal Society of London*, 2nd edn, London.

Swift, J. (1721), *Bubble: A Poem*, Edinburgh.

Temple, W. (1680), *Miscellanea*, London.

Tucker, J. (1755), *The Elements of Commerce and Theory of Taxes*, Bristol.

Turgot, A. (1973), *On Progress, Sociology and Economics*, trans. R. Meek (ed.), Cambridge: Cambridge University Press.

Voltaire, A. [1751] (1929), *Siècle de Louis XIV*, 14th edn, E. Bourgeois (ed.), Paris: Hachette.

— [1734] (1956), *Philosophical Letters*, in H. Block (ed.), *Candide and Other Writings*, New York: Modern Library, pp. 323–56.

— [1756] (2001), *Essai sur les Moeurs et l'esprit des Nations*, in *Les Oeuvres Complètes de Voltaire*, 3 vols (22–4), Oxford: Voltaire Foundation.

Xenophon (1923), *Oeconomicus*, trans. E. Marchant with text, London: Loeb Library.

## SECONDARY

Acemoglu, D. and J. Robinson (2012), *Why Nations Fail: The Origins of Power, Prosperity and Poverty*, London: Profile Books.

Allan, D. (1993), *Virtue, Learning and the Scottish Enlightenment*, Edinburgh: Edinburgh University Press.

Alvey, J. (2003), *Adam Smith: Optimist or Pessimist*, Aldershot: Ashgate.

Amrozowicz, M. (2013), 'Adam Smith: History and Poetics', in C. Berry, M. Paganelli and C. Smith (eds), *Oxford Handbook of Adam Smith*, Oxford: Oxford University Press, pp. 143–58.

Annas, J. (1993), *The Morality of Happiness*, New York: Oxford University Press.

Appleby, J. (1978), *Economic Thought and Ideology in Seventeenth-Century England*, Princeton: Princeton University Press.

Arena, V. (2011), 'Roman Sumptuary Legislation: Three Concepts of Liberty', *European Journal of Political Theory*, 10: 463–89.

Aspromourgos, T. (2009), *The Science of Wealth: Adam Smith and the Beginnings of Political Economy*, London: Routledge.

Baier, A. (1991), *A Progress of Sentiments: Reflections on Hume's Treatise*, Cambridge, MA: Harvard University Press.

Baker, K. (1975), *Condorcet: From Natural Philosophy to Social Mathematics*, Chicago: University of Chicago Press.

Baugh, D. (1983), 'Poverty, Protestantism and Political Economy', in S. Baxter (ed.), *England's Rise to Greatness*, Berkeley: University of California Press, pp. 63–107.

Benton, T. (1990), 'Adam Ferguson and the Enterprise Culture', in P. Hulme and L. Jordanova (eds), *The Enlightenment and its Shadows*, London: Routledge, pp. 63–120.

Berg, M. and E. Eger (2003), 'The Rise and Fall of the Luxury Debates', in M. Berg and E. Eger (eds), *Luxury in the Eighteenth Century*, Basingstoke: Palgrave, pp. 7–27.

Berry C. (1994), *The Idea of Luxury: A Conceptual and Historical Investigation*, Cambridge: Cambridge University Press.

— (1997), *Social Theory of the Scottish Enlightenment*, Edinburgh: Edinburgh University Press.

— (2000), 'Rude Religion: The Psychology of Polytheism in the Scottish Enlightenment', in P. Wood (ed.), *The Scottish Enlightenment: Essays in Re-Interpretation*, Rochester, NY: Rochester University Press, pp. 315–34.

— (2003a), 'Sociality and Socialisation', in A. Broadie (ed.), *The Cambridge Companion to the Scottish Enlightenment*, Cambridge: Cambridge University Press, pp. 243–57.

— (2003b), 'Lusty Women and Loose Imagination: Hume's Philosophical Anthropology of Chastity', *History of Political Thought*, 24: 415–33.

— (2004), 'Smith under Strain', *European Journal of Political Theory*, 3: 455–63.

— (2006a), 'Smith and Science', in K. Haakonssen (ed.), *The Cambridge Companion to Adam Smith*, Cambridge: Cambridge University Press, pp. 112–35.

— (2006b), 'Hume and the Customary Causes of Industry, Knowledge and Humanity', *History of Political Economy*, 38: 291–317.

220    *The Idea of Commercial Society in the Scottish Enlightenment*

— (2007), 'Hume's Universalism: The Science of Man and the Anthropological Point of View, *British Journal for the History of Philosophy*, 15: 535–50.

— (2008), 'Hume and Superfluous Value (or What's Wrong with Epictetus' Slippers)', in C. Wennerlind and M. Schabas (eds), *David Hume's Political Economy*, London: Routledge, pp. 49–64.

— (2009a), 'Ferguson and the Principle of Simultaneity', in E. Heath and V. Merolle (eds), *Adam Ferguson: Philosophy, Politics and Society*, London: Pickering and Chatto, pp. 143–53, pp. 214n–17n.

— (2009b), *David Hume*, London: Continuum.

— (2010), 'Creating Space for Civil Society: Conceptual Cartography in the Scottish Enlightenment', *Giornale di Storia Constituzionale*, 20: 49–60.

— (2011), 'Science and Superstition: Hume and Conservatism', *European Journal of Political Theory*, 10: 141–55.

— (2012), 'Adam Smith's Science of Human Nature', *History of Political Economy*, 44: 471–92.

Blaney, D. and N. Inayatullah (2010), *Savage Economics: Wealth, Poverty and the Temporal Walls of Capitalism*, London: Routledge.

Bonolas, P. (1987), 'Fénelon et le luxe dans le Télémaque', *Voltaire Studies*, 249: 81–90.

Booth, W. (1993), *Households: On the Moral Architecture of the Economy*, Ithaca, NY: Cornell University Press.

Bowles, P. (1985), 'The Origin of Property and the Development of Scottish Historical Science', *Journal of the History of Ideas*, 46: 197–209.

— (1986), 'John Millar, the Legislator and the Mode of Subsistence', *History of European Ideas*, 7: 237–51.

Boyd, R. (2004), *Uncivil Society: The Perils of Pluralism and the Making of Modern Liberalism*, Lanham, MD: Lexington Books.

— (2008), 'Manners and Morals: David Hume on Civility, Commerce and the Social Construction of Difference', in C. Wennerlind and M. Schabas (eds), *David Hume's Political Economy*, London: Routledge, pp. 65–85.

— (2013),'Adam Smith and Civil Society', in C. Berry, M. Paganelli and C. Smith (eds), *Oxford Handbook of Adam Smith*, Oxford: Oxford University Press, pp. 443–63.

Broadie, A. (2001), *The Scottish Enlightenment*, Edinburgh: Birlinn.

— (2006), 'Sympathy and the Impartial Spectator', in K. Haakonssen (ed.), *The Cambridge Companion to Adam Smith*, Cambridge: Cambridge University Press, pp. 158–88.

Brooke, C. (2012), *Philosophic Pride: Stoicism and Political Thought from Lipsius to Rousseau*, Princeton: Princeton University Press.

Brown, M. (1988), *Adam Smith's Economics*, London: Croom Helm.

Brown, S. (1997), 'William Robertson (1721–93) and the Scottish Enlightenment', in S. Brown (ed.), *William Robertson and the Expansion of Empire*, Cambridge: Cambridge University Press, pp. 7–35.

Brühlmeier, D. (1996), 'Die Geburt der Sozialwissenschaften aus dem Geiste der Moralphilosophie', in D. Brühlmeier, H. Holzhey and V. Mudroch (eds),

*Schottische Aufklärung: "A Hotbed of Genius"*, Berlin: Akademie Verlag, pp. 23–38.

Bryson, G. [1945] (1968), *Man and Society – the Scottish Enquiry of the Eighteenth Century*, New York: Kelley reprint.

Buckle, S. (1991), *Natural Law and the Theory of Property: Grotius to Hume*, Oxford: Clarendon Press.

Burtt, S. (1992), *Virtue Transformed: Political Argument in England, 1688–1740*, Cambridge: Cambridge University Press.

Caffentzis, G. (2001), 'Hume, Money and Civilization: Or Why Was Hume a Metallist?', *Hume Studies*, 27: 301–35.

— (2008), 'Fiction or Counterfeit? David Hume's Interpretations of Paper Money and Metallic Money', in C. Wennerlind and M. Schabas (eds), *David Hume's Political Economy*, London: Routledge, pp. 146–67.

Calkins, M. and P. Werhane (1998), 'Adam Smith, Aristotle and the Virtues of Commerce', *Journal of Value Inquiry*, 32: 43–60.

Cameron, A. (1995), *Bank of Scotland, 1695–1995*, Edinburgh: Mainstream.

Campbell, N. and R. Smellie (1983), *The Royal Society of Edinburgh (1783–1983)*, Edinburgh: RSE.

Campbell, R. H. (1982), 'The Enlightenment and the Economy', in R. H. Campbell and A. Skinner (eds), *Origins and Nature of the Scottish Enlightenment*, Edinburgh: John Donald, pp. 8–25.

Campbell, T. (1971), *Adam Smith's Science of Morals*, London: G. Allen and Unwin.

Cant, R. (1982), 'Origins of the Enlightenment in Scotland: the Universities', in R. Campbell and A. Skinner (eds), *Origins and Nature of the Scottish Enlightenment*, Edinburgh: John Donald, pp. 42–64.

Capaldi N. and D. Livingston (eds) (1990), *Liberty in Hume's 'History of England'*, Dordrecht: Kluwer Academic.

Carey, D. (2006), *Locke, Shaftesbury and Hutcheson: Contesting Diversity in the Enlightenment and Beyond*, Cambridge: Cambridge University Press.

Castiglione, D. (2000), '"That Noble Disquiet": Meanings of Liberty in the Discourse of the North', in S. Collini, D. Winch and J. Burrow (eds), *Economy, Politics and Society*, Cambridge: Cambridge University Press, pp. 48–69.

Chamley, P. (1975), 'The Conflict between Montesquieu and Hume', in A. Skinner and T. Wilson (eds), *Essays on Adam Smith*, Oxford: Clarendon Press, pp. 274–305.

Charles, L. (2008), 'French "New Politics" and the Dissemination of David Hume's *Political Discourses* on the Continent', in C. Wennerlind and M. Schabas (eds), *David Hume's Political Economy*, London: Routledge, pp. 81–202.

Chitnis, A. (1976), *The Scottish Enlightenment: A Social History*, London: Croom Helm.

Clark, I. (1970), 'From Protest to Reaction: The Moderate Regime in the Church of Scotland 1752–1805', in N. Phillipson and R. Mitchison (eds),

*Scotland in the Age of Improvement*, Edinburgh: Edinburgh University Press, pp. 200–24.

Coats, A. (1958), 'Changing Attitudes to Labour in the Mid-Eighteenth Century', *Economic History Review*, 11: 35–51.

— (1992), 'Economic Thought and Poor Law Policy in the Eighteenth Century', in *On the History of Economic Thought*, vol. 1, London: Routledge, pp. 85–100.

Cohon, R. (2008), *Hume's Morality: Feeling and Fabrication*, Oxford: Oxford University Press.

Collingwood, R. (1946), *The Idea of History*, Oxford: Clarendon Press.

Cropsey, J. [1957] (2001), *Polity and Economy. With Further Thoughts on the Principles of Adam Smith*, South Bend: St Augustine's Press.

Cunningham, A. (2005), 'David Hume's Account of Luxury', *Journal of the History of Economic Thought*, 27: 231–50.

Danford, J. (1980), 'Adam Smith, Equality and the Wealth of Nations', *American Political Science Review*, 24: 674–95.

— (1990), *David Hume and the Problem of Reason*, New Haven, CT: Yale University Press.

Daston, L. (1988), *Classical Probability in the Enlightenment*, Princeton: Princeton University Press.

Davie, G. (1981), *The Scottish Enlightenment*, pamphlet no. 99, London: Historical Association.

Davis, D. (1966), *The Problem of Slavery in Western Culture*, Ithaca, NY: Cornell University Press.

de Marchi, N. (1999), 'Adam Smith's Accommodation of "Altogether Endless" Desires', in M. Berg and H. Clifford (eds), *Consumers and Luxury*, Manchester: Manchester University Press, pp. 18–36.

Devine, T. (1985), 'The Union of 1707 and Scottish Development', *Scottish Economic and Social History*, 5: 23–40.

— (1990), *The Tobacco Lords: A Study of the Tobacco Merchants of Glasgow*, Edinburgh: Edinburgh University Press.

Dickey, L. (1986), 'Historicizing the "Adam Smith Problem": Conceptual, Historiographical and Textual Issues', *Journal of Modern History*, 58: 579–609.

Dickson, P. (1967), *The Financial Revolution in England*, London: Macmillan.

Donovan, A. (1982), 'William Cullen and the Research Tradition of Eighteenth-Century Scottish Chemistry', in R. Campbell and A. Skinner (eds), *Origins and Nature of the Scottish Enlightenment*, Edinburgh: John Donald, pp. 98–114.

Duke, M. (1979), 'David Hume and Monetary Adjustment', *History of Political Economy*, 11: 572–87.

Durie, A. (1979), *The Scottish Linen Industry in the Eighteenth Century*, Edinburgh: John Donald.

— (2010), 'Movement, Transport and Travel', in E. Foyster and C. Whatley (eds), *A History of Everyday Life in Scotland, 1600–1800*, Edinburgh: Edinburgh University Press, pp. 252–72.

Dwyer, J. (1987), *Virtuous Discourse: Sensibility and Community in Late Eighteenth-Century Scotland*, Edinburgh: John Donald.

Dwyer, J. and A. Murdoch (1983), 'Paradigms and Politics: Manners, Morals and the Rise of Henry Dundas', in J. Dwyer, R. Mason and A. Murdoch (eds), *New Perspectives on the Politics and Culture of Early Modern Scotland*, Edinburgh: John Donald, pp. 210–48.

Ehrenberg, J. (1999), *Civil Society: The Critical History of an Idea*, New York: New York University Press.

Elton, M. (2008), 'Moral Sense and Natural Reason', *The Review of Metaphysics*, 62: 79–110.

Emerson, R. (1973), 'The Social Composition of Enlightened Scotland: The Select Society of Edinburgh 1754–64, *Studies in Voltaire*, 114: 291–329.

— (1984), 'Conjectural History and the Scottish Philosophers', *Historical Papers of the Canadian Historical Association*, 63–90.

— (1986), 'Science and the Origins and Concerns of the Scottish Enlightenment', *History of Science*, 26: 333–66.

— (1989), 'The Religious, the Secular and the Worldly: Scotland 1680–1800', in J. Crimmins (ed.), *Religion, Secularization and Political Thought*, London: Routledge, pp. 68–89.

— (1992), *Professors and Patronage: The Aberdeen Universities in the Eighteenth Century*, Aberdeen: Aberdeen University Press.

— (1995a), 'Did the Scottish Enlightenment Emerge in an English Cultural Province?', *Lumen*, 15: 1–22.

— (1995b), 'Politics and the Glasgow Professors, 1690–1800', in A. Hook and R. Sher (eds), *The Glasgow Enlightenment*, East Linton: Tuckwell Press, pp. 1–39.

— (1998), 'Lord Bute and the Scottish Universities, 1760–92', in K. Schweizer (ed.), *Lord Bute: Essays in Re-Interpretation*, Leicester: Leicester University Press, pp. 147–79.

— (2008a), 'The Scottish Contexts for David Hume's Political-Economic Thinking', in C. Wennerlind and M. Schabas (eds), *David Hume's Political Economy*, London: Routledge, pp. 10–30.

— (2008b), *Academic Patronage in the Scottish Enlightenment: Glasgow, Edinburgh and St Andrews Universities*, Edinburgh: Edinburgh University Press.

— (2009), *Essays on David Hume, Medical Men and the Scottish Enlightenment*, Farnham: Ashgate.

Evans-Pritchard, E. (1981), *A History of Anthropological Thought*, London: Faber and Faber.

Evensky, J. (2005), *Adam Smith's Moral Philosophy*, Cambridge: Cambridge University Press.

Fauré, M. (1997), 'John Millar ou la culture politique d'un homme des

Lumières', in *L'Écosse des Lumières: Le XVIII siècle autrement*, Grenoble: Université de Stendhal, pp. 209–29.

Ferguson, J. (1958), *Moral Values in the Ancient World*, London: Methuen.

Filonowicz, J. (2008), *Fellow-Feeling and the Moral Life*, Cambridge: Cambridge University Press.

Finlay, C. (2006), 'Rhetoric and Citizenship in Adam Ferguson's *Essay on the History of Civil Society*', *History of Political Thought*, 27: 29–49.

— (2007), *Hume's Social Philosophy*, London: Continuum.

Fiori, S. and E. Pesciarelli, E. (1999), 'Adam Smith on the Relations of Subordination, Personal Incentives and the Division of Labour', *Scottish Journal of Political Economy*, 46: 91–106.

Fitzgibbon, A. (1995), *Adam Smith's System of Liberty*, Oxford: Clarendon Press.

Fleischacker, S. (1999), *A Third Concept of Liberty: Judgment and Freedom in Kant and Adam Smith*, Princeton: Princeton University Press.

— (2004), *On Adam Smith's* Wealth of Nations: *A Philosophical Companion*, Princeton: Princeton University Press.

— (2013), 'Smith on Equality', in C. Berry, M. Paganelli and C. Smith (eds), *Oxford Handbook of Adam Smith*, Oxford: Oxford University Press, pp. 486–500.

Foley, V. (1976), *The Social Physics of Adam Smith*, West Lafayette, IN: Purdue University Press.

Forbes, D. (1954),'Scientific Whiggism: Adam Smith and John Millar', *Cambridge Journal*, 7: 643–70.

— (1967), 'Adam Ferguson and the Idea of Community', in J. Young (ed.), *Edinburgh in the Age of Reason*, Edinburgh: Edinburgh University Press, pp. 40–7.

— (1975a), *Hume's Philosophical Politics*, Cambridge: Cambridge University Press.

— (1975b), 'Sceptical Whiggism, Commerce and Liberty', in A. Skinner and T. Wilson (eds), *Essays on Adam Smith*, Oxford: Clarendon Press, pp. 179–201.

— (1977), 'Hume's Science of Politics', in G. Morice, *David Hume: Bicentenary Papers*, Edinburgh: Edinburgh University Press, pp. 39–50.

— (1982), 'Natural Law and the Scottish Enlightenment', in R. Campbell and A. Skinner (eds), *Origins and Nature of the Scottish Enlightenment*, Edinburgh: John Donald, pp. 186–204.

Force, P. (2003), *Self-Interest before Adam Smith*, Cambridge: Cambridge University Press.

Forman-Barzilai, F. (2010), *Adam Smith and the Circles of Sympathy*, Cambridge: Cambridge University Press.

Foyster, E. and C. Whatley (2010), *A History of Everyday Life in Scotland, 1600–1800*, Edinburgh: Edinburgh University Press.

Francesconi, D. (1999), 'William Robertson on Historical Causation and Unintended Consequences', *Cromohs*: 1–18.

Frankel, C. (1948), *The Faith of Reason*, New York: Octagon Books.

Frazer, M. (2010), *The Enlightenment of Sympathy*, Oxford: Oxford University Press.

Fricke, C. (2013), 'Adam Smith: The Sympathetic Process and the Origin and Function of Conscience', in C. Berry, M. Paganelli and C. Smith (eds), *Oxford Handbook of Adam Smith*, Oxford: Oxford University Press, pp. 177–200.

Furniss, E. (1920), *The Position of the Laborer in a System of Nationalism*, Boston: Houghton Mifflin.

Gatch, L. (1996), 'To Redeem Metal with Paper: David Hume's Philosophy of Money', *Hume Studies*, 22: 169–91.

Gaukroger, S. (2001), *Francis Bacon and the Transformation of Early-Modern Philosophy*, Cambridge: Cambridge University Press.

Gay, P. (1967), *The Enlightenment: The Rise of Modern Paganism*, London: Weidenfeld and Nicolson.

Geertz, C. (1975), *The Interpretation of Cultures*, London: Hutchinson.

Giarrizzo, G. (1962), *David Hume: Politico e Storico*, Turin: Einaudi.

Goldsmith, M. (1994), 'Liberty, Virtue and the Rule of Law, 1689–1770', in D. Wootton (ed.), *Republicanism, Liberty and Commercial Society 1649–1776*, Stanford: Stanford University Press, pp. 197–232.

Golinski, J. (1988), 'Utility and Audience in Eighteenth-Century Chemistry: Case Studies of William Cullen and Joseph Priestley', *British Journal for the History of Science*, 21: 1–31.

Gordon, D. (1994), *Citizens without Sovereignty: Equality and Sociability in French Thought 1670–1789*, Princeton: Princeton University Press.

Griffin, M. (1976), *Seneca: A Philosopher in Politics*, Oxford: Clarendon Press.

Griswold, C. (1999), *Adam Smith and the Virtues of Enlightenment*, Cambridge: Cambridge University Press.

— (2010), 'Smith and Rousseau in Dialogue', *Adam Smith Review*, 8: 59–84.

Groenewegen, P. (1977), 'Adam Smith and the Division of Labour', *Australian Economic Papers*, 16: 161–74.

Guena, M. (2002), 'Republicanism and Commercial Society in the Scottish Enlightenment: The Case of Adam Ferguson', in M. van Gelderen and Q. Skinner (eds), *Republicanism: A Shared European Heritage*, Cambridge: Cambridge University Press, vol. 2, pp. 177–95.

Guthrie, D. (1950), 'William Cullen and his Times', in A. Kent (ed.), *An Eighteenth-Century Lectureship in Chemistry*, Glasgow: Jackson, pp. 49–65.

Haakonssen, K. (1981), *The Science of a Legislator*, Cambridge: Cambridge University Press.

— (1996), *Natural Law and Moral Philosophy: From Grotius to the Scottish Enlightenment*, Cambridge: Cambridge University Press.

Hamowy, R. (1987), *The Scottish Enlightenment and the Theory of Spontaneous Order*, Carbondale: Southern Illinois University Press.

Hanley, R. (2007), 'Adam Smith, Aristotle and Virtue Ethics', in E. Schliesser and L. Montes (eds), *New Voices on Smith*, London: Routledge, pp. 17–39.

— (2008a), 'Enlightened Nation Building: The "Science of the Legislator" in Adam Smith and Rousseau', *American Journal of Political Science*, 52: 219–34.

— (2008b), 'Commerce and Corruption: Rousseau's Diagnosis and Adam Smith's Cure', *European Journal of Political Theory*, 7: 137–58.

— (2009a), *Adam Smith and the Character of Virtue*, Cambridge: Cambridge University Press.

— (2009b), 'Social Science and Human Flourishing', *Journal of Scottish Philosophy*, 7: 29–46.

— (2013), 'Smith and Virtue', in C. Berry, M. Paganelli and C. Smith (eds), *Oxford Handbook of Adam Smith*, Oxford: Oxford University Press, pp. 219–40.

Hardin, R. (2007), *Hume's Moral and Political Theory*, Oxford: Oxford University Press.

Hargraves, N. (2002), 'The "Progress of Ambition": Character, Narrative and Philosophy in the Works of William Robertson', *Journal of the History of Ideas*, 63: 261–82.

Harkin, M. (2002), 'Natives and Nostalgia: The Problem of the "North American Savage" in Adam Smith's Historiography', *Scottish Studies Review*, 3: 21–32.

Harpham, E. (1984), 'Liberalism, Civic Humanism and the Case of Adam Smith', *American Political Science Review*, 78: 764–74.

Harris, J. (2010), 'Hume on the Moral Obligation to Justice', *Hume Studies*, 36: 25–50.

Harrison, J. (1981), *Hume's Theory of Justice*, Oxford: Clarendon Press.

Harte, N. (1976), 'State Control of Dress and Social Change in Pre-Industrial England', in D. C. Coleman and A. H. John (eds), *Trade, Government and Economy in Pre-Industrial England*, London: Weidenfeld and Nicolson, pp. 132–65.

Hayek, F. [1960] (1972), *The Constitution of Liberty*, Chicago: Gateway.

Heath, E. (2013), 'Adam Smith and Self-Interest', in C. Berry, M. Paganelli and C. Smith (eds), *Oxford Handbook of Adam Smith*, Oxford: Oxford University Press, pp. 241–64.

Heller, H. (2011), *The Birth of Capitalism: A Twenty-First Century Perspective*, London: Pluto Press.

Henderson, W. and W. Samuels (2004), 'The Etiology of Adam Smith on Division of Labor: Alternative Accounts and Smith's Methodology Applied to Them', in W. Henderson, K. Johnson, M. Johnson and W. Samuels (eds), *Essays in the History of Economics*, London: Routledge, pp. 8–85.

Herr, R. (1958), *The Eighteenth-Century Revolution in Spain*, Princeton: Princeton University Press.

Hill, C. (1968), *Puritanism and Revolution*, London: Panther Books.

Hill, L. (1999), 'Hume, Smith and Ferguson: Friendship in Commercial Society', *Critical Review of International Social and Political Philosophy*, 2: 33–49.

— (2006), *The Passionate Society: The Social, Political and Moral Thought of Adam Ferguson*, Dordrecht: Springer Press.

— (2007),'Adam Smith, Adam Ferguson and Karl Marx on the Division of Labour', *Journal of Classical Sociology*, 7: 339–66.

Himmelfarb, G. (1984), *The Idea of Poverty: England in the Early Industrial Age*, London: Faber and Faber.

Hirschman, A. (1977), *The Passions and the Interests*, Princeton: Princeton University Press.

Hobsbawm, E. (1980), 'Scottish Reformers of the Eighteenth Century and Capitalist Agriculture', in *Peasants in History*, Calcutta: Oxford University Press, pp. 3–29.

Hollander, S. (1973), *The Economics of Adam Smith*, Toronto: University of Toronto Press.

Hont, I. (2005), *Jealousy of Trade: International Competition and the Nation-State in Historical Perspective*, Cambridge, MA: Belknap Press.

— (2006), 'The Early Enlightenment Debate on Commerce and Luxury', in M. Goldie and R. Wokler (eds), *The Cambridge History of Eighteenth-Century Political Thought*, Cambridge: Cambridge University Press, pp. 379–418.

— (2009), 'Adam Smith's History of Law and Government as Political Theory', in R. Burke and R. Geuss (eds), *Political Judgement*, Cambridge: Cambridge University Press, pp. 131–71.

Hont, I and M. Ignatieff (1983), 'Needs and Justice in the Wealth of Nations', in I. Hont and M. Ignatieff (eds), *Wealth and Virtue*, Cambridge: Cambridge University Press, pp. 1–44.

Höpfl, H. (1978), 'From Savage to Scotsman: Conjectural History in the Scottish Enlightenment', *Journal of British Studies*, 7: 20–40.

Hoppit, J. (1990), 'Attitudes to Credit in Britain, 1680–1790', *The Historical Journal*, 33: 305–22.

Horne, T. (1990), *Property Rights and Society: Political Argument in Britain 1605–1834*, Chapel Hill: University of North Carolina Press.

Hundert, E. (1994), *The Enlightenment's Fable: Bernard Mandeville and the Discovery of Society*, Cambridge: Cambridge University Press.

Hunt, A. (1996), *Governance of the Consuming Passions*, London: Macmillan.

Hunter, M. (1992), 'Aikenhead the Atheist: The Context and Consequences of Articulate Irreligion in the Late Seventeenth Century', in M. Hunter and D. Wootton (eds), *Atheism from the Reformation to the Enlightenment*, Oxford: Clarendon Press, pp. 221–54.

Hutchinson, T. (1988), *Before Adam Smith: The Emergence of Political Economy 1662–1776*, Oxford: Blackwell.

Ignatieff, M. (1983), 'John Millar and Individualism', in I. Hont and M. Ignatieff (eds), *Wealth and Virtue*, Cambridge: Cambridge University Press, pp. 317–43.

— (1984), *The Needs of Strangers*, London: Chatto and Windus.

Immerwahr, J. (1992), 'Hume's Revised Racism', *Journal of the History of Ideas*, 53: 481–86.

Inwood, B. (1985), *Ethics and Human Action in Early Stoicism*, Oxford: Clarendon Press.

Ito, S. (2011), 'The Making of Institutional Credit in England, 1600 to 1688', *The European Journal of the History of Economic Thought*, 18: 487–519.

Jack, M. (1989), *Corruption and Progress: The Eighteenth-Century Debate*, New York: AMS Press.

Jardine, L. (1974), *Francis Bacon: Discovery and the Art of Discourse*, Cambridge: Cambridge University Press.

Johnson, E. (1937), *Predecessors of Adam Smith*, London: P. King.

Kelly, D. (2011), *The Propriety of Liberty*, Princeton: Princeton University Press.

Kennedy, G. (2005), *Adam Smith's Lost Legacy*, Basingstoke: Palgrave.

— (2011), 'Adam Smith and the Role of the Metaphor of an Invisible Hand', *Journal of the History of Economic Thought*, 33: 385–402.

— (2013), 'Adam Smith and Religion', in C. Berry, M. Paganelli and C. Smith (eds), *Oxford Handbook of Adam Smith*, Oxford: Oxford University Press, pp. 464–84.

Kennedy, T. (1995), 'William Leechman, Pulpit Eloquence and the Glasgow Enlightenment', in A. Hook and R. Sher (eds), *The Glasgow Enlightenment*, East Linton: Tuckwell Press, pp. 56–72.

Kent, A. (1950), 'William Cullen's History of Chemistry', in A. Kent (ed.), *An Eighteenth- Century Lectureship in Chemistry*, Glasgow: Jackson, pp. 49–77.

Kettler, D. (1965), *Social and Political Thought of Adam Ferguson*, Columbus: Ohio State University Press.

— (1977), 'History and Theory in Ferguson's *Essay on the History of Civil Society: A Reconsideration*', *Political Theory*, 5: 437–60.

Kidd, C. (1993), *Subverting Scotland's Past: Scottish Whig Historians and the Creation of an Anglo-British Identity 1689–c. 1800*, Cambridge: Cambridge University Press.

— (2004), 'Subscription, the Scottish Enlightenment and the Moderate Interpretation of History', *Journal of Ecclesiastical History*, 55: 502–19.

Krause, S. (2004), 'Hume and the (False) Luster of Justice', *Political Theory*, 32: 628–55.

Lamb, R. (1973), 'Adam Smith's Concept of Alienation', *Oxford Economic Papers*, 25: 275–85.

Langford, P. (1989), *A Polite and Commercial People: England 1727–1783*, Oxford: Oxford University Press.

Laudan, L. (1970), 'Thomas Reid and the Newtonian Turn in British Methodological Thought', in R. Butts and S. Davis (eds), *The Methodological Heritage of Newton*, Oxford: Oxford University Press, pp. 103–31.

Law, R. (1969), *James Watt and the Separate Condenser*, London: HMSO.

Lehmann, W. (1930), *Adam Ferguson and the Beginnings of Modern Sociology*, New York: Columbia University Press.

— (1971), *Henry Home, Lord Kames and the Scottish Enlightenment*, The Hague: M. Nifhoff.

Lenman, B. (1981), *Integration, Enlightenment and Industrialization: Scotland 1746–1832*, London: E. Arnold.

Letwin, W. (1964), *The Origins of Scientific Economics*, New York: Doubleday.

Lieberman, D. (1989), *The Province of Legislation Determined: Legal Theory in Eighteenth-Century Britain*, Cambridge: Cambridge University Press.

Lindgren, J. (1973), *The Social Philosophy of Adam Smith*, The Hague: Nijhoff.

Livingston, D. (1984), *Hume's Philosophy of Common Life*, Chicago: University of Chicago Press.

Lough, J. (1971), *The Encyclopédie*, London: Longman.

McArthur, N. (2007), *David Hume's Political Theory: Law, Commerce and the Constitution of Government*, Toronto: University of Toronto Press.

McDowall, G. (1983), 'Commerce, Virtue and Politics: Adam Ferguson's Constitutionalism', *Review of Politics*, 45: 536–52.

McElroy, D. (1969), *Scotland's Age of Improvement*, Pullman: Washington State University Press.

Macfie, A. (1967), *The Individual in Society: Papers on Adam Smith*, London: G. Allen and Unwin.

Macfie, A. and D. Raphael [1976] (1982), 'Introduction' to A. Smith *The Moral Sentiments*, Indianapolis: Liberty Press.

MacInnes, A. (1999), 'Scottish Jacobitism: In Search of a Movement', in T. Devine and J. Young (eds), *Eighteenth-Century Scotland: New Perspectives*, East Linton: Tuckwell Press, pp. 70–89.

McIntosh, J. (1998), *Church and Theology in Enlightenment Scotland: The Popular Party, 1740–1800*, East Linton: Tuckwell Press.

MacIntyre, A. (1998), *Whose Justice? Which Rationality?*, London: Duckworth.

McKenna, S. (2006), *Adam Smith: The Rhetoric of Propriety*, Albany: SUNY Press.

Mackie, J. (1954), *The University of Glasgow: 1451–1951*, Glasgow: Jackson.

McNally, D. (1988), *Political Economy and the Rise of Capitalism*, Berkeley: University of California Press.

MacRae, D. (1969), 'Adam Ferguson', in T. Raison (ed.), *Founding Fathers of Sociology*, Harmondsworth: Penguin Books, pp. 17–26.

Malcolm, N. (2002), *Aspects of Hobbes*, Oxford: Clarendon Press.

Manuel, F. (1959), *The Eighteenth Century Confronts the Gods*, Cambridge, MA: Harvard University Press.

Marshall, P. and G. Williams (1982), *The Great Map of Mankind*, London: Dent.

Martin, J. (1992), *Francis Bacon, the State and the Reform of Natural Philosophy*, Cambridge: Cambridge University Press.

Medema, S. and W. Samuels (2009), '"Only Three Duties": Adam Smith on the Role of Government', in J. Young (ed.), *Elgar Companion to Adam Smith*, Cheltenham: Edward Elgar, pp. 300–14.

Medick, H. (1973), *Naturzustand und Naturgeschichte der bürgerlichen Gesellschaft*, Göttingen: Vandenhoeck and Ruprecht.

Medick, H. and Z. Batscha (1988), *Einleitung: A. Ferguson Versuch über die Geschichte der bürgerlichen Gesellschaft*, Frankfurt-am-Main: Suhrkamp.

Medick, H. and A. Leppert-Fögen (1974), 'Frühe Sozialwissenschaft als Ideologie des kleinens Bürgertums: J. Millar of Glasgow', in H. Wehler (ed.), *Sozialgeschichte Heut*, Göttingen: Vandenhoeck and Ruprecht, pp. 22–48.

Meek, R. (1967), 'The Scottish Contribution to Marxist Sociology', in *Economics and Ideology*, London: Chapman and Hall, pp. 34–50.

— (1973), Introduction to *Turgot: On Progress. Sociology and Economics*, ed and trans. R. Meek, Cambridge: Cambridge University Press.

— (1976), *Social Science and the Ignoble Savage*, Cambridge: Cambridge University Press.

Mercer, P. (1972), *Sympathy and Ethics*, Oxford: Clarendon Press.

Miller, E. (1996), 'Sympathetic Exchange: Adam Smith and Punishment', *Ratio Juris*, 9: 182–97.

Mizuta H. (1975), 'Moral Philosophy and Civil Society', in A. Skinner and T. Wilson (eds), *Essays on Adam Smith*, Oxford: Clarendon Press, pp. 114–31.

— (1981), 'Two Adams in the Scottish Enlightenment: Adam Smith and Adam Ferguson on Progress', *Studies in Voltaire*, 191: 812–19.

Mokyr, J. (2009), *The Enlightened Economy: An Economic History of Britain 1700–1850*, New Haven, CT: Yale University Press.

Montes, L. (2004), *Adam Smith in Context*, London: Palgrave Macmillan.

— (2009), 'Adam Smith on the Standing Army versus Militia Issue: Wealth over Virtue', in J. Young (ed.), *The Elgar Companion to Adam Smith*, Cheltenham: Elgar, pp. 315–34.

Moore, J. (1977), 'Hume's Political Science and the Classical Republican Tradition', *Canadian Journal of Political Science*, 10: 809–39.

— (2000), 'Hutcheson's Theodicy', in P. Wood (ed.), *The Scottish Enlightenment: Essays in Re-Interpretation*, Rochester, NY: Rochester University Press, pp. 239–66.

— (2009), 'Montesquieu and the Scottish Enlightenment', in R. Kingston (ed.), *Montesquieu and his Legacy*, Albany: SUNY Press, pp. 179–95.

Moran, C. (2003), 'The Commerce of the Sexes: Gender and the Social Sphere in Scottish Enlightenment Accounts of Civil Society', in F. Trentman (ed.), *Paradoxes of Civil Society*, revd edn, New York: Berghahn, pp. 61–84.

Mossner, E. (1980), *Life of David Hume*, 2nd edn, Oxford: Clarendon Press.

Muldrew, C. (1998), *The Economy of Obligation: The Culture of Credit and Social Relations in Early Modern England*, Basingstoke: Macmillan.

Muller, J. (1993), *Adam Smith in his Time and Ours*, Princeton: Princeton University Press.

Murdoch, A. (1980), *The People Above: Politics and Administration in Mid-Eighteenth-Century Scotland*, Edinburgh: John Donald.

Murdoch, A. and R. Sher (1988), 'Literary and Learned Culture', in T. Devine and R. Mitchison (eds), *People and Society in Scotland*, vol. l, Edinburgh: John Donald, pp. 127–42.

Murphy, A. (2009), *The Origins of the English Financial Markets*, Cambridge: Cambridge University Press.

Murphy, J. (1993), *The Moral Economy of Labor*, New Haven, CT: Yale University Press.

Muzzarelli, M. (2009), 'Reconciling the Privilege of a Few with the Common Good: Sumptuary Laws in Medieval and Early Modern Europe', *J. Medieval and Early Modern Studies*, 39: 587–617.

Myers, M. (1983), *The Soul of Economic Man*, Chicago: University of Chicago Press.

Norrie, A. (1989), 'Punishment and Justice in Adam Smith, *Ratio Juris*, 2: 227–39.

Nussbaum, M. (1986), *The Fragility of Goodness*, Cambridge: Cambridge University Press.

Ostrom, E. (1998), 'A Behavioral Approach to the Rational Choice of Collective Action', *American Political Science Review*, 92: 1–22.

Otteson, J. (2002), *Adam Smith's Marketplace of Life*, Cambridge: Cambridge University Press.

Oz-Salzburger, F. (2008), 'Ferguson's Politics of Action', in E. Heath and V. Merolle (eds), *Adam Ferguson: History, Progress and Human Nature*, London: Pickering and Chatto, pp. 147–56, 214–17.

Paganelli, M. (2006), 'Vanity and the Daedalian Wings of Paper Money in Adam Smith', in E. Schliesser and L. Montes (eds), *New Voices on Adam Smith*, London: Routledge, pp. 271–89.

— (2010), 'The Moralizing Role of Distance in Adam Smith', *History of Political Economy*, 42: 425–41.

— (2013), 'Commercial Relations: From Adam Smith to Field Experiments', in C. Berry, M. Paganelli and C. Smith (eds), *Oxford Handbook of Adam Smith*, Oxford: Oxford University Press, pp. 333–50.

Pascal, R. (1938), 'Property and Society: The Scottish Historical School of the Eighteenth Century', *Modern Quarterly*, 1: 167–79.

Passmore, J. (1971), 'The Malleability of Man in Eighteenth-Century Thought', in E. Wassermann (ed.), *Aspects of the Eighteenth Century*, Baltimore: Johns Hopkins University Press, pp. 21–46.

Perez-Ramos, A. (1996), 'Bacon's Legacy', in M. Peltonen (ed.), *Cambridge Companion to Francis Bacon*, Cambridge: Cambridge University Press, pp. 311–34.

Pesciarelli, E. (1978), 'The Italian Contribution to the Four-Stages Theory', *History of Political Economy*, 10: 597–605.

Phillipson, N. (1973), 'Culture and Society in the Eighteenth-Century Province: The Case of Edinburgh and the Scottish Enlightenment', in L. Stone (ed.), *The University in Society*, vol.1, Princeton: Princeton University Press, pp. 407–48.

— (1976), 'Lawyers, Landowners and the Civic Leadership of Post-Union Scotland', *Juridical Review*, 21: 97–120.

— (1981), 'The Scottish Enlightenment', in R. Porter and M. Teich (eds), *The Enlightenment in National Context*, Cambridge: Cambridge University Press, pp. 19–40.

— (1987), 'Politics, Politeness and the Anglicisation of Early Eighteenth-Century Scottish Culture', in R. Mason (ed.), *Scotland and England 1286–1815*, Edinburgh: John Donald, pp. 226–46.

— (1997), 'Providence and Progress: An Introduction to the Historical Thought of William Robertson', in S. Brown (ed.), *William Robertson and the Expansion of Empire*, Cambridge: Cambridge University Press, pp. 55–73.

— (2000), 'Language, Sociability and History: Some Reflections on the Foundations of Adam Smith's Science of Man', in S. Collini, R. Whatmore and B. Young (eds), *Economy, Polity and Society: British Intellectual History 1750–1950*, Cambridge: Cambridge University Press, pp. 70–84.

— (2010), *Adam Smith: An Enlightened Life*, London: Allen Lane.

Pitts, J. (2005), *A Turn to Empire*, Princeton: Princeton University Press.

Pocock, J. (1975), *The Machiavellian Moment*, Princeton: Princeton University Press.

— (1983), 'Cambridge Paradigms and Scottish Philosophers', in I. Hont and M. Ignatieff (eds), *Wealth and Virtue*, Cambridge: Cambridge University Press, pp. 235–52.

— (1985), *Virtue, Commerce and History*, Cambridge: Cambridge University Press.

— (1999), *Barbarism and Religion: Narratives of Civil Government*, Cambridge: Cambridge University Press.

Poovey, M. (1988), *A History of the Modern Fact*, Chicago: University of Chicago Press.

Pulkkinen, O. (2003), *The Labyrinth of Politics: A Conceptual Approach to the Modes of the Political in the Scottish Enlightenment*, Jyväskylä: Jyväskylä Studies in Education, Psychology and Social Research.

Rae, J. [1895] (1965), *Life of Adam Smith*, J. Viner (ed.), New York: Kelly reprints.

Rahmatian, A. (2006), 'The Property Theory of Lord Kames (Henry Home)', *International Journal of Law in Context*, 2: 177–205.

Ranke, L. (1824), *Geschichte der Romanischen und Germanischen Völker*, Leipzig and Berlin: G. Reimer.

Raphael, D. (2007), *The Impartial Spectator: Adam Smith's Moral Philosophy*, Oxford: Oxford University Press.

Rashid, S. (1986), 'Adam Smith and the Division of Labour: A Historical View, *Scottish Journal of Political Economy*, 33: 292–7.

— (2009), 'Adam Smith and Economic Development', in J. Young (ed.), *The Elgar Companion to Adam Smith*, Cheltenham: Elgar, pp. 211–28.

Rasmussen, D. (2008), *The Problems and Promise of Commercial Society: Adam Smith's Response to Rousseau*, University Park: Pennsylvania State University Press.

— (2013), 'Adam Smith and Rousseau: Enlightenment and Counter-Enlightenment', in C. Berry, M. Paganelli and C. Smith (eds), *Oxford Handbook of Adam Smith*, Oxford: Oxford University Press, pp. 54–76.

Raynor, D. (1982), *Introduction: Sister Peg: A Pamphlet Hitherto Unknown by David Hume*, Cambridge: Cambridge University Press.

— (2008), 'Ferguson's Reflections Previous to the Establishment of a Militia', in E. Heath and V. Merolle (eds), *Adam Ferguson: History, Progress and Human Nature*, London: Pickering and Chatto, pp. 65–72, 196–7.

Rendall, J. (1978), *The Origins of the Scottish Enlightenment 1707–1776*, London: Macmillan.

Riley, P. (1978), *The Union of England and Scotland*, Manchester: Manchester University Press.

Rist, J. (1969), *Stoic Philosophy*, Cambridge: Cambridge University Press.

Roberts, M. (1998), 'The Concept of Luxury in British Political Economy: Adam Smith to Alfred Marshall', *History of Human Sciences*, 11: 23–47.

Robertson, J. (1983), 'The Scottish Enlightenment at the Limits of the Civic Tradition', in I. Hont and M. Ignatieff (eds), *Wealth and Virtue*, Cambridge: Cambridge University Press, pp. 137–78.

— (1985), *The Scottish Enlightenment and the Militia Issue*, Edinburgh: John Donald.

— (1986), 'Scottish Political Economy beyond the Civic Tradition: Government and Economic Development in the *Wealth of Nations*', *History of Political Thought*, 4: 451–82.

— (2005), *The Case for the Enlightenment; Scotland and Naples 1680–1760*, Cambridge: Cambridge University Press.

Robinson, E. (1964), Mathew Boulton and the Art of Parliamentary Lobbying', *Historical Journal*, 7: 209–29.

Robinson, J. (1962), *Economic Philosophy*, London: Watts.

Rockoff, H. (2011), 'Upon Daedalian Wings of Paper Money: Adam Smith and the Crisis of 1772', *Adam Smith Review*, 6: 237–68.

Rosen, F. (2000), 'The Idea of Utility in Adam Smith's "The Theory of Moral Sentiments"', *History of European Ideas*, 26: 79–103.

Rosenberg, N. (1965), 'Adam Smith on the Division of Labour: Two Views or One?', *Economica*, 32: 127–49.

— (1975), 'Adam Smith on Profits – Paradox Lost and Regained', in A. Skinner and T. Wilson (eds), *Essays on Adam Smith*, Oxford: Clarendon Press, pp. 377–89.

Ross, I. (1972), *Lord Kames and the Scotland of his Day*, Oxford: Clarendon Press.

— (2010), *The Life of Adam Smith*, 2nd edn, Oxford: Oxford University Press.

Rothschild, E. (2002), *Economic Sentiments: Adam Smith, Condorcet and the Enlightenment*, Cambridge, MA: Harvard University Press.

Salber Phillips, M. (2000), *Society and Sentiment: Genres of Historical Writing in Britain 1740–1820*, Princeton: Princeton University Press.

— (2006), 'Introduction', in John Millar, *An Historical View of the English Government*, Indianapolis: Liberty Press, pp. ix–xix.

Salter, J. (1994), 'Adam Smith on Justice and Distribution in Commercial Societies', *Scottish Journal of Political Economy*, 41: 299–314.

Sampson, R. (1956), *Progress in the Age of Reason*, London: Heinemann.

Schabas, M. (1994), 'Market Contracts in the Age of Hume', in N. de Marchi and M. Morgan (eds), *Higgling: Transactors and their Markets*, Durham, NC: Duke University Press, pp. 117–34.

— (2005), *The Natural Origins of Economics*, Chicago: University of Chicago Press.

— (2008), 'Temporal Dimensions in Hume's Monetary Theory', in C. Wennerlind and M. Schabas (eds), *David Hume's Political Economy*, London: Routledge, pp. 127–45.

Schofield, M. (2007), 'Epictetus on Cynicism', in T. Scaltas and A. Mason (eds), *The Philosophy of Epictetus*, Oxford: Oxford University Press, pp. 71–86.

Schumpeter, J. (1986), *History of Economic Analysis*, London: Allen and Unwin.

Scott, W. [1937] (1965), *Adam Smith as Student and Professor*, New York: Kelley reprints.

— [1900] (1966), *Francis Hutcheson*, New York: Kelley reprints.

Sebastiani, S. (1998), 'Storia Universale e Teoria Stadiale negli "Sketches on the History of Man" di Lord Kames', *Studi Storici*, 39: 113–36.

— (2005), '"Race", Women and Progress in the Scottish Enlightenment', in S. Knott and B. Taylor (eds), *Women, Gender and Enlightenment*, Basingstoke: Palgrave, pp. 75–96.

Seki, G. (2003), 'Policy Debate on Economic Developments in Scotland: The 1720s to the 1730s', in T. Sakamoto and H. Tanaka (eds), *The Rise of Political Economy in the Scottish Enlightenment*, London: Routledge, pp. 22–38.

Sen, A. (2011), 'Uses and Abuses of Adam Smith', *History of Political Economy*, 43: 257–71.

Sen, A. and E. Rothschild (2006), 'Adam Smith's Economics', in K. Haakonssen (ed.), *The Cambridge Companion to Adam Smith*, Cambridge: Cambridge University Press, pp. 319–65.

Shackleton, R. (1961), *Montesquieu: A Critical Biography*, Oxford: Oxford University Press.

Shaw, J. (1983), *The Management of Scottish Society 1707–64*, Edinburgh: John Donald.

Sher, R. (1985), *Church and University in the Scottish Enlightenment*, Edinburgh: Edinburgh University Press.

— (1989), 'Adam Ferguson, Adam Smith and the Problem of National Defense', *Journal of Modern History*, 61: 240–68.

— (2006), *The Enlightenment and the Book: Scottish Authors and their Publishers in Eighteenth-Century Britain and America*, Chicago: University of Chicago Press.

Shklar, J. (1969), *Men and Citizens: A Study of Rousseau's Social Theory*, Cambridge: Cambridge University Press.

Shovlin, J. (2006), *The Political Economy of Virtue: Luxury, Patriotism and the Origins of the French Revolution*, Ithaca, NY: Cornell University Press.

Simmel, G. [1907] (1990), *The Philosophy of Money*, D. Frisby (ed.), London: Routledge.

Simon, F. (2013), 'Adam Smith and the Law', in C. Berry, M. Paganelli and C. Smith (eds), *Oxford Handbook of Adam Smith*, Oxford: Oxford University Press, pp. 393–416.

Skinner, A. (1995), 'Adam Smith and the Role of the State: Education as a Public Service', in S. Copley and K. Sutherland (eds), *Adam Smith's Wealth of Nations: New Interdisciplinary Essays*, Manchester: Manchester University Press, pp. 70–96.

— (1996), *A System of Social Science*, Oxford: Clarendon Press.

Skoczylas, A. (2001), *Mr Simson's Knotty Case: Divinity, Politics and Due Process in Early Eighteenth-Century Scotland*, Montreal and Kingston: McGill-Queen's University Press.

Smith, C. (2006), *Adam Smith's Political Philosophy: The Invisible Hand and Spontaneous Order*, London: Routledge.

— (2008), 'Ferguson the Active Genius of Mankind', in E. Heath and V. Merolle (eds), *Adam Ferguson: History, Progress and Human Nature*, London: Pickering and Chatto, pp. 157–70, 217–22.

— (2009), 'The Scottish Enlightenment, Unintended Consequences and the Science of Man', *Scottish Journal of Philosophy*, 7: 9–28.

Smout, C. (1969), *A History of the Scottish People 1560–1830*, London: Collins.

— (1999), 'The Improvers and the Scottish Environment: Soils, Bogs and Woods', in T. Devine, T. and J. Young (eds), *Eighteenth-Century Scotland: New Perspectives*, East Linton: Tuckwell Press, pp. 210–24.

— (2012), 'A New Look at the Scottish Improvers', *Scottish Historical Review*, 91: 125–49.

Sombart, W. (1913), *Luxus und Kapitalismus*, Munich: Duncker and Humblot.

Spadafora, D. (1990), *The Idea of Progress in Eighteenth-Century Britain*, New Haven, CT: Yale University Press.

Stalley, R. (2012), 'Adam Smith and the Theory of Punishment', *Journal of Scottish Philosophy*, 10: 69–89.

Starobinski, J. (1993), *Blessings in Disguise; or the Morality of Evil*, trans A. Goldhammer, Cambridge: Polity Press.

Stein, P. (1988), 'The Four Stages Theory of the Development of Societies', in P. Stein, *The Character and Influence of the Roman Civil Law*, London: The Hambledon Press, pp. 395–409.

Stewart, J. (1992), *Opinion and Reform in Hume's Political Philosophy*, Princeton: Princeton University Press.

Suderman, J. (2007), *Orthodoxy and Enlightenment: George Campbell in the Eighteenth Century*, Montreal and Kingston: McGill-Queen's University Press.

Susato, R. (2006), 'Hume's Nuanced Defense of Luxury', *Hume Studies*, 32: 167–86.

Tanaka, H. (2007), 'Beyond the Ambivalent View of Commercial Society: Commerce, Industry and Alienation in the Scottish Enlightenment', *International Journal of Public Affairs*, 3: 32–55.

Tanaka, S. (2003), 'The Main Themes of Moral Philosophy and the Formation of Political Economy in Adam Smith', in T. Sakamoto and H. Tanaka (eds), *The Rise of Political Economy in the Scottish Enlightenment*, London: Routledge, pp. 134–49.

Teggart, F. (1941), *Theory and Process of History*, Berkeley: University of California Press.

Tegos, S. (2013), 'Adam Smith Theorist of Corruption', in C. Berry, M. Paganelli and C. Smith (eds), *Oxford Handbook of Adam Smith*, Oxford: Oxford University Press, pp. 353–71.

Teichgraeber III, R. (1986), *'Free Trade' and Moral Philosophy*, Durham, NC: Duke University Press.

Thompson, E. (1991a), 'The Moral Economy of the English Crowd in the Eighteenth Century', in *Customs in Common*, London: Merlin Press, pp. 185–258.

— (1991b), 'Moral Economy Revisited', *Customs in Common*, London: Merlin Press, pp. 267–351.

Thomson, J. [1822] (1859), An *Account of the Life and Lectures of William Cullen*, 2 vols, Edinburgh: Blackwood.

Thornhill, C. (2011), *A Sociology of Constitutions and State Legitimacy in Historical-Sociological Perspective*, Cambridge: Cambridge University Press.

Tierney, B. (1959), *Medieval Poor Law*, Berkeley: University of California Press.

Tomkins, A. (2009), 'On Republican Constitutionalism in the Age of Commerce: Reflections from the Scottish Enlightenment', in S. Besson and J. Marti (eds), *Legal Republicanism*, Oxford: Oxford University Press, pp. 317–36.

Tooby J and L. Cosmides (1992), 'The Psychological Foundations of Culture', in J. Barkow, L. Cosmides and J. Tooby (eds), *The Adapted Mind: Evolutionary Psychology and the Generation of Culture*, New York: Oxford University Press, pp. 19–136.

Trevor-Roper, H. (1977), 'The Scottish Enlightenment', *Blackwood's Magazine*, 322: 371–88.

Turco, L. (2003), 'Moral Sense and the Foundations of Morals', in A. Broadie (ed.), *The Cambridge Companion to the Scottish Enlightenment*, Cambridge: Cambridge University Press, pp. 136–56.

Ulman, L. (1990), *The Minutes of the Aberdeen Philosophical Society 1758–1773*, Aberdeen: Aberdeen University Press.

Varty, J. (1997), 'Civic or Commercial? Adam Ferguson's Concept of Civil Society', in R. Fine and S. Rai (eds), *Civil Society: Democratic Perspectives*, London: Frank Cass, pp. 29–48.

Vereker, C. (1967), *Eighteenth-Century Optimism*, Liverpool: Liverpool University Press.

Vickers, D. (1960), *Studies in the Theory of Money*, London: Peter Owen.

— (1975), 'Adam Smith and the Status of the Theory of Money', in A. Skinner and T. Wilson (eds), *Essays on Adam Smith*, Oxford: Clarendon Press, pp. 482–503.

Viner, J. (1927), 'Adam Smith and Laissez-Faire', *Journal of Political Economy*, 35: 198–232.

Vivenza, G. (2001), *Adam Smith and the Classics*, Oxford: Oxford University Press.

Vlachos, G. (1955), *Essai sur la politique de Hume*, Paris: Institut Français Athènes.

Voges, F. (1986), 'Moderate and Evangelical Thinking in the later Eighteenth Century: Differences and Shared Attitudes', *Scottish Church History Society Records*, 22: 141–57.

Vyverberg, H. (1958), *Historical Pessimism in the French Enlightenment*, Cambridge, MA: Harvard University Press.

Wahnbaeck, T. (2004), *Luxury and Public Happiness: Political Economy in the Italian Enlightenment*, Oxford: Clarendon Press.

Waszek, N. (1984), 'Two Concepts of Morality: A Distinction of Adam Smith's Ethics and its Stoic Origin', *Journal of the History of Ideas*, 45: 591–606.

Webster, C. (1975), *The Great Instauration: Science, Medicine and Reform 1626–1660*, London: Duckworth.

Weinstein, J. (2006), 'Sympathy, Difference and Education: Social Unity in the Work of Adam Smith', *Economics and Philosophy*, 22: 79–111.

Wences Simon, M. (2006), *Sociedad Civil y Virtud Civica en Adam Ferguson*, Madrid: Centro de Estudios Politicos y Constitucionales.

Wennerlind, C. (2001), 'The Link between David Hume's *Treatise of Human Nature* and his Fiduciary Theory of Money', *History of Political Economy*, 33: 139–60.

— (2002), 'David Hume's Political Philosophy: A Theory of Commercial Modernization', *Hume Studies*, 28: 247–70.

— (2005), 'David Hume's Monetary Theory Revisited', *Journal of Political Economy*, 28: 247–70.

— (2008), 'An Artificial Virtue and the Oil of Commerce: A Synthetic View of Hume's Theory of Money', in C. Wennerlind and M. Schabas (eds), *David Hume's Political Economy*, London: Routledge, pp. 105–26.

— (2011), *Casualties of Credit: The English Financial Revolution 1620–1720*, Cambridge, MA: Harvard University Press.

Werhane, P. (1991), *Adam Smith and his Legacy for Modern Capitalism*, New York: Oxford University Press.

West, E. (1964), 'Adam Smith's Two Views on the Division of Labour', *Economica*, 31: 23–32.

— (1969), 'The Political Economy of Alienation: Karl Marx and Adam Smith', *Oxford Economic Papers*, 21: 1–23.

— (1975), Adam Smith and Alienation: A Rejoinder', *Oxford Economic Papers*, 27: 295–311.

Whatley, C. (2006), *The Scots and the Union*, Edinburgh: Edinburgh University Press.

Winch, D. (1978), *Adam Smith's Politics*, Cambridge: Cambridge University Press.

— (1983), 'Adam Smith's "Enduring Particular Result"', in I. Hont and M. Ignatieff (eds), *Wealth and Virtue*, Cambridge: Cambridge University Press, pp. 253–69.

— (1988), 'Adam Smith and the Liberal Tradition', in K. Haakonssen (ed.), *Traditions of Liberalism*, St Leonards NSW: Centre for Independent Studies, pp. 83–104.

Withers, C. (2007), *Placing the Enlightenment: Thinking Geographically about the Age of Reason*, Chicago: University of Chicago Press.

Withers, C. and P. Wood (eds) (2002), *Science and Medicine in the Scottish Enlightenment*, East Linton: Tuckwell Press.

Wolin, S. (1960), *Politics and Vision: Continuity and Innovation in Western Political Thought*, Boston: Little, Brown.

Womersley, D. (1986), 'The Historical Writings of William Robertson', *Journal of the History of Ideas*, 47: 497–506.

Wood, P. (2003), 'Science in the Scottish Enlightenment', in A. Broadie (ed.), *The Cambridge Companion to the Scottish Enlightenment*, Cambridge: Cambridge University Press, pp. 94–116.

Wootton, D. (1986), 'Introduction', in *Divine Right and Democracy*', London: Penguin Books, pp. 22–86.

Young, James D. (1979), *The Rousing of the Scottish Working Class*, London: Croom Helm.

Young, Jeffrey T. (1997), *Economics as a Moral Science: The Political Economy of Adam Smith*, Cheltenham: Elgar.

— (2005), 'Unintended Order and Intervention: Adam Smith's Theory of the Role of the State', in S. Medema and P. Boettke (eds), *The Role of Government in the History of Economic Thought* (supplement to vol. 37 of *History of Political Economy*), Durham, NC: Duke University Press, pp. 91–119.

Youngson, A. (1972), *After the Forty-Five: The Economic Impact on the Scottish Highlands*, Edinburgh: Edinburgh University Press.

Zeller, E. (1885), *Socrates and the Socratic Schools*, 3 vols, trans. O. Reichel, London: Longmans Green.

# Index